Essentials of Programming Languages

third edition

Essentials of Programming Languages

third edition

Daniel P. Friedman

Mitchell Wand

The MIT Press
Cambridge, Massachusetts
London, England

MIT Press books may be purchased at special quantity discounts for business or sales promotional use. For information, please email special_sales@mitpress.mit.edu or write to Special Sales Department, The MIT Press, 55 Hayward Street, Cambridge, MA 02142.

This book was set in LATEX 2_ε by the authors, and was printed and bound in the United States of America.

Library of Congress Cataloging-in-Publication Data

Friedman, Daniel P.
Essentials of programming languages / Daniel P. Friedman, Mitchell Wand.
—3rd ed.
  p.   cm.
Includes bibliographical references and index.
ISBN 978-0-262-06279-4 (hbk. : alk. paper)
1. Programming Languages (Electronic computers). I. Wand, Mitchell. II. Title.

QA76.7.F73 2008
005.1—dc22   2007039723

10 9 8 7 6 5 4 3 2 1

Contents

Foreword

This book brings you face-to-face with the most fundamental idea in computer programming:

> *The interpreter for a computer language is just another program.*

It sounds obvious, doesn't it? But the implications are profound. If you are a computational theorist, the interpreter idea recalls Gödel's discovery of the limitations of formal logical systems, Turing's concept of a universal computer, and von Neumann's basic notion of the stored-program machine. If you are a programmer, mastering the idea of an interpreter is a source of great power. It provokes a real shift in mindset, a basic change in the way you think about programming.

I did a lot of programming before I learned about interpreters, and I produced some substantial programs. One of them, for example, was a large data-entry and information-retrieval system written in PL/I. When I implemented my system, I viewed PL/I as a fixed collection of rules established by some unapproachable group of language designers. I saw my job as not to modify these rules, or even to understand them deeply, but rather to pick through the (very) large manual, selecting this or that feature to use. The notion that there was some underlying structure to the way the language was organized, and that I might want to override some of the language designers' decisions, never occurred to me. I didn't know how to create embedded sublanguages to help organize my implementation, so the entire program seemed like a large, complex mosaic, where each piece had to be carefully shaped and fitted into place, rather than a cluster of languages, where the pieces could be flexibly combined. If you don't understand interpreters, you can still write programs; you can even be a competent programmer. But you can't be a master.

There are three reasons why as a programmer you should learn about interpreters.

First, you will need at some point to implement interpreters, perhaps not interpreters for full-blown general-purpose languages, but interpreters just the same. Almost every complex computer system with which people interact in flexible ways—a computer drawing tool or an information-retrieval system, for example—includes some sort of interpreter that structures the interaction. These programs may include complex individual operations—shading a region on the display screen, or performing a database search—but the interpreter is the glue that lets you combine individual operations into useful patterns. Can you use the result of one operation as the input to another operation? Can you name a sequence of operations? Is the name local or global? Can you parameterize a sequence of operations, and give names to its inputs? And so on. No matter how complex and polished the individual operations are, it is often the quality of the glue that most directly determines the power of the system. It's easy to find examples of programs with good individual operations, but lousy glue; looking back on it, I can see that my PL/I database program certainly had lousy glue.

Second, even programs that are not themselves interpreters have important interpreter-like pieces. Look inside a sophisticated computer-aided design system and you're likely to find a geometric recognition language, a graphics interpreter, a rule-based control interpreter, and an object-oriented language interpreter all working together. One of the most powerful ways to structure a complex program is as a collection of languages, each of which provides a different perspective, a different way of working with the program elements. Choosing the right kind of language for the right purpose, and understanding the implementation tradeoffs involved: that's what the study of interpreters is about.

The third reason for learning about interpreters is that programming techniques that explicitly involve the structure of language are becoming increasingly important. Today's concern with designing and manipulating class hierarchies in object-oriented systems is only one example of this trend. Perhaps this is an inevitable consequence of the fact that our programs are becoming increasingly complex—thinking more explicitly about languages may be our best tool for dealing with this complexity. Consider again the basic idea: the interpreter itself is just a program. But that program is written in some language, whose interpreter is itself just a program written in some language whose interpreter is itself ... Perhaps the whole distinction between program and programming language is a misleading idea, and future programmers will see themselves not as writing programs in particular, but as creating new languages for each new application.

Friedman and Wand have done a landmark job, and their book will change the landscape of programming-language courses. They don't just *tell* you about interpreters; they *show* them to you. The core of the book is a tour de force sequence of interpreters starting with an abstract high-level language and progressively making linguistic features explicit until we reach a state machine. You can actually run this code, study and modify it, and change the way these interpreters handle scoping, parameter-passing, control structure, etc.

Having used interpreters to study the execution of languages, the authors show how the same ideas can be used to analyze programs without running them. In two new chapters, they show how to implement type checkers and inferencers, and how these features interact in modern object-oriented languages.

Part of the reason for the appeal of this approach is that the authors have chosen a good tool—the Scheme language, which combines the uniform syntax and data-abstraction capabilities of Lisp with the lexical scoping and block structure of Algol. But a powerful tool becomes most powerful in the hands of masters. The sample interpreters in this book are outstanding models. Indeed, since they are *runnable* models, I'm sure that these interpreters and analyzers will find themselves at the cores of many programming systems over the coming years.

This is not an easy book. Mastery of interpreters does not come easily, and for good reason. The language designer is a further level removed from the end user than is the ordinary application programmer. In designing an application program, you think about the specific tasks to be performed, and consider what features to include. But in designing a language, you consider the various applications people might want to implement, and the ways in which they might implement them. Should your language have static or dynamic scope, or a mixture? Should it have inheritance? Should it pass parameters by reference or by value? Should continuations be explicit or implicit? It all depends on how you expect your language to be used, which kinds of programs should be easy to write, and which you can afford to make more difficult.

Also, interpreters really *are* subtle programs. A simple change to a line of code in an interpreter can make an enormous difference in the behavior of the resulting language. Don't think that you can just skim these programs—very few people in the world can glance at a new interpreter and predict from that how it will behave even on relatively simple programs. So study these programs. Better yet, *run* them—this is working code. Try interpreting some simple expressions, then more complex ones. Add error messages. Modify the interpreters. Design your own variations. Try to really master these programs, not just get a vague feeling for how they work.

If you do this, you will change your view of your programming, and your view of yourself as a programmer. You'll come to see yourself as a designer of languages rather than only a user of languages, as a person who chooses the rules by which languages are put together, rather than only a follower of rules that other people have chosen.

Postscript to the Third Edition

The foreword above was written only seven years ago. Since then, information applications and services have entered the lives of people around the world in ways that hardly seemed possible in 1990. They are powered by an ever—growing collection of programming languages and programming frameworks—all erected on an ever-expanding platform of interpreters.

Do you want to create Web pages? In 1990, that meant formatting static text and graphics, in effect, creating a program to be run by browsers executing only a single "print" statement. Today's dynamic Web pages make full use of scripting languages (another name for interpreted languages) like Javascript. The browser programs can be complex, and including asynchronous calls to a Web server that is typically running a program in a completely different programming framework possibly with a host of services, each with its own individual language.

Or you might be creating a bot for enhancing the performance of your avatar in a massive online multiplayer game like World of Warcraft. In that case, you're probably using a scripting language like Lua, possibly with an object-oriented extension to help in expressing classes of behaviors.

Or maybe you're programming a massive computing cluster to do indexing and searching on a global scale. If so, you might be writing your programs using the map-reduce paradigm of functional programming to relieve you of dealing explicitly with the details of how the individual processors are scheduled.

Or perhaps you're developing new algorithms for sensor networks, and exploring the use of lazy evaluation to better deal with parallelism and data aggregation. Or exploring transformation systems like XSLT for controlling Web pages. Or designing frameworks for transforming and remixing multimedia streams. Or ...

So many new applications! So many new languages! So many new interpreters!

As ever, novice programmers, even capable ones, can get along viewing each new framework individually, working within its fixed set of rules. But creating new frameworks requires skills of the master: understanding the principles that run across languages, appreciating which language features are best suited for which type of application, and knowing how to craft the interpreters that bring these languages to life. These are the skills you will learn from this book.

Hal Abelson
Cambridge, Massachusetts
September 2007

Preface

Goal

This book is an analytic study of programming languages. Our goal is to provide a deep, working understanding of the essential concepts of programming languages. These essentials have proved to be of enduring importance; they form a basis for understanding future developments in programming languages.

Most of these essentials relate to the semantics, or meaning, of program elements. Such meanings reflect how program elements are interpreted as the program executes. Programs called interpreters provide the most direct, executable expression of program semantics. They process a program by directly analyzing an abstract representation of the program text. We therefore choose interpreters as our primary vehicle for expressing the semantics of programming language elements.

The most interesting question about a program as object is, "What does it do?" The study of interpreters tells us this. Interpreters are critical because they reveal nuances of meaning, and are the direct path to more efficient compilation and to other kinds of program analyses.

Interpreters are also illustrative of a broad class of systems that transform information from one form to another based on syntax structure. Compilers, for example, transform programs into forms suitable for interpretation by hardware or virtual machines. Though general compilation techniques are beyond the scope of this book, we do develop several elementary program translation systems. These reflect forms of program analysis typical of compilation, such as control transformation, variable binding resolution, and type checking.

The following are some of the strategies that distinguish our approach.

1. Each new concept is explained through the use of a small language. These languages are often cumulative: later languages may rely on the features of earlier ones.

2. Language processors such as interpreters and type checkers are used to explain the behavior of programs in a given language. They express language design decisions in a manner that is both formal (unambiguous and complete) and executable.

3. When appropriate, we use interfaces and specifications to create data abstractions. In this way, we can change data representation without changing programs. We use this to investigate alternative implementation strategies.

4. Our language processors are written both at the very high level needed to produce a concise and comprehensible view of semantics and at the much lower level needed to understand implementation strategies.

5. We show how simple algebraic manipulation can be used to predict the behavior of programs and to derive their properties. In general, however, we make little use of mathematical notation, preferring instead to study the behavior of programs that constitute the implementations of our languages.

6. The text explains the key concepts, while the exercises explore alternative designs and other issues. For example, the text deals with static binding, but dynamic binding is discussed in the exercises. One thread of exercises applies the concept of lexical addressing to the various languages developed in the book.

We provide several views of programming languages using widely varying levels of abstraction. Frequently our interpreters provide a very high-level view that expresses language semantics in a very concise fashion, not far from that of formal mathematical semantics. At the other extreme, we demonstrate how programs may be transformed into a very low-level form characteristic of assembly language. By accomplishing this transformation in small stages, we maintain a clear connection between the high-level and low-level views.

We have made some significant changes to this edition. We have included informal contracts with all nontrivial definitions. This has the effect of clarifying the chosen abstractions. In addition, the chapter on modules is completely new. To make implementations simpler, the source language for chapters 3, 4, 5, 7, and 8 assumes that exactly one argument can be passed to a function; we have included exercises that support multiargument procedures. Chapter 6 is completely new, since we have opted for a first-order compositional continuation-passing-style transform rather than a relational one. Also, because of the nature of tail-form expressions, we use multiargument procedures here, and in the objects and classes chapter, we do the same, though there it is not so necessary. Every chapter has been revised and many new exercises have been added.

Organization

The first two chapters provide the foundations for a careful study of programming languages. Chapter 1 emphasizes the connection between inductive data specification and recursive programming and introduces several notions related to the scope of variables. Chapter 2 introduces a data type facility. This leads to a discussion of data abstraction and examples of representational transformations of the sort used in subsequent chapters.

Chapter 3 uses these foundations to describe the behavior of programming languages. It introduces interpreters as mechanisms for explaining the runtime behavior of languages and develops an interpreter for a simple, lexically scoped language with first-class procedures and recursion. This interpreter is the basis for much of the material in the remainder of the book. The chapter ends by giving a thorough treatment of a language that uses indices in place of variables and as a result variable lookup can be via a list reference.

Chapter 4 introduces a new component, the state, which maps locations to values. Once this is added, we can look at various questions of representation. In addition, it permits us to explore call-by-reference, call-by-name, and call-by-need parameter-passing mechanisms.

Chapter 5 rewrites our basic interpreter in continuation-passing style. The control structure that is needed to run the interpreter thereby shifts from recursion to iteration. This exposes the control mechanisms of the interpreted language, and strengthens one's intuition for control issues in general. It also allows us to extend the language with trampolining, exception-handling, and multithreading mechanisms.

Chapter 6 is the companion to the previous chapter. There we show how to transform our familiar interpreter into continuation-passing style; here we show how to accomplish this for a much larger class of programs. Continuation-passing style is a powerful programming tool, for it allows any sequential control mechanism to be implemented in almost any language. The algorithm is also an example of an abstractly specified source-to-source program transformation.

Chapter 7 turns the language of chapter 3 into a typed language. First we implement a type checker. Then we show how the types in a program can be deduced by a unification-based type inference algorithm.

Chapter 8 builds typed modules relying heavily on an understanding of the previous chapter. Modules allow us to build and enforce abstraction boundaries, and they offer a new kind of scoping.

Chapter 9 presents the basic concepts of object-oriented languages, centered on classes. We first develop an efficient run-time architecture, which is used as the basis for the material in the second part of the chapter. The second part combines the ideas of the type checker of chapter 7 with those of the object-oriented language of the first part, leading to a conventional typed object-oriented language. This requires introducing new concepts including interfaces, abstract methods, and casting.

For Further Reading explains where each of the ideas in the book has come from. This is a personal walk-through allowing the reader the opportunity to visit each topic from the original paper, though in some cases, we have just chosen an accessible source.

Finally, appendix B describes our SLLGEN parsing system.

The dependencies of the various chapters are shown in the figure below.

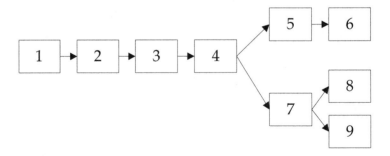

Usage

This material has been used in both undergraduate and graduate courses. Also, it has been used in continuing education courses for professional programmers. We assume background in data structures and experience both in a procedural language such as C, C++, or Java, and in Scheme, ML, Python, or Haskell.

Exercises are a vital part of the text and are scattered throughout. They range in difficulty from being trivial if related material is understood [⋆], to requiring many hours of thought and programming work [⋆ ⋆ ⋆]. A great deal of material of applied, historical, and theoretical interest resides within them. We recommend that each exercise be read and some thought be given as to how to solve it. Although we write our program interpretation and transformation systems in Scheme, any language that supports both first-class procedures and assignment (ML, Common Lisp, Python, Ruby, etc.) is adequate for working the exercises.

Exercise 0.1 [⋆] We often use phrases like "some languages have property X." For each such phrase, find one or more languages that have the property and one or more languages that do not have the property. Feel free to ferret out this information from any descriptive book on programming languages (say Scott (2005), Sebesta (2007), or Pratt & Zelkowitz (2001)).

This is a hands-on book: everything discussed in the book may be implemented within the limits of a typical university course. Because the abstraction facilities of functional programming languages are especially suited to this sort of programming, we can write substantial language-processing systems that are nevertheless compact enough that one can understand and manipulate them with reasonable effort.

The web site, available through the publisher, includes complete Scheme code for all of the interpreters and analyzers in this book. The code is written in PLT Scheme. We chose this Scheme implementation because its module system and programming environment provide a substantial advantage to the student. The code is largely R^5RS-compatible, and should be easily portable to any full-featured Scheme implementation.

Acknowledgments

We are indebted to countless colleagues and students who used and critiqued the first two editions of this book and provided invaluable assistance in the long gestation of this third edition. We are especially grateful for the contributions of the following individuals, to whom we offer a special word of thanks. Olivier Danvy encouraged our consideration of a first-order compositional continuation-passing algorithm and proposed some interesting exercises. Matthias Felleisen's keen analysis has improved the design of several chapters. Amr Sabry made many useful suggestions and found at least one extremely subtle bug in a draft of chapter 9. Benjamin Pierce offered a number of insightful observations after teaching from the first edition, almost all of which we have incorporated. Gary Leavens provided exceptionally thorough and valuable comments on early drafts of the second edition, including a large number of detailed suggestions for change. Stephanie Weirich found a subtle bug in the type inference code of the second edition of chapter 7. Ryan Newton, in addition to reading a draft of the second edition, assumed the onerous task of suggesting a difficulty level for each exercise for that edition. Chung-chieh Shan taught from an early draft of the third edition and provided copious and useful comments.

Kevin Millikin, Arthur Lee, Roger Kirchner, Max Hailperin, and Erik Hilsdale all used early drafts of the second edition. Will Clinger, Will Byrd, Joe Near, and Kyle Blocher all used drafts of this edition. Their comments have been extremely valuable. Ron Garcia, Matthew Flatt, Shriram Krishnamurthi, Steve Ganz, Gregor Kiczales, Marlene Miller, Galen Williamson, Dipanwita Sarkar, Steven Bogaerts, Albert Rossi, Craig Citro, Christopher Dutchyn, Jeremy Siek, and Neil Ching also provided careful reading and useful comments.

Several people deserve special thanks for assisting us with this book. We want to thank Neil Ching for developing the index. Jonathan Sobel and Erik Hilsdale built several prototype implementations and contributed many ideas as we experimented with the design of the `define-datatype` and `cases` syntactic extensions. The Programming Language Team, and especially Matthias Felleisen, Matthew Flatt, Robby Findler, and Shriram Krishnamurthi, were very helpful in providing compatibility with their DrScheme system. Kent Dybvig developed the exceptionally efficient and robust Chez Scheme implementation, which the authors have used for decades. Will Byrd has provided invaluable assistance during the entire process. Matthias Felleisen strongly urged us to adopt compatibility with DrScheme's module system, which is evident in the implementation that can be found at `http://mitpress.mit.edu/eopl3`.

Some have earned special mention for their thoughtfulness and concern for our well-being. George Springer and Larry Finkelstein have each supplied invaluable support. Bob Prior, our wonderful editor at MIT Press, deserves special thanks for his encouragement in getting us to attack the writing of this edition. Ada Brunstein, Bob's successor, also deserves thanks for making our transition to a new editor so smoothly. Indiana University's School of Informatics and Northeastern University's College of Computer and Information Science have created an environment that has allowed us to undertake this project. Mary Friedman's gracious hosting of several week-long writing sessions did much to accelerate our progress.

We want to thank Christopher T. Haynes for his collaboration on the first two editions. Unfortunately, his interests have shifted elsewhere, and he has not continued with us on this edition.

Finally, we are most grateful to our families for tolerating our passion for working on the book. Thank you Rob, Shannon, Rachel, Sara, and Mary; and thank you Rebecca and Joshua, Jennifer and Stephen, Joshua and Georgia, and Barbara.

This edition has been in the works for a while and we have likely overlooked someone who has helped along the way. We regret any oversight. You see this written in books all the time and wonder why anyone would write it. Of course, you regret any oversight. But, when you have an army of helpers (it takes a village), you really feel a sense of obligation not to forget anyone. So, if you were overlooked, we are truly sorry.

— D.P.F. and M.W.

1 *Inductive Sets of Data*

This chapter introduces the basic programming tools we will need to write interpreters, checkers and similar programs that form the heart of a programming language processor.

Because the syntax of a program in a language is usually a nested or tree-like structure, recursion will be at the core of our techniques. Section 1.1 and section 1.2 introduce methods for inductively specifying data structures and show how such specifications may be used to guide the construction of recursive programs. Section 1.3 shows how to extend these techniques to more complex problems. The chapter concludes with an extensive set of exercises. These exercises are the heart of this chapter. They provide experience that is essential for mastering the technique of recursive programming upon which the rest of this book is based.

1.1 Recursively Specified Data

When writing code for a procedure, we must know precisely what kinds of values may occur as arguments to the procedure, and what kinds of values are legal for the procedure to return. Often these sets of values are complex. In this section we introduce formal techniques for specifying sets of values.

1.1.1 Inductive Specification

Inductive specification is a powerful method of specifying a set of values. To illustrate this method, we use it to describe a certain subset S of the natural numbers $N = \{0, 1, 2, \ldots\}$.

Definition 1.1.1 *A natural number n is in S if and only if*

1. $n = 0$, *or*

2. $n - 3 \in S$.

Let us see how we can use this definition to determine what natural numbers are in S. We know that $0 \in S$. Therefore $3 \in S$, since $(3 - 3) = 0$ and $0 \in S$. Similarly $6 \in S$, since $(6 - 3) = 3$ and $3 \in S$. Continuing in this way, we can conclude that all multiples of 3 are in S.

What about other natural numbers? Is $1 \in S$? We know that $1 \neq 0$, so the first condition is not satisfied. Furthermore, $(1 - 3) = -2$, which is not a natural number and thus is not a member of S. Therefore the second condition is not satisfied. Since 1 satisfies neither condition, $1 \notin S$. Similarly, $2 \notin S$. What about 4? $4 \in S$ only if $1 \in S$. But $1 \notin S$, so $4 \notin S$, as well. Similarly, we can conclude that if n is a natural number and is not a multiple of 3, then $n \notin S$.

From this argument, we conclude that S is the set of natural numbers that are multiples of 3.

We can use this definition to write a procedure to decide whether a natural number n is in S.

```
in-S? : N → Bool
usage: (in-S? n) = #t if n is in S, #f otherwise
(define in-S?
  (lambda (n)
    (if (zero? n) #t
      (if (>= (- n 3) 0)
        (in-S? (- n 3))
        #f)))))
```

Here we have written a recursive procedure in Scheme that follows the definition. The notation **in-S?** : $N \rightarrow Bool$ is a comment, called the *contract* for this procedure. It means that `in-S?` is intended to be a procedure that takes a natural number and produces a boolean. Such comments are helpful for reading and writing code.

To determine whether $n \in S$, we first ask whether $n = 0$. If it is, then the answer is true. Otherwise we need to see whether $n - 3 \in S$. To do this, we first check to see whether $(n - 3) \geq 0$. If it is, we then can use our procedure to see whether it is in S. If it is not, then n cannot be in S.

Here is an alternative way of writing down the definition of S.

Definition 1.1.2 *Define the set S to be the smallest set contained in N and satisfying the following two properties:*

1. $0 \in S$, and

2. if $n \in S$, then $n + 3 \in S$.

A "smallest set" is the one that satisfies properties 1 and 2 and that is a subset of any other set satisfying properties 1 and 2. It is easy to see that there can be only one such set: if S_1 and S_2 both satisfy properties 1 and 2, and both are smallest, then $S_1 \subseteq S_2$ (since S_1 is smallest), and $S_2 \subseteq S_1$ (since S_2 is smallest), hence $S_1 = S_2$. We need this extra condition, because otherwise there are many sets that satisfy the remaining two conditions (see exercise 1.3).

Here is yet another way of writing the definition:

$$\frac{}{0 \in S}$$

$$\frac{n \in S}{(n + 3) \in S}$$

This is simply a shorthand notation for the preceding version of the definition. Each entry is called a *rule of inference*, or just a *rule*; the horizontal line is read as an "if-then." The part above the line is called the *hypothesis* or the *antecedent*; the part below the line is called the *conclusion* or the *consequent*. When there are two or more hypotheses listed, they are connected by an implicit "and" (see definition 1.1.5). A rule with no hypotheses is called an *axiom*. We often write an axiom without the horizontal line, like

$$0 \in S$$

The rules are interpreted as saying that a natural number n is in S if and only if the statement "$n \in S$" can be derived from the axioms by using the rules of inference finitely many times. This interpretation automatically makes S the smallest set that is closed under the rules.

These definitions all say the same thing. We call the first version a *top-down* definition, the second version a *bottom-up* definition, and the third version a *rules-of-inference* version.

Let us see how this works on some other examples.

Definition 1.1.3 (list of integers, top-down) *A Scheme list is a* list of integers *if and only if either*

1. *it is the empty list, or*

2. *it is a pair whose car is an integer and whose cdr is a list of integers.*

We use *Int* to denote the set of all integers, and *List-of-Int* to denote the set of lists of integers.

Definition 1.1.4 (list of integers, bottom-up) *The set List-of-Int is the smallest set of Scheme lists satisfying the following two properties:*

1. *() ∈ List-of-Int, and*

2. *if n ∈ Int and l ∈ List-of-Int, then (n . l) ∈ List-of-Int.*

Here we use the infix "*.*" to denote the result of the cons operation in Scheme. The phrase (*n . l*) denotes a Scheme pair whose car is *n* and whose cdr is *l*.

Definition 1.1.5 (list of integers, rules of inference)

$$() \in \textit{List-of-Int}$$

$$\frac{n \in \textit{Int} \qquad l \in \textit{List-of-Int}}{(n \, . \, l) \in \textit{List-of-Int}}$$

These three definitions are equivalent. We can show how to use them to generate some elements of *List-of-Int*.

1. () is a list of integers, because of property 1 of definition 1.1.4 or the first rule of definition 1.1.5.

2. (14 . ()) is a list of integers, because of property 2 of definition 1.1.4, since 14 is an integer and () is a list of integers. We can also write this as an instance of the second rule for *List-of-Int*.

$$\frac{14 \in \textit{Int} \qquad () \in \textit{List-of-Int}}{(14 \, . \, ()) \in \textit{List-of-Int}}$$

3. (3 . (14 . ())) is a list of integers, because of property 2, since 3
   is an integer and (14 . ()) is a list of integers. We can write this as
   another instance of the second rule for *List-of-Int*.

$$\frac{3 \in Int \qquad (14 . ()) \in List\text{-}of\text{-}Int}{(3 . (14 . ())) \in List\text{-}of\text{-}Int}$$

4. (-7 . (3 . (14 . ()))) is a list of integers, because of property 2,
   since -7 is a integer and (3 . (14 . ())) is a list of integers. Once
   more we can write this as an instance of the second rule for *List-of-Int*.

$$\frac{-7 \in Int \qquad (3 . (14 . ())) \in List\text{-}of\text{-}Int}{(-7 . (3 . (14 . ()))) \in List\text{-}of\text{-}Int}$$

5. Nothing is a list of integers unless it is built in this fashion.

Converting from dot notation to list notation, we see that (), (14), (3
14), and (-7 3 14) are all members of *List-of-Int*.

We can also combine the rules to get a picture of the entire chain of reasoning that shows that (-7 . (3 . (14 . ()))) ∈ *List-of-Int*. The tree-like
picture below is called a *derivation* or *deduction tree*.

$$\frac{-7 \in N \quad \dfrac{3 \in N \quad \dfrac{14 \in N \qquad () \in List\text{-}of\text{-}Int}{(14 . ()) \in List\text{-}of\text{-}Int}}{(3 . (14 . ())) \in List\text{-}of\text{-}Int}}{(-7 . (3 . (14 . ()))) \in List\text{-}of\text{-}Int}$$

Exercise 1.1 [⋆] Write inductive definitions of the following sets. Write each definition in all three styles (top-down, bottom-up, and rules of inference). Using your
rules, show the derivation of some sample elements of each set.

1. $\{3n + 2 \mid n \in N\}$
2. $\{2n + 3m + 1 \mid n, m \in N\}$
3. $\{(n, 2n + 1) \mid n \in N\}$
4. $\{(n, n^2) \mid n \in N\}$ Do not mention squaring in your rules. As a hint, remember the
   equation $(n + 1)^2 = n^2 + 2n + 1$.

Exercise 1.2 [⋆⋆] What sets are defined by the following pairs of rules? Explain why.

1. $(0, 1) \in S$ $\dfrac{(n, k) \in S}{(n + 1, k + 7) \in S}$

2. $(0,1) \in S$ $\dfrac{(n,k) \in S}{(n+1,2k) \in S}$

3. $(0,0,1) \in S$ $\dfrac{(n,i,j) \in S}{(n+1,j,i+j) \in S}$

4.   [★★★] $(0,1,0) \in S$ $\dfrac{(n,i,j) \in S}{(n+1,i+2,i+j) \in S}$

Exercise 1.3 [★] Find a set T of natural numbers such that $0 \in T$, and whenever $n \in T$, then $n+3 \in T$, but $T \neq S$, where S is the set defined in definition 1.1.2.

1.1.2   Defining Sets Using Grammars

The previous examples have been fairly straightforward, but it is easy to imagine how the process of describing more complex data types becomes quite cumbersome. To help with this, we show how to specify sets with *grammars*. Grammars are typically used to specify sets of strings, but we can use them to define sets of values as well.

For example, we can define the set *List-of-Int* by the grammar

$$\begin{aligned}
\textit{List-of-Int} &::= \; () \\
\textit{List-of-Int} &::= \; (\textit{Int} \;\; . \;\; \textit{List-of-Int})
\end{aligned}$$

Here we have two rules corresponding to the two properties in definition 1.1.4 above. The first rule says that the empty list is in *List-of-Int*, and the second says that if n is in *Int* and l is in *List-of-Int*, then $(n \;\; . \;\; l)$ is in *List-of-Int*. This set of rules is called a *grammar*.

Let us look at the pieces of this definition. In this definition we have

- **Nonterminal Symbols**. These are the names of the sets being defined. In this case there is only one such set, but in general, there might be several sets being defined. These sets are sometimes called *syntactic categories*.

  We will use the convention that nonterminals and sets have names that are capitalized, but we will use lower-case names when referring to their elements in prose. This is simpler than it sounds. For example, *Expression* is a nonterminal, but we will write $e \in \textit{Expression}$ or "*e* is an expression."

  Another common convention, called *Backus-Naur Form* or *BNF*, is to surround the word with angle brackets, e.g. ⟨expression⟩.

- **Terminal Symbols**. These are the characters in the external representation, in this case ., (, and). We typically write these using a typewriter font, e.g. lambda.

- **Productions**. The rules are called *productions*. Each production has a left-hand side, which is a nonterminal symbol, and a right-hand side, which consists of terminal and nonterminal symbols. The left- and right-hand sides are usually separated by the symbol ::=, read *is* or *can be*. The right-hand side specifies a method for constructing members of the syntactic category in terms of other syntactic categories and *terminal symbols*, such as the left parenthesis, right parenthesis, and the period.

Often some syntactic categories mentioned in a production are left undefined when their meaning is sufficiently clear from context, such as *Int*.

Grammars are often written using some notational shortcuts. It is common to omit the left-hand side of a production when it is the same as the left-hand side of the preceding production. Using this convention our example would be written as

$$List\text{-}of\text{-}Int ::= ()$$
$$::= (Int \ . \ List\text{-}of\text{-}Int)$$

One can also write a set of rules for a single syntactic category by writing the left-hand side and ::= just once, followed by all the right-hand sides separated by the special symbol "|" (vertical bar, read *or*). The grammar for *List-of-Int* could be written using "|" as

$$List\text{-}of\text{-}Int ::= () \quad | \quad (Int \quad . \quad List\text{-}of\text{-}Int)$$

Another shortcut is the *Kleene star*, expressed by the notation $\{\ldots\}^*$. When this appears in a right-hand side, it indicates a sequence of any number of instances of whatever appears between the braces. Using the Kleene star, the definition of *List-of-Int* is simply

$$List\text{-}of\text{-}Int ::= (\{Int\}^*)$$

This includes the possibility of no instances at all. If there are zero instances, we get the empty string.

A variant of the star notation is *Kleene plus* $\{\ldots\}^+$, which indicates a sequence of *one* or more instances. Substituting $^+$ for * in the example above would define the syntactic category of non-empty lists of integers.

Still another variant of the star notation is the *separated list* notation. For example, we write $\{Int\}^{*(c)}$ to denote a sequence of any number of instances of the nonterminal *Int*, separated by the non-empty character sequence c. This includes the possibility of no instances at all. If there are zero instances, we get the empty string. For example, $\{Int\}^{*(,)}$ includes the strings

```
8
14, 12
7, 3, 14, 16
```

and $\{Int\}^{*(,)}$ includes the strings

```
8
14; 12
7; 3; 14; 16
```

These notational shortcuts are not essential. It is always possible to rewrite the grammar without them.

If a set is specified by a grammar, a *syntactic derivation* may be used to show that a given data value is a member of the set. Such a derivation starts with the nonterminal corresponding to the set. At each step, indicated by an arrow ⇒, a nonterminal is replaced by the right-hand side of a corresponding rule, or with a known member of its syntactic class if the class was left undefined. For example, the previous demonstration that (14 . ()) is a list of integers may be formalized with the syntactic derivation

> *List-of-Int*
> ⇒ (*Int* . *List-of-Int*)
> ⇒ (14 . *List-of-Int*)
> ⇒ (14 . ())

The order in which nonterminals are replaced does not matter. Thus, here is another derivation of (14 . ()).

> *List-of-Int*
> ⇒ (*Int* . *List-of-Int*)
> ⇒ (*Int* . ())
> ⇒ (14 . ())

Exercise 1.4 [⋆] Write a derivation from *List-of-Int* to (-7 . (3 . (14 . ()))).

Let us consider the definitions of some other useful sets.

1. Many symbol manipulation procedures are designed to operate on lists that contain only symbols and other similarly restricted lists. We call these lists *s-lists*, defined as follows:

Definition 1.1.6 (s-list, s-exp)

$$S\text{-}list ::= (\{S\text{-}exp\}^*)$$
$$S\text{-}exp ::= Symbol \mid S\text{-}list$$

An s-list is a list of s-exps, and an s-exp is either an s-list or a symbol. Here are some s-lists.

```
(a b c)
(an (((s-list)) (with () lots) ((of) nesting)))
```

We may occasionally use an expanded definition of s-list with integers allowed, as well as symbols.

2. A binary tree with numeric leaves and interior nodes labeled with symbols may be represented using three-element lists for the interior nodes by the grammar:

Definition 1.1.7 (binary tree)

$$Bintree ::= Int \mid (Symbol \ Bintree \ Bintree)$$

Here are some examples of such trees:

```
1
2
(foo 1 2)
(bar 1 (foo 1 2))
(baz
  (bar 1 (foo 1 2))
  (biz 4 5))
```

3. The *lambda calculus* is a simple language that is often used to study the theory of programming languages. This language consists only of variable references, procedures that take a single argument, and procedure calls. We can define it with the grammar:

Definition 1.1.8 (lambda expression)

$$\begin{aligned} LcExp ::=&\ Identifier \\ ::=&\ (\texttt{lambda}\ (Identifier)\ LcExp) \\ ::=&\ (LcExp\ LcExp) \end{aligned}$$

where an identifier is any symbol other than lambda.

The identifier in the second production is the name of a variable in the body of the `lambda` expression. This variable is called the *bound variable* of the expression, because it binds or captures any occurrences of the variable in the body. Any occurrence of that variable in the body refers to this one.

To see how this works, consider the lambda calculus extended with arithmetic operators. In that language,

```
(lambda (x) (+ x 5))
```

is an expression in which x is the bound variable. This expression describes a procedure that adds 5 to its argument. Therefore, in

```
((lambda (x) (+ x 5)) (- x 7))
```

the last occurrence of x does not refer to the x that is bound in the `lambda` expression. We discuss this in section 1.2.4, where we introduce `occurs-free?`.

This grammar defines the elements of *LcExp* as Scheme values, so it becomes easy to write programs that manipulate them.

These grammars are said to be *context-free* because a rule defining a given syntactic category may be applied in any context that makes reference to that syntactic category. Sometimes this is not restrictive enough. Consider binary search trees. A node in a binary search tree is either empty or contains an integer and two subtrees

$$Binary\text{-}search\text{-}tree ::= \text{()} \quad | \quad (Int \;\; Binary\text{-}search\text{-}tree \;\; Binary\text{-}search\text{-}tree)$$

This correctly describes the structure of each node but ignores an important fact about binary search trees: all the keys in the left subtree are less than (or equal to) the key in the current node, and all the keys in the right subtree are greater than the key in the current node.

Because of this additional constraint, not every syntactic derivation from *Binary-search-tree* leads to a correct binary search tree. To determine whether a particular production can be applied in a particular syntactic derivation, we have to look at the context in which the production is applied. Such constraints are called *context-sensitive constraints* or *invariants*.

Context-sensitive constraints also arise when specifying the syntax of programming languages. For instance, in many languages every variable must be declared before it is used. This constraint on the use of variables is sensitive to the context of their use. Formal methods can be used to specify context-sensitive constraints, but these methods are far more complicated than the ones we consider in this chapter. In practice, the usual approach is first to specify a context-free grammar. Context-sensitive constraints are then added using other methods. We show an example of such techniques in chapter 7.

1.1.3   Induction

Having described sets inductively, we can use the inductive definitions in two ways: to prove theorems about members of the set and to write programs that manipulate them. Here we present an example of such a proof; writing the programs is the subject of the next section.

Theorem 1.1.1 *Let t be a binary tree, as defined in definition 1.1.7. Then t contains an odd number of nodes.*

Proof: The proof is by induction on the size of t, where we take the size of t to be the number of nodes in t. The induction hypothesis, $IH(k)$, is that any tree of size $\leq k$ has an odd number of nodes. We follow the usual prescription for an inductive proof: we first prove that $IH(0)$ is true, and we then prove that whenever k is an integer such that IH is true for k, then IH is true for $k + 1$ also.

1. There are no trees with 0 nodes, so $IH(0)$ holds trivially.

2. Let k be an integer such that $IH(k)$ holds, that is, any tree with $\leq k$ nodes actually has an odd number of nodes. We need to show that $IH(k + 1)$ holds as well: that any tree with $\leq k + 1$ nodes has an odd number of nodes. If t has $\leq k + 1$ nodes, there are exactly two possibilities according to the definition of a binary tree:

   (a) t could be of the form n, where n is an integer. In this case, t has exactly one node, and one is odd.

   (b) t could be of the form $(sym\ t_1\ t_2)$, where sym is a symbol and t_1 and t_2 are trees. Now t_1 and t_2 must have fewer nodes than t. Since t has $\leq k + 1$ nodes, t_1 and t_2 must have $\leq k$ nodes. Therefore they are covered by $IH(k)$, and they must each have an odd number of nodes, say $2n_1 + 1$ and $2n_2 + 1$ nodes, respectively. Hence the total number of nodes in the tree, counting the two subtrees and the root, is

$$(2n_1 + 1) + (2n_2 + 1) + 1 = 2(n_1 + n_2 + 1) + 1$$

which is once again odd.

This completes the proof of the claim that $IH(k + 1)$ holds and therefore completes the induction. □

The key to the proof is that the substructures of a tree t are always smaller than t itself. This pattern of proof is called *structural induction*.

Proof by Structural Induction

To prove that a proposition $IH(s)$ is true for all structures s, prove the following:

1. *IH is true on simple structures (those without substructures).*

2. *If IH is true on the substructures of s, then it is true on s itself.*

Exercise 1.5 [★★] Prove that if $e \in LcExp$, then there are the same number of left and right parentheses in e.

1.2   Deriving Recursive Programs

We have used the method of inductive definition to characterize complicated sets. We have seen that we can analyze an element of an inductively defined set to see how it is built from smaller elements of the set. We have used this idea to write a procedure `in-S?` to decide whether a natural number is in the set S. We now use the same idea to define more general procedures that compute on inductively defined sets.

Recursive procedures rely on an important principle:

The Smaller-Subproblem Principle

If we can reduce a problem to a smaller subproblem, we can call the procedure that solves the problem to solve the subproblem.

The solution returned for the subproblem may then be used to solve the original problem. This works because each time we call the procedure, it is called with a smaller problem, until eventually it is called with a problem that can be solved directly, without another call to itself.

We illustrate this idea with a sequence of examples.

1.2.1   `list-length`

The standard Scheme procedure `length` determines the number of elements in a list.

```
> (length '(a b c))
3
> (length '((x) ()))
2
```

Let us write our own procedure, called `list-length`, that does the same thing.

We begin by writing down the *contract* for the procedure. The contract specifies the sets of possible arguments and possible return values for the procedure. The contract also may include the intended usage or behavior of the procedure. This helps us keep track of our intentions both as we write and afterwards. In code, this would be a comment; we typeset it for readability.

list-length : *List* → *Int*
usage: (list-length *l*) = the length of *l*
```
(define list-length
  (lambda (lst)
    ...))
```

We can define the set of lists by

$$List ::= () \mid (Scheme\ value . List)$$

Therefore we consider each possibility for a list. If the list is empty, then its length is 0.

list-length : *List* → *Int*
usage: (list-length *l*) = the length of *l*
```
(define list-length
  (lambda (lst)
    (if (null? lst)
      0
      ...)))
```

If a list is non-empty, then its length is one more than the length of its cdr. This gives us a complete definition.

list-length : *List* → *Int*
usage: (list-length *l*) = the length of *l*
```
(define list-length
  (lambda (lst)
    (if (null? lst)
        0
        (+ 1 (list-length (cdr lst))))))
```

We can watch list-length compute by using its definition.

```
(list-length '(a (b c) d))
= (+ 1 (list-length '((b c) d)))
= (+ 1 (+ 1 (list-length '(d))))
= (+ 1 (+ 1 (+ 1 (list-length '()))))
= (+ 1 (+ 1 (+ 1 0)))
= 3
```

1.2.2 nth-element

The standard Scheme procedure list-ref takes a list lst and a zero-based index n and returns element number n of lst.

```
> (list-ref '(a b c) 1)
b
```

Let us write our own procedure, called nth-element, that does the same thing.

Again we use the definition of *List* above.

What should (nth-element *lst n*) return when *lst* is empty? In this case, (nth-element *lst n*) is asking for an element of an empty list, so we report an error.

What should (nth-element *lst n*) return when *lst* is non-empty? The answer depends on *n*. If $n = 0$, the answer is simply the car of *lst*.

What should (nth-element *lst n*) return when *lst* is non-empty and $n \neq 0$? In this case, the answer is the $(n-1)$-st element of the cdr of *lst*. Since $n \in N$ and $n \neq 0$, we know that $n - 1$ must also be in N, so we can find the $(n-1)$-st element by recursively calling nth-element.

This leads us to the definition

nth-element : *List* × *Int* → *SchemeVal*
usage: (nth-element *lst* *n*) = the *n*-th element of *lst*

```
(define nth-element
  (lambda (lst n)
    (if (null? lst)
      (report-list-too-short n)
      (if (zero? n)
        (car lst)
        (nth-element (cdr lst) (- n 1))))))

(define report-list-too-short
  (lambda (n)
    (eopl:error 'nth-element
      "List too short by ~s elements.~%" (+ n 1))))
```

Here the notation **nth-element** : *List* × *Int* → *SchemeVal* means that **nth-element** is a procedure that takes two arguments, a list and an integer, and returns a Scheme value. This is the same notation that is used in mathematics when we write $f : A \times B \to C$.

The procedure `report-list-too-short` reports an error condition by calling `eopl:error`. The procedure `eopl:error` aborts the computation. Its first argument is a symbol that allows the error message to identify the procedure that called `eopl:error`. The second argument is a string that is then printed in the error message. There must then be an additional argument for each instance of the character sequence ~s in the string. The values of these arguments are printed in place of the corresponding ~s when the string is printed. A ~% is treated as a new line. After the error message is printed, the computation is aborted. This procedure `eopl:error` is not part of standard Scheme, but most implementations of Scheme provide such a facility. We use procedures named `report-` to report errors in a similar fashion throughout the book.

Watch how `nth-element` computes its answer:

```
    (nth-element '(a b c d e) 3)
  = (nth-element   '(b c d e) 2)
  = (nth-element     '(c d e) 1)
  = (nth-element       '(d e) 0)
  = d
```

Here `nth-element` recurs on shorter and shorter lists, and on smaller and smaller numbers.

If error checking were omitted, we would have to rely on car and cdr to complain about being passed the empty list, but their error messages would be less helpful. For example, if we received an error message from car, we might have to look for uses of car throughout our program.

Exercise 1.6 [*] If we reversed the order of the tests in nth-element, what would go wrong?

Exercise 1.7 [**] The error message from nth-element is uninformative. Rewrite nth-element so that it produces a more informative error message, such as "(a b c) does not have 8 elements."

1.2.3 `remove-first`

The procedure remove-first should take two arguments: a symbol, *s*, and a list of symbols, *los*. It should return a list with the same elements arranged in the same order as *los*, except that the first occurrence of the symbol *s* is removed. If there is no occurrence of *s* in *los*, then *los* is returned.

```
> (remove-first 'a '(a b c))
(b c)
> (remove-first 'b '(e f g))
(e f g)
> (remove-first 'a4 '(c1 a4 c1 a4))
(c1 c1 a4)
> (remove-first 'x '())
()
```

Before we start writing the definition of this procedure, we must complete the problem specification by defining the set *List-of-Symbol* of lists of symbols. Unlike the s-lists introduced in the last section, these lists of symbols do not contain sublists.

$$\textit{List-of-Symbol} ::= ()\ \mid\ (\textit{Symbol}\ .\ \textit{List-of-Symbol})$$

A list of symbols is either the empty list or a list whose car is a symbol and whose cdr is a list of symbols.

If the list is empty, there are no occurrences of *s* to remove, so the answer is the empty list.

remove-first : *Sym* × *Listof(Sym)* → *Listof(Sym)*
usage: (remove-first s *los*) returns a list with
the same elements arranged in the same
order as *los*, except that the first
occurrence of the symbol *s* is removed.

```
(define remove-first
  (lambda (s los)
    (if (null? los)
      '()
      ...)))
```

Here we have written the contract with *Listof(Sym)* instead of *List-of-Symbol*. This notation will allow us to avoid many definitions like the ones above.

If *los* is non-empty, is there some case where we can determine the answer immediately? If the first element of *los* is *s*, say $los = (s\ s_1\ \ldots\ s_{n-1})$, the first occurrence of *s* is as the first element of *los*. So the result of removing it is just $(s_1\ \ldots\ s_{n-1})$.

remove-first : *Sym* × *Listof(Sym)* → *Listof(Sym)*

```
(define remove-first
  (lambda (s los)
    (if (null? los)
      '()
      (if (eqv? (car los) s)
        (cdr los)
        ...))))
```

If the first element of *los* is not *s*, say $los = (s_0\ s_1\ \ldots\ s_{n-1})$, then we know that s_0 is not the first occurrence of *s*. Therefore the first element of the answer must be s_0, which is the value of the expression (car los). Furthermore, the first occurrence of *s* in *los* must be its first occurrence in $(s_1\ \ldots\ s_{n-1})$. So the rest of the answer must be the result of removing the first occurrence of *s* from the cdr of *los*. Since the cdr of *los* is shorter than *los*, we may recursively call remove-first to remove *s* from the cdr of *los*. So the cdr of the answer can be obtained as the value of (remove-first s (cdr los)). Since we know how to find the car and cdr of the answer, we can find the whole answer by combining them with cons, using the expression (cons (car los) (remove-first s (cdr los))). With this, the complete definition of remove-first becomes

```
remove-first : Sym × Listof(Sym) → Listof(Sym)
(define remove-first
  (lambda (s los)
    (if (null? los)
      '()
      (if (eqv? (car los) s)
        (cdr los)
        (cons (car los) (remove-first s (cdr los)))))))
```

Exercise 1.8 [*] In the definition of `remove-first`, if the last line were replaced by `(remove-first s (cdr los))`, what function would the resulting procedure compute? Give the contract, including the usage statement, for the revised procedure.

Exercise 1.9 [**] Define `remove`, which is like `remove-first`, except that it removes *all* occurrences of a given symbol from a list of symbols, not just the first.

1.2.4 occurs-free?

The procedure `occurs-free?` should take a variable *var*, represented as a Scheme symbol, and a lambda-calculus expression *exp* as defined in definition 1.1.8, and determine whether or not *var* occurs free in *exp*. We say that a variable *occurs free* in an expression *exp* if it has some occurrence in *exp* that is not inside some `lambda` binding of the same variable. For example,

```
> (occurs-free? 'x 'x)
#t
> (occurs-free? 'x 'y)
#f
> (occurs-free? 'x '(lambda (x) (x y)))
#f
> (occurs-free? 'x '(lambda (y) (x y)))
#t
> (occurs-free? 'x '((lambda (x) x) (x y)))
#t
> (occurs-free? 'x '(lambda (y) (lambda (z) (x (y z)))))
#t
```

We can solve this problem by following the grammar for lambda-calculus expressions

$$LcExp ::= Identifier$$
$$::= (\texttt{lambda} \ (Identifier) \ LcExp)$$
$$::= (LcExp \ LcExp)$$

We can summarize these cases in the rules:

- If the expression e is a variable, then the variable x occurs free in e if and only if x is the same as e.

- If the expression e is of the form (lambda (y) e'), then the variable x occurs free in e if and only if y is different from x and x occurs free in e'.

- If the expression e is of the form (e_1 e_2), then x occurs free in e if and only if it occurs free in e_1 or e_2. Here, we use "or" to mean *inclusive or*, meaning that this includes the possibility that x occurs free in both e_1 and e_2. We will generally use "or" in this sense.

You should convince yourself that these rules capture the notion of occurring "not inside a lambda-binding of x."

Exercise 1.10 [⋆] We typically use "or" to mean "inclusive or." What other meanings can "or" have?

Then it is easy to define occurs-free?. Since there are three alternatives to be checked, we use a Scheme cond rather than an if. In Scheme, (or exp_1 exp_2) returns a true value if either exp_1 or exp_2 returns a true value.

occurs-free? : *Sym* × *LcExp* → *Bool*
usage: returns #t if the symbol *var* occurs free
               in *exp*, otherwise returns #f.
```
(define occurs-free?
  (lambda (var exp)
    (cond
      ((symbol? exp) (eqv? var exp))
      ((eqv? (car exp) 'lambda)
       (and
         (not (eqv? var (car (cadr exp))))
         (occurs-free? var (caddr exp))))
      (else
        (or
          (occurs-free? var (car exp))
          (occurs-free? var (cadr exp)))))))
```

This procedure is not as readable as it might be. It is hard to tell, for example, that (car (cadr exp)) refers to the declaration of a variable in a lambda expression, or that (caddr exp) refers to its body. We show how to improve this situation considerably in section 2.5.

1.2.5   `subst`

The procedure `subst` should take three arguments: two symbols, `new` and `old`, and an s-list, `slist`. All elements of `slist` are examined, and a new list is returned that is similar to `slist` but with all occurrences of `old` replaced by instances of `new`.

```
> (subst 'a 'b '((b c) (b () d)))
((a c) (a () d))
```

Since `subst` is defined over s-lists, its organization should reflect the definition of s-lists (definition 1.1.6)

$$S\text{-}list ::= (\{S\text{-}exp\}^*)$$
$$S\text{-}exp ::= Symbol \mid S\text{-}list$$

The Kleene star gives a concise description of the set of s-lists, but it is not so helpful for writing programs. Therefore our first step is to rewrite the grammar to eliminate the use of the Kleene star. The resulting grammar suggests that our procedure should recur on the car and cdr of an s-list.

$$S\text{-}list ::= ()$$
$$::= (S\text{-}exp \; . \; S\text{-}list)$$
$$S\text{-}exp ::= Symbol \mid S\text{-}list$$

This example is more complex than our previous ones because the grammar for its input contains two nonterminals, *S-list* and *S-exp*. Therefore we will have two procedures, one for dealing with *S-list* and one for dealing with *S-exp*:

subst : *Sym* × *Sym* × *S-list* → *S-list*
```
(define subst
  (lambda (new old slist)
    ...))
```

subst-in-s-exp : *Sym* × *Sym* × *S-exp* → *S-exp*
```
(define subst-in-s-exp
  (lambda (new old sexp)
    ...))
```

Let us first work on `subst`. If the list is empty, there are no occurrences of `old` to replace.

subst : *Sym* × *Sym* × *S-list* → *S-list*
```
(define subst
  (lambda (new old slist)
    (if (null? slist)
      '()
      ...)))
```

If `slist` is non-empty, its car is a member of *S-exp* and its cdr is another s-list. In this case, the answer should be a list whose car is the result of changing `old` to `new` in the car of `slist`, and whose cdr is the result of changing `old` to `new` in the cdr of `slist`. Since the car of `slist` is an element of *S-exp*, we solve the subproblem for the car using `subst-in-s-exp`. Since the cdr of `slist` is an element of *S-list*, we recur on the cdr using `subst`:

subst : *Sym* × *Sym* × *S-list* → *S-list*
```
(define subst
  (lambda (new old slist)
    (if (null? slist)
      '()
      (cons
        (subst-in-s-exp new old (car slist))
        (subst new old (cdr slist))))))
```

Now we can move on to `subst-in-s-exp`. From the grammar, we know that the symbol expression `sexp` is either a symbol or an s-list. If it is a symbol, we need to ask whether it is the same as the symbol `old`. If it is, the answer is `new`; if it is some other symbol, the answer is the same as `sexp`. If `sexp` is an s-list, then we can recur using `subst` to find the answer.

subst-in-s-exp : *Sym* × *Sym* × *S-exp* → *S-exp*
```
(define subst-in-s-exp
  (lambda (new old sexp)
    (if (symbol? sexp)
      (if (eqv? sexp old) new sexp)
      (subst new old sexp))))
```

Since we have strictly followed the definition of *S-list* and *S-exp*, this recursion is guaranteed to halt. Since `subst` and `subst-in-s-exp` call each other recursively, we say they are *mutually recursive*.

The decomposition of `subst` into two procedures, one for each syntactic category, is an important technique. It allows us to think about one syntactic category at a time, which greatly simplifies our thinking about more complicated programs.

Exercise 1.11 [⋆] In the last line of subst-in-s-exp, the recursion is on sexp and not a smaller substructure. Why is the recursion guaranteed to halt?

Exercise 1.12 [⋆] Eliminate the one call to subst-in-s-exp in subst by replacing it by its definition and simplifying the resulting procedure. The result will be a version of subst that does not need subst-in-s-exp. This technique is called *inlining*, and is used by optimizing compilers.

Exercise 1.13 [⋆ ⋆] In our example, we began by eliminating the Kleene star in the grammar for *S-list*. Write subst following the original grammar by using map.

We've now developed a recipe for writing procedures that operate on inductively defined data sets. We summarize it as a slogan.

Follow the Grammar!

When defining a procedure that operates on inductively defined data, the structure of the program should be patterned after the structure of the data.

More precisely:

- Write one procedure for each nonterminal in the grammar. The procedure will be responsible for handling the data corresponding to that nonterminal, and nothing else.

- In each procedure, write one alternative for each production corresponding to that nonterminal. You may need additional case structure, but this will get you started. For each nonterminal that appears in the right-hand side, write a recursive call to the procedure for that nonterminal.

1.3   Auxiliary Procedures and Context Arguments

The *Follow-the-Grammar* recipe is powerful, but sometimes it is not sufficient. Consider the procedure number-elements. This procedure should take any list $(v_0 \ v_1 \ v_2 \ \ldots)$ and return the list $((0 \ v_0) \ (1 \ v_1) \ (2 \ v_2) \ \ldots)$.

A straightforward decomposition of the kind we've used so far does not solve this problem, because there is no obvious way to build the value of (number-elements lst) from the value of (number-elements (cdr lst)) (but see exercise 1.36).

To solve this problem, we need to *generalize* the problem. We write a new procedure number-elements-from that takes an additional argument n

that specifies the number to start from. This procedure is easy to write, by recursion on the list.

number-elements-from : *Listof(SchemeVal)* $\times$ *Int* $\rightarrow$ *Listof(List(Int, SchemeVal))*

usage: (number-elements-from ' (v_0 v_1 v_2 ...) n)
         = ((n v_0) ($n+1$ v_1) ($n+2$ v_2) ...)
```
(define number-elements-from
  (lambda (lst n)
    (if (null? lst) '()
      (cons
        (list n (car lst))
        (number-elements-from (cdr lst) (+ n 1)))))))
```

Here the contract header tells us that this procedure takes two arguments, a list (containing any Scheme values) and an integer, and returns a list of things, each of which is a list consisting of two elements: an integer and a Scheme value.

Once we have defined number-elements-from, it's easy to write the desired procedure.

number-elements : *List* $\rightarrow$ *Listof(List(Int, SchemeVal))*
```
(define number-elements
  (lambda (lst
    (number-elements-from lst 0)))
```

There are two important observations to be made here. First, the procedure number-elements-from has a specification that is *independent* of the specification of number-elements. It's very common for a programmer to write a procedure that simply calls some auxiliary procedure with some additional constant arguments. Unless we can understand what that auxiliary procedure does for *every* value of its arguments, then we can't possibly understand what the calling procedure does. This gives us a slogan:

No Mysterious Auxiliaries!

When defining an auxiliary procedure, always specify what it does on all *arguments, not just the initial values.*

Second, the two arguments to number-elements-from play two different roles. The first argument is the list we are working on. It gets smaller at every recursive call. The second argument, however, is an abstraction

of the *context* in which we are working. In this example, when we call
`number-elements`, we end up calling `number-elements-from` on each
sublist of the original list. The second argument tells us the position of the
sublist in the original list. This need not decrease at a recursive call; indeed it
grows, because we are passing over another element of the original list. We
sometimes call this a *context argument* or *inherited attribute*.

As another example, consider the problem of summing all the values in a
vector.

If we were summing the values in a list, we could follow the grammar to
recur on the cdr of the list. This would get us a procedure like

```
list-sum  :  Listof(Int)  →  Int
(define list-sum
  (lambda (loi)
    (if (null? loi)
        0
        (+ (car loi)
           (list-sum (cdr loi)))))))
```

But it is not possible to proceed in this way with vectors, because they do not
decompose as readily.

Since we cannot decompose vectors, we generalize the problem to compute the sum of part of the vector. The specification of our problem is to
compute

$$\sum_{i=0}^{i=length(v)-1} v_i$$

where v is a vector of integers. We generalize it by turning the upper bound
into a parameter n, so that the new task is to compute

$$\sum_{i=0}^{i=n} v_i$$

where $0 \leq n < length(v)$.

This procedure is straightforward to write from its specification, using
induction on its second argument n.

partial-vector-sum : *Vectorof(Int)* × *Int* → *Int*
usage: if $0 \le n < length(v)$, then

$$(\texttt{partial-vector-sum } v \ n) = \sum_{i=0}^{i=n} v_i$$

```
(define partial-vector-sum
  (lambda (v n)
    (if (zero? n)
      (vector-ref v 0)
      (+ (vector-ref v n)
        (partial-vector-sum v (- n 1))))))
```

Since *n* decreases steadily to zero, a proof of correctness for this program would proceed by induction on *n*. Because $0 \le n$ and $n \ne 0$, we can deduce that $0 \le (n-1)$, so that the recursive call to the procedure `partial-vector-sum` satisfies its contract.

It is now a simple matter to solve our original problem. The procedure `partial-vector-sum` doesn't apply if the vector is of length 0, so we need to handle that case separately.

vector-sum : *Vectorof(Int)* → *Int*
usage: (vector-sum *v*) = $\displaystyle\sum_{i=0}^{i=length(v)-1} v_i$

```
(define vector-sum
  (lambda (v)
    (let ((n (vector-length v)))
      (if (zero? n)
        0
        (partial-vector-sum v (- n 1))))))
```

There are many other situations in which it may be helpful or necessary to introduce auxiliary variables or procedures to solve a problem. Always feel free to do so, provided that you can give an independent specification of what the new procedure is intended to do.

Exercise 1.14 [⋆⋆] Given the assumption $0 \le n < length(v)$, prove that `partial-vector-sum` is correct.

1.4 Exercises

Getting the knack of writing recursive programs involves practice. Thus we conclude this chapter with a sequence of exercises.

In each of these exercises, assume that s is a symbol, n is a nonnegative integer, 1st is a list, loi is a list of integers, los is a list of symbols, slist is an s-list, and x is any Scheme value; and similarly s1 is a symbol, los2 is a list of symbols, x1 is a Scheme value, etc. Also assume that pred is a predicate, that is, a procedure that takes any Scheme value and always returns either #t or #f. Make no other assumptions about the data unless further restrictions are given as part of a particular problem. For these exercises, there is no need to check that the input matches the description; for each procedure, assume that its input values are members of the specified sets.

Define, test, and debug each procedure. Your definition should include a contract and usage comment in the style we have used in this chapter. Feel free to define auxiliary procedures, but each auxiliary procedure you define should have its own specification, as in section 1.3.

To test these procedures, first try all the given examples. Then use other examples to test these procedures, since the given examples are not adequate to reveal all possible errors.

Exercise 1.15 [⋆] (duple n x) returns a list containing n copies of x.

```
> (duple 2 3)
(3 3)
> (duple 4 '(ha ha))
((ha ha) (ha ha) (ha ha) (ha ha))
> (duple 0 '(blah))
()
```

Exercise 1.16 [⋆] (invert lst), where lst is a list of 2-lists (lists of length two), returns a list with each 2-list reversed.

```
> (invert '((a 1) (a 2) (1 b) (2 b)))
((1 a) (2 a) (b 1) (b 2))
```

Exercise 1.17 [⋆] (down lst) wraps parentheses around each top-level element of lst.

```
> (down '(1 2 3))
((1) (2) (3))
> (down '((a) (fine) (idea)))
(((a)) ((fine)) ((idea)))
> (down '(a (more (complicated)) object))
((a) ((more (complicated))) (object))
```

Exercise 1.18 [⋆] (swapper s1 s2 slist) returns a list the same as slist, but with all occurrences of s1 replaced by s2 and all occurrences of s2 replaced by s1.

```
> (swapper 'a 'd '(a b c d))
(d b c a)
> (swapper 'a 'd '(a d () c d))
(d a () c a)
> (swapper 'x 'y '((x) y (z (x))))
((y) x (z (y)))
```

Exercise 1.19 [⋆⋆] (list-set lst n x) returns a list like lst, except that the n-th element, using zero-based indexing, is x.

```
> (list-set '(a b c d) 2 '(1 2))
(a b (1 2) d)
> (list-ref (list-set '(a b c d) 3 '(1 5 10)) 3)
(1 5 10)
```

Exercise 1.20 [⋆] (count-occurrences s slist) returns the number of occurrences of s in slist.

```
> (count-occurrences 'x '((f x) y (((x z) x))))
3
> (count-occurrences 'x '((f x) y (((x z) () x))))
3
> (count-occurrences 'w '((f x) y (((x z) x))))
0
```

Exercise 1.21 [⋆⋆] (product sos1 sos2), where sos1 and sos2 are each a list of symbols without repetitions, returns a list of 2-lists that represents the Cartesian product of sos1 and sos2. The 2-lists may appear in any order.

```
> (product '(a b c) '(x y))
((a x) (a y) (b x) (b y) (c x) (c y))
```

Exercise 1.22 [⋆⋆] (filter-in pred lst) returns the list of those elements in lst that satisfy the predicate pred.

```
> (filter-in number? '(a 2 (1 3) b 7))
(2 7)
> (filter-in symbol? '(a (b c) 17 foo))
(a foo)
```

Exercise 1.23 [⋆⋆] (list-index pred lst) returns the 0-based position of the first element of lst that satisfies the predicate pred. If no element of lst satisfies the predicate, then list-index returns #f.

```
> (list-index number? '(a 2 (1 3) b 7))
1
> (list-index symbol? '(a (b c) 17 foo))
0
> (list-index symbol? '(1 2 (a b) 3))
#f
```

Exercise 1.24 [★★] (every? pred lst) returns #f if any element of lst fails to satisfy pred, and returns #t otherwise.

```
> (every? number? '(a b c 3 e))
#f
> (every? number? '(1 2 3 5 4))
#t
```

Exercise 1.25 [★★] (exists? pred lst) returns #t if any element of lst satisfies pred, and returns #f otherwise.

```
> (exists? number? '(a b c 3 e))
#t
> (exists? number? '(a b c d e))
#f
```

Exercise 1.26 [★★] (up lst) removes a pair of parentheses from each top-level element of lst. If a top-level element is not a list, it is included in the result, as is. The value of (up (down lst)) is equivalent to lst, but (down (up lst)) is not necessarily lst. (See exercise 1.17.)

```
> (up '((1 2) (3 4)))
(1 2 3 4)
> (up '((x (y)) z))
(x (y) z)
```

Exercise 1.27 [★★] (flatten slist) returns a list of the symbols contained in slist in the order in which they occur when slist is printed. Intuitively, flatten removes all the inner parentheses from its argument.

```
> (flatten '(a b c))
(a b c)
> (flatten '((a) () (b ()) () (c)))
(a b c)
> (flatten '((a b) c (((d)) e)))
(a b c d e)
> (flatten '(a b (() (c))))
(a b c)
```

Exercise 1.28 [★★] (merge loi1 loi2), where loi1 and loi2 are lists of integers that are sorted in ascending order, returns a sorted list of all the integers in loi1 and loi2.

```
> (merge '(1 4) '(1 2 8))
(1 1 2 4 8)
> (merge '(35 62 81 90 91) '(3 83 85 90))
(3 35 62 81 83 85 90 90 91)
```

Exercise 1.29 [★★] (sort loi) returns a list of the elements of loi in ascending order.

```
> (sort '(8 2 5 2 3))
(2 2 3 5 8)
```

Exercise 1.30 [★★] (sort/predicate pred loi) returns a list of elements sorted by the predicate.

```
> (sort/predicate < '(8 2 5 2 3))
(2 2 3 5 8)
> (sort/predicate > '(8 2 5 2 3))
(8 5 3 2 2)
```

Exercise 1.31 [★] Write the following procedures for calculating on a bintree (definition 1.1.7): leaf and interior-node, which build bintrees, leaf?, which tests whether a bintree is a leaf, and lson, rson, and contents-of, which extract the components of a node. contents-of should work on both leaves and interior nodes.

Exercise 1.32 [★] Write a procedure double-tree that takes a bintree, as represented in definition 1.1.7, and produces another bintree like the original, but with all the integers in the leaves doubled.

Exercise 1.33 [★★] Write a procedure mark-leaves-with-red-depth that takes a bintree (definition 1.1.7), and produces a bintree of the same shape as the original, except that in the new tree, each leaf contains the integer of nodes between it and the root that contain the symbol red. For example, the expression

```
(mark-leaves-with-red-depth
  (interior-node 'red
    (interior-node 'bar
      (leaf 26)
      (leaf 12))
    (interior-node 'red
      (leaf 11)
      (interior-node 'quux
        (leaf 117)
        (leaf 14))
```

which is written using the procedures defined in exercise 1.31, should return the bintree

```
(red
  (bar 1 1)
  (red 2 (quux 2 2)))
```

Exercise 1.34 [★★★] Write a procedure `path` that takes an integer n and a binary search tree `bst` (page 10) that contains the integer n, and returns a list of `lefts` and `rights` showing how to find the node containing n. If n is found at the root, it returns the empty list.

```
> (path 17 '(14 (7 () (12 () ()))
                (26 (20 (17 () ())
                        ())
                    (31 () ()))))
(right left left)
```

Exercise 1.35 [★★★] Write a procedure `number-leaves` that takes a bintree, and produces a bintree like the original, except the contents of the leaves are numbered starting from 0. For example,

```
(number-leaves
  (interior-node 'foo
    (interior-node 'bar
      (leaf 26)
      (leaf 12))
    (interior-node 'baz
      (leaf 11)
      (interior-node 'quux
        (leaf 117)
        (leaf 14))
```

should return

```
(foo
  (bar 0 1)
  (baz
    2
    (quux 3 4)))
```

Exercise 1.36 [★★★] Write a procedure g such that `number-elements` from page 23 could be defined as

```
(define number-elements
  (lambda (lst)
    (if (null? lst) '()
        (g (list 0 (car lst)) (number-elements (cdr lst))))))
```

2 *Data Abstraction*

2.1   Specifying Data via Interfaces

Every time we decide to represent a certain set of quantities in a particular way, we are defining a new data type: the data type whose values are those representations and whose operations are the procedures that manipulate those entities.

The representation of these entities is often complex, so we do not want to be concerned with their details when we can avoid them. We may also decide to change the representation of the data. The most efficient representation is often a lot more difficult to implement, so we may wish to develop a simple implementation first and only change to a more efficient representation if it proves critical to the overall performance of a system. If we decide to change the representation of some data for any reason, we must be able to locate all parts of a program that are dependent on the representation. This is accomplished using the technique of *data abstraction*.

Data abstraction divides a data type into two pieces: an *interface* and an *implementation*. The interface tells us what the data of the type represents, what the operations on the data are, and what properties these operations may be relied on to have. The *implementation* provides a specific representation of the data and code for the operations that make use of that data representation.

A data type that is abstract in this way is said to be an *abstract data type*. The rest of the program, the *client* of the data type, manipulates the new data only through the operations specified in the interface. Thus if we wish to change the representation of the data, all we must do is change the implementation of the operations in the interface.

This is a familiar idea: when we write programs that manipulate files, most of the time we care only that we can invoke procedures that perform the open, close, read, and other typical operations on files. Similarly, most of the time, we don't care how integers are actually represented inside the machine. Our only concern is that we can perform the arithmetic operations reliably.

When the client manipulates the values of the data type only through the procedures in the interface, we say that the client code is *representation-independent*, because then the code does not rely on the representation of the values in the data type.

All the knowledge about how the data is represented must therefore reside in the code of the implementation. The most important part of an implementation is the specification of how the data is represented. We use the notation $\lceil v \rceil$ for "the representation of data v."

To make this clearer, let us consider a simple example: the data type of natural numbers. The data to be represented are the natural numbers. The interface is to consist of four procedures: zero, is-zero?, successor, and predecessor. Of course, not just any set of procedures will be acceptable as an implementation of this interface. A set of procedures will be acceptable as implementations of zero, is-zero?, successor, and predecessor only if they satisfy the four equations

$$(\texttt{zero}) = \lceil 0 \rceil$$
$$(\texttt{is-zero?}\ \lceil n \rceil) = \begin{cases} \texttt{\#t} & n = 0 \\ \texttt{\#f} & n \neq 0 \end{cases}$$
$$(\texttt{successor}\ \lceil n \rceil) = \lceil n + 1 \rceil \quad (n \geq 0)$$
$$(\texttt{predecessor}\ \lceil n + 1 \rceil) = \lceil n \rceil \quad (n \geq 0)$$

This specification does not dictate how these natural numbers are to be represented. It requires only that these procedures conspire to produce the specified behavior. Thus, the procedure zero must return the representation of 0. The procedure successor, given the representation of the number n, must return the representation of the number $n + 1$, and so on. The specification says nothing about (predecessor (zero)), so under this specification any behavior would be acceptable.

We can now write client programs that manipulate natural numbers, and we are guaranteed that they will get correct answers, no matter what representation is in use. For example,

```
(define plus
  (lambda (x y)
    (if (is-zero? x)
        y
        (successor (plus (predecessor x) y)))))
```

will satisfy (plus $\lceil x \rceil$ $\lceil y \rceil$) = $\lceil x + y \rceil$, no matter what implementation of the natural numbers we use.

Most interfaces will contain some *constructors* that build elements of the data type, and some *observers* that extract information from values of the data type. Here we have three constructors, zero, successor, and predecessor, and one observer, is-zero?.

There are many possible representations of this interface. Let us consider three of them.

1. *Unary representation:* In the unary representation, the natural number n is represented by a list of n #t's. Thus, 0 is represented by (), 1 is represented by (#t), 2 is represented by (#t #t), etc. We can define this representation inductively by:

   $$\lceil 0 \rceil = ()$$
   $$\lceil n + 1 \rceil = (\text{#t} \; . \; \lceil n \rceil)$$

   In this representation, we can satisfy the specification by writing

   ```
   (define zero (lambda () '()))
   (define is-zero? (lambda (n) (null? n)))
   (define successor (lambda (n) (cons #t n)))
   (define predecessor (lambda (n) (cdr n)))
   ```

2. *Scheme number representation:* In this representation, we simply use Scheme's internal representation of numbers (which might itself be quite complicated!). We let $\lceil n \rceil$ be the Scheme integer n, and define the four required entities by

   ```
   (define zero (lambda () 0))
   (define is-zero? (lambda (n) (zero? n)))
   (define successor (lambda (n) (+ n 1)))
   (define predecessor (lambda (n) (- n 1)))
   ```

3. *Bignum representation:* In the bignum representation, numbers are represented in base N, for some large integer N. The representation becomes a list consisting of numbers between 0 and $N - 1$ (sometimes called *bigits* rather than digits). This representation makes it easy to represent integers that are much larger than can be represented in a machine word. For our purposes, it is convenient to keep the list with least-significant bigit first. We can define the representation inductively by

$$\lceil n \rceil = \begin{cases} () & n = 0 \\ (r \ . \ \lceil q \rceil) & n = qN + r, \ 0 \le r < N \end{cases}$$

So if $N = 16$, then $\lceil 33 \rceil = (1 \ 2)$ and $\lceil 258 \rceil = (2 \ 0 \ 1)$, since

$$258 = 2 \times 16^0 + 0 \times 16^1 + 1 \times 16^2$$

None of these implementations enforces data abstraction. There is nothing to prevent a client program from looking at the representation and determining whether it is a list or a Scheme integer. On the other hand, some languages provide direct support for data abstractions: they allow the programmer to create new interfaces and check that the new data is manipulated only through the procedures in the interface. If the representation of a type is hidden, so it cannot be exposed by any operation (including printing), the type is said to be *opaque.* Otherwise, it is said to be *transparent.*

Scheme does not provide a standard mechanism for creating new opaque types. Thus we settle for an intermediate level of abstraction: we define interfaces and rely on the writer of the client program to be discreet and use only the procedures in the interfaces.

In chapter 8, we discuss ways in which a language can enforce such protocols.

Exercise 2.1 [$\star$] Implement the four required operations for bigits. Then use your implementation to calculate the factorial of 10. How does the execution time vary as this argument changes? How does the execution time vary as the base changes? Explain why.

Exercise 2.2 [$\star\star$] Analyze each of these proposed representations critically. To what extent do they succeed or fail in satisfying the specification of the data type?

Exercise 2.3 [$\star\star$] Define a representation of all the integers (negative and nonnegative) as diff-trees, where a diff-tree is a list defined by the grammar

Diff-tree ::= (one) | (diff *Diff-tree Diff-tree*)

The list (one) represents 1.   If t_1 represents n_1 and t_2 represents n_2, then
(diff t_1 t_2) is a representation of $n_1 - n_2$.

So both (one) and (diff (one) (diff (one) (one))) are representations of
1; (diff (diff (one) (one)) (one)) is a representation of -1.

1. Show that every number has infinitely many representations in this system.

2. Turn this representation of the integers into an implementation by writing zero,
   is-zero?, successor, and predecessor, as specified on page 32, except that
   now the negative integers are also represented. Your procedures should take as
   input any of the multiple legal representations of an integer in this scheme. For
   example, if your successor procedure is given any of the infinitely many legal
   representations of 1, it should produce one of the legal representations of 2. It is
   permissible for different legal representations of 1 to yield different legal representations of 2.

3. Write a procedure diff-tree-plus that does addition in this representation.
   Your procedure should be optimized for the diff-tree representation, and should
   do its work in a constant amount of time (independent of the size of its inputs). In
   particular, it should not be recursive.

2.2   Representation Strategies for Data Types

When data abstraction is used, programs have the property of representation
independence: programs are independent of the particular representation
used to implement an abstract data type. It is then possible to change the
representation by redefining the small number of procedures belonging to
the interface. We frequently rely on this property in later chapters.

In this section we introduce some strategies for representing data types.
We illustrate these choices using a data type of *environments*. An environment
associates a value with each element of a finite set of variables. An environment may be used to associate variables with their values in a programming
language implementation. A compiler may also use an environment to associate each variable name with information about that variable.

Variables may be represented in any way we please, so long as we can
check two variables for equality. We choose to represent variables using
Scheme symbols, but in a language without a symbol data type, variables
could be represented by strings, by references into a hash table, or even by
numbers (see section 3.6).

2.2.1   The Environment Interface

An environment is a function whose domain is a finite set of variables, and whose range is the set of all Scheme values. Since we adopt the usual mathematical convention that a finite function is a finite set of ordered pairs, then we need to represent all sets of the form $\{(var_1, val_1), \ldots, (var_n, val_n)\}$ where the var_i are distinct variables and the val_i are any Scheme values. We sometimes call the value of the variable *var* in an environment *env* its *binding* in *env*.

The interface to this data type has three procedures, specified as follows:

$$(\texttt{empty-env}) \qquad\qquad = \lceil \emptyset \rceil$$
$$(\texttt{apply-env}\ \lceil f \rceil\ var) \qquad = f(var)$$
$$(\texttt{extend-env}\ var\ v\ \lceil f \rceil) \quad = \lceil g \rceil,$$
$$\text{where } g(var_1) = \begin{cases} v & \text{if } var_1 = var \\ f(var_1) & \text{otherwise} \end{cases}$$

The procedure `empty-env`, applied to no arguments, must produce a representation of the empty environment; `apply-env` applies a representation of an environment to a variable and (`extend-env` *var val env*) produces a new environment that behaves like *env*, except that its value at variable *var* is *val*. For example, the expression

```
> (define e
    (extend-env 'd 6
      (extend-env 'y 8
        (extend-env 'x 7
          (extend-env 'y 14
            (empty-env))))))
```

defines an environment *e* such that $e(d) = 6$, $e(x) = 7$, $e(y) = 8$, and *e* is undefined on any other variables. This is, of course, only one of many different ways of building this environment. For instance, in the example above the binding of y to 14 is overridden by its later binding to 8.

As in the previous example, we can divide the procedures of the interface into constructors and observers. In this example, `empty-env` and `extend-env` are the constructors, and `apply-env` is the only observer.

Exercise 2.4 [⋆⋆] Consider the data type of *stacks* of values, with an interface consisting of the procedures `empty-stack`, `push`, `pop`, `top`, and `empty-stack?`. Write a specification for these operations in the style of the example above. Which operations are constructors and which are observers?

2.2.2 Data Structure Representation

We can obtain a representation of environments by observing that every environment can be built by starting with the empty environment and applying `extend-env` n times, for some $n \geq 0$, e.g.,

```
(extend-env varₙ valₙ
   ...
   (extend-env var₁ val₁
     (empty-env))...)
```

So every environment can be built by an expression in the following grammar:

$$Env\text{-}exp ::= \text{(empty-env)}$$
$$::= \text{(extend-env } Identifier \ Scheme\text{-}value \ Env\text{-}exp\text{)}$$

We could represent environments using the same grammar to describe a set of lists. This would give the implementation shown in figure 2.1. The procedure `apply-env` looks at the data structure `env` representing an environment, determines what kind of environment it represents, and does the right thing. If it represents the empty environment, then an error is reported. If it represents an environment built by `extend-env`, then it checks to see if the variable it is looking for is the same as the one bound in the environment. If it is, then the saved value is returned. Otherwise, the variable is looked up in the saved environment.

This is a very common pattern of code. We call it the *interpreter recipe*:

The Interpreter Recipe

1. *Look at a piece of data.*

2. *Decide what kind of data it represents.*

3. *Extract the components of the datum and do the right thing with them.*

Env = (empty-env) | (extend-env *Var SchemeVal Env*)
Var = *Sym*

empty-env : () $\rightarrow$ *Env*
```
(define empty-env
  (lambda () (list 'empty-env)))
```

extend-env : *Var* $\times$ *SchemeVal* $\times$ *Env* $\rightarrow$ *Env*
```
(define extend-env
  (lambda (var val env)
    (list 'extend-env var val env)))
```

apply-env : *Env* $\times$ *Var* $\rightarrow$ *SchemeVal*
```
(define apply-env
  (lambda (env search-var)
    (cond
      ((eqv? (car env) 'empty-env)
       (report-no-binding-found search-var))
      ((eqv? (car env) 'extend-env)
       (let ((saved-var (cadr env))
             (saved-val (caddr env))
             (saved-env (cadddr env)))
         (if (eqv? search-var saved-var)
             saved-val
             (apply-env saved-env search-var))))
      (else
        (report-invalid-env env)))))

(define report-no-binding-found
  (lambda (search-var)
    (eopl:error 'apply-env "No binding for ~s" search-var)))

(define report-invalid-env
  (lambda (env)
    (eopl:error 'apply-env "Bad environment: ~s" env)))
```

Figure 2.1   A data-structure representation of environments

Exercise 2.5 [⋆] We can use any data structure for representing environments, if we can distinguish empty environments from non-empty ones, and in which one can extract the pieces of a non-empty environment. Implement environments using a representation in which the empty environment is represented as the empty list, and in which `extend-env` builds an environment that looks like

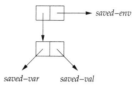

This is called an *a-list* or *association-list* representation.

Exercise 2.6 [⋆] Invent at least three different representations of the environment interface and implement them.

Exercise 2.7 [⋆] Rewrite `apply-env` in figure 2.1 to give a more informative error message.

Exercise 2.8 [⋆] Add to the environment interface an observer called `empty-env?` and implement it using the a-list representation.

Exercise 2.9 [⋆] Add to the environment interface an observer called `has-binding?` that takes an environment *env* and a variable *s* and tests to see if *s* has an associated value in *env*. Implement it using the a-list representation.

Exercise 2.10 [⋆] Add to the environment interface a constructor `extend-env*`, and implement it using the a-list representation. This constructor takes a list of variables, a list of values of the same length, and an environment, and is specified by

$$(\text{extend-env*} \ (var_1 \ \ldots \ var_k) \ (val_1 \ \ldots \ val_k) \ \lceil f \rceil) = \lceil g \rceil,$$
$$\text{where } g(var) = \begin{cases} val_i & \text{if } var = var_i \text{ for some } i \text{ such that } 1 \le i \le k \\ f(var) & \text{otherwise} \end{cases}$$

Exercise 2.11 [⋆⋆] A naive implementation of `extend-env*` from the preceding exercise requires time proportional to *k* to run. It is possible to represent environments so that `extend-env*` requires only constant time: represent the empty environment by the empty list, and represent a non-empty environment by the data structure

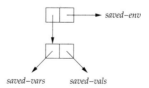

Such an environment might look like

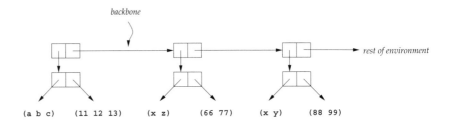

This is called the *ribcage* representation. The environment is represented as a list of pairs called *ribs*; each left rib is a list of variables and each right rib is the corresponding list of values.

Implement the environment interface, including `extend-env*`, in this representation.

2.2.3   Procedural Representation

The environment interface has an important property: it has exactly one observer, `apply-env`. This allows us to represent an environment as a Scheme procedure that takes a variable and returns its associated value.

To do this, we define `empty-env` and `extend-env` to return procedures that, when applied, do the same thing that `apply-env` did in the preceding section. This gives us the following implementation.

Env = *Var* → *SchemeVal*

empty-env : () → *Env*
```
(define empty-env
  (lambda ()
    (lambda (search-var)
      (report-no-binding-found search-var))))
```

extend-env : *Var* × *SchemeVal* × *Env* → *Env*
```
(define extend-env
  (lambda (saved-var saved-val saved-env)
    (lambda (search-var)
      (if (eqv? search-var saved-var)
        saved-val
        (apply-env saved-env search-var)))))
```

apply-env : *Env* × *Var* → *SchemeVal*
```
(define apply-env
  (lambda (env search-var)
    (env search-var)))
```

If the empty environment, created by invoking `empty-env`, is passed any variable whatsoever, it indicates with an error message that the given variable is not in its domain. The procedure `extend-env` returns a new procedure that represents the extended environment. This procedure, when passed a variable `search-var`, checks to see if the variable it is looking for is the same as the one bound in the environment. If it is, then the saved value is returned. Otherwise, the variable is looked up in the saved environment.

We call this a *procedural representation*, in which the data is represented by its *action under* `apply-env`.

The case of a data type with a single observer is less rare than one might think. For example, if the data being represented is a set of functions, then it can be represented by its action under application. In this case, we can extract the interface and the procedural representation by the following recipe:

1. Identify the lambda expressions in the client code whose evaluation yields values of the type. Create a constructor procedure for each such lambda expression. The parameters of the constructor procedure will be the free variables of the lambda expression. Replace each such lambda expression in the client code by an invocation of the corresponding constructor.

2. Define an `apply-` procedure like `apply-env` above. Identify all the places in the client code, including the bodies of the constructor procedures, where a value of the type is applied. Replace each such application by an invocation of the `apply-` procedure.

If these steps are carried out, the interface will consist of all the constructor procedures and the `apply-` procedure, and the client code will be representation-independent: it will not rely on the representation, and we will be free to substitute another implementation of the interface, such as the one we describe in section 2.2.2.

If the implementation language does not allow higher-order procedures, then one can perform the additional step of implementing the resulting interface using a data structure representation and the interpreter recipe, as in the preceding section. This process is called *defunctionalization*. The derivation of the data structure representation of environments is a simple example of defunctionalization. The relation between procedural and defunctionalized representations will be a recurring theme in this book.

Exercise 2.12 [⋆] Implement the stack data type of exercise 2.4 using a procedural representation.

Exercise 2.13 [⋆ ⋆] Extend the procedural representation to implement `empty-env?` by representing the environment by a list of two procedures: one that returns the value associated with a variable, as before, and one that returns whether or not the environment is empty.

Exercise 2.14 [⋆ ⋆] Extend the representation of the preceding exercise to include a third procedure that implements `has-binding?` (see exercise 2.9).

2.3   Interfaces for Recursive Data Types

We spent much of chapter 1 manipulating recursive data types. For example, we defined lambda-calculus expressions in definition 1.1.8 by the grammar

$$
\begin{aligned}
\textit{Lc-exp} ::=\ & \textit{Identifier} \\
::=\ & (\texttt{lambda}\ \ (\textit{Identifier})\ \ \textit{Lc-exp}) \\
::=\ & (\textit{Lc-exp}\ \ \textit{Lc-exp})
\end{aligned}
$$

and we wrote procedures like `occurs-free?`. As we mentioned at the time, the definition of `occurs-free?` in section 1.2.4 is not as readable as it might be. It is hard to tell, for example, that `(car (cadr exp))` refers to the declaration of a variable in a `lambda` expression, or that `(caddr exp)` refers to its body.

We can improve this situation by introducing an interface for lambda-calculus expressions. Our interface will have constructors and two kinds of observers: predicates and extractors.

The constructors are:

var-exp $: \textit{Var} \rightarrow \textit{Lc-exp}$
lambda-exp $: \textit{Var} \times \textit{Lc-exp} \rightarrow \textit{Lc-exp}$
app-exp $: \textit{Lc-exp} \times \textit{Lc-exp} \rightarrow \textit{Lc-exp}$

The predicates are:

var-exp? $: \textit{Lc-exp} \rightarrow \textit{Bool}$
lambda-exp? $: \textit{Lc-exp} \rightarrow \textit{Bool}$
app-exp? $: \textit{Lc-exp} \rightarrow \textit{Bool}$

Finally, the extractors are

var-exp->var	: *Lc-exp* → *Var*
lambda-exp->bound-var	: *Lc-exp* → *Var*
lambda-exp->body	: *Lc-exp* → *Lc-exp*
app-exp->rator	: *Lc-exp* → *Lc-exp*
app-exp->rand	: *Lc-exp* → *Lc-exp*

Each of these extracts the corresponding portion of the lambda-calculus expression. We can now write a version of `occurs-free?` that depends only on the interface.

occurs-free? : *Sym* × *LcExp* → *Bool*
```
(define occurs-free?
  (lambda (search-var exp)
    (cond
      ((var-exp? exp) (eqv? search-var (var-exp->var exp)))
      ((lambda-exp? exp)
       (and
         (not (eqv? search-var (lambda-exp->bound-var exp)))
         (occurs-free? search-var (lambda-exp->body exp))))
      (else
        (or
          (occurs-free? search-var (app-exp->rator exp))
          (occurs-free? search-var (app-exp->rand exp)))))))
```

This works on any representation of lambda-calculus expressions, so long as they are built using these constructors.

We can write down a general recipe for designing an interface for a recursive data type:

Designing an interface for a recursive data type

1. *Include one constructor for each kind of data in the data type.*

2. *Include one predicate for each kind of data in the data type.*

3. *Include one extractor for each piece of data passed to a constructor of the data type.*

Exercise 2.15 [⋆] Implement the lambda-calculus expression interface for the representation specified by the grammar above.

Exercise 2.16 [⋆] Modify the implementation to use a representation in which there are no parentheses around the bound variable in a `lambda` expression.

Exercise 2.17 [⋆] Invent at least two other representations of the data type of lambda-calculus expressions and implement them.

Exercise 2.18 [⋆] We usually represent a sequence of values as a list. In this representation, it is easy to move from one element in a sequence to the next, but it is hard to move from one element to the preceding one without the help of context arguments. Implement non-empty bidirectional sequences of integers, as suggested by the grammar

$$NodeInSequence ::= (Int \ \ Listof(Int) \ \ Listof(Int))$$

The first list of numbers is the elements of the sequence preceding the current one, in reverse order, and the second list is the elements of the sequence after the current one. For example, (6 (5 4 3 2 1) (7 8 9)) represents the list (1 2 3 4 5 6 7 8 9), with the focus on the element 6.

In this representation, implement the procedure number->sequence, which takes a number and produces a sequence consisting of exactly that number. Also implement current-element, move-to-left, move-to-right, insert-to-left, insert-to-right, at-left-end?, and at-right-end?.

For example:

```
> (number->sequence 7)
(7 () ())
> (current-element '(6 (5 4 3 2 1) (7 8 9)))
6
> (move-to-left '(6 (5 4 3 2 1) (7 8 9)))
(5 (4 3 2 1) (6 7 8 9))
> (move-to-right '(6 (5 4 3 2 1) (7 8 9)))
(7 (6 5 4 3 2 1) (8 9))
> (insert-to-left 13 '(6 (5 4 3 2 1) (7 8 9)))
(6 (13 5 4 3 2 1) (7 8 9))
> (insert-to-right 13 '(6 (5 4 3 2 1) (7 8 9)))
(6 (5 4 3 2 1) (13 7 8 9))
```

The procedure move-to-right should fail if its argument is at the right end of the sequence, and the procedure move-to-left should fail if its argument is at the left end of the sequence.

Exercise 2.19 [⋆] A binary tree with empty leaves and with interior nodes labeled with integers could be represented using the grammar

$$Bintree ::= () \ \ | \ \ (Int \ \ Bintree \ \ Bintree)$$

In this representation, implement the procedure number->bintree, which takes a number and produces a binary tree consisting of a single node containing that number. Also implement current-element, move-to-left-son, move-to-right-son, at-leaf?, insert-to-left, and insert-to-right. For example,

```
> (number->bintree 13)
(13 () ())
> (define t1 (insert-to-right 14
                (insert-to-left 12
                  (number->bintree 13))))
> t1
(13
  (12 () ())
  (14 () ()))
> (move-to-left t1)
(12 () ())
> (current-element (move-to-left t1))
12
> (at-leaf? (move-to-right (move-to-left t1)))
#t
> (insert-to-left 15 t1)
(13
  (15
    (12 () ())
    ())
  (14 () ()))
```

Exercise 2.20 [⋆ ⋆ ⋆] In the representation of binary trees in exercise 2.19 it is easy to move from a parent node to one of its sons, but it is impossible to move from a son to its parent without the help of context arguments. Extend the representation of lists in exercise 2.18 to represent nodes in a binary tree. As a hint, consider representing the portion of the tree above the current node by a reversed list, as in exercise 2.18.

In this representation, implement the procedures from exercise 2.19. Also implement move-up, at-root?, and at-leaf?.

2.4   A Tool for Defining Recursive Data Types

For complicated data types, applying the recipe for constructing an interface can quickly become tedious. In this section, we introduce a tool for automatically constructing and implementing such interfaces in Scheme. The interfaces constructed by this tool will be similar, but not identical, to the interface constructed in the preceding section.

Consider again the data type of lambda-calculus expressions, as discussed in the preceding section. We can implement an interface for lambda-calculus expressions by writing

```
(define-datatype lc-exp lc-exp?
  (var-exp
    (var identifier?))
  (lambda-exp
    (bound-var identifier?)
    (body lc-exp?))
  (app-exp
    (rator lc-exp?)
    (rand lc-exp?)))
```

Here the names var-exp, var, bound-var, app-exp, rator, and rand abbreviate *variable expression, variable, bound variable, application expression, operator,* and *operand,* respectively.

This expression declares three constructors, var-exp, lambda-exp, and app-exp, and a single predicate lc-exp?. The three constructors check their arguments with the predicates identifier? and lc-exp? to make sure that the arguments are valid, so if an lc-exp is constructed using only these constructors, we can be certain that it and all its subexpressions are legal lc-exps. This allows us to ignore many checks while processing lambda expressions.

In place of the various predicates and extractors, we use the form cases to determine the variant to which an object of a data type belongs, and to extract its components. To illustrate this form, we can rewrite occurs-free? (page 43) using the data type lc-exp:

occurs-free? : *Sym* × *LcExp* → *Bool*
```
(define occurs-free?
  (lambda (search-var exp)
    (cases lc-exp exp
      (var-exp (var) (eqv? var search-var))
      (lambda-exp (bound-var body)
        (and
          (not (eqv? search-var bound-var))
          (occurs-free? search-var body)))
      (app-exp (rator rand)
        (or
          (occurs-free? search-var rator)
          (occurs-free? search-var rand))))))
```

To see how this works, assume that exp is a lambda-calculus expression that was built by app-exp. For this value of exp, the app-exp case would be selected, rator and rand would be bound to the two subexpressions, and the expression

```
(or
  (occurs-free? search-var rator)
  (occurs-free? search-var rand))
```

would be evaluated, just as if we had written

```
(if (app-exp? exp)
  (let ((rator (app-exp->rator exp))
        (rand (app-exp->rand exp)))
    (or
      (occurs-free? search-var rator)
      (occurs-free? search-var rand)))
  ...)
```

The recursive calls to occurs-free? work similarly to finish the calculation.

In general, a define-datatype declaration has the form

```
(define-datatype type-name type-predicate-name
  { (variant-name   { (field-name  predicate) }*) }+)
```

This creates a data type, named *type-name*, with some *variants*. Each variant has a variant-name and zero or more fields, each with its own field-name and associated predicate. No two types may have the same name and no two variants, even those belonging to different types, may have the same name. Also, type names cannot be used as variant names. Each field predicate must be a Scheme predicate.

For each variant, a new constructor procedure is created that is used to create data values belonging to that variant. These procedures are named after their variants. If there are n fields in a variant, its constructor takes n arguments, tests each of them with its associated predicate, and returns a new value of the given variant with the i-th field containing the i-th argument value.

The *type-predicate-name* is bound to a predicate. This predicate determines if its argument is a value belonging to the named type.

A record can be defined as a data type with a single variant. To distinguish data types with only one variant, we use a naming convention. When there is a single variant, we name the constructor a-*type-name* or an-*type-name*; otherwise, the constructors have names like *variant-name-type-name*.

Data types built by `define-datatype` may be mutually recursive. For example, consider the grammar for s-lists from section 1.1:

$$S\text{-}list ::= (\{S\text{-}exp\}^*)$$
$$S\text{-}exp ::= Symbol \mid S\text{-}list$$

The data in an s-list could be represented by the data type `s-list` defined by

```
(define-datatype s-list s-list?
  (empty-s-list)
  (non-empty-s-list
    (first s-exp?)
    (rest s-list?)))

(define-datatype s-exp s-exp?
  (symbol-s-exp
    (sym symbol?))
  (s-list-s-exp
    (slst s-list?)))
```

The data type `s-list` gives its own representation of lists by using `(empty-s-list)` and `non-empty-s-list` in place of `()` and `cons`; if we wanted to specify that Scheme lists be used instead, we could have written

```
(define-datatype s-list s-list?
  (an-s-list
    (sexps (list-of s-exp?))))

(define list-of
  (lambda (pred)
    (lambda (val)
      (or (null? val)
        (and (pair? val)
          (pred (car val))
          ((list-of pred) (cdr val)))))))
```

Here (`list-of` *pred*) builds a predicate that tests to see if its argument is a list, and that each of its elements satisfies *pred*.

The general syntax of `cases` is

```
(cases type-name expression
  {(variant-name ({field-name}*) consequent)}*
  (else default))
```

The form specifies the type, the expression yielding the value to be examined, and a sequence of clauses. Each clause is labeled with the name of a variant of the given type and the names of its fields. The `else` clause is optional. First, *expression* is evaluated, resulting in some value v of *type-name*. If v is a variant of *variant-name*, then the corresponding clause is selected. Each of the *field-names* is bound to the value of the corresponding field of v. Then the *consequent* is evaluated within the scope of these bindings and its value returned. If v is not one of the variants, and an `else` clause has been specified, *default* is evaluated and its value returned. If there is no `else` clause, then there must be a clause for *every* variant of that data type.

The form `cases` binds its variables positionally: the i-th variable is bound to the value in the i-th field. So we could just as well have written

```
(app-exp (exp1 exp2)
  (or
    (occurs-free? search-var exp1)
    (occurs-free? search-var exp2)))
```

instead of

```
(app-exp (rator rand)
  (or
    (occurs-free? search-var rator)
    (occurs-free? search-var rand)))
```

The forms `define-datatype` and `cases` provide a convenient way of defining an inductive data type, but it is not the only way. Depending on the application, it may be valuable to use a special-purpose representation that is more compact or efficient, taking advantage of special properties of the data. These advantages are gained at the expense of having to write the procedures in the interface by hand.

The form `define-datatype` is an example of a *domain-specific language*. A domain-specific language is a small language for describing a single task among a small, well-defined set of tasks. In this case, the task was defining a recursive data type. Such a language may lie inside a general-purpose language, as `define-datatype` does, or it may be a standalone language with its own set of tools. In general, one constructs such a language by identifying the possible variations in the set of tasks, and then designing a language that describes those variations. This is often a very useful strategy.

Exercise 2.21 [⋆] Implement the data type of environments, as in section 2.2.2, using define-datatype. Then include has-binding? of exercise 2.9.

Exercise 2.22 [⋆] Using define-datatype, implement the stack data type of exercise 2.4.

Exercise 2.23 [⋆] The definition of lc-exp ignores the condition in definition 1.1.8 that says "*Identifier* is any symbol other than lambda." Modify the definition of identifier? to capture this condition. As a hint, remember that any predicate can be used in define-datatype, even ones you define.

Exercise 2.24 [⋆] Here is a definition of binary trees using define-datatype.

```
(define-datatype bintree bintree?
  (leaf-node
    (num integer?))
  (interior-node
    (key symbol?)
    (left bintree?)
    (right bintree?)))
```

Implement a bintree-to-list procedure for binary trees, so that (bintree-to-list (interior-node 'a (leaf-node 3) (leaf-node 4))) returns the list

```
(interior-node
  a
  (leaf-node 3)
  (leaf-node 4))
```

Exercise 2.25 [⋆⋆] Use cases to write max-interior, which takes a binary tree of integers (as in the preceding exercise) with at least one interior node and returns the symbol associated with an interior node with a maximal leaf sum.

```
> (define tree-1
    (interior-node 'foo (leaf-node 2) (leaf-node 3)))
> (define tree-2
    (interior-node 'bar (leaf-node -1) tree-1))
> (define tree-3
    (interior-node 'baz tree-2 (leaf-node 1)))
> (max-interior tree-2)
foo
> (max-interior tree-3)
baz
```

The last invocation of max-interior might also have returned foo, since both the foo and baz nodes have a leaf sum of 5.

Exercise 2.26 [⋆ ⋆] Here is another version of exercise 1.33. Consider a set of trees given by the following grammar:

> *Red-blue-tree* ::= *Red-blue-subtree*
> *Red-blue-subtree* ::= (red-node *Red-blue-subtree Red-blue-subtree*)
> ::= (blue-node {*Red-blue-subtree*}*)
> ::= (leaf-node *Int*)

Write an equivalent definition using define-datatype, and use the resulting interface to write a procedure that takes a tree and builds a tree of the same shape, except that each leaf node is replaced by a leaf node that contains the number of red nodes on the path between it and the root.

2.5 Abstract Syntax and Its Representation

A grammar usually specifies a particular representation of an inductive data type: one that uses the strings or values generated by the grammar. Such a representation is called *concrete syntax*, or *external* representation.

Consider, for example, the set of lambda-calculus expressions defined in definition 1.1.8. This gives a concrete syntax for lambda-calculus expressions. We might have used some other concrete syntax for lambda-calculus expressions. For example, we could have written

> *Lc-exp* ::= *Identifier*
> ::= proc *Identifier* => *Lc-exp*
> ::= *Lc-exp* (*Lc-exp*)

to define lambda-calculus expressions as a different set of strings.

In order to process such data, we need to convert it to an *internal* representation. The define-datatype form provides a convenient way of defining such an internal representation. We call this *abstract syntax*. In the abstract syntax, terminals such as parentheses need not be stored, because they convey no information. On the other hand, we want to make sure that the data structure allows us to determine what kind of lambda-calculus expression it represents, and to extract its components. The data type lc-exp on page 46 allows us to do both of these things easily.

It is convenient to visualize the internal representation as an *abstract syntax tree*. Figure 2.2 shows the abstract syntax tree of the lambda-calculus expression (lambda (x) (f (f x))), using the data type lc-exp. Each internal node of the tree is labeled with the associated production name. Edges are labeled with the name of the corresponding nonterminal occurrence. Leaves correspond to terminal strings.

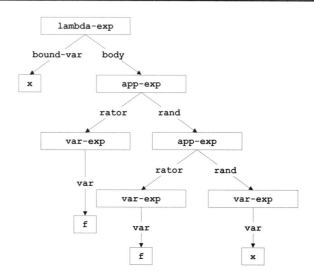

Figure 2.2   Abstract syntax tree for (lambda (x) (f (f x)))

To create an abstract syntax for a given concrete syntax, we must name
each production of the concrete syntax and each occurrence of a nonterminal
in each production. It is straightforward to generate define-datatype
declarations for the abstract syntax. We create one define-datatype for
each nonterminal, with one variant for each production.

We can summarize the choices we have made in figure 2.2 using the following concise notation:

> *Lc-exp* ::= *Identifier*
> > var-exp (var)
>
> ::= (lambda (*Identifier*) *Lc-exp*)
> > lambda-exp (bound-var body)
>
> ::= (*Lc-exp* *Lc-exp*)
> > app-exp (rator rand)

Such notation, which specifies both concrete and abstract syntax, is used
throughout this book.

Having made the distinction between concrete syntax, which is primarily
useful for humans, and abstract syntax, which is primarily useful for computers, we now consider how to convert from one syntax to the other.

If the concrete syntax is a set of strings of characters, it may be a complex undertaking to derive the corresponding abstract syntax tree. This task is called *parsing* and is performed by a *parser*. Because writing a parser is difficult in general, it is best performed by a tool called a *parser generator*. A parser generator takes as input a grammar and produces a parser. Since the grammars are processed by a tool, they must be written in some machine-readable language: a domain-specific language for writing grammars. There are many parser generators available.

If the concrete syntax is given as a set of lists, the parsing process is considerably simplified. For example, the grammar for lambda-calculus expressions at the beginning of this section specified a set of lists, as did the grammar for `define-datatype` on page 47. In this case, the Scheme `read` routine automatically parses strings into lists and symbols. It is then easier to parse these list structures into abstract syntax trees as in `parse-expression`.

parse-expression : *SchemeVal* → *LcExp*
```
(define parse-expression
  (lambda (datum)
    (cond
      ((symbol? datum) (var-exp datum))
      ((pair? datum)
       (if (eqv? (car datum) 'lambda)
         (lambda-exp
           (car (cadr datum))
           (parse-expression (caddr datum)))
         (app-exp
           (parse-expression (car datum))
           (parse-expression (cadr datum)))))
      (else (report-invalid-concrete-syntax datum)))))
```

It is usually straightforward to convert an abstract syntax tree back to a list-and-symbol representation. If we do this, the Scheme print routines will then display it in a list-based concrete syntax. This is performed by `unparse-lc-exp`:

unparse-lc-exp : *LcExp* → *SchemeVal*
```
(define unparse-lc-exp
  (lambda (exp)
    (cases lc-exp exp
      (var-exp (var) var)
      (lambda-exp (bound-var body)
        (list 'lambda (list bound-var)
          (unparse-lc-exp body)))
      (app-exp (rator rand)
        (list
```

```
                        (unparse-lc-exp rator) (unparse-lc-exp rand))))))
```

Exercise 2.27 [⋆] Draw the abstract syntax tree for the lambda calculus expressions

```
((lambda (a) (a b)) c)

(lambda (x)
  (lambda (y)
    ((lambda (x)
        (x y))
     x)))
```

Exercise 2.28 [⋆] Write an unparser that converts the abstract syntax of an lc-exp into a string that matches the second grammar in this section (page 52).

Exercise 2.29 [⋆] Where a Kleene star or plus (page 7) is used in concrete syntax, it is most convenient to use a *list* of associated subtrees when constructing an abstract syntax tree. For example, if the grammar for lambda-calculus expressions had been

> *Lc-exp* ::= *Identifier*
>   `var-exp (var)`
>
>   ::= (lambda ({*Identifier*}*) *Lc-exp*)
>   `lambda-exp (bound-vars body)`
>
>   ::= (*Lc-exp* {*Lc-exp*}*)
>   `app-exp (rator rands)`

then the predicate for the `bound-vars` field could be (`list-of identifier?`), and the predicate for the `rands` field could be (`list-of lc-exp?`). Write a `define-datatype` and a parser for this grammar that works in this way.

Exercise 2.30 [⋆ ⋆] The procedure `parse-expression` as defined above is fragile: it does not detect several possible syntactic errors, such as (a b c), and aborts with inappropriate error messages for other expressions, such as (lambda). Modify it so that it is robust, accepting any s-exp and issuing an appropriate error message if the s-exp does not represent a lambda-calculus expression.

Exercise 2.31 [⋆ ⋆] Sometimes it is useful to specify a concrete syntax as a sequence of symbols and integers, surrounded by parentheses. For example, one might define the set of *prefix lists* by

Prefix-list ::= (*Prefix-exp*)
Prefix-exp ::= *Int*
         ::= - *Prefix-exp* *Prefix-exp*

so that (- - 3 2 - 4 - 12 7) is a legal prefix list. This is sometimes called *Polish prefix notation*, after its inventor, Jan Łukasiewicz. Write a parser to convert a prefix-list to the abstract syntax

```
(define-datatype prefix-exp prefix-exp?
  (const-exp
    (num integer?))
  (diff-exp
    (operand1 prefix-exp?)
    (operand2 prefix-exp?)))
```

so that the example above produces the same abstract syntax tree as the sequence of constructors

```
(diff-exp
  (diff-exp
    (const-exp 3)
    (const-exp 2))
  (diff-exp
    (const-exp 4)
    (diff-exp
      (const-exp 12)
      (const-exp 7))))
```

As a hint, consider writing a procedure that takes a list and produces a prefix-exp and the list of leftover list elements.

3 *Expressions*

In this chapter, we study the binding and scoping of variables. We do this by presenting a sequence of small languages that illustrate these concepts. We write specifications for these languages, and implement them using interpreters, following the interpreter recipe from chapter 1. Our specifications and interpreters take a context argument, called the *environment*, which keeps track of the meaning of each variable in the expression being evaluated.

3.1   Specification and Implementation Strategy

Our specification will consist of assertions of the form

$$(\texttt{value-of}\ exp\ \rho) = val$$

meaning that the value of expression exp in environment ρ should be val. We write down rules of inference and equations, like those in chapter 1, that will enable us to derive such assertions. We use the rules and equations by hand to find the intended value of some expressions.

But our goal is to write a program that implements our language. The overall picture is shown in figure 3.1(a). We start with the text of the program written in the language we are implementing. This is called the *source language* or the *defined language*. Program text (a program in the source language) is passed through a front end that converts it to an abstract syntax tree. The syntax tree is then passed to the interpreter, which is a program that looks at a data structure and performs some actions that depend on its structure. Of course the interpreter is itself written in some language. We call that language the *implementation language* or the *defining language*. Most of our implementations will follow this pattern.

Another common organization is shown in figure 3.1(b). There the interpreter is replaced by a compiler, which translates the abstract syntax tree into a program in some other language (the *target language*), and that program is executed. That target language may be executed by an interpreter, as in figure 3.1(b), or it may be translated into some even lower-level language for execution.

Most often, the target language is a machine language, which is interpreted by a hardware machine. Yet another possibility is that the target machine is a special-purpose language that is simpler than the original and for which it is relatively simple to write an interpreter. This allows the program to be compiled once and then executed on many different hardware platforms. For historical reasons, such a target language is often called a *byte code*, and its interpreter is called a *virtual machine*.

A compiler is typically divided into two parts: an *analyzer* that attempts to deduce useful information about the program, and a *translator* that does the translation, possibly using information from the analyzer. Each of these phases may be specified either by rules of inference or a special-purpose specification language, and then implemented. We study some simple analyzers and translators in chapters 6 and 7.

No matter what implementation strategy we use, we need a *front end* that converts programs into abstract syntax trees. Because programs are just strings of characters, our front end needs to group these characters into meaningful units. This grouping is usually divided into two stages: *scanning* and *parsing*.

Scanning is the process of dividing the sequence of characters into words, numbers, punctuation, comments, and the like. These units are called *lexical items*, *lexemes*, or most often *tokens*. We refer to the way in which a program should be divided up into tokens as the *lexical specification* of the language. The scanner takes a sequence of characters and produces a sequence of tokens.

Parsing is the process of organizing the sequence of tokens into hierarchical syntactic structures such as expressions, statements, and blocks. This is like organizing (diagramming) a sentence into clauses. We refer to this as the *syntactic* or *grammatical* structure of the language. The parser takes a sequence of tokens from the scanner and produces an abstract syntax tree.

The standard approach to building a front end is to use a *parser generator*. A parser generator is a program that takes as input a lexical specification and a grammar, and produces as output a scanner and parser for them.

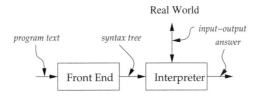

(a) Execution via interpreter

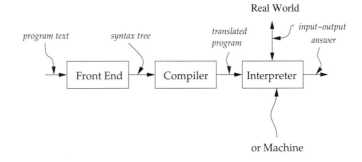

(b) Execution via Compiler

Figure 3.1 Block diagrams for a language-processing system

Parser generator systems are available for most major languages. If no parser generator is available, or none is suitable for the application, one can choose to build a scanner and parser by hand. This process is described in compiler textbooks. The parsing technology and associated grammars we use are designed for simplicity in the context of our very specialized needs.

Another approach is to ignore the details of the concrete syntax and to write our expressions as list structures, as we did for lambda-calculus expressions with the procedure `parse-expression` in section 2.5 and exercise 2.31.

Program   ::= *Expression*
           `a-program (exp1)`

Expression ::= *Number*
           `const-exp (num)`

Expression ::= -(*Expression* , *Expression*)
           `diff-exp (exp1 exp2)`

Expression ::= `zero?` (*Expression*)
           `zero?-exp (exp1)`

Expression ::= `if` *Expression* `then` *Expression* `else` *Expression*
           `if-exp (exp1 exp2 exp3)`

Expression ::= *Identifier*
           `var-exp (var)`

Expression ::= `let` *Identifier* = *Expression* `in` *Expression*
           `let-exp (var exp1 body)`

Figure 3.2   Syntax for the LET language

3.2   LET: A Simple Language

We begin by specifying a very simple language, which we call LET, after its
most interesting feature.

3.2.1   Specifying the Syntax

Figure 3.2 shows the syntax of our simple language. In this language, a program is just an expression. An expression is either an integer constant, a
difference expression, a zero-test expression, a conditional expression, a variable, or a `let` expression.

Here is a simple expression in this language and its representation as
abstract syntax.

```
(scan&parse "-(55, -(x,11))")
#(struct:a-program
   #(struct:diff-exp
      #(struct:const-exp 55)
      #(struct:diff-exp
         #(struct:var-exp x)
         #(struct:const-exp 11))))
```

3.2.2 Specification of Values

An important part of the specification of any programming language is the set of values that the language manipulates. Each language has at least two such sets: the *expressed values* and the *denoted values*. The expressed values are the possible values of expressions, and the denoted values are the values bound to variables.

In the languages of this chapter, the expressed and denoted values will always be the same. They will start out as

$$ExpVal = Int + Bool$$
$$DenVal = Int + Bool$$

Chapter 4 presents languages in which expressed and denoted values are different.

In order to make use of this definition, we will need an interface for the data type of expressed values. Our interface will have the entries

num-val	: $Int \rightarrow ExpVal$
bool-val	: $Bool \rightarrow ExpVal$
expval->num	: $ExpVal \rightarrow Int$
expval->bool	: $ExpVal \rightarrow Bool$

We assume that `expval->num` and `expval->bool` are undefined when given an argument that is not a number or a boolean, respectively.

3.2.3 Environments

If we are going to evaluate expressions containing variables, we will need to know the value associated with each variable. We do this by keeping those values in an *environment*, as defined in section 2.2.

An environment is a function whose domain is a finite set of variables and whose range is the denoted values. We use some abbreviations when writing about environments.

- ρ ranges over environments.
- [] denotes the empty environment.
- $[var = val]\rho$ denotes (extend-env *var val* ρ).
- $[var_1 = val_1, var_2 = val_2]\rho$ abbreviates $[var_1 = val_1]([var_2 = val_2]\rho)$, etc.
- $[var_1 = val_1, var_2 = val_2, \ldots]$ denotes the environment in which the value of var_1 is val_1, etc.

We will occasionally write down complicated environments using indentation to improve readability. For example, we might write

```
[x=3]
 [y=7]
  [u=5] ρ
```

to abbreviate

```
(extend-env 'x 3
  (extend-env 'y 7
    (extend-env 'u 5 ρ)))
```

3.2.4 Specifying the Behavior of Expressions

There are six kinds of expressions in our language: one for each production with *Expression* as its left-hand side. Our interface for expressions will contain seven procedures: six constructors and one observer. We use *ExpVal* to denote the set of expressed values.

constructors:

const-exp	: $Int \rightarrow Exp$
zero?-exp	: $Exp \rightarrow Exp$
if-exp	: $Exp \times Exp \times Exp \rightarrow Exp$
diff-exp	: $Exp \times Exp \rightarrow Exp$
var-exp	: $Var \rightarrow Exp$
let-exp	: $Var \times Exp \times Exp \rightarrow Exp$

observer:

value-of	: $Exp \times Env \rightarrow ExpVal$

Before starting on an implementation, we write down a specification for the behavior of these procedures. Following the interpreter recipe, we expect that `value-of` will look at the expression, determine what kind of expression it is, and return the appropriate value.

```
(value-of (const-exp n) ρ) = (num-val n)

(value-of (var-exp var) ρ) = (apply-env ρ var)

(value-of (diff-exp exp₁ exp₂) ρ)
= (num-val
    (-
      (expval->num (value-of exp₁ ρ))
      (expval->num (value-of exp₂ ρ)))))
```

The value of a constant expression in any environment is the constant value. The value of a variable reference in an environment is determined by looking up the variable in the environment. The value of a difference expression in some environment is the difference between the value of the first operand in that environment and the value of the second operand in that environment. Of course, to be precise we have to make sure that the values of the operands are numbers, and we have to make sure that value of the result is a number represented as an expressed value.

Figure 3.3 shows how these rules work together to specify the value of an expression built by these constructors. In this and our other examples, we write *«exp»* to denote the AST for expression *exp*. We also write $\lceil n \rceil$ in place of (num-val *n*), and $\lfloor val \rfloor$ in place of (expval->num *val*). We will also use the fact that $\lfloor \lceil n \rceil \rfloor = n$.

Exercise 3.1 [⋆] In figure 3.3, list all the places where we used the fact that $\lfloor \lceil n \rceil \rfloor = n$.

Exercise 3.2 [⋆ ⋆] Give an expressed value *val* ∈ *ExpVal* for which $\lceil \lfloor val \rfloor \rceil \neq val$.

3.2.5   Specifying the Behavior of Programs

In our language, a whole program is just an expression. In order to find the value of such an expression, we need to specify the values of the free variables in the program. So the value of a program is just the value of that expression in a suitable initial environment. We choose our initial environment to be [i=1,v=5,x=10].

```
(value-of-program exp)
= (value-of exp [i=⌈1⌉,v=⌈5⌉,x=⌈10⌉])
```

3.2.6   Specifying Conditionals

The next portion of the language introduces an interface for booleans in our language. The language has one constructor of booleans, zero?, and one observer of booleans, the if expression.

The value of a zero? expression is a true value if and only if the value of its operand is zero. We can write this as a rule of inference like those in definition 1.1.5. We use bool-val as a constructor to turn a boolean into an expressed value, and expval->num as an extractor to check whether an expressed value is an integer, and if so, to return the integer.

Let $\rho = $ `[i=1,v=5,x=10]`.

```
(value-of
  <<-(-(x,3), -(v,i))>>
  ρ)

= ⌈(-
    ⌊(value-of <<-(x,3)>> ρ)⌋
    ⌊(value-of <<-(v,i)>> ρ)⌋)⌉

= ⌈(-
    (-
      ⌊(value-of <<x>> ρ)⌋
      ⌊(value-of <<3>> ρ)⌋)
    ⌊(value-of <<-(v,i)>> ρ)⌋)⌉

= ⌈(-
    (-
      10
      ⌊(value-of <<3>> ρ)⌋)
    (value-of <<-(v,i)>> ρ))⌉

= ⌈(-
    (-
      10
      3)
    ⌊(value-of <<-(v,i)>> ρ)⌋)⌉

= ⌈(-
    7
    ⌊(value-of <<-(v,i)>> ρ)⌋)⌉
```

```
= ⌈(-
    7
    (-
      ⌊(value-of <<v>> ρ)⌋
      ⌊(value-of <<i>> ρ)⌋)))⌉

= ⌈(-
    7
    (-
      5
      ⌊(value-of <<i>> ρ)⌋)))⌉

= ⌈(-
    7
    (-
      5
      1))⌉

= ⌈(-
    7
    4)⌉

= ⌈3⌉
```

Figure 3.3 A simple calculation using the specification

$$\frac{(\text{value-of } exp_1 \; \rho) = val_1}{\begin{array}{l} (\text{value-of } (\text{zero?-exp } exp_1) \; \rho) \\ = \begin{cases} (\text{bool-val #t}) & \text{if } (\text{expval->num } val_1) = 0 \\ (\text{bool-val #f}) & \text{if } (\text{expval->num } val_1) \neq 0 \end{cases} \end{array}}$$

An `if` expression is an observer of boolean values. To determine the value of an `if` expression (`if-exp` exp_1 exp_2 exp_3), we must first determine the value of the subexpression exp_1. If this value is a true value, the value of the entire `if-exp` should be the value of the subexpression exp_2; otherwise it should be the value of the subexpression exp_3. This is also easy to write as a rule of inference. We use `expval->bool` to extract the boolean part of an expressed value, just as we used `expval->num` in the preceding example.

$$\frac{(\text{value-of } exp_1 \; \rho) = val_1}{\begin{array}{l} (\text{value-of } (\text{if-exp } exp_1 \; exp_2 \; exp_3) \; \rho) \\ = \begin{cases} (\text{value-of } exp_2 \; \rho) & \text{if } (\text{expval->bool } val_1) = \text{#t} \\ (\text{value-of } exp_3 \; \rho) & \text{if } (\text{expval->bool } val_1) = \text{#f} \end{cases} \end{array}}$$

Rules of inference like this make the intended behavior of any individual expression easy to specify, but they are not very good for displaying a deduction. An antecedent like (`value-of` exp_1 ρ) = val_1 denotes a subcomputation, so a calculation should be a tree, much like the one on page 5. Unfortunately, such trees can be difficult to read. We therefore often recast our rules as equations. We can then use substitution of equals for equals to display a calculation.

For an `if-exp`, the equational specification is

```
(value-of (if-exp exp₁ exp₂ exp₃) ρ)
= (if (expval->bool (value-of exp₁ ρ))
     (value-of exp₂ ρ)
     (value-of exp₃ ρ))
```

Figure 3.4 shows a simple calculation using these rules.

3.2.7   Specifying `let`

Next we address the problem of creating new variable bindings with a `let` expression. We add to the interpreted language a syntax in which the keyword `let` is followed by a declaration, the keyword `in`, and the body. For example,

Let $\rho = $ [x=$\lceil 33 \rceil$,y=$\lceil 22 \rceil$].

```
(value-of
  <<if zero?(-(x,11)) then -(y,2) else -(y,4)>>
  ρ)

= (if (expval->bool (value-of <<zero?(-(x,11))>> ρ))
     (value-of <<-(y,2)>> ρ)
     (value-of <<-(y,4)>> ρ))

= (if (expval->bool (bool-val #f))
     (value-of <<-(y,2)>> ρ)
     (value-of <<-(y,4)>> ρ))

= (if #f
     (value-of <<-(y,2)>> ρ)
     (value-of <<-(y,4)>> ρ))

= (value-of <<-(y,4)>> ρ)

= ⌈18⌉
```

Figure 3.4   A simple calculation for a conditional expression

```
let x = 5
in -(x,3)
```

The `let` variable is bound in the body, much as a `lambda` variable is bound (see section 1.2.4).

The entire `let` form is an expression, as is its body, so `let` expressions may be nested, as in

```
let z = 5
in let x = 3
   in let y = -(x,1)     % here x = 3
      in let x = 4
         in -(z, -(x,y)) % here x = 4
```

In this example, the reference to x in the first difference expression refers to the outer declaration, whereas the reference to x in the other difference expression refers to the inner declaration, and thus the entire expression's value is 3.

The right-hand side of the `let` is also an expression, so it can be arbitrarily complex. For example,

```
let x = 7
in let y = 2
   in let y = let x = -(x,1)
              in -(x,y)
      in -(-(x,8), y)
```

Here the x declared on the third line is bound to 6, so the value of y is 4, and the value of the entire expression is $((-1) - 4) = -5$.

We can write down the specification as a rule.

$$\frac{\texttt{(value-of } exp_1 \; \rho) = val_1}{\begin{array}{l}\texttt{(value-of (let-exp } var \; exp_1 \; body) \; \rho) \\ \texttt{= (value-of } body \; [var = val_1]\rho)\end{array}}$$

As before, it is often more convenient to recast this as the equation

$$\texttt{(value-of (let-exp } var \; exp_1 \; body) \; \rho)$$
$$\texttt{= (value-of } body \; [var = \texttt{(value-of } exp_1 \; \rho)]\rho)$$

Figure 3.5 shows an example. There ρ_0 denotes an arbitrary environment.

3.2.8   Implementing the Specification of LET

Our next task is to implement this specification as a set of Scheme procedures. Our implementation uses SLLGEN as a front end, which means that expressions will be represented by a data type like the one in figure 3.6. The representation of expressed values in our implementation is shown in figure 3.7. The data type declares the constructors `num-val` and `bool-val` for converting integers and booleans to expressed values. We also define extractors for converting from an expressed value back to either an integer or a boolean. The extractors report an error if an expressed value is not of the expected kind.

```
(value-of
  <<let x = 7
     in let y = 2
        in let y = let x = -(x,1) in -(x,y)
           in -(-(x,8),y)>>
  ρ₀)
```

$$= \text{(value-of}$$
```
    <<let y = 2
       in let y = let x = -(x,1) in -(x,y)
          in -(-(x,8),y)>>
    [x=⌈7⌉]ρ₀)
```

$$= \text{(value-of}$$
```
    <<let y = let x = -(x,1) in -(x,y)
       in -(-(x,8),y)>>
    [y=⌈2⌉][x=⌈7⌉]ρ₀)
```

Let $\rho_1 = [y=\lceil 2 \rceil][x=\lceil 7 \rceil]\rho_0$.

$$= \text{(value-of}$$
```
    <<-(-(x,8),y)>>
    [y=(value-of <<let x = -(x,1) in -(x,y)>> ρ₁)]
    ρ₁)
```

$$= \text{(value-of}$$
```
    <<-(-(x,8),y)>>
    [y=(value-of <<-(x,2)>> [x=(value-of <<-(x,1)>> ρ₁)]ρ₁)]ρ₁)]
    ρ₁)
```

$$= \text{(value-of}$$
```
    <<-(-(x,8),y)>>
    [y=(value-of <<-(x,2)>> [x=⌈6⌉]ρ₁)]
    ρ₁)
```

$$= \text{(value-of}$$
```
    <<-(-(x,8),y)>>
    [y=⌈4⌉]ρ₁)
```

$$= \lceil (- \ (- \ 7 \ 8) \ 4) \rceil$$

$$= \lceil -5 \rceil$$

Figure 3.5 An example of let

```
(define-datatype program program?
  (a-program
    (exp1 expression?)))

(define-datatype expression expression?
  (const-exp
    (num number?))
  (diff-exp
    (exp1 expression?)
    (exp2 expression?))
  (zero?-exp
    (exp1 expression?))
  (if-exp
    (exp1 expression?)
    (exp2 expression?)
    (exp3 expression?))
  (var-exp
    (var identifier?))
  (let-exp
    (var identifier?)
    (exp1 expression?)
    (body expression?)))
```

Figure 3.6 Syntax data types for the LET language

We can use any implementation of environments, provided that it meets the specification in section 2.2. The procedure init-env constructs the specified initial environment used by value-of-program.

init-env : () $\rightarrow$ *Env*
usage: (init-env) = $[i=\lceil 1 \rceil, v=\lceil 5 \rceil, x=\lceil 10 \rceil]$
```
(define init-env
  (lambda ()
    (extend-env
     'i (num-val 1)
     (extend-env
      'v (num-val 5)
      (extend-env
       'x (num-val 10)
       (empty-env))))))
```

```
(define-datatype expval expval?
  (num-val
    (num number?))
  (bool-val
    (bool boolean?))))
```

expval->num : *ExpVal* → *Int*
```
(define expval->num
  (lambda (val)
    (cases expval val
      (num-val (num) num)
      (else (report-expval-extractor-error 'num val)))))
```

expval->bool : *ExpVal* → *Bool*
```
(define expval->bool
  (lambda (val)
    (cases expval val
      (bool-val (bool) bool)
      (else (report-expval-extractor-error 'bool val)))))
```

Figure 3.7   Expressed values for the LET language

Now we can write down the interpreter, shown in figures 3.8 and 3.9. The main procedure is `run`, which takes a string, parses it, and hands the result to `value-of-program`. The most interesting procedure is `value-of`, which takes an expression and an environment and uses the interpreter recipe to calculate the answer required by the specification. In the listing below we have inserted the relevant specification rules to show how the code for `value-of` comes from the specification.

In the following exercises, and throughout the book, the phrase "extend the language by adding ..." means to write down additional rules or equations to the language specification, and to implement the feature by adding or modifying the associated interpreter.

Exercise 3.3 [⋆] Why is subtraction a better choice than addition for our single arithmetic operation?

Exercise 3.4 [⋆] Write out the derivation of figure 3.4 as a derivation tree in the style of the one on page 5.

```
run : String → ExpVal
(define run
  (lambda (string)
    (value-of-program (scan&parse string))))
```

```
value-of-program : Program → ExpVal
(define value-of-program
  (lambda (pgm)
    (cases program pgm
      (a-program (exp1)
        (value-of exp1 (init-env))))))
```

```
value-of : Exp × Env → ExpVal
(define value-of
  (lambda (exp env)
    (cases expression exp
```

$$(\texttt{value-of (const-exp } n)\ \rho) = n$$

```
      (const-exp (num) (num-val num))
```

$$(\texttt{value-of (var-exp } var)\ \rho) = (\texttt{apply-env } \rho\ var)$$

```
      (var-exp (var) (apply-env env var))
```

$$(\texttt{value-of (diff-exp } exp_1\ exp_2)\ \rho) =$$
$$\lceil(\texttt{- }\lfloor(\texttt{value-of } exp_1\ \rho)\rfloor\ \lfloor(\texttt{value-of } exp_2\ \rho)\rfloor)\rceil$$

```
      (diff-exp (exp1 exp2)
        (let ((val1 (value-of exp1 env))
              (val2 (value-of exp2 env)))
          (let ((num1 (expval->num val1))
                (num2 (expval->num val2)))
            (num-val
              (- num1 num2)))))))
```

Figure 3.8 Interpreter for the LET language

$$\frac{(\text{value-of } exp_1 \ \rho) = val_1}{\begin{array}{l} (\text{value-of } (\text{zero?-exp } exp_1) \ \rho) \\ \quad = \begin{cases} (\text{bool-val } \#\text{t}) & \text{if } (\text{expval->num } val_1) = 0 \\ (\text{bool-val } \#\text{f}) & \text{if } (\text{expval->num } val_1) \neq 0 \end{cases} \end{array}}$$

```
(zero?-exp (exp1)
  (let ((val1 (value-of exp1 env)))
    (let ((num1 (expval->num val1)))
      (if (zero? num1)
          (bool-val #t)
          (bool-val #f)))))
```

$$\frac{(\text{value-of } exp_1 \ \rho) = val_1}{\begin{array}{l} (\text{value-of } (\text{if-exp } exp_1 \ exp_2 \ exp_3) \ \rho) \\ \quad = \begin{cases} (\text{value-of } exp_2 \ \rho) & \text{if } (\text{expval->bool } val_1) = \#\text{t} \\ (\text{value-of } exp_3 \ \rho) & \text{if } (\text{expval->bool } val_1) = \#\text{f} \end{cases} \end{array}}$$

```
(if-exp (exp1 exp2 exp3)
  (let ((val1 (value-of exp1 env)))
    (if (expval->bool val1)
        (value-of exp2 env)
        (value-of exp3 env))))
```

$$\frac{(\text{value-of } exp_1 \ \rho) = val_1}{\begin{array}{l} (\text{value-of } (\text{let-exp } var \ exp_1 \ body) \ \rho) \\ \quad = (\text{value-of } body \ [var = val_1]\rho) \end{array}}$$

```
(let-exp (var exp1 body)
  (let ((val1 (value-of exp1 env)))
    (value-of body
      (extend-env var val1 env)))))))))
```

Figure 3.9   Interpreter for the LET language, continued

Exercise 3.5 [⋆] Write out the derivation of figure 3.5 as a derivation tree in the style of the one on page 5.

Exercise 3.6 [⋆] Extend the language by adding a new operator minus that takes one argument, n, and returns $-n$. For example, the value of minus(-(minus(5),9)) should be 14.

Exercise 3.7 [⋆] Extend the language by adding operators for addition, multiplication, and integer quotient.

Exercise 3.8 [⋆] Add a numeric equality predicate `equal?` and numeric order predicates `greater?` and `less?` to the set of operations in the defined language.

Exercise 3.9 [⋆⋆] Add list processing operations to the language, including `cons`, `car`, `cdr`, `null?` and `emptylist`. A list should be able to contain any expressed value, including another list. Give the definitions of the expressed and denoted values of the language, as in section 3.2.2. For example,

```
let x = 4
in cons(x,
        cons(cons(-(x,1),
                  emptylist),
              emptylist))
```

should return an expressed value that represents the list `(4 (3))`.

Exercise 3.10 [⋆⋆] Add an operation `list` to the language. This operation should take any number of arguments, and return an expressed value containing the list of their values. For example,

```
let x = 4
in list(x, -(x,1), -(x,3))
```

should return an expressed value that represents the list `(4 3 1)`.

Exercise 3.11 [⋆] In a real language, one might have many operators such as those in the preceding exercises. Rearrange the code in the interpreter so that it is easy to add new operators.

Exercise 3.12 [⋆] Add to the defined language a facility that adds a `cond` expression. Use the grammar

Expression ::= `cond` {*Expression* `==>` *Expression*}* `end`

In this expression, the expressions on the left-hand sides of the `==>`'s are evaluated in order until one of them returns a true value. Then the value of the entire expression is the value of the corresponding right-hand expression. If none of the tests succeeds, the expression should report an error.

Exercise 3.13 [⋆] Change the values of the language so that integers are the only expressed values. Modify `if` so that the value 0 is treated as false and all other values are treated as true. Modify the predicates accordingly.

Exercise 3.14 [⋆⋆] As an alternative to the preceding exercise, add a new nonterminal *Bool-exp* of boolean expressions to the language. Change the production for conditional expressions to say

Expression ::= `if` *Bool-exp* `then` *Expression* `else` *Expression*

Write suitable productions for *Bool-exp* and implement `value-of-bool-exp`. Where do the predicates of exercise 3.8 wind up in this organization?

Exercise 3.15 [⋆] Extend the language by adding a new operation `print` that takes one argument, prints it, and returns the integer 1. Why is this operation not expressible in our specification framework?

Exercise 3.16 [⋆ ⋆] Extend the language so that a `let` declaration can declare an arbitrary number of variables, using the grammar

$$Expression ::= \texttt{let} \ \{Identifier = Expression\}^* \ \texttt{in} \ Expression$$

As in Scheme's `let`, each of the right-hand sides is evaluated in the current environment, and the body is evaluated with each new variable bound to the value of its associated right-hand side. For example,

```
let x = 30
in let x = -(x,1)
       y = -(x,2)
   in -(x,y)
```

should evaluate to 1.

Exercise 3.17 [⋆⋆] Extend the language with a `let*` expression that works like Scheme's `let*`, so that

```
let x = 30
in let* x = -(x,1)  y = -(x,2)
     in -(x,y)
```

should evaluate to 2.

Exercise 3.18 [⋆ ⋆] Add an expression to the defined language:

$$Expression ::= \texttt{unpack} \ \{Identifier\}^* \ = \ Expression \ \texttt{in} \ Expression$$

so that `unpack x y z = lst in ...` binds x, y, and z to the elements of `lst` if `lst` is a list of exactly three elements, and reports an error otherwise. For example, the value of

```
let u = 7
in unpack x y = cons(u,cons(3,emptylist))
     in -(x,y)
```

should be 4.

3.3   PROC: A Language with Procedures

So far our language has only the operations that were included in the original language. For our interpreted language to be at all useful, we must allow new procedures to be created. We call the new language PROC.

We will follow the design of Scheme, and let procedures be expressed values in our language, so that

$$ExpVal = Int + Bool + Proc$$
$$DenVal = Int + Bool + Proc$$

where *Proc* is a set of values representing procedures. We will think of *Proc* as an abstract data type. We consider its interface and specification below.

We will also need syntax for procedure creation and calling. This is given by the productions

$$Expression ::= \texttt{proc}\ (Identifier)\ Expression$$
$$\boxed{\texttt{proc-exp (var body)}}$$

$$Expression ::= (Expression\ Expression)$$
$$\boxed{\texttt{call-exp (rator rand)}}$$

In (`proc-exp` *var body*), the variable *var* is the *bound variable* or *formal parameter*. In a procedure call (`call-exp` exp_1 exp_2), the expression exp_1 is the *operator* and exp_2 is the *operand* or *actual parameter*. We use the word *argument* to refer to the value of an actual parameter.

Here are two simple programs in this language.

```
let f = proc (x) -(x,11)
in (f (f 77))

(proc (f) (f (f 77))
 proc (x) -(x,11))
```

The first program creates a procedure that subtracts 11 from its argument. It calls the resulting procedure f, and then applies f twice to 77, yielding the answer 55. The second program creates a procedure that takes its argument and applies it twice to 77. The program then applies this procedure to the subtract-11 procedure. The result is again 55.

We now turn to the data type *Proc*. Its interface consists of the constructor `procedure`, which tells how to build a procedure value, and the observer `apply-procedure`, which tells how to apply a procedure value.

Our next task is to determine what information must be included in a value representing a procedure. To do this, we consider what happens when we write a `proc` expression in an arbitrary position in our program.

The lexical scope rule tells us that when a procedure is applied, its body is evaluated in an environment that binds the formal parameter of the procedure to the argument of the call. Variables occurring free in the procedure should also obey the lexical binding rule. Consider the expression

```
let x = 200
in let f = proc (z) -(z,x)
   in let x = 100
      in let g = proc (z) -(z,x)
         in -((f 1), (g 1))
```

Here we evaluate the expression proc (z) -(z,x) twice. The first time we do it, x is bound to 200, so by the lexical scope rule, the result is a procedure that subtracts 200 from its argument. We name this procedure f. The second time we do it, x is bound to 100, so the resulting procedure should subtract 100 from its argument. We name this procedure g.

These two procedures, created from identical expressions, must behave differently. We conclude that the value of a proc expression must depend in some way on the environment in which it is evaluated. Therefore the constructor procedure must take three arguments: the bound variable, the body, and the environment. The specification for a proc expression is

```
(value-of (proc-exp var body) ρ)
= (proc-val (procedure var body ρ))
```

where proc-val is a constructor, like bool-val or num-val, that builds an expressed value from a *Proc*.

At a procedure call, we want to find the value of the operator and the operand. If the value of the operator is a proc-val, then we want to apply it to the value of the operand.

```
(value-of (call-exp rator rand) ρ)
= (let ((proc (expval->proc (value-of rator ρ)))
        (arg (value-of rand ρ)))
    (apply-procedure proc arg))
```

Here we rely on a tester expval->proc, like expval->num, to test whether the value of (value-of *rator* ρ), an expressed value, was constructed by proc-val, and if so to extract the underlying procedure.

Last, we consider what happens when apply-procedure is invoked. As we have seen, the lexical scope rule tells us that when a procedure is applied, its body is evaluated in an environment that binds the formal parameter of the procedure to the argument of the call. Furthermore any other variables must have the same values they had at procedure-creation time. Therefore these procedures should satisfy the condition

```
(apply-procedure (procedure var body ρ) val)
= (value-of body [var=val] ρ)
```

3.3.1   An Example

Let's do an example to show how the pieces of the specification fit together. This is a calculation using the *specification*, not the implementation, since we have not yet written down the implementation of procedures. Let ρ be any environment.

```
(value-of
  <<let x = 200
    in let f = proc (z) -(z,x)
        in let x = 100
            in let g = proc (z) -(z,x)
                in -((f 1), (g 1))>>
  ρ)

= (value-of
    <<let f = proc (z) -(z,x)
      in let x = 100
          in let g = proc (z) -(z,x)
              in -((f 1), (g 1))>>
    [x=⌈200⌉]ρ)


= (value-of
    <<let x = 100
      in let g = proc (z) -(z,x)
          in -((f 1), (g 1))>>
    [f=(proc-val (procedure z <<-(z,x)>> [x=⌈200⌉]ρ))]
      [x=⌈200⌉]ρ)

= (value-of
    <<let g = proc (z) -(z,x)
      in -((f 1), (g 1))>>
    [x=⌈100⌉]
      [f=(proc-val (procedure z <<-(z,x)>> [x=⌈200⌉]ρ))]
        [x=⌈200⌉]ρ)
```

```
= (value-of
    <<-((f 1), (g 1))>>
    [g=(proc-val (procedure z <<-(z,x)>>
                         [x=⌈100⌉] [f=...] [x=⌈200⌉] ρ))]
     [x=⌈100⌉]
      [f=(proc-val (procedure z <<-(z,x)>> [x=⌈200⌉] ρ))]
       [x=⌈200⌉] ρ)
```

```
= ⌈(-
    (value-of <<(f 1)>>
      [g=(proc-val (procedure z <<-(z,x)>>
                           [x=⌈100⌉] [f=...] [x=⌈200⌉] ρ))]
       [x=⌈100⌉]
        [f=(proc-val (procedure z <<-(z,x)>> [x=⌈200⌉] ρ))]
         [x=⌈200⌉] ρ)
    (value-of <<(g 1)>>
      [g=(proc-val (procedure z <<-(z,x)>>
                           [x=⌈100⌉] [f=...] [x=⌈200⌉] ρ))]
       [x=⌈100⌉]
        [f=(proc-val (procedure z <<-(z,x)>> [x=⌈200⌉] ρ))]
         [x=⌈200⌉] ρ))⌉
```

```
= ⌈(-
    (apply-procedure
     (procedure z <<-(z,x)>> [x=⌈200⌉] ρ)
     ⌈1⌉)
    (apply-procedure
     (procedure z <<-(z,x)>> [x=⌈100⌉] [f=...] [x=⌈200⌉] ρ)
     ⌈1⌉))⌉
```

```
= ⌈(-
    (value-of <<-(z,x)>> [z=⌈1⌉] [x=⌈200⌉] ρ)
    (value-of <<-(z,x)>> [z=⌈1⌉] [x=⌈100⌉] [f=...] [x=⌈200⌉] ρ))⌉
```

```
= ⌈(- -199 -99)⌉
```

```
= ⌈-100⌉
```

Here f is bound to a procedure that subtracts 200 from its argument, and g is bound to a procedure that subtracts 100 from its argument, so the value of (f 1) is −199 and the value of (g 1) is −99.

3.3.2 Representing Procedures

According to the recipe described in section 2.2.3, we can employ a procedural representation for procedures by their action under `apply-procedure`. To do this we define `procedure` to have a value that is an implementation-language procedure that expects an argument, and returns the value required by the specification

```
(apply-procedure (procedure var body ρ) val)
= (value-of body (extend-env var val ρ))
```

Therefore the entire implementation is

proc? : *SchemeVal* → *Bool*
```
(define proc?
  (lambda (val)
    (procedure? val)))
```

procedure : *Var* × *Exp* × *Env* → *Proc*
```
(define procedure
  (lambda (var body env)
    (lambda (val)
      (value-of body (extend-env var val env)))))
```

apply-procedure : *Proc* × *ExpVal* → *ExpVal*
```
(define apply-procedure
  (lambda (proc1 val)
    (proc1 val)))
```

The function `proc?`, as defined here, is somewhat inaccurate, since not every Scheme procedure is a possible procedure in our language. We need it only for defining the data type `expval`.

Alternatively, we could use a data structure representation like that of section 2.2.2.

proc? : *SchemeVal* → *Bool*
procedure : *Var* × *Exp* × *Env* → *Proc*
```
(define-datatype proc proc?
  (procedure
    (var identifier?)
    (body expression?)
    (saved-env environment?)))
```

apply-procedure : *Proc* × *ExpVal* → *ExpVal*
```
(define apply-procedure
  (lambda (proc1 val)
    (cases proc proc1
      (procedure (var body saved-env)
        (value-of body (extend-env var val saved-env))))))
```

These data structures are often called *closures*, because they are self-contained: they contain everything the procedure needs in order to be applied. We sometimes say the procedure is *closed over* or *closed in* its creation environment.

Each of these implementations evidently satisfies the specification for the procedure interface.

In either implementation, we add an alternative to the data type `expval`

```
(define-datatype expval expval?
  (num-val
    (num number?))
  (bool-val
    (bool boolean?))
  (proc-val
    (proc proc?)))
```

and we need to add two new clauses to `value-of`

```
(proc-exp (var body)
  (proc-val (procedure var body env)))

(call-exp (rator rand)
  (let ((proc (expval->proc (value-of rator env)))
        (arg (value-of rand env)))
    (apply-procedure proc arg)))
```

Reminder: be sure to write down specifications for each language extension. See the note on page 70.

Exercise 3.19 [⋆] In many languages, procedures must be created and named at the same time. Modify the language of this section to have this property by replacing the `proc` expression with a `letproc` expression.

Exercise 3.20 [⋆] In PROC, procedures have only one argument, but one can get the effect of multiple argument procedures by using procedures that return other procedures. For example, one might write code like

```
let f = proc (x) proc (y) ...
in ((f 3) 4)
```

This trick is called *Currying*, and the procedure is said to be *Curried*. Write a Curried procedure that takes two arguments and returns their sum. You can write $x + y$ in our language by writing $-(x, -(0, y))$.

Exercise 3.21 [⋆ ⋆] Extend the language of this section to include procedures with multiple arguments and calls with multiple operands, as suggested by the grammar

$$Expression ::= \texttt{proc} (\{Identifier\}^{*(,)}) Expression$$
$$Expression ::= (Expression \{Expression\}^*)$$

Exercise 3.22 [★★★] The concrete syntax of this section uses different syntax for a built-in operation, such as difference, from a procedure call. Modify the concrete syntax so that the user of this language need not know which operations are built-in and which are defined procedures. This exercise may range from very easy to hard, depending on the parsing technology being used.

Exercise 3.23 [★★] What is the value of the following PROC program?

```
let makemult = proc (maker)
                  proc (x)
                   if zero?(x)
                   then 0
                   else -(((maker maker) -(x,1)), -4)
in let times4 = proc (x) ((makemult makemult) x)
   in (times4 3)
```

Use the tricks of this program to write a procedure for factorial in PROC. As a hint, remember that you can use Currying (exercise 3.20) to define a two-argument procedure times.

Exercise 3.24 [★★] Use the tricks of the program above to write the pair of mutually recursive procedures, odd and even, as in exercise 3.32.

Exercise 3.25 [★] The tricks of the previous exercises can be generalized to show that we can define any recursive procedure in PROC. Consider the following bit of code:

```
let makerec = proc (f)
                let d = proc (x)
                          proc (z) ((f (x x)) z)
                in proc (n) ((f (d d)) n)
in let maketimes4 = proc (f)
                      proc (x)
                       if zero?(x)
                       then 0
                       else -((f -(x,1)), -4)
   in let times4 = (makerec maketimes4)
      in (times4 3)
```

Show that it returns 12.

Exercise 3.26 [★★] In our data-structure representation of procedures, we have kept the entire environment in the closure. But of course all we need are the bindings for the free variables. Modify the representation of procedures to retain only the free variables.

Exercise 3.27 [★] Add a new kind of procedure called a traceproc to the language. A traceproc works exactly like a proc, except that it prints a trace message on entry and on exit.

Exercise 3.28 [⋆⋆] *Dynamic binding* (or *dynamic scoping*) is an alternative design for procedures, in which the procedure body is evaluated in an environment obtained by extending the environment at the point of call. For example in

```
let a = 3
in let p = proc (x) -(x,a)
       a = 5
   in -(a,(p 2))
```

the a in the procedure body would be bound to 5, not 3. Modify the language to use dynamic binding. Do this twice, once using a procedural representation for procedures, and once using a data-structure representation.

Exercise 3.29 [⋆⋆] Unfortunately, programs that use dynamic binding may be exceptionally difficult to understand. For example, under lexical binding, consistently renaming the bound variables of a procedure can never change the behavior of a program: we can even remove all variables and replace them by their lexical addresses, as in section 3.6. But under dynamic binding, this transformation is unsafe.

For example, under dynamic binding, the procedure proc (z) a returns the value of the variable a in its caller's environment. Thus, the program

```
let a = 3
in let p = proc (z) a
   in let f = proc (x) (p 0)
      in let a = 5
         in (f 2)
```

returns 5, since a's value at the call site is 5. What if f's formal parameter were a?

3.4   LETREC: A Language with Recursive Procedures

We now define a new language LETREC, which adds recursion to our language. Since our language has only one-argument procedures, we make our life simpler by having our letrec expressions declare only a single one-argument procedure, for example

```
letrec double(x)
          = if zero?(x) then 0 else -((double -(x,1)), -2)
in (double 6)
```

The left-hand side of a recursive declaration is the name of the recursive procedure and its bound variable. To the right of the = is the procedure body. The production for this is

> *Expression* ::= letrec *Identifier* (*Identifier*) = *Expression* in *Expression*
>
> > letrec-exp (p-name b-var p-body letrec-body)

The value of a `letrec` expression is the value of the body in an environment that has the desired behavior:

```
(value-of
  (letrec-exp proc-name bound-var proc-body letrec-body)
  ρ)
= (value-of
    letrec-body
    (extend-env-rec proc-name bound-var proc-body ρ))
```

Here we have added a new procedure `extend-env-rec` to the environment interface. But we still need to answer the question: What is the desired behavior of (`extend-env-rec` *proc-name bound-var proc-body* ρ)?

We specify the behavior of this environment as follows: Let ρ_1 be the environment produced by (`extend-env-rec` *proc-name bound-var proc-body* ρ). Then what should (`apply-env` ρ_1 *var*) return?

1. If the variable *var* is the same as *proc-name*, then (`apply-env` ρ_1 *var*) should produce a closure whose bound variable is *bound-var*, whose body is *proc-body*, and with an environment in which *proc-name* is bound to this procedure. But we already have such an environment, namely ρ_1 itself! So

   ```
   (apply-env ρ₁ proc-name)
   = (proc-val (procedure bound-var proc-body ρ₁))
   ```

2. If *var* is not the same as *proc-name*, then

   $$(\texttt{apply-env }\rho_1\ \textit{var}) = (\texttt{apply-env }\rho\ \textit{var})$$

Figures 3.10 and 3.11 show an example. There in the last line of figure 3.11, the recursive call to `double` finds the original `double` procedure, as desired.

We can implement `extend-env-rec` in any way that satisfies these requirements. We'll do it here for the abstract-syntax representation. Some other implementation strategies are discussed in the exercises.

In an abstract-syntax representation, we add a new variant for an `extend-env-rec` in figure 3.12. The `env` on the next-to-last line of `apply-env` corresponds to ρ_1 in the discussion above.

Exercise 3.30 [⋆] What is the purpose of the call to `proc-val` on the next-to-last line of `apply-env`?

Exercise 3.31 [⋆] Extend the language above to allow the declaration of a recursive procedure of possibly many arguments, as in exercise 3.21.

```
(value-of <<letrec double(x) = if zero?(x)
                                then 0
                                else -((double -(x,1)), -2)
              in (double 6)>> ρ₀)

= (value-of <<(double 6)>>
     (extend-env-rec double x <<if zero?(x) ...>> ρ₀))

= (apply-procedure
     (value-of <<double>> (extend-env-rec double x
                             <<if zero?(x) ...>> ρ₀))
     (value-of <<6>> (extend-env-rec double x
                         <<if zero?(x) ...>> ρ₀)))

= (apply-procedure
     (procedure x <<if zero?(x) ...>>
        (extend-env-rec double x <<if zero?(x) ...>> ρ₀))
     ⌈6⌉)

= (value-of
     <<if zero?(x) ...>>
    [x=⌈6⌉] (extend-env-rec
                 double x <<if zero?(x) ...>> ρ₀))

...

= (-
     (value-of
       <<(double -(x,1))>>
      [x=⌈6⌉] (extend-env-rec
                   double x <<if zero?(x) ...>> ρ₀))
     -2)
```

Figure 3.10   A calculation with `extend-env-rec`

Exercise 3.32 [⋆ ⋆] Extend the language above to allow the declaration of any number of mututally recursive unary procedures, for example:

```
letrec
   even(x) = if zero?(x) then 1 else (odd -(x,1))
   odd(x)  = if zero?(x) then 0 else (even -(x,1))
in (odd 13)
```

```
=  (-
     (apply-procedure
       (value-of
         <<double>>
         [x=⌈6⌉] (extend-env-rec
                            double x <<if zero?(x) ...>> ρ₀))
       (value-of
         <<-(x,1)>>
         [x=⌈6⌉] (extend-env-rec
                            double x <<if zero?(x) ...>> ρ₀)))
     -2)

=  (-
     (apply-procedure
       (procedure x <<if zero?(x) ...>>
         (extend-env-rec double x <<if zero?(x) ...>> ρ₀))
       ⌈5⌉)
     -2)

=  ...
```

Figure 3.11   A calculation with `extend-env-rec`, cont'd.

Exercise 3.33 [⋆ ⋆] Extend the language above to allow the declaration of any number of mutually recursive procedures, each of possibly many arguments, as in exercise 3.21.

Exercise 3.34 [⋆ ⋆ ⋆] Implement `extend-env-rec` in the procedural representation of environments from section 2.2.3.

Exercise 3.35 [⋆] The representations we have seen so far are inefficient, because they build a new closure every time the procedure is retrieved. But the closure is the same every time. We can build the closures only once, by putting the value in a vector of length 1 and building an explicit circular structure, like

```
(define-datatype environment environment?
  (empty-env)
  (extend-env
    (var identifier?)
    (val expval?)
    (env environment?))
  (extend-env-rec
    (p-name identifier?)
    (b-var identifier?)
    (body expression?)
    (env environment?)))

(define apply-env
  (lambda (env search-var)
    (cases environment env
      (empty-env ()
        (report-no-binding-found search-var))
      (extend-env (saved-var saved-val saved-env)
        (if (eqv? saved-var search-var)
          saved-val
          (apply-env saved-env search-var)))
      (extend-env-rec (p-name b-var p-body saved-env)
        (if (eqv? search-var p-name)
          (proc-val (procedure b-var p-body env))
          (apply-env saved-env search-var))))))
```

Figure 3.12   extend-env-rec added to environments.

Here's the code to build this data structure.

```
(define extend-env-rec
  (lambda (p-name b-var body saved-env)
    (let ((vec (make-vector 1)))
      (let ((new-env (extend-env p-name vec saved-env)))
        (vector-set! vec 0
          (proc-val (procedure b-var body new-env)))
        new-env))))
```

Complete the implementation of this representation by modifying the definitions of the environment data type and apply-env accordingly. Be sure that apply-env always returns an expressed value.

Exercise 3.36 [⋆ ⋆] Extend this implementation to handle the language from exercise 3.32.

Exercise 3.37 [⋆] With dynamic binding (exercise 3.28), recursive procedures may be bound by `let`; no special mechanism is necessary for recursion. This is of historical interest; in the early years of programming language design other approaches to recursion, such as those discussed in section 3.4, were not widely understood. To demonstrate recursion via dynamic binding, test the program

```
let fact = proc (n) add1(n)
in let fact = proc (n)
                if zero?(n)
                then 1
                else *(n, (fact -(n,1)))
     in (fact 5)
```

using both lexical and dynamic binding. Write the mutually recursive procedures `even` and `odd` as in section 3.4 in the defined language with dynamic binding.

3.5   Scoping and Binding of Variables

We have now seen a variety of situations in which variables are declared and used. We now discuss these ideas in a more systematic way.

In most programming languages, variables may appear in two different ways: as *references* or as *declarations*. A variable reference is a use of the variable. For example, in the Scheme expression

```
(f x y)
```

all the variables, f, x, and y, appear as references. However, in

```
(lambda (x) (+ x 3))
```

or

```
(let ((x (+ y 7))) (+ x 3))
```

the first occurrence of x is a declaration: it introduces the variable as a name for some value. In the `lambda` expression, the value of the variable will be supplied when the procedure is called. In the `let` expression, the value of the variable is obtained from the value of the expression (+ y 7).

We say that a variable reference is *bound by* the declaration with which it is associated, and that it is *bound to* its value. We have already seen examples of a variable being bound by a declaration, in section 1.2.4.

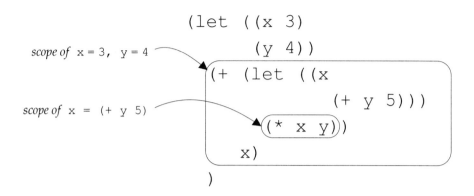

Figure 3.13   A simple contour diagram

Declarations in most programming languages have a limited scope, so that the same variable name may be used for different purposes in different parts of a program. For example, we have repeatedly used `lst` as a bound variable, and in each case its scope was limited to the body of the corresponding lambda expression.

Every programming language must have some rules to determine the declaration to which each variable reference refers. These rules are typically called *scoping* rules. The portion of the program in which a declaration is valid is called the *scope* of the declaration.

We can determine which declaration is associated with each variable use without executing the program. Properties like this, which can be computed without executing the program, are called *static* properties.

To find which declaration corresponds to a given use of a variable, we search *outward* from the use until we find a declaration of the variable. Here is a simple example in Scheme.

```
(let ((x 3)              Call this x1
      (y 4))
    (+ (let ((x           Call this x2
              (+ y 5)))
          (* x y))        Here x refers to x2
       x))                Here x refers to x1
```

In this example, the inner x is bound to 9, so the value of the expression is

```
(let ((x 3)
      (y 4))
  (+ (let ((x
              (+ y 5)))
       (* x y))
     x))

= (+ (let ((x
              (+ 4 5)))
       (* x 4))
     3)

= (+ (let ((x 9))
       (* x 4))
     3)

= (+ 36
     3)

= 39
```

Scoping rules like this are called *lexical scoping* rules, and the variables declared in this way are called *lexical variables*.

Under lexical scoping, we can create a hole in a scope by redeclaring a variable. Such an inner declaration *shadows* the outer one. For instance, in the example above, the inner x shadows the outer one in the multiplication (* x y).

Lexical scopes are nested: each scope lies entirely within another scope. We can illustrate this with a *contour diagram*. Figure 3.13 shows the contour diagram for the example above. A box surrounds each scope, and a vertical line connects each declaration to its scope.

Figure 3.14 shows a more complicated program with the contours drawn in. Here there are three occurrences of the expression (+ x y z), on lines 5, 7, and 8. Line 5 is within the scope of x2 and z2, which is within the scope of z1, which is within the scope of x1 and y1. So at line 5, x refers to x2, y refers to y1, and z refers to z2. Line 7 is within the scope of x4 and y2, which is within the scope of x2 and z2, which is within the scope of z1, which is within the scope of x1 and y1. So at line 7, x refers to x4, y refers to y2, and z refers to z2. Last, line 8 is within the scope of x3, which is within the scope of x2 and z2, which is within the scope of z1, which is within the scope of x1 and y1. So at line 8, x refers to x3, y refers to y1, and z refers to z2.

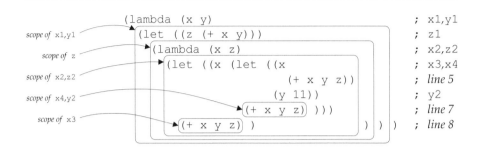

Figure 3.14   A more complicated contour diagram

The association between a variable and its value is called a *binding*. For our language, we can look at the specification to see how the binding is created.

A variable declared by a `proc` is bound when the procedure is applied.

```
(apply-procedure (procedure var body ρ) val)
= (value-of body (extend-env var val ρ))
```

A `let`-variable is bound by the value of its right-hand side.

```
(value-of (let-exp var val body) ρ)
= (value-of body (extend-env var val ρ))
```

A variable declared by a `letrec` is bound using its right-hand side as well.

```
(value-of
  (letrec-exp proc-name bound-var proc-body letrec-body)
  ρ)
= (value-of
    letrec-body
    (extend-env-rec proc-name bound-var proc-body ρ))
```

The *extent* of a binding is the time interval during which the binding is maintained. In our little language, as in Scheme, all bindings have *semi-infinite* extent, meaning that once a variable gets bound, that binding must be maintained indefinitely (at least potentially). This is because the binding might be hidden inside a closure that is returned. In languages with semi-infinite extent, the garbage collector collects bindings when they are no longer reachable. This is only determinable at run-time, so we say that this is a *dynamic* property.

Regrettably, "dynamic" is sometimes used to mean "during the evaluation of an expression" but other times is used to mean "not calculable in
advance." If we did not allow a procedure to be used as the value of a `let`,
then the let-bindings would expire at the end of the evaluation of the `let`
body. This is called *dynamic* extent, and it is a *static* property. Because the
extent is a static property, we can predict exactly when a binding can be discarded. Dynamic binding, as in exercise 3.28 *et seq.*, behaves similarly.

3.6 Eliminating Variable Names

Execution of the scoping algorithm may then be viewed as a journey outward from a variable reference. In this journey a number of contours may be
crossed before arriving at the associated declaration. The number of contours
crossed is called the *lexical* (or *static*) *depth* of the variable reference. It is cus-
tomary to use "zero-based indexing," thereby not counting the last contour
crossed. For example, in the Scheme expression

```
(lambda (x)
  ((lambda (a)
    (x a))
  x))
```

the reference to x on the last line and the reference to a have lexical depth
zero, while the reference to x in the third line has lexical depth one.

We could, therefore, get rid of variable names entirely, and write something like

```
(nameless-lambda
  ((nameless-lambda
    (#1 #0))
  #0))
```

Here each `nameless-lambda` declares a new anonymous variable, and
each variable reference is replaced by its lexical depth; this number uniquely
identifies the declaration to which it refers. These numbers are called *lexical
addresses* or *de Bruijn indices*. Compilers routinely calculate the lexical address
of each variable reference. Once this has been done, the variable names may
be discarded unless they are required to provide debugging information.

This way of recording the information is useful because the lexical address
predicts just where in the environment any particular variable will be found.

Consider the expression

```
let x = exp₁
in let y = exp₂
   in -(x,y)
```

in our language. In the difference expression, the lexical depths of y and x are 0 and 1, respectively.

Now assume that the values of *exp₁* and *exp₂*, in the appropriate environments, are *val₁* and *val₂*. Then the value of this expression is

```
(value-of
  <<let x = exp₁
     in let y = exp₂
        in -(x,y) >>
   ρ)
=
(value-of
  <<let y = exp₂
     in -(x,y) >>
   [x=val₁] ρ)
=
(value-of
  <<-(x,y) >>
   [y=val₂] [x=val₁] ρ)
```

so that when the difference expression is evaluated, y is at depth 0 and x is at depth 1, just as predicted by their lexical depths.

If we are using an association-list representation of environments (see exercise 2.5), then the environment will look like

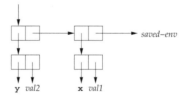

so that the values of x and y will be found by taking either 1 cdr or 0 cdrs in the environment, regardless of the values *val₁* and *val₂*.

The same thing works for procedure bodies. Consider

```
let a = 5
in proc (x) -(x,a)
```

In the body of the procedure, x is at lexical depth 0 and a is at depth 1.

The value of this expression is

```
(value-of
  <<let a = 5 in proc (x) -(x,a)>>
  ρ)
= (value-of <<proc (x) -(x,a)>>
    (extend-env a ⌈5⌉ ρ))
= (proc-val (procedure x <<-(x,a)>> [a=⌈5⌉]ρ))
```

The body of this procedure can only be evaluated by `apply-procedure`:

```
(apply-procedure
  (procedure x <<-(x,a)>> [a=⌈5⌉]ρ)
  ⌈7⌉)
= (value-of <<-(x,a)>>
    [x=⌈7⌉] [a=⌈5⌉]ρ)
```

So again every variable is found in the environment at the place predicted by its lexical depth.

3.7   Implementing Lexical Addressing

We now implement the lexical-address analysis we sketched above. We write a procedure `translation-of-program` that takes a program and removes all the variables from the declarations, and replaces every variable reference by its lexical depth.

For example, the program

```
let x = 37
in proc (y)
    let z = -(y,x)
    in -(x,y)
```

is translated to

```
#(struct:a-program
  #(struct:nameless-let-exp
    #(struct:const-exp 37)
    #(struct:nameless-proc-exp
      #(struct:nameless-let-exp
        #(struct:diff-exp
          #(struct:nameless-var-exp 0)
          #(struct:nameless-var-exp 1))
        #(struct:diff-exp
          #(struct:nameless-var-exp 2)
          #(struct:nameless-var-exp 1))))))
```

We then write a new version of `value-of-program` that will find the value of such a nameless program, without putting variables in the environment.

3.7.1   The Translator

We are writing a translator, so we need to know the source language and the target language. The target language will have things like `nameless-var-exp` and `nameless-let-exp` that were not in the source language, and it will lose the things in the source language that these constructs replace, like `var-exp` and `let-exp`.

We can either write out `define-datatype`'s for each language, or we can set up a single `define-datatype` that includes both. Since we are using SLLGEN as our front end, it is easier to do the latter. We add to the SLLGEN grammar the productions

$$Expression ::= \texttt{\%lexref } number$$
$$\boxed{\texttt{nameless-var-exp (num)}}$$

$$Expression ::= \texttt{\%let } Expression \texttt{ in } Expression$$
$$\boxed{\texttt{nameless-let-exp (exp1 body)}}$$

$$Expression ::= \texttt{\%lexproc } Expression$$
$$\boxed{\texttt{nameless-proc-exp (body)}}$$

We use names starting with `%` for these new constructs because `%` is normally the comment character in our language.

Our translator will reject any program that has one of these new nameless constructs (`nameless-var-exp`, `nameless-let-exp`, or `nameless-proc-exp`), and our interpreter will reject any program that has one of the old nameful constructs (`var-exp`, `let-exp`, or `proc-exp`) that are supposed to be replaced.

To calculate the lexical address of any variable reference, we need to know the scopes in which it is enclosed. This is *context* information, so it should be like the inherited attributes in section 1.3.

So `translation-of` will take two arguments: an expression and a *static environment*. The static environment will be a list of variables, representing the scopes within which the current expression lies. The variable declared in the innermost scope will be the first element of the list.

For example, when we translate the last line of the example above, the static environment should be

$$(\texttt{z y x})$$

So looking up a variable in the static environment means finding its position in the static environment, which gives a lexical address: looking up x will give 2, looking up y will give 1, and looking up z will give 0.

Senv = *Listof* (*Sym*)
Lexaddr = *N*

empty-senv : () → *Senv*
```
(define empty-senv
  (lambda ()
    '()))
```

extend-senv : *Var* × *Senv* → *Senv*
```
(define extend-senv
  (lambda (var senv)
    (cons var senv)))
```

apply-senv : *Senv* × *Var* → *Lexaddr*
```
(define apply-senv
  (lambda (senv var)
    (cond
      ((null? senv)
       (report-unbound-var var))
      ((eqv? var (car senv))
       0)
      (else
        (+ 1 (apply-senv (cdr senv) var))))))
```

Figure 3.15   Implementation of static environments

Entering a new scope will mean adding a new element to the static environment. We introduce a procedure extend-senv to do this.

Since the static environment is just a list of variables, these procedures are easy to implement and are shown in figure 3.15.

For the translator, we have two procedures, translation-of, which handles expressions, and translation-of-program, which handles programs.

We are trying to translate an expression e which is sitting inside the declarations represented by senv. To do this, we recursively copy the tree, as we did in exercises 1.33 or 2.26, except that

1. Every var-exp is replaced by a nameless-var-exp with the right lexical address, which we compute by calling apply-senv.

2. Every `let-exp` is replaced by a `nameless-let-exp`. The right-hand side of the new expression will be the translation of the right-hand side of the old expression. This is in the same scope as the original, so we translate it in the same static environment `senv`. The body of the new expression will be the translation of the body of the old expression. But the body now lies in a new scope, with the additional bound variable *var*. So we translate the body in the static environment `(extend-senv` *var* `senv)`.

3. Every `proc-exp` is replaced by a `nameless-proc-exp`, with the body translated with respect to the new scope, represented by the static environment `(extend-senv` *var* `senv)`.

The code for `translation-of` is shown in figure 3.16.

The procedure `translation-of-program` runs `translation-of` in a suitable initial static environment.

translation-of-program : *Program* → *Nameless-program*
```
(define translation-of-program
  (lambda (pgm)
    (cases program pgm
      (a-program (exp1)
        (a-program
          (translation-of exp1 (init-senv)))))))
```

init-senv : () → *Senv*
```
(define init-senv
  (lambda ()
    (extend-senv 'i
      (extend-senv 'v
        (extend-senv 'x
          (empty-senv))))))
```

3.7.2   The Nameless Interpreter

Our interpreter takes advantage of the predictions of the lexical-address analyzer to avoid explicitly searching for variables at run time.

Since there are no more variables in our programs, we won't be able to put variables in our environments, but since we know exactly where to look in each environment, we don't need them!

translation-of : *Exp* × *Senv* → *Nameless-exp*

```
(define translation-of
  (lambda (exp senv)
    (cases expression exp
      (const-exp (num) (const-exp num))
      (diff-exp (exp1 exp2)
        (diff-exp
          (translation-of exp1 senv)
          (translation-of exp2 senv)))
      (zero?-exp (exp1)
        (zero?-exp
          (translation-of exp1 senv)))
      (if-exp (exp1 exp2 exp3)
        (if-exp
          (translation-of exp1 senv)
          (translation-of exp2 senv)
          (translation-of exp3 senv)))
      (var-exp (var)
        (nameless-var-exp
          (apply-senv senv var)))
      (let-exp (var exp1 body)
        (nameless-let-exp
          (translation-of exp1 senv)
          (translation-of body
            (extend-senv var senv))))
      (proc-exp (var body)
        (nameless-proc-exp
          (translation-of body
            (extend-senv var senv))))
      (call-exp (rator rand)
        (call-exp
          (translation-of rator senv)
          (translation-of rand senv)))
      (else
        (report-invalid-source-expression exp)))))
```

Figure 3.16   The lexical-address translator

Our top-level procedure will be `run`:

run : *String* → *ExpVal*
```
(define run
  (lambda (string)
    (value-of-program
      (translation-of-program
        (scan&parse string)))))
```

Instead of having full-fledged environments, we will have nameless environments, with the following interface:

nameless-environment?	: *SchemeVal* → *Bool*
empty-nameless-env	: *()* → *Nameless-env*
extend-nameless-env	: *Expval* × *Nameless-env* → *Nameless-env*
apply-nameless-env	: *Nameless-env* × *Lexaddr* → *DenVal*

We can implement a nameless environment as a list of denoted values, so that `apply-nameless-env` is simply a call to `list-ref`. The implementation is shown in figure 3.17.

At the last line of the example on page 93, the nameless environment will look like

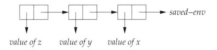

Having changed the environment interface, we need to look at all the code that depends on that interface. There are only two things in our interpreter that use environments: procedures and `value-of`.

The revised specification for procedures is just the old one with the variable name removed.

```
(apply-procedure (procedure body ρ) val)
= (value-of body (extend-nameless-env val ρ))
```

We can implement this by defining

procedure : *Nameless-exp* × *Nameless-env* → *Proc*
```
(define-datatype proc proc?
  (procedure
    (body expression?)
    (saved-nameless-env nameless-environment?)))
```

nameless-environment? : *SchemeVal* → *Bool*
```
(define nameless-environment?
  (lambda (x)
    ((list-of expval?) x)))
```

empty-nameless-env : () → *Nameless-env*
```
(define empty-nameless-env
  (lambda ()
    '()))
```

extend-nameless-env : *ExpVal* × *Nameless-env* → *Nameless-env*
```
(define extend-nameless-env
  (lambda (val nameless-env)
    (cons val nameless-env)))
```

apply-nameless-env : *Nameless-env* × *Lexaddr* → *ExpVal*
```
(define apply-nameless-env
  (lambda (nameless-env n)
    (list-ref nameless-env n)))
```

Figure 3.17 Nameless environments

---

apply-procedure : *Proc* × *ExpVal* → *ExpVal*
```
(define apply-procedure
  (lambda (proc1 val)
    (cases proc proc1
      (procedure (body saved-nameless-env)
        (value-of body
          (extend-nameless-env val saved-nameless-env))))))
```

Now we can write `value-of`. Most cases are the same as in the earlier interpreters except that where we used `env` we now use `nameless-env`. We do have new cases, however, that correspond to `var-exp`, `let-exp`, and `proc-exp`, which we replace by cases for `nameless-var-exp`, `nameless-let-exp`, and `nameless-proc-exp`, respectively. The implementation is shown in figure 3.18. A `nameless-var-exp` gets looked up in the environment. A `nameless-let-exp` evaluates its right-hand side exp_1, and then evalutes its body in an environment extended by the value of the right-hand side. This is just what an ordinary `let` does, but without the variables. A `nameless-proc` produces a `proc`, which is then applied by `apply-procedure`.

---

value-of : *Nameless-exp* × *Nameless-env* → *ExpVal*

```
(define value-of
  (lambda (exp nameless-env)
    (cases expression exp

      (const-exp (num)    ...as before...)
      (diff-exp (exp1 exp2)   ...as before...)
      (zero?-exp (exp1)    ...as before...)
      (if-exp (exp1 exp2 exp3) ...as before...)
      (call-exp (rator rand)   ...as before...)

      (nameless-var-exp (n)
        (apply-nameless-env nameless-env n))

      (nameless-let-exp (exp1 body)
        (let ((val (value-of exp1 nameless-env)))
          (value-of body
            (extend-nameless-env val nameless-env))))

      (nameless-proc-exp (body)
        (proc-val
          (procedure body nameless-env)))

      (else
        (report-invalid-translated-expression exp)))))
```

Figure 3.18   value-of for the nameless interpreter

Last, here's the new value-of-program:

value-of-program : *Nameless-program* → *ExpVal*

```
(define value-of-program
  (lambda (pgm)
    (cases program pgm
      (a-program (exp1)
        (value-of exp1 (init-nameless-env))))))
```

Exercise 3.38 [⋆] Extend the lexical address translator and interpreter to handle cond from exercise 3.12.

Exercise 3.39 [⋆] Extend the lexical address translator and interpreter to handle pack and unpack from exercise 3.18.

Exercise 3.40 [⋆ ⋆] Extend the lexical address translator and interpreter to handle letrec. Do this by modifying the context argument to translation-of so that it keeps track of not only the name of each bound variable, but also whether it was bound by letrec or not. For a reference to a variable that was bound by a letrec, generate a new kind of reference, called a nameless-letrec-var-exp. You can then continue to use the nameless environment representation above, and the interpreter can do the right thing with a nameless-letrec-var-exp.

Exercise 3.41 [⋆ ⋆] Modify the lexical address translator and interpreter to handle let expressions, procedures, and procedure calls with multiple arguments, as in exercise 3.21. Do this using a nameless version of the ribcage representation of environments (exercise 2.11). For this representation, the lexical address will consist of two nonnegative integers: the lexical depth, to indicate the number of contours crossed, as before; and a position, to indicate the position of the variable in the declaration.

Exercise 3.42 [⋆ ⋆ ⋆] Modify the lexical address translator and interpreter to use the trimmed representation of procedures from exercise 3.26. For this, you will need to translate the body of the procedure not (extend-senv *var senv*), but in a new static environment that tells exactly where each variable will be kept in the trimmed representation.

Exercise 3.43 [⋆ ⋆ ⋆] The translator can do more than just keep track of the names of variables. For example, consider the program

```
let x = 3
in let f = proc (y) -(y,x)
   in (f 13)
```

Here we can tell statically that at the procedure call, f will be bound to a procedure whose body is -(y,x), where x has the same value that it had at the procedure-creation site. Therefore we could avoid looking up f in the environment entirely. Extend the translator to keep track of "known procedures" and generate code that avoids an environment lookup at the call of such a procedure.

Exercise 3.44 [⋆ ⋆ ⋆] In the preceding example, the only use of f is as a known procedure. Therefore the procedure built by the expression proc (y) -(y,x) is never used. Modify the translator so that such a procedure is never constructed.

4 *State*

4.1 Computational Effects

So far, we have only considered the *value* produced by a computation. But a computation may have *effects* as well: it may read, print, or alter the state of memory or a file system. In the real world, we are *always* interested in effects: if a computation doesn't display its answer, it doesn't do us any good!

What's the difference between producing a value and producing an effect? An effect is *global*: it is seen by the entire computation. An effect affects the entire computation (pun intended).

We will be concerned primarily with a single effect: assignment to a location in memory. How does assignment differ from binding? As we have seen, binding is local, but variable assignment is potentially global. It is about the *sharing* of values between otherwise unrelated portions of the computation. Two procedures can share information if they both know about the same location in memory. A single procedure can share information with a future invocation of itself by leaving the information in a known location.

We model memory as a finite map from *locations* to a set of values called the *storable values*. For historical reasons, we call this the *store*. The storable values in a language are typically, but not always, the same as the expressed values of the language. This choice is part of the design of a language.

A data structure that represents a location is called a *reference*. A location is a place in memory where a value can be stored, and a reference is a data structure that refers to that place. The distinction between locations and references may be seen by analogy: a location is like a file and a reference is like a URL. The URL refers to the file, and the file contains some data. Similarly, a reference denotes a location, and the location contains some data.

References are sometimes called *L-values*. This name reflects the association of such data structures with variables appearing on the left-hand side of assignment statements. Analogously, expressed values, such as the values of the right-hand side expressions of assignment statements, are known as *R-values*.

We consider two designs for a language with a store. We call these designs *explicit references* and *implicit references*.

4.2   EXPLICIT-REFS: A Language with Explicit References

In this design, we add references as a new kind of expressed value. So we have

$$ExpVal = Int + Bool + Proc + Ref(ExpVal)$$
$$DenVal = ExpVal$$

Here *Ref(ExpVal)* means the set of references to locations that contain expressed values.

We leave the binding structures of the language unchanged, but we add three new operations to create and use references.

- `newref`, which allocates a new location and returns a reference to it.

- `deref`, which dereferences a reference: that is, it returns the contents of the location that the reference represents.

- `setref`, which changes the contents of the location that the reference represents.

We call the resulting language EXPLICIT-REFS. Let's write some programs using these constructs.

Below are two procedures, `even` and `odd`. They each take an argument, which they ignore, and return 1 or 0 depending on whether the contents of the location x is even or odd. They communicate not by passing data explicitly, but by changing the contents of the variable they share.

This program determines whether or not 13 is odd, and therefore returns 1. The procedures `even` and `odd` do not refer to their arguments; instead they look at the contents of the location to which x is bound.

```
let x = newref(0)
in letrec even(dummy)
            = if zero?(deref(x))
              then 1
              else begin
                      setref(x, -(deref(x),1));
                      (odd 888)
                   end
         odd(dummy)
            = if zero?(deref(x))
              then 0
              else begin
                      setref(x, -(deref(x),1));
                      (even 888)
                   end
   in begin setref(x,13); (odd 888) end
```

This program uses multideclaration `letrec` (exercise 3.32) and a `begin` expression (exercise 4.4). A `begin` expression evaluates its subexpressions in order and returns the value of the last one.

We pass a dummy argument to `even` and `odd` to stay within the framework of our unary language; if we had procedures of any number of arguments (exercise 3.21) we could have made these procedures of no arguments.

This style of communication is convenient when two procedures might share many quantities; one needs to assign only to the few quantities that change from one call to the next. Similarly, one procedure might call another procedure not directly but through a long chain of procedure calls. They could communicate data directly through a shared variable, without the intermediate procedures needing to know about it. Thus communication through a shared variable can be a kind of information hiding.

Another use of assignment is to create hidden state through the use of private variables. Here is an example.

```
let g = let counter = newref(0)
        in proc (dummy)
              begin
                setref(counter, -(deref(counter), -1));
                deref(counter)
              end
in let a = (g 11)
   in let b = (g 11)
      in -(a,b)
```

Here the procedure g keeps a private variable that stores the number of times g has been called. Hence the first call to g returns 1, the second call to g returns 2, and the entire program has the value -1.

Here is a picture of the environment in which g is bound.

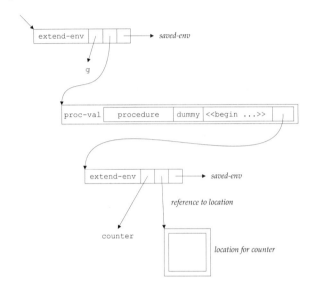

We can think of this as the different invocations of g sharing information with each other. This technique is used by the Scheme procedure gensym to create unique symbols.

Exercise 4.1 [⋆] What would have happened had the program been instead

```
let g = proc (dummy)
          let counter = newref(0)
          in begin
               setref(counter, -(deref(counter), -1));
               deref(counter)
             end
in let a = (g 11)
   in let b = (g 11)
      in -(a,b)
```

In EXPLICIT-REFS, we can store any expressed value, and references are expressed values. This means we can store a reference in a location. Consider the program

```
let x = newref(newref(0))
in begin
     setref(deref(x), 11);
     deref(deref(x))
   end
```

This program allocates a new location containing 0. It then binds x to a location containing a reference to the first location. Hence the value of deref(x) is a reference to the first location. So when the program evaluates the setref, it is the first location that is modified, and the entire program returns 11.

4.2.1   Store-Passing Specifications

In our language, any expression may have an effect. To specify these effects, we need to describe what store should be used for each evaluation and how each evaluation can modify the store.

In our specifications, we use σ to range over stores. We write $[l = v]\sigma$ to mean a store just like σ, except that location l is mapped to v. When we refer to a particular value of σ, we sometimes call it the *state* of the store.

We use *store-passing specfications*. In a store-passing specification, the store is passed as an explicit argument to value-of and is returned as an explicit result from value-of. Thus we write

$$(\texttt{value-of } exp_1 \; \rho \; \sigma_0) = (val_1, \sigma_1)$$

This asserts that expression exp_1, evaluated in environment ρ and with the store in state σ_0, returns the value val_1 and leaves the store in a possibly different state σ_1.

Thus we can specify an effect-free operation like const-exp by writing

$$(\texttt{value-of } (\texttt{const-exp } n) \; \rho \; \sigma) = (n, \sigma)$$

showing that the store is unchanged by evaluation of this expression.

The specification for diff-exp shows how we specify sequential behavior.

$$\frac{(\texttt{value-of } exp_1 \; \rho \; \sigma_0) = (val_1, \sigma_1) \quad (\texttt{value-of } exp_2 \; \rho \; \sigma_1) = (val_2, \sigma_2)}{(\texttt{value-of } (\texttt{diff-exp } exp_1 \; exp_2) \; \rho \; \sigma_0) = (\lceil \lfloor val_1 \rfloor - \lfloor val_2 \rfloor \rceil, \sigma_2)}$$

Here we evaluate exp_1 starting with the store in state σ_0. exp_1 returns value val_1, but it might also have some effects that leave the store in state σ_1. We then evaluate exp_2 starting with the store in the state that exp_1 left it, namely σ_1. exp_2 similarly returns a value val_2 and leaves the store in state σ_2. Then the entire expression returns $val_1 - val_2$ without further effect on the store, so it leaves the store in state σ_2.

Let's try a conditional.

$$\frac{(\texttt{value-of} \; exp_1 \; \rho \; \sigma_0) = (val_1, \sigma_1)}{\begin{array}{l} (\texttt{value-of} \; (\texttt{if-exp} \; exp_1 \; exp_2 \; exp_3) \; \rho \; \sigma_0) \\ \quad = \begin{cases} (\texttt{value-of} \; exp_2 \; \rho \; \sigma_1) & \text{if} \, (\texttt{expval->bool} \, val_1) = \texttt{\#t} \\ (\texttt{value-of} \; exp_3 \; \rho \; \sigma_1) & \text{if} \, (\texttt{expval->bool} \, val_1) = \texttt{\#f} \end{cases} \end{array}}$$

Starting in state σ_0, an if-exp evaluates its test expression exp_1, returning the value val_1 and leaving the store in state σ_1. The result of the entire expression is then either the result of exp_2 or exp_3, each evaluated in the current environment ρ and in the state σ_1 in which exp_1 left the store.

Exercise 4.2 [$\star$] Write down the specification for a zero?-exp.

Exercise 4.3 [$\star$] Write down the specification for a call-exp.

Exercise 4.4 [$\star\star$] Write down the specification for a begin expresssion.

$$Expression ::= \texttt{begin} \; Expression \; \{; \; Expression\}^* \; \texttt{end}$$

A begin expression may contain one or more subexpressions separated by semi-colons. These are evaluated in order and the value of the last is returned.

Exercise 4.5 [$\star\star$] Write down the specification for list (exercise 3.10).

4.2.2 Specifying Operations on Explicit References

In EXPLICIT-REFS, we have three new operations that must be specified: newref, deref, and setref. These are given by the grammar

$$Expression ::= \texttt{newref} \; (Expression)$$
$$\boxed{\texttt{newref-exp (exp1)}}$$

$$Expression ::= \texttt{deref} \; (Expression)$$
$$\boxed{\texttt{deref-exp (exp1)}}$$

$$Expression ::= \texttt{setref} \; (Expression \; , \; Expression)$$
$$\boxed{\texttt{setref-exp (exp1 exp2)}}$$

We can specify the behavior of these operations as follows.

$$\frac{(\texttt{value-of} \; exp \; \rho \; \sigma_0) = (val, \sigma_1) \qquad l \notin \text{dom}(\sigma_1)}{(\texttt{value-of} \; (\texttt{newref-exp} \; exp) \; \rho \; \sigma_0) = ((\texttt{ref-val} \; l), [l = val] \, \sigma_1)}$$

This rule says that `newref-exp` evaluates its operand. It extends the resulting store by allocating a new location l and puts the value *val* of its argument in that location. Then it returns a reference to a location l that is new. This means that it is not already in the domain of σ_1.

$$\frac{(\texttt{value-of}\ exp\ \rho\ \sigma_0) = (l, \sigma_1)}{(\texttt{value-of}\ (\texttt{deref-exp}\ exp)\ \rho\ \sigma_0) = (\sigma_1(l), \sigma_1)}$$

This rule says that a `deref-exp` evaluates its operand, leaving the store in state σ_1. The value of that argument should be a reference to a location l. The `deref-exp` then returns the contents of l in σ_1, without any further change to the store.

$$\frac{(\texttt{value-of}\ exp_1\ \rho\ \sigma_0) = (l, \sigma_1) \quad (\texttt{value-of}\ exp_2\ \rho\ \sigma_1) = (val, \sigma_2)}{(\texttt{value-of}\ (\texttt{setref-exp}\ exp_1\ exp_2)\ \rho\ \sigma_0) = (\lceil 23 \rceil, [l{=}val]\,\sigma_2)}$$

This rule says that a `setref-exp` evaluates its operands from left to right. The value of the first operand must be a reference to a location l. The `setref-exp` then updates the resulting store by putting the value *val* of the second argument in location l. What should a `setref-exp` return? It could return anything. To emphasize the arbitrary nature of this choice, we have specified that it returns 23. Because we are not interested in the value returned by a `setref-exp`, we say that this expression is executed *for effect*, rather than for its value.

Exercise 4.6 [⋆] Modify the rule given above so that a `setref-exp` returns the value of the right-hand side.

Exercise 4.7 [⋆] Modify the rule given above so that a `setref-exp` returns the old contents of the location.

4.2.3   Implementation

The specification language we have used so far makes it easy to describe the desired behavior of effectful computations, but it does not embody a key fact about the store: a reference ultimately refers to a real location in a memory that exists in the real world. Since we have only one real world, our program can only keep track of one state σ of the store.

In our implementations, we take advantage of this fact by modeling the store using Scheme's own store. Thus we model an effect as a Scheme effect.

We represent the state of the store as a Scheme value, but we do not explicitly pass and return it, as the specification suggests. Instead, we keep the state in a single global variable, to which all the procedures of the implementation have access. This is much like even/odd example, where we used a shared location instead of passing an explicit argument. By using a single global variable, we also use as little as possible of our understanding of Scheme effects.

We still have to choose how to model the store as a Scheme value. We choose the simplest possible model: we represent the store as a list of expressed values, and a reference is a number that denotes a position in the list. A new reference is allocated by appending a new value to the list; and updating the store is modeled by copying over as much of the list as necessary. The code is shown in figures 4.1 and 4.2.

This representation is extremely inefficient. Ordinary memory operations require approximately constant time, but in our representation these operations require time proportional to the size of the store. No real implementation would ever do this, of course, but it suffices for our purposes.

We add a new variant, ref-val, to the data type for expressed values, and we modify value-of-program to initialize the store before each evaluation.

value-of-program : *Program* → *ExpVal*
```
(define value-of-program
  (lambda (pgm)
    (initialize-store!)
    (cases program pgm
      (a-program (exp1)
        (value-of exp1 (init-env))))))
```

Now we can write clauses in value-of for newref, deref, and setref. The clauses are shown in figure 4.3.

We can instrument our system by adding some procedures that convert environments, procedures, and stores to a more readable form, and we can instrument our system by printing messages at key points in the code. We also use procedures that convert environments, procedures, and stores to a more readable form. The resulting logs give a detailed picture of our system in action. A typical example is shown in figures 4.4 and 4.5. This trace shows, among other things, that the arguments to the subtraction are evaluated from left to right.

empty-store : () → *Sto*
```
(define empty-store
  (lambda () '()))
```

usage: A Scheme variable containing the current state
  of the store. Initially set to a dummy value.
```
(define the-store 'uninitialized)
```

get-store : () → *Sto*
```
(define get-store
  (lambda () the-store))
```

initialize-store! : () → *Unspecified*
usage: (initialize-store!) sets the-store to the empty store
```
(define initialize-store!
  (lambda ()
    (set! the-store (empty-store))))
```

reference? : *SchemeVal* → *Bool*
```
(define reference?
  (lambda (v)
    (integer? v)))
```

newref : *ExpVal* → *Ref*
```
(define newref
  (lambda (val)
    (let ((next-ref (length the-store)))
      (set! the-store (append the-store (list val)))
      next-ref)))
```

deref : *Ref* → *ExpVal*
```
(define deref
  (lambda (ref)
    (list-ref the-store ref)))
```

Figure 4.1   A naive model of the store

```
setref! : Ref × ExpVal → Unspecified
usage: sets the-store to a state like the original, but with
  position ref containing val.
(define setref!
  (lambda (ref val)
    (set! the-store
      (letrec
        ((setref-inner
            usage: returns a list like store1, except that
            position ref1 contains val.
            (lambda (store1 ref1)
              (cond
                ((null? store1)
                 (report-invalid-reference ref the-store))
                ((zero? ref1)
                 (cons val (cdr store1)))
                (else
                  (cons
                    (car store1)
                    (setref-inner
                      (cdr store1) (- ref1 1))))))))
        (setref-inner the-store ref)))))
```

Figure 4.2   A naive model of the store, continued

Exercise 4.8 [⋆] Show exactly where in our implementation of the store these operations take linear time rather than constant time.

Exercise 4.9 [⋆] Implement the store in constant time by representing it as a Scheme vector. What is lost by using this representation?

Exercise 4.10 [⋆] Implement the begin expression as specified in exercise 4.4.

Exercise 4.11 [⋆] Implement list from exercise 4.5.

Exercise 4.12 [⋆ ⋆ ⋆] Our understanding of the store, as expressed in this interpreter, depends on the meaning of effects in Scheme. In particular, it depends on us knowing *when* these effects take place in a Scheme program. We can avoid this dependency by writing an interpreter that more closely mimics the specification. In this interpreter, value-of would return both a value and a store, just as in the specification. A fragment of this interpreter appears in figure 4.6. We call this a *store-passing interpreter*. Extend this interpreter to cover all of the language EXPLICIT-REFS.

Every procedure that might modify the store returns not just its usual value but also a new store. These are packaged in a data type called answer. Complete this definition of value-of.

```
(newref-exp (exp1)
  (let ((v1 (value-of exp1 env)))
    (ref-val (newref v1))))

(deref-exp (exp1)
  (let ((v1 (value-of exp1 env)))
    (let ((ref1 (expval->ref v1)))
      (deref ref1))))

(setref-exp (exp1 exp2)
  (let ((ref (expval->ref (value-of exp1 env))))
    (let ((val2 (value-of exp2 env)))
      (begin
        (setref! ref val2)
        (num-val 23)))))
```

Figure 4.3 value-of clauses for explicit-reference operators

Exercise 4.13 [★★★] Extend the interpreter of the preceding exercise to have procedures of multiple arguments.

4.3 IMPLICIT-REFS: A Language with Implicit References

The explicit reference design gives a clear account of allocation, dereferencing, and mutation because all these operations are explicit in the programmer's code.

Most programming languages take common patterns of allocation, dereferencing, and mutation, and package them up as part of the language. Then the programmer need not worry about when to perform these operations, because they are built into the language.

In this design, every variable denotes a reference. Denoted values are references to locations that contain expressed values. References are no longer expressed values. They exist only as the bindings of variables.

$$
\begin{aligned}
ExpVal &= Int + Bool + Proc \\
DenVal &= Ref(ExpVal)
\end{aligned}
$$

Locations are created with each binding operation: at each procedure call, let, or letrec.

```
> (run "
let x = newref(22)
in let f = proc (z) let zz = newref(-(z,deref(x)))
                    in deref(zz)
   in -((f 66), (f 55))")

entering let x
newref: allocating location 0
entering body of let x with env =
((x #(struct:ref-val 0))
 (i #(struct:num-val 1))
 (v #(struct:num-val 5))
 (x #(struct:num-val 10)))
store =
((0 #(struct:num-val 22)))

entering let f
entering body of let f with env =
((f
  (procedure
    z
    ...
    ((x #(struct:ref-val 0))
     (i #(struct:num-val 1))
     (v #(struct:num-val 5))
     (x #(struct:num-val 10)))))
 (x #(struct:ref-val 0))
 (i #(struct:num-val 1))
 (v #(struct:num-val 5))
 (x #(struct:num-val 10)))
store =
((0 #(struct:num-val 22)))

entering body of proc z with env =
((z #(struct:num-val 66))
 (x #(struct:ref-val 0))
 (i #(struct:num-val 1))
 (v #(struct:num-val 5))
 (x #(struct:num-val 10)))
store =
((0 #(struct:num-val 22)))
```

Figure 4.4   Trace of an evaluation in EXPLICIT-REFS.

```
entering let zz
newref: allocating location 1
entering body of let zz with env =
((zz #(struct:ref-val 1))
 (z #(struct:num-val 66))
 (x #(struct:ref-val 0))
 (i #(struct:num-val 1))
 (v #(struct:num-val 5))
 (x #(struct:num-val 10)))
store =
((0 #(struct:num-val 22)) (1 #(struct:num-val 44)))

entering body of proc z with env =
((z #(struct:num-val 55))
 (x #(struct:ref-val 0))
 (i #(struct:num-val 1))
 (v #(struct:num-val 5))
 (x #(struct:num-val 10)))
store =
((0 #(struct:num-val 22)) (1 #(struct:num-val 44)))

entering let zz
newref: allocating location 2
entering body of let zz with env =
((zz #(struct:ref-val 2))
 (z #(struct:num-val 55))
 (x #(struct:ref-val 0))
 (i #(struct:num-val 1))
 (v #(struct:num-val 5))
 (x #(struct:num-val 10)))
store =
((0 #(struct:num-val 22))
 (1 #(struct:num-val 44))
 (2 #(struct:num-val 33)))

#(struct:num-val 11)
>
```

Figure 4.5   Trace of an evaluation in EXPLICIT-REFS, continued

```
(define-datatype answer answer?
  (an-answer
    (val expval?)
    (store store?)))
```

value-of : *Exp* × *Env* × *Sto* → *ExpVal*
```
(define value-of
  (lambda (exp env store)
    (cases expression exp
      (const-exp (num)
        (an-answer (num-val num) store))
      (var-exp (var)
        (an-answer
          (apply-store store (apply-env env var))
          store))
      (if-exp (exp1 exp2 exp3)
        (cases answer (value-of exp1 env store)
          (an-answer (val new-store)
            (if (expval->bool val)
              (value-of exp2 env new-store)
              (value-of exp3 env new-store)))))
      (deref-exp (exp1)
        (cases answer (value-of exp1 env store)
          (an-answer (v1 new-store)
            (let ((ref1 (expval->ref v1)))
              (an-answer (deref ref1) new-store)))))
      ...)))
```

Figure 4.6   Store-passing interpreter for exercise 4.12

When a variable appears in an expression, we first look up the identifier in the environment to find the location to which it is bound, and then we look up in the store to find the value at that location. Hence we have a "two-level" system for var-exp.

The contents of a location can be changed by a set expression. We use the syntax

$$Expression ::= \text{set } Identifier = Expression$$
$$\boxed{\text{assign-exp (var exp1)}}$$

Here the *Identifier* is not part of an expression, so it does not get dereferenced. In this design, we say that variables are *mutable*, meaning changeable.

```
let x = 0
in letrec even(dummy)
            = if zero?(x)
                then 1
                else begin
                        set x = -(x,1);
                        (odd 888)
                     end
          odd(dummy)
            = if zero?(x)
                then 0
                else begin
                        set x = -(x,1);
                        (even 888)
                     end
    in begin set x = 13; (odd -888) end

let g = let count = 0
        in proc (dummy)
            begin
              set count = -(count,-1);
              count
            end
in let a = (g 11)
   in let b = (g 11)
      in -(a,b)
```

Figure 4.7   odd and even in IMPLICIT-REFS

This design is called *call-by-value*, or *implicit references*. Most programming languages, including Scheme, use some variation on this design.

Figure 4.7 has our two sample programs in this design. Because references are no longer expressed values, we can't make chains of references, as we did in the last example in section 4.2.

4.3.1   Specification

We can write the rules for dereference and `set` easily. The environment now always binds variables to locations, so when a variable appears as an expression, we need to dereference it:

$$(\text{value-of } (\text{var-exp } \mathit{var}) \; \rho \; \sigma) = (\sigma(\rho(\mathit{var})), \sigma)$$

Assignment works as one might expect: we look up the left-hand side in the environment, getting a location, we evaluate the right-hand side in the environment, and we modify the desired location. As with `setref`, the value returned by a `set` expression is arbitrary. We choose to have it return the expressed value 27.

$$\frac{(\texttt{value-of}\ exp_1\ \rho\ \sigma_0) = (val_1, \sigma_1)}{(\texttt{value-of}\ (\texttt{assign-exp}\ var\ exp_1)\ \rho\ \sigma_0) = (\lceil 27 \rceil, [\rho(var) = val_1]\sigma_1)}$$

We also need to rewrite the rules for procedure call and `let` to show the modified store. For procedure call, the rule becomes

$$(\texttt{apply-procedure}\ (\texttt{procedure}\ var\ body\ \rho)\ val\ \sigma)$$
$$= (\texttt{value-of}\ body\ [var = l]\rho\ [l = val]\sigma)$$

where l is a location not in the domain of σ.

The rule for (`let-exp` var exp_1 $body$) is similar. The right-hand side exp_1 is evaluated, and the value of the `let` expression is the value of the body, evaluated in an environment where the variable var is bound to a new location containing the value of exp_1.

Exercise 4.14 [⋆] Write the rule for `let`.

4.3.2 The Implementation

Now we are ready to modify the interpreter. In `value-of`, we dereference at each `var-exp`, just like the rules say

```
(var-exp (var) (deref (apply-env env var)))
```

and we write the obvious code for a `assign-exp`

```
(assign-exp (var exp1)
  (begin
    (setref!
      (apply-env env var)
      (value-of exp1 env))
    (num-val 27)))
```

What about creating references? New locations should be allocated at every new binding. There are exactly four places in the language where new bindings are created: in the initial environment, in a `let`, in a procedure call, and in a `letrec`.

In the initial environment, we explicitly allocate new locations.

For `let`, we change the corresponding line in `value-of` to allocate a new location containing the value, and to bind the variable to a reference to that location.

```
(let-exp (var exp1 body)
  (let ((val1 (value-of exp1 env)))
    (value-of body
      (extend-env var (newref val1) env))))
```

For a procedure call, we similarly change `apply-procedure` to call `newref`.

apply-procedure : *Proc* × *ExpVal* → *ExpVal*
```
(define apply-procedure
  (lambda (proc1 val)
    (cases proc proc1
      (procedure (var body saved-env)
        (value-of body
          (extend-env var (newref val) saved-env))))))
```

Last, to handle `letrec`, we replace the `extend-env-rec` clause in `apply-env` to return a reference to a location containing the appropriate closure. Since we are using multideclaration `letrec` (exercise 3.32), `extend-env-rec` takes a list of procedure names, a list of bound variables, a list of procedure bodies, and a saved environment. The procedure `location` takes a variable and a list of variables and returns either the position of the variable in the list, or `#f` if it is not present.

```
(extend-env-rec (p-names b-vars p-bodies saved-env)
  (let ((n (location search-var p-names)))
    (if n
      (newref
        (proc-val
          (procedure
            (list-ref b-vars n)
            (list-ref p-bodies n)
            env)))
      (apply-env saved-env search-var))))
```

Figure 4.8 shows a simple evaluation in IMPLICIT-REFS, using the same instrumentation as before.

```
> (run  "
let f = proc (x) proc (y)
          begin
            set x = -(x,-1);
            -(x,y)
          end
in ((f 44) 33)")
newref: allocating location 0
newref: allocating location 1
newref: allocating location 2
entering let f
newref: allocating location 3
entering body of let f with env =
((f 3) (i 0) (v 1) (x 2))
store =
((0 #(struct:num-val 1))
 (1 #(struct:num-val 5))
 (2 #(struct:num-val 10))
 (3 (procedure x ... ((i 0) (v 1) (x 2)))))

newref: allocating location 4
entering body of proc x with env =
((x 4) (i 0) (v 1) (x 2))
store =
((0 #(struct:num-val 1))
 (1 #(struct:num-val 5))
 (2 #(struct:num-val 10))
 (3 (procedure x ... ((i 0) (v 1) (x 2))))
 (4 #(struct:num-val 44)))

newref: allocating location 5
entering body of proc y with env =
((y 5) (x 4) (i 0) (v 1) (x 2))
store =
((0 #(struct:num-val 1))
 (1 #(struct:num-val 5))
 (2 #(struct:num-val 10))
 (3 (procedure x ... ((i 0) (v 1) (x 2))))
 (4 #(struct:num-val 44))
 (5 #(struct:num-val 33)))

#(struct:num-val 12)
>
```

Figure 4.8   Sample evaluation in IMPLICIT-REFS

Exercise 4.15 [⋆] In figure 4.8, why are variables in the environment bound to plain integers rather than expressed values, as in figure 4.5?

Exercise 4.16 [⋆] Now that variables are mutable, we can build recursive procedures by assignment. For example

```
letrec times4(x) = if zero?(x)
                       then 0
                       else -((times4 -(x,1)), -4)
in (times4 3)
```

can be replaced by

```
let times4 = 0
in begin
    set times4 = proc (x)
                     if zero?(x)
                     then 0
                     else -((times4 -(x,1)), -4);
    (times4 3)
   end
```

Trace this by hand and verify that this translation works.

Exercise 4.17 [⋆ ⋆] Write the rules for and implement multiargument procedures and `let` expressions.

Exercise 4.18 [⋆ ⋆] Write the rule for and implement multiprocedure `letrec` expressions.

Exercise 4.19 [⋆ ⋆] Modify the implementation of multiprocedure `letrec` so that each closure is built only once, and only one location is allocated for it. This is like exercise 3.35.

Exercise 4.20 [⋆ ⋆] In the language of this section, all variables are mutable, as they are in Scheme. Another alternative is to allow both mutable and immutable variable bindings:

$$ExpVal = Int + Bool + Proc$$
$$DenVal = Ref(ExpVal) + ExpVal$$

Variable assignment should work only when the variable to be assigned to has a mutable binding. Dereferencing occurs implicitly when the denoted value is a reference.

Modify the language of this section so that `let` introduces immutable variables, as before, but mutable variables are introduced by a `letmutable` expression, with syntax given by

$Expression ::=$ `letmutable` *Identifier* $=$ *Expression* `in` *Expression*

Exercise 4.21 [⋆⋆] We suggested earlier the use of assignment to make a program more modular by allowing one procedure to communicate information to a distant procedure without requiring intermediate procedures to be aware of it. Very often such an assignment should only be temporary, lasting for the execution of a procedure call. Add to the language a facility for *dynamic assignment* (also called *fluid binding*) to accomplish this. Use the production

Expression ::= setdynamic *Identifier* = *Expression* during *Expression*

| setdynamic-exp (*var exp*$_1$ *body*) |

The effect of the setdynamic expression is to assign temporarily the value of *exp*$_1$ to *var*, evaluate *body*, reassign *var* to its original value, and return the value of *body*. The variable *var* must already be bound. For example, in

```
let x = 11
in let p = proc (y) -(y,x)
   in -(setdynamic x = 17 during (p 22),
        (p 13))
```

the value of x, which is free in procedure p, is 17 in the call (p 22), but is reset to 11 in the call (p 13), so the value of the expression is $5 - 2 = 3$.

Exercise 4.22 [⋆⋆] So far our languages have been expression-oriented: the primary syntactic category of interest has been expressions and we have primarily been interested in their values. Extend the language to model the simple statement-oriented language whose specification is sketched below. Be sure to *Follow the Grammar* by writing separate procedures to handle programs, statements, and expressions.

Values As in IMPLICIT-REFS.

Syntax Use the following syntax:

$$
\begin{aligned}
Program &::= Statement \\
Statement &::= Identifier = Expression \\
&::= \texttt{print}\ Expression \\
&::= \{\ \{Statement\}^{*(;)}\ \} \\
&::= \texttt{if}\ Expression\ Statement\ Statement \\
&::= \texttt{while}\ Expression\ Statement \\
&::= \texttt{var}\ \{Identifier\}^{*(,)}\ ;\ Statement
\end{aligned}
$$

The nonterminal *Expression* refers to the language of expressions of IMPLICIT-REFS, perhaps with some extensions.

Semantics A program is a statement. A statement does not return a value, but acts by modifying the store and by printing.

Assignment statements work in the usual way. A print statement evaluates its actual parameter and prints the result. The if statement works in the usual way. A block statement, defined in the last production for *Statement*, binds each of the declared variables to an uninitialized reference and then executes the body of the block. The scope of these bindings is the body.

Write the specification for statements using assertions like

$$(\text{result-of } \textit{stmt } \rho \; \sigma_0) = \sigma_1$$

Examples Here are some examples.

```
(run "var x,y; {x = 3; y = 4; print +(x,y)}")   % Example 1
7
(run "var x,y,z; {x = 3;                         % Example 2
                  y = 4;
                  z = 0;
                  while not(zero?(x))
                    {z = +(z,y); x = -(x,1)};
                  print z}")
12
(run " var x; {x = 3;                            % Example 3
               print x;
               var x; {x = 4; print x};
               print x}")
3
4
3
(run "var f,x; {f = proc(x,y) *(x,y);            % Example 4
                x = 3;
                print (f 4 x)}")
12
```

Example 3 illustrates the scoping of the block statement.

Example 4 illustrates the interaction between statements and expressions. A procedure value is created and stored in the variable f. In the last line, this procedure is applied to the actual parameters 4 and x; since x is bound to a reference, it is dereferenced to obtain 3.

Exercise 4.23 [⋆] Add to the language of exercise 4.22 read statements of the form read *var*. This statement reads a nonnegative integer from the input and stores it in the given variable.

Exercise 4.24 [⋆] A do-while statement is like a while statement, except that the test is performed *after* the execution of the body. Add do-while statements to the language of exercise 4.22.

Exercise 4.25 [⋆] Extend the block statement of the language of exercise 4.22 to allow variables to be initialized. In your solution, does the scope of a variable include the initializer for variables declared later in the same block statement?

Exercise 4.26 [★ ★ ★] Extend the solution to the preceding exercise so that procedures declared in a single block are mutually recursive. Consider restricting the language so that the variable declarations in a block are followed by the procedure declarations.

Exercise 4.27 [★ ★] Extend the language of the preceding exercise to include *subroutines*. In our usage a subroutine is like a procedure, except that it does not return a value and its body is a statement, rather than an expression. Also, add subroutine calls as a new kind of statement and extend the syntax of blocks so that they may be used to declare both procedures and subroutines. How does this affect the denoted and expressed values? What happens if a procedure is referenced in a subroutine call, or vice versa?

4.4   MUTABLE-PAIRS: A Language with Mutable Pairs

In exercise 3.9 we added lists to our language, but these were immutable: there was nothing like Scheme's set-car! or set-cdr! for them.

Now, let's add mutable pairs to IMPLICIT-REFS. Pairs will be expressed values, and will have the following operations:

newpair : $Expval \times Expval \rightarrow MutPair$
left : $MutPair \rightarrow Expval$
right : $MutPair \rightarrow Expval$
setleft : $MutPair \times Expval \rightarrow Unspecified$
setright : $MutPair \times Expval \rightarrow Unspecified$

A pair consists of two locations, each of which is independently assignable. This gives us the domain equations:

$$
\begin{aligned}
ExpVal &= Int + Bool + Proc + MutPair \\
DenVal &= Ref(ExpVal) \\
MutPair &= Ref(ExpVal) \times Ref(ExpVal)
\end{aligned}
$$

We call this language MUTABLE-PAIRS.

4.4.1   Implementation

We can implement this literally using the reference data type from our preceding examples. The code is shown in figure 4.9.

Once we've done this, it is straightforward to add these to the language. We add a mutpair-val variant to our data type of expressed values, and five new lines to value-of. These are shown in figure 4.10. We arbitrarily choose to make setleft return 82 and setright return 83. The trace of an example, using the same instrumentation as before, is shown in figures 4.11 and 4.12.

```
(define-datatype mutpair mutpair?
  (a-pair
    (left-loc reference?)
    (right-loc reference?)))
```

make-pair : *ExpVal* × *ExpVal* → *MutPair*
```
(define make-pair
  (lambda (val1 val2)
    (a-pair
      (newref val1)
      (newref val2))))
```

left : *MutPair* → *ExpVal*
```
(define left
  (lambda (p)
    (cases mutpair p
      (a-pair (left-loc right-loc)
        (deref left-loc)))))
```

right : *MutPair* → *ExpVal*
```
(define right
  (lambda (p)
    (cases mutpair p
      (a-pair (left-loc right-loc)
        (deref right-loc)))))
```

setleft : *MutPair* × *ExpVal* → *Unspecified*
```
(define setleft
  (lambda (p val)
    (cases mutpair p
      (a-pair (left-loc right-loc)
        (setref! left-loc val)))))
```

setright : *MutPair* × *ExpVal* → *Unspecified*
```
(define setright
  (lambda (p val)
    (cases mutpair p
      (a-pair (left-loc right-loc)
        (setref! right-loc val)))))
```

Figure 4.9   Naive implementation of mutable pairs

```
(newpair-exp (exp1 exp2)
  (let ((val1 (value-of exp1 env))
        (val2 (value-of exp2 env)))
    (mutpair-val (make-pair val1 val2))))

(left-exp (exp1)
  (let ((val1 (value-of exp1 env)))
    (let ((p1 (expval->mutpair val1)))
      (left p1))))

(right-exp (exp1)
  (let ((val1 (value-of exp1 env)))
    (let ((p1 (expval->mutpair val1)))
      (right p1))))

(setleft-exp (exp1 exp2)
  (let ((val1 (value-of exp1 env))
        (val2 (value-of exp2 env)))
    (let ((p (expval->mutpair val1)))
      (begin
        (setleft p val2)
        (num-val 82)))))

(setright-exp (exp1 exp2)
  (let ((val1 (value-of exp1 env))
        (val2 (value-of exp2 env)))
    (let ((p (expval->mutpair val1)))
      (begin
        (setright p val2)
        (num-val 83)))))
```

Figure 4.10 Integrating mutable pairs into the interpreter

4.4.2 Another Representation of Mutable Pairs

The representation of a mutable pair as two references does not take advantage of all we know about *MutPair*. The two locations in a pair are independently assignable, but they are not independently allocated. We know that they will be allocated together: if the left part of a pair is one location, then the right part is in the next location. So we can instead represent the pair by a reference to its left. The code for this is shown in figure 4.13. Nothing else need change.

```
> (run "let glo = pair(11,22)
in let f = proc (loc)
          let d1 = setright(loc, left(loc))
          in let d2 = setleft(glo, 99)
          in -(left(loc),right(loc))
in (f glo)")
;; allocating cells for init-env
newref: allocating location 0
newref: allocating location 1
newref: allocating location 2
entering let glo
;; allocating cells for the pair
newref: allocating location 3
newref: allocating location 4
;; allocating cell for glo
newref: allocating location 5
entering body of let glo with env =
((glo 5) (i 0) (v 1) (x 2))
store =
((0 #(struct:num-val 1))
 (1 #(struct:num-val 5))
 (2 #(struct:num-val 10))
 (3 #(struct:num-val 11))
 (4 #(struct:num-val 22))
 (5 #(struct:mutpair-val #(struct:a-pair 3 4))))

entering let f
;; allocating cell for f
newref: allocating location 6
entering body of let f with env =
((f 6) (glo 5) (i 0) (v 1) (x 2))
store =
((0 #(struct:num-val 1))
 (1 #(struct:num-val 5))
 (2 #(struct:num-val 10))
 (3 #(struct:num-val 11))
 (4 #(struct:num-val 22))
 (5 #(struct:mutpair-val #(struct:a-pair 3 4)))
 (6 (procedure loc ... ((glo 5) (i 0) (v 1) (x 2)))))
```

Figure 4.11   Trace of evaluation in MUTABLE-PAIRS

```
;; allocating cell for loc
newref: allocating location 7
entering body of proc loc with env =
((loc 7) (glo 5) (i 0) (v 1) (x 2))
store =
((0 #(struct:num-val 1))
 (1 #(struct:num-val 5))
 (2 #(struct:num-val 10))
 (3 #(struct:num-val 11))
 (4 #(struct:num-val 22))
 (5 #(struct:mutpair-val #(struct:a-pair 3 4)))
 (6 (procedure loc ... ((glo 5) (i 0) (v 1) (x 2))))
 (7 #(struct:mutpair-val #(struct:a-pair 3 4))))

#(struct:num-val 88)
>
```

Figure 4.12   Trace of evaluation in MUTABLE-PAIRS, cont'd

Similarly, one could represent any aggregate object in the heap by a pointer to its first location. However, a pointer does not by itself identify an area of memory unless it is supplemented by information about the length of the area (see exercise 4.30). The lack of length information is a source of classic security errors, such as out-of-bounds array writes.

Exercise 4.28 [⋆ ⋆] Write down the specification rules for the five mutable-pair operations.

Exercise 4.29 [⋆ ⋆] Add arrays to this language. Introduce new operators `newarray`, `arrayref`, and `arrayset` that create, dereference, and update arrays. This leads to

$$ArrVal = (Ref(ExpVal))^*$$
$$ExpVal = Int + Bool + Proc + ArrVal$$
$$DenVal = Ref(ExpVal)$$

Since the locations in an array are consecutive, use a representation like the second representation above. What should be the result of the following program?

mutpair? : *SchemeVal* → *Bool*
```
(define mutpair?
  (lambda (v)
    (reference? v)))
```

make-pair : *ExpVal* × *ExpVal* → *MutPair*
```
(define make-pair
  (lambda (val1 val2)
    (let ((ref1 (newref val1)))
      (let ((ref2 (newref val2)))
        ref1))))
```

left : *MutPair* → *ExpVal*
```
(define left
  (lambda (p)
    (deref p)))
```

right : *MutPair* → *ExpVal*
```
(define right
  (lambda (p)
    (deref (+ 1 p))))
```

setleft : *MutPair* × *ExpVal* → *Unspecified*
```
(define setleft
  (lambda (p val)
    (setref! p val)))
```

setright : *MutPair* × *ExpVal* → *Unspecified*
```
(define setright
  (lambda (p val)
    (setref! (+ 1 p) val)))
```

Figure 4.13 Alternate representation of mutable pairs

```
let a = newarray(2,-99)
    p = proc (x)
          let v = arrayref(x,1)
          in arrayset(x,1,-(v,-1))
in begin arrayset(a,1,0); (p a); (p a); arrayref(a,1) end
```

Here `newarray(2,-99)` is intended to build an array of size 2, with each location in the array containing -99. `begin` expressions are defined in exercise 4.4. Make the array indices zero-based, so an array of size 2 has indices 0 and 1.

Exercise 4.30 [⋆ ⋆] Add to the language of exercise 4.29 a procedure `arraylength`, which returns the size of an array. Your procedure should work in constant time. Make sure that `arrayref` and `arrayset` check to make sure that their indices are within the length of the array.

4.5   Parameter-Passing Variations

When a procedure body is executed, its formal parameter is bound to a denoted value. Where does that value come from? It must be passed from the actual parameter in the procedure call. We have already seen two ways in which a parameter can be passed:

- Natural parameter passing, in which the denoted value is the same as the expressed value of the actual parameter (page 75).

- Call-by-value, in which the denoted value is a reference to a location containing the expressed value of the actual parameter (section 4.3). This is the most commonly used form of parameter-passing.

In this section, we explore some alternative parameter-passing mechanisms.

4.5.1   CALL-BY-REFERENCE

Consider the following expression:

```
let p = proc (x) set x = 4
in let a = 3
   in begin (p a); a end
```

Under call-by-value, the denoted value associated with x is a reference that initially contains the same value as the reference associated with a, but these references are distinct. Thus the assignment to x has no effect on the contents of a's reference, so the value of the entire expression is 3.

With call-by-value, when a procedure assigns a new value to one of its parameters, this cannot possibly be seen by its caller. Of course, if the parameter passed to the caller contains a mutable pair, as in section 4.4, then the effect of `setleft` or `setright` will be visible to a caller. But the effect of a `set` is not.

Though this isolation between the caller and callee is generally desirable, there are times when it is valuable to allow a procedure to be passed locations with the expectation that they will be assigned by the procedure. This may be accomplished by passing the procedure a reference to the location of the caller's variable, rather than the contents of the variable. This parameter-passing mechanism is called *call-by-reference*. If an operand is simply a variable reference, a reference to the variable's location is passed. The formal parameter of the procedure is then bound to this location. If the operand is some other kind of expression, then the formal parameter is bound to a new location containing the value of the operand, just as in call-by-value. Using call-by-reference in the above example, the assignment of 4 to x has the effect of assigning 4 to a, so the entire expression would return 4, not 3.

When a call-by-reference procedure is called and the actual parameter is a variable, what is passed is the *location* of that variable, rather than the contents of that location, as in call-by-value. For example, consider

```
let f = proc (x) set x = 44
in let g = proc (y) (f y)
   in let z = 55
      in begin (g z); z end
```

When the procedure g is called, y is bound to the location of z, not the contents of that location. Similarly, when f is called, x becomes bound to that same location. So x, y, and z will all be bound to the same location, and the effect of the set x = 44 is to set that location to 44. Hence the value of the entire expression is 44. A trace of the execution of this expression is shown in figures 4.14 and 4.15; in this example, x, y, and z all wind up bound to location 5.

A typical use of call-by-reference is to return multiple values. A procedure can return one value in the normal way and assign others to parameters that are passed by reference. For another sort of example, consider the problem of swapping the values in two variables:

```
let swap = proc (x) proc (y)
              let temp = x
              in begin
                   set x = y;
                   set y = temp
                 end
in let a = 33
   in let b = 44
      in begin
           ((swap a) b);
           -(a,b)
         end
```

Under call-by-reference, this swaps the values of a and b, so it returns 11. If this program were run with our existing call-by-value interpreter, however, it would return -11, because the assignments inside the swap procedure then have no effect on variables a and b.

Under call-by-reference, variables still denote references to expressed values, just as they did under call-by-value:

$$ExpVal \;\; = \;\; Int + Bool + Proc$$
$$DenVal \;\; = \;\; Ref(ExpVal)$$

The only thing that changes is the allocation of new locations. Under call-by-value, a new location is created for every evaluation of an operand; under call-by-reference, a new location is created for every evaluation of an operand *other than a variable*.

This is easy to implement. The function `apply-procedure` must change, because it is no longer true that a new location is allocated for every procedure call. That responsibility must be moved upstream, to the `call-exp` line in `value-of`, which will have the information to make that decision.

apply-procedure : *Proc* × *Ref* → *ExpVal*
```
(define apply-procedure
  (lambda (proc1 val)
    (cases proc proc1
      (procedure (var body saved-env)
        (value-of body
          (extend-env var val saved-env))))))
```

We then modify the `call-exp` line in `value-of`, and introduce a new function `value-of-operand` that makes the necessary decision.

```
(call-exp (rator rand)
  (let ((proc (expval->proc (value-of rator env)))
        (arg (value-of-operand rand env)))
    (apply-procedure proc arg)))
```

The procedure `value-of-operand` checks to see if the operand is a variable. If it is, then the reference that the variable denotes is returned and then passed to the procedure by `apply-procedure`. Otherwise, the operand is evaluated, and a reference to a new location containing that value is returned.

value-of-operand : *Exp* × *Env* → *Ref*
```
(define value-of-operand
  (lambda (exp env)
    (cases expression exp
      (var-exp (var) (apply-env env var))
      (else
        (newref (value-of exp env))))))
```

We could modify `let` to work in a similar fashion, but we have chosen not to do so, so that some call-by-value functionality will remain in the language.

More than one call-by-reference parameter may refer to the same location, as in the following program.

```
let b = 3
in let p = proc (x) proc(y)
           begin
             set x = 4;
             y
           end
   in ((p b) b)
```

This yields 4 since both x and y refer to the same location, which is the binding of b. This phenomenon is known as *variable aliasing*. Here x and y are aliases (names) for the same location. Generally, we do not expect an assignment to one variable to change the value of another, so aliasing makes it very difficult to understand programs.

Exercise 4.31 [*] Write out the specification rules for CALL-BY-REFERENCE.

Exercise 4.32 [*] Extend the language CALL-BY-REFERENCE to have procedures of multiple arguments.

Exercise 4.33 [* *] Extend the language CALL-BY-REFERENCE to support call-by-value procedures as well.

Exercise 4.34 [*] Add a call-by-reference version of `let`, called `letref`, to the language. Write the specification and implement it.

Exercise 4.35 [* *] We can get some of the benefits of call-by-reference without leaving the call-by-value framework. Extend the language IMPLICIT-REFS by adding a new expression

$$Expression ::= \texttt{ref } Identifier$$
$$\boxed{\texttt{ref-exp (var)}}$$

This differs from the language EXPLICIT-REFS, since references are only of variables. This allows us to write familiar programs such as swap within our call-by-value language. What should be the value of this expression?

```
let a = 3
in let b = 4
   in let swap = proc (x) proc (y)
                   let temp = deref(x)
                   in begin
                        setref(x,deref(y));
                        setref(y,temp)
                      end
      in begin ((swap ref a) ref b); -(a,b) end
```

Here we have used a version of `let` with multiple declarations (exercise 3.16). What are the expressed and denoted values of this language?

```
>  (run "
let f = proc (x) set x = 44
in let g = proc (y) (f y)
in let z = 55
in begin
    (g z);
    z
  end")
newref: allocating location 0
newref: allocating location 1
newref: allocating location 2
entering let f
newref: allocating location 3
entering body of let f with env =
((f 3) (i 0) (v 1) (x 2))
store =
((0 #(struct:num-val 1))
 (1 #(struct:num-val 5))
 (2 #(struct:num-val 10))
 (3 (procedure x ... ((i 0) (v 1) (x 2)))))

entering let g
newref: allocating location 4
entering body of let g with env =
((g 4) (f 3) (i 0) (v 1) (x 2))
store =
((0 #(struct:num-val 1))
 (1 #(struct:num-val 5))
 (2 #(struct:num-val 10))
 (3 (procedure x ... ((i 0) (v 1) (x 2))))
 (4 (procedure y ... ((f 3) (i 0) (v 1) (x 2)))))

entering let z
newref: allocating location 5
entering body of let z with env =
((z 5) (g 4) (f 3) (i 0) (v 1) (x 2))
store =
((0 #(struct:num-val 1))
 (1 #(struct:num-val 5))
 (2 #(struct:num-val 10))
 (3 (procedure x ... ((i 0) (v 1) (x 2))))
 (4 (procedure y ... ((f 3) (i 0) (v 1) (x 2))))
 (5 #(struct:num-val 55)))
```

Figure 4.14   Sample evaluation in CALL-BY-REFERENCE

```
entering body of proc y with env =
((y 5) (f 3) (i 0) (v 1) (x 2))
store =
((0 #(struct:num-val 1))
 (1 #(struct:num-val 5))
 (2 #(struct:num-val 10))
 (3 (procedure x ... ((i 0) (v 1) (x 2))))
 (4 (procedure y ... ((f 3) (i 0) (v 1) (x 2))))
 (5 #(struct:num-val 55)))

entering body of proc x with env =
((x 5) (i 0) (v 1) (x 2))
store =
((0 #(struct:num-val 1))
 (1 #(struct:num-val 5))
 (2 #(struct:num-val 10))
 (3 (procedure x ... ((i 0) (v 1) (x 2))))
 (4 (procedure y ... ((f 3) (i 0) (v 1) (x 2))))
 (5 #(struct:num-val 55)))

#(struct:num-val 44)
>
```

Figure 4.15 Sample evaluation in CALL-BY-REFERENCE, cont'd

Exercise 4.36 [*] Most languages support arrays, in which case array references are generally treated like variable references under call-by-reference. If an operand is an array reference, then the location referred to, rather than its contents, is passed to the called procedure. This allows, for example, a swap procedure to be used in commonly occurring situations in which the values in two array elements are to be exchanged. Add array operators like those of exercise 4.29 to the call-by-reference language of this section, and extend `value-of-operand` to handle this case, so that, for example, a procedure application like

```
((swap (arrayref a i)) (arrayref a j))
```

will work as expected. What should happen in the case of

```
((swap (arrayref a (arrayref a i))) (arrayref a j))?
```

Exercise 4.37 [* *] *Call-by-value-result* is a variation on call-by-reference. In call-by-value-result, the actual parameter must be a variable. When a parameter is passed, the formal parameter is bound to a new reference initialized to the value of the actual parameter, just as in call-by-value. The procedure body is then executed normally. When the procedure body returns, however, the value in the new reference is copied back into the reference denoted by the actual parameter. This may be more efficient than call-by-reference because it can improve memory locality. Implement call-by-value-result and write a program that produces different answers using call-by-value-result and call-by-reference.

4.5.2   Lazy Evaluation: CALL-BY-NAME and CALL-BY-NEED

All the parameter-passing mechanisms we have discussed so far are *eager*: they always find a value for each operand. We now turn to a very different form of parameter passing, called *lazy evaluation*. Under lazy evaluation, an operand in a procedure call is not evaluated until it is needed by the procedure body. If the body never refers to the parameter, then there is no need to evaluate it.

This can potentially avoid non-termination. For example, consider

```
letrec infinite-loop (x) = infinite-loop(-(x,-1))
in let f = proc (z) 11
   in (f (infinite-loop 0))
```

Here `infinite-loop` is a procedure that, when called, never terminates. `f` is a procedure that, when called, never refers to its argument and always returns 11. Under any of the mechanisms considered so far, this program will fail to terminate. Under lazy evaluation, however, this program will return 11, because the operand `(infinite-loop 1)` is never evaluated.

We now modify our language to use lazy evaluation. Under lazy evaluation, we do not evaluate an operand expression until it is needed. Therefore we associate the bound variable of a procedure with an unevaluated operand. When the procedure body needs the value of its bound variable, the associated operand is evaluated. We sometimes say that the operand is *frozen* when it is passed unevaluated to the procedure, and that it is *thawed* when the procedure evaluates it.

Of course we will also have to include the environment in which that procedure is to be evaluated. To do this, we introduce a new data type of *thunks*. A thunk consists of an expression and an environment.

```
(define-datatype thunk thunk?
  (a-thunk
    (exp1 expression?)
    (env environment?)))
```

When a procedure needs to use the value of its bound variable, it will evaluate the associated thunk.

Our situation is somewhat more complicated, because we need to accommodate both lazy evaluation, effects, and eager evaluation (for `let`). We therefore let our denoted values be references to locations containing either expressed values or thunks.

$$
\begin{aligned}
DenVal &= Ref(ExpVal + Thunk) \\
ExpVal &= Int + Bool + Proc
\end{aligned}
$$

Our policy for allocating new locations will be similar to the one we used for call-by-reference: If the operand is a variable, then we pass its denotation, which is a reference. Otherwise, we pass a reference to a new location containing a thunk for the unevaluated argument.

value-of-operand : *Exp* × *Env* → *Ref*
```
(define value-of-operand
  (lambda (exp env)
    (cases expression exp
      (var-exp (var) (apply-env env var))
      (else
        (newref (a-thunk exp env)))))))
```

When we evaluate a `var-exp`, we first find the location to which the variable is bound. If the location contains an expressed value, then that value is returned as the value of the `var-exp`. If it instead contains a thunk, then the thunk is evaluated, and that value is returned. This design is called *call by name*.

```
(var-exp (var)
  (let ((ref1 (apply-env env var)))
    (let ((w (deref ref1)))
      (if (expval? w)
          w
          (value-of-thunk w)))))
```

The procedure `value-of-thunk` is defined as

value-of-thunk : *Thunk* → *ExpVal*
```
(define value-of-thunk
  (lambda (th)
    (cases thunk th
      (a-thunk (exp1 saved-env)
        (value-of exp1 saved-env)))))
```

Alternatively, once we find the value of the thunk, we can install that expressed value in the same location, so that the thunk will not be evaluated again. This arrangement is called *call by need*.

```
(var-exp (var)
  (let ((ref1 (apply-env env var)))
    (let ((w (deref ref1)))
      (if (expval? w)
          w
          (let ((val1 (value-of-thunk w)))
            (begin
              (setref! ref1 val1)
              val1))))))
```

This is an instance of a general strategy called *memoization*.

An attraction of lazy evaluation in all its forms is that in the absence of effects, it supports reasoning about programs in a particularly simple way. The effect of a procedure call can be modeled by replacing the call with the body of the procedure, with every reference to a formal parameter in the body replaced by the corresponding operand. This evaluation strategy is the basis for the lambda calculus, where it is called *β-reduction*.

Unfortunately, call-by-name and call-by-need make it difficult to determine the order of evaluation, which in turn is essential to understanding a program with effects. If there are no effects, though, this is not a problem. Thus lazy evaluation is popular in functional programming languages (those with no effects), and rarely found elsewhere.

Exercise 4.38 [⋆] The example below shows a variation of exercise 3.25 that works under call-by-need. Does the original program in exercise 3.25 work under call-by-need? What happens if the program below is run under call-by-value? Why?

```
let makerec = proc (f)
                let d = proc (x) (f (x x))
                in (f (d d))
in let maketimes4 = proc (f)
                      proc (x)
                        if zero?(x)
                        then 0
                        else -((f -(x,1)), -4)
   in let times4 = (makerec maketimes4)
      in (times4 3)
```

Exercise 4.39 [⋆] In the absence of effects, call-by-name and call-by-need always give the same answer. Construct an example in which call-by-name and call-by-need give different answers.

Exercise 4.40 [⋆] Modify value-of-operand so that it avoids making thunks for constants and procedures.

Exercise 4.41 [⋆ ⋆] Write out the specification rules for call-by-name and call-by-need.

Exercise 4.42 [⋆ ⋆] Add a lazy let to the call-by-need interpreter.

5 Continuation-Passing Interpreters

In chapter 3, we used the concept of environments to explore the behavior of bindings, which establish the data context in which each portion of a program is executed. Here we will do the same for the *control context* in which each portion of a program is executed. We will introduce the concept of a *continuation* as an abstraction of the control context, and we will write interpreters that take a continuation as an argument, thus making the control context explicit.

Consider the following definition of the factorial function in Scheme.

```
(define fact
  (lambda (n)
    (if (zero? n) 1 (* n (fact (- n 1))))))
```

We can use a derivation to model a calculation with `fact`:

```
   (fact 4)
 = (* 4 (fact 3))
 = (* 4 (* 3 (fact 2)))
 = (* 4 (* 3 (* 2 (fact 1))))
 = (* 4 (* 3 (* 2 (* 1 (fact 0)))))
 = (* 4 (* 3 (* 2 (* 1 1))))
 = (* 4 (* 3 (* 2 1)))
 = (* 4 (* 3 2))
 = (* 4 6)
 = 24
```

This is the natural recursive definition of factorial. Each call of `fact` is made with a promise that the value returned will be multiplied by the value of n at the time of the call. Thus `fact` is invoked in larger and larger *control contexts* as the calculation proceeds. Compare this behavior to that of the following procedures.

```
(define fact-iter
  (lambda (n)
    (fact-iter-acc n 1)))

(define fact-iter-acc
  (lambda (n a)
    (if (zero? n) a (fact-iter-acc (- n 1) (* n a)))))
```

With these definitions, we calculate:

```
  (fact-iter 4)
= (fact-iter-acc 4 1)
= (fact-iter-acc 3 4)
= (fact-iter-acc 2 12)
= (fact-iter-acc 1 24)
= (fact-iter-acc 0 24)
= 24
```

Here, `fact-iter-acc` is always invoked in the same control context: in this case, no context at all. When `fact-iter-acc` calls itself, it does so at the "tail end" of an execution of `fact-iter-acc`. No promise is made to do anything with the returned value other than to return it as the result of the call to `fact-iter-acc`. We call this a *tail call*. Thus each step in the derivation above has the form (`fact-iter-acc` *n a*).

When a procedure such as `fact` executes, additional control information is recorded with each recursive call, and this information is retained until the call returns. This reflects growth of the control context in the first derivation above. Such a process is said to exhibit *recursive control behavior*.

By contrast, no additional control information need be recorded when `fact-iter-acc` calls itself. This is reflected in the derivation by recursive calls occurring at the same level within the expression (on the outside in the derivation above). In such cases the system does not need an ever-increasing amount of memory for control contexts as the depth of recursion (the number of recursive calls without corresponding returns) increases. A process that uses a bounded amount of memory for control information is said to exhibit *iterative control behavior*.

Why do these programs exhibit different control behavior? In the recursive definition of factorial, the procedure `fact` is called *in an operand position*. We need to save context around this call because we need to remember that after the evaluation of the procedure call, we still need to finish evaluating the operands and executing the outer call, in this case to the waiting multiplication. This leads us to an important principle:

> **It is evaluation of operands, not the calling of procedures, that
> makes the control context grow.**

In this chapter we will learn how to track and manipulate control contexts. Our central tool will be the data type of *continuations*. Continuations are an abstraction of the notion of control context, much as environments are an abstraction of data contexts. We will explore continuations by writing an interpreter that explicitly passes a continuation parameter, just as our previous interpreters explicitly passed an environment parameter. Once we do this for the simple cases, we can see how to add to our language facilities that manipulate control contexts in more complicated ways, such as exceptions and threads.

In chapter 6 we show how the same techniques we used to transform the interpreter can be applied to any program. We say that a program transformed in this manner is in *continuation-passing style*. Chapter 6 also shows several other important uses of continuations.

5.1 A Continuation-Passing Interpreter

In our new interpreter, the major procedures such as `value-of` will take a third parameter. This new parameter, the *continuation*, is intended to be an abstraction of the control context in which each expression is evaluated.

We begin with an interpreter in figure 5.1 of the language LETREC of section 3.4. We refer to the result of `value-of-program` as a *FinalAnswer* to emphasize that this expressed value is the final value of the program.

Our goal is to rewrite the interpreter so that no call to `value-of` builds control context. When the control context needs to grow, we extend the continuation parameter, much as we extended the environment in the interpreters of chapter 3 as the program builds up data context. By making the control context explicit, we can see how it grows and shrinks, and later, in sections 5.4–5.5 we will use it to add new control behavior to our language.

Now, we know that an environment is a representation of a function from symbols to denoted values. What does a continuation represent? The continuation of an expression represents a procedure that takes the result of the expression and completes the computation. So our interface must include a procedure `apply-cont` that takes a continuation `cont` and an expressed value `val` and finishes the computation as specified by `cont`. The contract for `apply-cont` will be

FinalAnswer = *ExpVal*

value-of-program : *Program* $\rightarrow$ *FinalAnswer*
```
(define value-of-program
  (lambda (pgm)
    (cases program pgm
      (a-program (exp1)
        (value-of exp1 (init-env))))))
```

value-of : *Exp* $\times$ *Env* $\rightarrow$ *ExpVal*
```
(define value-of
  (lambda (exp env)
    (cases expression exp
      (const-exp (num) (num-val num))
      (var-exp (var) (apply-env env var))
      (diff-exp (exp1 exp2)
        (let ((num1 (expval->num (value-of exp1 env)))
              (num2 (expval->num (value-of exp2 env))))
          (num-val (- num1 num2))))
      (zero?-exp (exp1)
        (let ((num1 (expval->num (value-of exp1 env))))
          (if (zero? num1) (bool-val #t) (bool-val #f))))
      (if-exp (exp1 exp2 exp3)
        (if (expval->bool (value-of exp1 env))
          (value-of exp2 env)
          (value-of exp3 env)))
      (let-exp (var exp1 body)
        (let ((val1 (value-of exp1 env)))
          (value-of body (extend-env var val1 env))))
      (proc-exp (var body)
        (proc-val (procedure var body env)))
      (call-exp (rator rand)
        (let ((proc1 (expval->proc (value-of rator env)))
              (arg   (value-of rand env)))
          (apply-procedure proc1 arg)))
      (letrec-exp (p-name b-var p-body letrec-body)
        (value-of letrec-body
          (extend-env-rec p-name b-var p-body env))))))
```

apply-procedure : *Proc* $\times$ *ExpVal* $\rightarrow$ *ExpVal*
```
(define apply-procedure
  (lambda (proc1 val)
    (cases proc proc1
      (procedure (var body saved-env)
        (value-of body (extend-env var val saved-env))))))
```

Figure 5.1   Environment-passing Interpreter

FinalAnswer = *ExpVal*
apply-cont : *Cont* × *ExpVal* → *FinalAnswer*

We call the result of `apply-cont` a *FinalAnswer* to remind ourselves that it is the final value of the computation: it will not be used by any other part of our program.

What kind of continuation-builders will be included in the interface? We will discover these continuation-builders as we analyze the interpreter. To begin, we will need a continuation-builder for the context that says there is nothing more to do with the value of the computation. We call this continuation (`end-cont`), and we will specify it by

```
(apply-cont (end-cont) val)
= (begin
    (eopl:printf "End of computation.~%")
    val)
```

Invoking (`end-cont`) prints out an end-of-computation message and returns the value of the program. Because (`end-cont`) prints out a message, we can tell how many times it has been invoked. In a correct completed computation, it should be invoked exactly once.

We rewrite `value-of-program` as:

value-of-program : *Program* → *FinalAnswer*
```
(define value-of-program
  (lambda (pgm)
    (cases program pgm
      (a-program (exp1)
        (value-of/k exp1 (init-env) (end-cont))))))
```

We can now begin to write `value-of/k`. We consider each of the alternatives in `value-of` in turn. The first few lines of `value-of` simply calculate a value and return it, without calling `value-of` again. In the continuation-passing interpreter, these same lines send the same value to the continuation by calling `apply-cont`:

value-of/k : *Exp* × *Env* × *Cont* → *FinalAnswer*
```
(define value-of/k
  (lambda (exp env cont)
    (cases expression exp
      (const-exp (num) (apply-cont cont (num-val num)))
      (var-exp (var) (apply-cont cont (apply-env env var)))
      (proc-exp (var body)
        (apply-cont cont
          (proc-val (procedure var body env))))
      ...)))
```

Up to now the only possible value of cont has been the end continuation, but that will change momentarily. It is easy to check that if the program consists of an expression of one of these forms, the value of the expression will be supplied to end-cont (through apply-cont).

The behavior of letrec is almost as simple: it creates a new environment without calling value-of, and then evaluates the body in the new environment. The value of the body becomes the value of the entire expression. That means that the body is performed in the same control context as the entire expression. Therefore the value of the body should be returned to the continuation of the entire expression. Therefore we write

```
(letrec-exp (p-name b-var p-body letrec-body)
  (value-of/k letrec-body
    (extend-env-rec p-name b-var p-body env)
    cont))
```

This illustrates a general principle:

Tail Calls Don't Grow the Continuation

If the value of exp_1 is returned as the value of exp_2, then exp_1 and exp_2 should run in the same continuation.

It would not be correct to write

```
(letrec-exp (p-name b-var p-body letrec-body)
  (apply-cont cont
    (value-of/k letrec-body
      (extend-env-rec p-name b-var p-body env)
      (end-cont))))
```

because the call to value-of/k is in an operand position: it appears as an operand to apply-cont. In addition, using the continuation (end-cont) causes the end-of-computation message to be printed before the computation is finished, so an error like this is easy to detect.

Let us next consider a zero? expression. In a zero? expression, we want to evaluate the argument, and then return a value to the continuation depending on the value of the argument. So we evaluate the argument in a new continuation that will look at the returned value and do the right thing.

So in `value-of/k` we write

```
(zero?-exp (exp1)
  (value-of/k exp1 env
    (zero1-cont cont)))
```

where (`zero1-cont cont`) is a continuation with the property that

```
(apply-cont (zero1-cont cont) val)
= (apply-cont cont
    (bool-val
      (zero? (expval->num val))))
```

Just as with `letrec`, we could not write in `value-of/k`

```
(zero?-exp (exp1)
  (let ((val (value-of/k exp1 env (end-cont))))
    (apply-cont cont
      (bool-val
        (zero? (expval->num val))))))
```

because the call to `value-of/k` is in operand position. The right-hand side of a `let` is in operand position, because (`let` ((*var* *exp₁*)) *exp₂*) is equivalent to ((`lambda` (*var*) *exp₂*) *exp₁*). The value of the call to `value-of/k` eventually becomes the operand of `expval->num`. As before, if we ran this code, the end-of-computation message would appear twice: once in the middle of the computation and once at the real end.

A `let` expression is just slightly more complicated than a `zero?` expression: after evaluating the right-hand side, we evaluate the body in a suitably extended environment. The original code for `let` was

```
(let-exp (var exp1 body)
  (let ((val1 (value-of exp1 env)))
    (value-of body
      (extend-env var val1 env))))
```

In the continuation-passing interpreter, we need to evaluate `exp1` in a context that will finish the computation. So in `value-of/k` we write

```
(let-exp (var exp1 body)
  (value-of/k exp1 env
    (let-exp-cont var body env cont)))
```

and we add to our continuations interface the specification

```
(apply-cont (let-exp-cont var body env cont) val)
= (value-of/k body (extend-env var val env) cont)
```

The value of the body of the `let` expression becomes the value of the `let` expression, so the body of the `let` expression is evaluated in the same continuation as the entire `let` expression. This is another instance of the Tail Calls Don't Grow the Continuation principle.

Let us move on to `if` expressions. In an `if` expression, the first thing evaluated is the test, but the result of the test is not the value of the entire expression. We need to build a new continuation that will see if the result of the test expression is a true value, and evaluate either the true expression or the false expression. So in `value-of/k` we write

```
(if-exp (exp1 exp2 exp3)
  (value-of/k exp1 env
    (if-test-cont exp2 exp3 env cont)))
```

where `if-test-cont` is a new continuation-builder subject to the specification

```
(apply-cont (if-test-cont exp2 exp3 env cont) val)
= (if (expval->bool val)
    (value-of/k exp2 env cont)
    (value-of/k exp3 env cont))
```

So far, we have four continuation-builders. We can implement them using either a procedural representation or a data structure representation. The procedural representation is in figure 5.2 and the data structure representation, using `define-datatype`, is in figure 5.3.

Here is a sample calculation that shows how these pieces fit together. As we did in section 3.3, we write «*exp*» to denote the abstract syntax tree associated with the expression *exp*. Assume ρ_0 is an environment in which b is bound to (bool-val #t) and assume $cont_0$ is the initial continuation, which is the value of (end-cont). The commentary is informal and should be checked against the definition of `value-of/k` and the specification of `apply-cont`. This example is contrived because we have `letrec` to introduce procedures but we do not yet have a way to invoke them.

Cont = *ExpVal* → *FinalAnswer*

end-cont : () → *Cont*
```
(define end-cont
  (lambda ()
    (lambda (val)
      (begin
        (eopl:printf "End of computation.~%")
        val)))))
```

zero1-cont : *Cont* → *Cont*
```
(define zero1-cont
  (lambda (cont)
    (lambda (val)
      (apply-cont cont
        (bool-val
          (zero? (expval->num val)))))))
```

let-exp-cont : *Var* × *Exp* × *Env* × *Cont* → *Cont*
```
(define let-exp-cont
  (lambda (var body env cont)
    (lambda (val)
      (value-of/k body (extend-env var val env) cont))))
```

if-test-cont : *Exp* × *Exp* × *Env* × *Cont* → *Cont*
```
(define if-test-cont
  (lambda (exp2 exp3 env cont)
    (lambda (val)
      (if (expval->bool val)
        (value-of/k exp2 env cont)
        (value-of/k exp3 env cont)))))
```

apply-cont : *Cont* × *ExpVal* → *FinalAnswer*
```
(define apply-cont
  (lambda (cont v)
    (cont v)))
```

Figure 5.2   Procedural representation of continuations

```
(define-datatype continuation continuation?
  (end-cont)
  (zero1-cont
    (cont continuation?))
  (let-exp-cont
    (var identifier?)
    (body expression?)
    (env environment?)
    (cont continuation?))
  (if-test-cont
    (exp2 expression?)
    (exp3 expression?)
    (env environment?)
    (cont continuation?)))
```

apply-cont : *Cont* × *ExpVal* → *FinalAnswer*
```
(define apply-cont
  (lambda (cont val)
    (cases continuation cont
      (end-cont ()
        (begin
          (eopl:printf "End of computation.~%")
          val))
      (zero1-cont (saved-cont)
        (apply-cont saved-cont
          (bool-val
            (zero? (expval->num val)))))
      (let-exp-cont (var body saved-env saved-cont)
        (value-of/k body
          (extend-env var val saved-env) saved-cont))
      (if-test-cont (exp2 exp3 saved-env saved-cont)
        (if (expval->bool val)
          (value-of/k exp2 saved-env saved-cont)
          (value-of/k exp3 saved-env saved-cont))))))
```

Figure 5.3   Data structure representation of continuations

```
(value-of/k <<letrec p(x) = x in if b then 3 else 4>>
  ρ₀ cont₀)
```
= *letting* ρ_1 *be* (extend-env-rec ... ρ_0)
```
(value-of/k <<if b then 3 else 4>> ρ₁ cont₀)
```
= *next, evaluate the test expression*
```
(value-of/k <<b>> ρ₁ (test-cont <<3>> <<4>> ρ₁ cont₀))
```
= *send the value of* b *to the continuation*
```
(apply-cont (test-cont <<3>> <<4>> ρ₁ cont₀)
            (bool-val #t))
```
= *evaluate the then-expression*
```
(value-of/k <<3>> ρ₁ cont₀)
```
= *send the value of the expression to the continuation*
```
(apply-cont cont₀ (num-val 3))
```
= *invoke the final continuation with the final answer*
```
(begin (eopl:printf ...) (num-val 3))
```

Difference expressions add a new wrinkle to our interpreter because they must evaluate both operands. We begin as we did with if, evaluating the first argument:

```
(diff-exp (exp1 exp2)
  (value-of/k exp1 env
    (diff1-cont exp2 env cont)))
```

When (diff1-cont exp2 env cont) receives a value, it should evaluate exp2 in a context that saves the value of exp1. We specify this by writing

```
(apply-cont (diff1-cont exp2 env cont) val1)
= (value-of/k exp2 env
    (diff2-cont val1 cont))
```

When a (diff2-cont val1 cont) receives a value, we know the values of both operands so we can proceed to send their difference to cont, which has been waiting to receive it. The specification is

```
(apply-cont (diff2-cont val1 cont) val2)
= (let ((num1 (expval->num val1))
        (num2 (expval->num val2)))
    (apply-cont cont
      (num-val (- num1 num2))))
```

Let's watch this system do an example.

```
(value-of/k
  <<-(-(44,11),3)>>
  ρ0
  #(struct:end-cont))
```
= *start working on first operand*
```
(value-of/k
  <<-(44,11)>>
  ρ0
  #(struct:diff1-cont <<3>> ρ0
      #(struct:end-cont)))
```
= *start working on first operand*
```
(value-of/k
  <<44>>
  ρ0
  #(struct:diff1-cont <<11>> ρ0
      #(struct:diff1-cont <<3>> ρ0
          #(struct:end-cont))))
```
= *send value of <<44>> to continuation*
```
(apply-cont
  #(struct:diff1-cont <<11>> ρ0
      #(struct:diff1-cont <<3>> ρ0
          #(struct:end-cont)))
  (num-val 44))
```
= *now start working on second operand*
```
(value-of/k
  <<11>>
  ρ0
  #(struct:diff2-cont (num-val 44)
      #(struct:diff1-cont <<3>> ρ0
          #(struct:end-cont))))
```
= *send value to continuation*
```
(apply-cont
  #(struct:diff2-cont (num-val 44)
      #(struct:diff1-cont <<3>> ρ0
          #(struct:end-cont)))
  (num-val 11))
```
= $44 - 11$ *is 33, send that to the continuation*
```
(apply-cont
  #(struct:diff1-cont <<3>> ρ0
      #(struct:end-cont))
  (num-val 33))
```

```
=  start working on second operand <<3>>
(value-of/k
  <<3>>
  ρ₀
  #(struct:diff2-cont (num-val 33)
     #(struct:end-cont)))
=  send value to continuation
(apply-cont
  #(struct:diff2-cont (num-val 33)
     #(struct:end-cont))
  (num-val 3))
=  33 − 3 is 30, send that to the continuation
(apply-cont
  #(struct:end-cont)
  (num-val 30))
```

`apply-cont` prints out the completion message `"End of computation"` and returns `(num-val 30)` as the final answer of the computation.

The last thing in our language is procedure application. In the environment-passing interpreter, we wrote

```
(call-exp (rator rand)
  (let ((proc1 (expval->proc (value-of rator env)))
        (val (value-of rand env)))
    (apply-procedure proc1 val)))
```

Here we have two calls to consider, as we did in `diff-exp`. So we must choose one of them to be first, and then we must transform the remainder to handle the second. Furthermore, we will have to pass the continuation to `apply-procedure`, because `apply-procedure` contains a call to `value-of/k`.

We choose the evaluation of the operator to be first, so in `value-of/k` we write

```
(call-exp (rator rand)
  (value-of/k rator env
    (rator-cont rand env cont)))
```

As with `diff-exp`, a `rator-cont` will evaluate the operand in a suitable continuation:

```
(apply-cont (rator-cont rand env cont) val1)
= (value-of/k rand env
    (rand-cont val1 cont))
```

When a `rand-cont` receives a value, it is ready to call the procedure:

```
(apply-cont (rand-cont val1 cont) val2)
= (let ((proc1 (expval->proc val1)))
    (apply-procedure/k proc1 val2 cont))
```

Last, we must modify `apply-procedure` to fit in this continuation-passing style:

apply-procedure/k : *Proc* × *ExpVal* × *Cont* → *FinalAnswer*
```
(define apply-procedure/k
  (lambda (proc1 val cont)
    (cases proc proc1
      (procedure (var body saved-env)
        (value-of/k body
          (extend-env var val saved-env)
          cont)))))
```

This completes the presentation of the continuation-passing interpreter. The complete interpreter is shown in figures 5.4 and 5.5. The complete specification of the continuations is shown in figure 5.6.

Now we can check the assertion that it is evaluation of actual parameters, not the calling of procedures, that requires growing the control context. In particular, if we evaluate a procedure call $(exp_1\ exp_2)$ in some continuation $cont_1$, the body of the procedure to which exp_1 evaluates will also be evaluated in the continuation $cont_1$.

But procedure calls do not themselves grow control contexts. Consider the evaluation of $(exp_1\ exp_2)$, where the value of exp_1 is some procedure $proc_1$ and the value of exp_2 is some expressed value val_2.

```
(value-of/k << (exp1 exp2) >> ρ1 cont1)
= evaluate operator
(value-of/k <<exp1>> ρ1
  (rator-cont <<exp2>> ρ1 cont1))
= send the procedure to the continuation
(apply-cont
  (rator-cont <<exp2>> ρ1 cont1)
  proc1)
= evaluate the operand
(value-of/k <<exp2>> ρ1
  (rand-cont proc1 cont1))
= send the argument to the continuation
(apply-cont
  (rand-cont proc1 cont1)
  val2)
= apply the procedure
(apply-procedure/k proc1 val2 cont1)
```

So the procedure is applied, and its body is evaluated, in the same continuation in which it was called. It is the evaluation of operands, not the entry into a procedure body, that requires control context.

Exercise 5.1 [⋆] Implement this data type of continuations using the procedural representation.

Exercise 5.2 [⋆] Implement this data type of continuations using a data-structure representation.

Exercise 5.3 [⋆] Add `let2` to this interpreter. A `let2` expression is like a `let` expression, except that it defines exactly two variables.

Exercise 5.4 [⋆] Add `let3` to this interpreter. A `let3` expression is like a `let` expression, except that it defines exactly three variables.

Exercise 5.5 [⋆] Add lists to the language, as in exercise 3.9.

Exercise 5.6 [⋆ ⋆] Add a `list` expression to the language, as in exercise 3.10. As a hint, consider adding two new continuation-builders, one for evaluating the first element of the list and one for evaluating the rest of the list.

Exercise 5.7 [⋆ ⋆] Add multideclaration `let` (exercise 3.16) to this interpreter.

Exercise 5.8 [⋆ ⋆] Add multiargument procedures (exercise 3.21) to this interpreter.

Exercise 5.9 [⋆ ⋆] Modify this interpreter to implement the IMPLICIT-REFS language. As a hint, consider including a new continuation-builder (`set-rhs-cont env var cont`).

Exercise 5.10 [⋆ ⋆] Modify the solution to the previous exercise so that the environment is not kept in the continuation.

Exercise 5.11 [⋆ ⋆] Add the `begin` expression of exercise 4.4 to the continuation-passing interpreter. Be sure that no call to `value-of` or `value-of-rands` occurs in a position that would build control context.

Exercise 5.12 [⋆] Instrument the interpreter of figures 5.4–5.6 to produce output similar to that of the calculation on page 150.

Exercise 5.13 [⋆] Translate the definitions of `fact` and `fact-iter` into the LETREC language. You may add a multiplication operator to the language. Then, using the instrumented interpreter of the previous exercise, compute (`fact 4`) and (`fact-iter 4`). Compare them to the calculations at the beginning of this chapter. Find (⋆ 4 (⋆ 3 (⋆ 2 (`fact 1`)))) in the trace of (`fact 4`). What is the continuation of `apply-procedure/k` for this call of (`fact 1`)?

Exercise 5.14 [⋆] The instrumentation of the preceding exercise produces voluminous output. Modify the instrumentation to track instead only the *size* of the largest continuation used during the calculation. We measure the size of a continuation by the number of continuation-builders employed in its construction, so the

value-of-program : *Program* → *FinalAnswer*
```
(define value-of-program
  (lambda (pgm)
    (cases program pgm
      (a-program (exp1)
        (value-of/k exp1 (init-env) (end-cont))))))
```

value-of/k : *Exp* × *Env* × *Cont* → *FinalAnswer*
```
(define value-of/k
  (lambda (exp env cont)
    (cases expression exp
      (const-exp (num) (apply-cont cont (num-val num)))
      (var-exp (var) (apply-cont cont (apply-env env var)))
      (proc-exp (var body)
        (apply-cont cont
          (proc-val
            (procedure var body env))))
      (letrec-exp (p-name b-var p-body letrec-body)
        (value-of/k letrec-body
          (extend-env-rec p-name b-var p-body env)
          cont))
      (zero?-exp (exp1)
        (value-of/k exp1 env
          (zero1-cont cont)))
      (if-exp (exp1 exp2 exp3)
        (value-of/k exp1 env
          (if-test-cont exp2 exp3 env cont)))
      (let-exp (var exp1 body)
        (value-of/k exp1 env
          (let-exp-cont var body env cont)))
      (diff-exp (exp1 exp2)
        (value-of/k exp1 env
          (diff1-cont exp2 env cont)))
      (call-exp (rator rand)
        (value-of/k rator env
          (rator-cont rand env cont))))))
```

Figure 5.4   Continuation-passing interpreter (part 1)

```
apply-procedure/k : Proc × ExpVal × Cont → FinalAnswer
(define apply-procedure/k
  (lambda (proc1 val cont)
    (cases proc proc1
      (procedure (var body saved-env)
        (value-of/k body
          (extend-env var val saved-env)
          cont)))))
```

Figure 5.5   Continuation-passing interpreter (part 2)

---

size of the largest continuation in the calculation on page 150 is 3. Then calculate the values of fact and fact-iter applied to several operands. Confirm that the size of the largest continuation used by fact grows linearly with its argument, but the size of the largest continuation used by fact-iter is a constant.

Exercise 5.15 [⋆] Our continuation data type contains just the single constant, end-cont, and all the other continuation-builders have a single continuation argument. Implement continuations by representing them as lists, where (end-cont) is represented by the empty list, and each other continuation is represented by a non-empty list whose car contains a distinctive data structure (called *frame* or *activation record*) and whose cdr contains the embedded continuation. Observe that the interpreter treats these lists like a stack (of frames).

Exercise 5.16 [⋆ ⋆] Extend the continuation-passing interpreter to the language of exercise 4.22. Pass a continuation argument to result-of, and make sure that no call to result-of occurs in a position that grows a control context. Since a statement does not return a value, distinguish between ordinary continuations and continuations for statements; the latter are usually called *command continuations*. The interface should include a procedure apply-command-cont that takes a command continuation and invokes it. Implement command continuations both as data structures and as zero-argument procedures.

5.2   A Trampolined Interpreter

One might now be tempted to transcribe the interpreter into an ordinary procedural language, using a data structure representation of continuations to avoid the need for higher-order procedures. Most procedural languages, however, make it difficult to do this translation: instead of growing control context only when necessary, they add to the control context (the stack!) on every procedure call. Since the procedure calls in our system never return until the very end of the computation, the stack in these systems continues to grow until that time.

```
(apply-cont (end-cont) val)
= (begin
    (eopl:printf
      "End of computation.~%")
    val)

(apply-cont (diff1-cont exp2 env cont) val1)
= (value-of/k exp2 env (diff2-cont val1 cont))

(apply-cont (diff2-cont val1 cont) val2)
= (let ((num1 (expval->num val1))
        (num2 (expval->num val2)))
    (apply-cont cont (num-val (- num1 num2))))

(apply-cont (rator-cont rand env cont) val1)
= (value-of/k rand env (rand-cont val1 cont))

(apply-cont (rand-cont val1 cont) val2)
= (let ((proc1 (expval->proc val1)))
    (apply-procedure/k proc1 val2 cont))

(apply-cont (zero1-cont cont) val)
= (apply-cont cont (bool-val (zero? (expval->num val))))

(apply-cont (if-test-cont exp2 exp3 env cont) val)
= (if (expval->bool val)
    (value-of/k exp2 env cont)
    (value-of/k exp3 env cont))

(apply-cont (let-exp-cont var body env cont) val1)
= (value-of/k body (extend-env var val1 env) cont)
```

Figure 5.6   Specification of continuations for figure 5.4

This behavior is not entirely irrational: in such languages almost every procedure call occurs on the right-hand side of an assignment statement, so that almost every procedure call must grow the control context to keep track of the pending assignment. Hence the architecture is optimized for this most common case. Furthermore, most languages store environment information on the stack, so every procedure call must generate a control context that remembers to remove the environment information from the stack.

In such languages, one solution is to use a technique called *trampolining*. To avoid having an unbounded chain of procedure calls, we break the chain by having one of the procedures in the interpreter actually return a zero-argument procedure. This procedure, when called, will continue the computation. The entire computation is driven by a procedure called a *trampoline* that bounces from one procedure call to the next. For example, we can insert a (lambda () ...) around the body of apply-procedure/k, since in our language no expression would run more than a bounded amount of time without performing a procedure call.

The resulting code is shown in figure 5.7, which also shows all the tail calls in the interpreter. Since we have modified apply-procedure/k to return a procedure, rather than an *ExpVal*, we must rewrite its contract and also the contracts of all the procedures that call it. We must therefore review the contracts of all the procedures in the interpreter.

We begin with value-of-program. Since this is the procedure that is used to invoke the interpreter, its contract is unchanged. It calls value-of/k and passes the result to trampoline. Since we are now doing something with the result of value-of/k, that result is something other than a *FinalAnswer*. How can that be, since we have not changed the code of value-of/k? The procedure value-of/k calls apply-cont tail-recursively, and apply-cont calls apply-procedure/k tail-recursively, so any result of apply-procedure/k could appear as the result of value-of/k. And, of course, we have modified apply-procedure/k to return something different than it did before.

We introduce the set *Bounce* for the possible results of the value-of/k. (We call it *Bounce* because it is the input to trampoline.) What kind of values could appear in this set? value-of/k calls itself and apply-cont tail-recursively, and these are the only tail-recursive calls it makes. So the only values that could appear as results of value-of/k are those that appear as results of apply-cont. Also, apply-procedure/k calls value-of/k tail-recursively, so whatever *Bounce* is, it is the set of results of value-of/k, apply-cont, and apply-procedure/k.

The procedures `value-of/k` and `apply-cont` just call other procedures tail-recursively. The only procedure that actually puts values in *Bounce* is `apply-procedure/k`. What kind of values are these? Let's look at the code.

```
(define apply-procedure/k
  (lambda (proc1 val cont)
    (lambda ()
      (cases procedure proc1
        (... (value-of/k ...))))))
```

We see that `apply-procedure/k` returns a procedure of no arguments, which when called returns either an *ExpVal* or the result of a call to one of `value-of/k`, `apply-cont`, or `apply-procedure/k`, that is, a *Bounce*. So the possible values of `apply-procedure/k` are described by the set

$$ExpVal \cup (() \rightarrow Bounce)$$

These are the same as the possible results of `value-of/k`, so we conclude that

$$Bounce = ExpVal \cup (() \rightarrow Bounce)$$

and that the contracts should be

> **value-of-program** : *Program* → *FinalAnswer*
> **trampoline** : *Bounce* → *FinalAnswer*
> **value-of/k** : *Exp* × *Env* × *Cont* → *Bounce*
> **apply-cont** : *Cont* × *ExpVal* → *Bounce*
> **apply-procedure/k** : *Proc* × *ExpVal* × *Cont* → *Bounce*

The procedure `trampoline` satisfies its contract: it is initially passed a *Bounce*. If its argument is an *ExpVal* (and hence a *FinalAnswer*), then it returns it. Otherwise the argument must be a procedure that returns a *Bounce*. So it invokes the procedure on no arguments, and calls itself with the resulting value, which will always be a *Bounce*. (We will see in section 7.4 how to automate reasoning like this.)

Each zero-argument procedure returned by `apply-procedure/k` represents a snapshot of the computation in progress. We could choose to return such a snapshot at different places in the computation; we see in section 5.5 how this idea can be utilized to simulate atomic actions in multithreaded programs.

Bounce = *ExpVal* ∪ (() → *Bounce*)

value-of-program : *Program* → *FinalAnswer*
```
(define value-of-program
  (lambda (pgm)
    (cases program pgm
      (a-program (exp)
        (trampoline
          (value-of/k exp (init-env) (end-cont)))))))
```

trampoline : *Bounce* → *FinalAnswer*
```
(define trampoline
  (lambda (bounce)
    (if (expval? bounce)
      bounce
      (trampoline (bounce)))))
```

value-of/k : *Exp* × *Env* × *Cont* → *Bounce*
```
(define value-of/k
  (lambda (exp env cont)
    (cases expression exp
      (... (value-of/k ...))
      (... (apply-cont ...)))))
```

apply-cont : *Cont* × *ExpVal* → *Bounce*
```
(define apply-cont
  (lambda (cont val)
    (cases continuation cont
      (... val)
      (... (value-of/k ...))
      (... (apply-cont ...))
      (... (apply-procedure/k ...)))))
```

apply-procedure/k : *Proc* × *ExpVal* × *Cont* → *Bounce*
```
(define apply-procedure/k
  (lambda (proc1 val cont)
    (lambda ()
      (cases procedure proc1
        (... (value-of/k ...))))))
```

Figure 5.7   Procedural representation of trampolining

Exercise 5.17 [⋆] Modify the trampolined interpreter to wrap (lambda () ...) around each call (there's only one) to apply-procedure/k. Does this modification require changing the contracts?

Exercise 5.18 [⋆] The trampoline system in figure 5.7 uses a procedural representation of a *Bounce*. Replace this by a data structure representation.

Exercise 5.19 [⋆] Instead of placing the (lambda () ...) around the body of apply-procedure/k, place it around the body of apply-cont. Modify the contracts to match this change. Does the definition of *Bounce* need to change? Then replace the procedural representation of *Bounce* with a data-structure representation, as in exercise 5.18.

Exercise 5.20 [⋆] In exercise 5.19, the last bounce before trampoline returns a *FinalAnswer* is always something like (apply-cont (end-cont) val), where *val* is some *ExpVal*. Optimize your representation of bounces in exercise 5.19 to take advantage of this fact.

Exercise 5.21 [⋆ ⋆] Implement a trampolining interpreter in an ordinary procedural language. Use a data structure representation of the snapshots as in exercise 5.18, and replace the recursive call to trampoline in its own body by an ordinary while or other looping construct.

Exercise 5.22 [⋆ ⋆ ⋆] One could also attempt to transcribe the environment-passing interpreters of chapter 3 in an ordinary procedural language. Such a transcription would fail in all but the simplest cases, for the same reasons as suggested above. Can the technique of trampolining be used in this situation as well?

5.3   An Imperative Interpreter

In chapter 4, we saw how assignment to shared variables could sometimes be used in place of binding. Consider the familiar example of even and odd at the top of figure 5.8. It could be replaced by the program below it in figure 5.8. There the shared variable x allows communication between the two procedures. In the top example, the procedure bodies look for the relevant data in the environment; in the other program, they look for the relevant data in the store.

Consider a trace of the computation at the bottom of figure 5.8. This could be a trace of either computation. It could be a trace of the first computation, in which we keep track of the procedure being called and its argument, or it could be a trace of the second, in which we keep track of the procedure being called and the contents of the register x.

Yet a third interpretation of this trace would be as the trace of *goto*s (called a flowchart program), in which we keep track of the location of the program counter and the contents of the register x.

```
letrec
 even(x) = if zero?(x)
             then 1
             else (odd sub1(x))
 odd(x) = if zero?(x)
             then 0
             else (even sub1(x))
in (odd 13)
```

```
let x = 0
in letrec
     even() = if zero?(x)
                 then 1
                 else let d = set x = sub1(x)
                         in (odd)
     odd() = if zero?(x)
                 then 0
                 else let d = set x = sub1(x)
                         in (even)
    in let d = set x = 13
        in (odd)
```

```
        x = 13;
        goto odd;
even:  if (x=0) then return(1)
               else {x = x-1;
                      goto odd;}
odd:   if (x=0) then return(0)
               else {x = x-1;
                      goto even;}
```

```
  (odd  13)
= (even 12)
= (odd  11)
...
= (odd   1)
= (even  0)
= 1
```

Figure 5.8   Three programs with a common trace

But this works only because in the original code the calls to even and odd do not grow any control context: they are tail calls. We could not carry out this transformation for fact, because the trace of fact grows unboundedly: the "program counter" appears not at the outside of the trace, as it does here, but inside a control context.

We can carry out this transformation for any procedure that does not require control context. This leads us to an important principle:

> **A 0-argument tail call is the same as a jump.**

If a group of procedures call each other only by tail calls, then we can translate the calls to use assignment instead of binding, and then we can translate such an assignment program into a flowchart program, as we did in figure 5.8.

In this section, we will use this principle to translate the continuation-passing interpreter into a form suitable for transcription into a language without higher-order procedures.

We begin with the interpreter of figures 5.4 and 5.5, using a data structure representation of continuations. The data structure representation is shown in figures 5.9 and 5.10.

Our first task is to list the procedures that will communicate via shared registers. These procedures, with their formal parameters, are:

```
(value-of/k exp env cont)
(apply-cont cont val)
(apply-procedure/k proc1 val cont)
```

So we will need five global registers: exp, env, cont, val, and proc1. Each of the three procedures above will be replaced by a zero-argument procedure, and each call to one of these procedures will be replaced by code that stores the value of each actual parameter in the corresponding register and then invokes the new zero-argument procedure. So the fragment

```
(define value-of/k
  (lambda (exp env cont)
    (cases expression exp
      (const-exp (num) (apply-cont cont (num-val num)))
      ...)))
```

can be replaced by

```
(define-datatype continuation continuation?
  (end-cont)
  (zero1-cont
    (saved-cont continuation?))
  (let-exp-cont
    (var identifier?)
    (body expression?)
    (saved-env environment?)
    (saved-cont continuation?))
  (if-test-cont
    (exp2 expression?)
    (exp3 expression?)
    (saved-env environment?)
    (saved-cont continuation?))
  (diff1-cont
    (exp2 expression?)
    (saved-env environment?)
    (saved-cont continuation?))
  (diff2-cont
    (val1 expval?)
    (saved-cont continuation?))
  (rator-cont
    (rand expression?)
    (saved-env environment?)
    (saved-cont continuation?))
  (rand-cont
    (val1 expval?)
    (saved-cont continuation?)))
```

Figure 5.9 Data structure implementation of continuations (part 1)

```
(define value-of/k
  (lambda ()
    (cases expression exp
      (const-exp (num)
        (set! cont cont)
        (set! val (num-val num))
        (apply-cont))
      ...)))
```

We can now systematically go through each of our four procedures and perform this transformation. We will also have to transform the body of

apply-cont : *Cont* × *ExpVal* → *FinalAnswer*

```
(define apply-cont
  (lambda (cont val)
    (cases continuation cont
      (end-cont ()
        (begin
          (eopl:printf
            "End of computation.~%")
          val))
      (zero1-cont (saved-cont)
        (apply-cont saved-cont
          (bool-val
            (zero? (expval->num val)))))
      (let-exp-cont (var body saved-env saved-cont)
        (value-of/k body
          (extend-env var val saved-env) saved-cont))
      (if-test-cont (exp2 exp3 saved-env saved-cont)
        (if (expval->bool val)
          (value-of/k exp2 saved-env saved-cont)
          (value-of/k exp3 saved-env saved-cont)))
      (diff1-cont (exp2 saved-env saved-cont)
        (value-of/k exp2
          saved-env (diff2-cont val saved-cont)))
      (diff2-cont (val1 saved-cont)
        (let ((num1 (expval->num val1))
              (num2 (expval->num val)))
          (apply-cont saved-cont
            (num-val (- num1 num2)))))
      (rator-cont (rand saved-env saved-cont)
        (value-of/k rand saved-env
          (rand-cont val saved-cont)))
      (rand-cont (val1 saved-cont)
        (let ((proc (expval->proc val1)))
          (apply-procedure/k proc val saved-cont))))))
```

Figure 5.10   Data structure implementation of continuations (part 2) `value-of-program`, since that is where `value-of/k` is initially called. There are just three easy-to-resolve complications:

1. Often a register is unchanged from one procedure call to another. This yields an assignment like `(set! cont cont)` in the example above. We can safely omit such assignments.

2. We must make sure that no field name in a `cases` expression happens to be the same as a register name. In this situation, the field shadows the register, so the register becomes inaccessible. For example, if in `value-of-program` we had written

```
(cases program pgm
  (a-program (exp)
    (value-of/k exp (init-env) (end-cont))))
```

then `exp` would be locally bound, so we could not assign to the global register `exp`. The solution is to rename the local variable to avoid the conflict:

```
(cases program pgm
  (a-program (exp1)
    (value-of/k exp1 (init-env) (end-cont))))
```

Then we can write

```
(cases program pgm
  (a-program (exp1)
    (set! cont (end-cont))
    (set! exp exp1)
    (set! env (init-env))
    (value-of/k)))
```

We have already carefully chosen the field names in our data types to avoid such conflicts.

3. An additional complication may arise if a register is used twice in a single call. Consider transforming a first call in `(cons (f (car x)) (f (cdr x)))`, where x is the formal parameter of f. A naive transformation of this call would be:

```
(begin
  (set! x (car x))
  (set! cont (arg1-cont x cont))
  (f))
```

But this is incorrect, because it loads the register x with the new value of x, when the old value of x was intended. The solution is either to reorder the assignments so the right values are loaded into the registers, or to use temporary variables. Most occurrences of this bug can be avoided by assigning to the continuation variable first:

```
(begin
  (set! cont (arg1-cont x cont))
  (set! x (car x))
  (f))
```

Occasionally, temporary variables are unavoidable; consider `(f y x)` where x and y are the formal parameters of f. Again, this complication does not arise in our example.

The result of performing this translation on our interpreter is shown in figures 5.11–5.14. This process is called *registerization*. It is an easy process to translate this into an imperative language that supports gotos.

Exercise 5.23 [*] What happens if you remove the "goto" line in one of the branches of this interpreter? Exactly how does the interpreter fail?

Exercise 5.24 [*] Devise examples to illustrate each of the complications mentioned above.

Exercise 5.25 [* *] Registerize the interpreter for multiargument procedures (exercise 3.21).

Exercise 5.26 [*] Convert this interpreter to a trampoline by replacing each call to `apply-procedure/k` with `(set! pc apply-procedure/k)` and using a driver that looks like

```
(define trampoline
  (lambda (pc)
    (if pc (trampoline (pc)) val)))
```

```
(define exp 'uninitialized)
(define env 'uninitialized)
(define cont 'uninitialized)
(define val 'uninitialized)
(define proc1 'uninitialized)
```

value-of-program : *Program* → *FinalAnswer*
```
(define value-of-program
  (lambda (pgm)
    (cases program pgm
      (a-program (exp1)
        (set! cont (end-cont))
        (set! exp exp1)
        (set! env (init-env))
        (value-of/k)))))
```

value-of/k : () → *FinalAnswer*
usage: : relies on registers
```
        exp  : Exp
        env  : Env
        cont : Cont
(define value-of/k
  (lambda ()
    (cases expression exp
      (const-exp (num)
        (set! val (num-val num))
        (apply-cont))
      (var-exp (var)
        (set! val (apply-env env var))
        (apply-cont))
      (proc-exp (var body)
        (set! val (proc-val (procedure var body env)))
        (apply-cont))
      (letrec-exp (p-name b-var p-body letrec-body)
        (set! exp letrec-body)
        (set! env (extend-env-rec p-name b-var p-body env))
        (value-of/k))
```

Figure 5.11   Imperative interpreter (part 1)

```
(zero?-exp (exp1)
  (set! cont (zero1-cont cont))
  (set! exp exp1)
  (value-of/k))
(let-exp (var exp1 body)
  (set! cont (let-exp-cont var body env cont))
  (set! exp exp1)
  (value-of/k))
(if-exp (exp1 exp2 exp3)
  (set! cont (if-test-cont exp2 exp3 env cont))
  (set! exp exp1)
  (value-of/k))
(diff-exp (exp1 exp2)
  (set! cont (diff1-cont exp2 env cont))
  (set! exp exp1)
  (value-of/k))
(call-exp (rator rand)
  (set! cont (rator-cont rand env cont))
  (set! exp rator)
  (value-of/k))))))
```

Figure 5.12   Imperative interpreter (part 2)

Exercise 5.27 [⋆] Invent a language feature for which setting the cont variable last requires a temporary variable.

Exercise 5.28 [⋆] Instrument this interpreter as in exercise 5.12. Since continuations are represented the same way, reuse that code. Verify that the imperative interpreter of this section generates *exactly* the same traces as the interpreter in exercise 5.12.

Exercise 5.29 [⋆] Apply the transformation of this section to fact-iter (page 139).

Exercise 5.30 [⋆ ⋆] Modify the interpreter of this section so that procedures rely on dynamic binding, as in exercise 3.28. As a hint, consider transforming the interpreter of exercise 3.28 as we did in this chapter; it will differ from the interpreter of this section only for those portions of the original interpreter that are different. Instrument the interpreter as in exercise 5.28. Observe that just as there is only one continuation in the state, there is only one environment that is pushed and popped, and furthermore, it is pushed and popped in parallel with the continuation. We can conclude that dynamic bindings have *dynamic extent*: that is, a binding to a formal parameter lasts exactly until that procedure returns. This is different from lexical bindings, which can persist indefinitely if they wind up in a closure.

```
apply-cont : ()  →  FinalAnswer
usage:   : reads registers
         cont : Cont
         val  : ExpVal
(define apply-cont
  (lambda ()
    (cases continuation cont
      (end-cont ()
        (eopl:printf "End of computation.~%")
        val)
      (zero1-cont (saved-cont)
        (set! cont saved-cont)
        (set! val (bool-val (zero? (expval->num val))))
        (apply-cont))
      (let-exp-cont (var body saved-env saved-cont)
        (set! cont saved-cont)
        (set! exp body)
        (set! env (extend-env var val saved-env))
        (value-of/k))
      (if-test-cont (exp2 exp3 saved-env saved-cont)
        (set! cont saved-cont)
        (if (expval->bool val)
          (set! exp exp2)
          (set! exp exp3))
        (set! env saved-env)
        (value-of/k))
```

Figure 5.13   Imperative interpreter (part 3)

Exercise 5.31 [⋆] Eliminate the remaining `let` expressions in this code by using additional global registers.

Exercise 5.32 [⋆ ⋆] Improve your solution to the preceding exercise by minimizing the number of global registers used. You can get away with fewer than 5. You may use no data structures other than those already used by the interpreter.

Exercise 5.33 [⋆ ⋆] Translate the interpreter of this section into an imperative language. Do this twice: once using zero-argument procedure calls in the host language, and once replacing each zero-argument procedure call by a `goto`. How do these alternatives perform as the computation gets longer?

```
      (diff1-cont (exp2 saved-env saved-cont)
        (set! cont (diff2-cont val saved-cont))
        (set! exp exp2)
        (set! env saved-env)
        (value-of/k))
      (diff2-cont (val1 saved-cont)
        (let ((num1 (expval->num val1))
              (num2 (expval->num val)))
          (set! cont saved-cont)
          (set! val (num-val (- num1 num2)))
          (apply-cont)))
      (rator-cont (rand saved-env saved-cont)
        (set! cont (rand-cont val saved-cont))
        (set! exp rand)
        (set! env saved-env)
        (value-of/k))
      (rand-cont (rator-val saved-cont)
        (let ((rator-proc (expval->proc rator-val)))
          (set! cont saved-cont)
          (set! proc1 rator-proc)
          (set! val val)
          (apply-procedure/k))))))
```

apply-procedure/k : () $\rightarrow$ *FinalAnswer*
usage: : relies on registers
     proc1 : *Proc*
     val   : *ExpVal*
     cont   : *Cont*

```
(define apply-procedure/k
  (lambda ()
    (cases proc proc1
      (procedure (var body saved-env)
        (set! exp body)
        (set! env (extend-env var val saved-env))
        (value-of/k)))))
```

Figure 5.14   Imperative interpreter (part 4)

Exercise 5.34 [⋆ ⋆] As noted on page 157, most imperative languages make it difficult to do this translation, because they use the stack for all procedure calls, even tail calls. Furthermore, for large interpreters, the pieces of code linked by goto's may be too large for some compilers to handle. Translate the interpreter of this section into an imperative language, circumventing this difficulty by using the technique of trampolining, as in exercise 5.26.

5.4 Exceptions

So far we have used continuations only to manage the ordinary flow of control in our languages. But continuations allow us to alter the control context as well. Let us consider adding *exception handling* to our defined language. We add to the language two new productions:

Expression ::= try *Expression* catch (*Identifier*) *Expression*

> try-exp (exp1 var handler-exp)

Expression ::= raise *Expression*

> raise-exp (exp)

A try expression evaluates its first argument in the context of the exception handler described by the catch clause. If this expression returns normally, its value becomes the value of the entire try expression, and the exception handler is removed.

A raise expression evaluates its single expression and raises an exception with that value. The value is sent to the most recently installed exception handler and is bound to the variable of the handler. The body of the handler is then evaluated. The handler body can either return a value, which becomes the value of the associated try expression, or it can *propagate* the exception by raising another exception; in this case the exception would be sent to the next most recently installed exception handler.

Here's an example, where we assume for the moment that we have added strings to the language.

```
let list-index =
    proc (str)
      letrec inner (lst)
        = if null?(lst)
          then raise("ListIndexFailed")
          else if string-equal?(car(lst), str)
               then 0
               else -((inner cdr(lst)), -1)
```

The procedure `list-index` is a Curried procedure that takes a string and list of strings, and returns the position of the string in the list. If the desired list element is not found, `inner` raises an exception and passes `"ListIndexFailed"` to the most recently installed handler, skipping over all the pending subtractions.

The handler can take advantage of knowledge at the call site to handle the exception appropriately.

```
let find-member-number =
    proc (member-name)
      ... try ((list-index member-name) member-list)
          catch (exn)
            raise("CantFindMemberNumber")
```

The procedure `find-member-number` takes a string and uses `list-index` to find the position of the string in the list `member-list`. The caller of `find-member-number` has no reason to know about `list-index`, so `find-member-number` translates the error message into an exception that its caller can understand.

Yet another possibility, depending on the purpose of the program, is that `find-member-number` might return some default number if the member's name is not in the list.

```
let find-member-number =
    proc (member-name)
      ... try ((list-index member-name) member-list)
          catch (exn)
            the-default-member-number
```

In both these programs, we have ignored the value of the exception. In other situations, the value passed by `raise` might include some partial information that the caller could utilize.

Implementing this exception-handling mechanism using the continuation-passing interpreter is straightforward. We begin with the `try` expression. In the data-structure representation, we add two continuation-builders:

```
(try-cont
  (var identifier?)
  (handler-exp expression?)
  (env environment?)
  (cont continuation?))
(raise1-cont
  (saved-cont continuation?))
```

and we add to `value-of/k` the following clause for `try`:

```
(try-exp (exp1 var handler-exp)
  (value-of/k exp1 env
    (try-cont var handler-exp env cont)))
```

What happens when the body of the `try` expression is evaluated? If the body returns normally, then that value should be sent to the continuation of the `try` expression, in this case `cont`:

(apply-cont (try-cont *var handler-exp env cont*) *val*)
= (apply-cont *cont val*)

What happens if an exception is raised? First, of course, we need to evaluate the argument to `raise`.

```
(raise-exp (exp1)
  (value-of/k exp1 env
    (raise1-cont cont)))
```

When the value of `exp1` is returned to `raise1-cont`, we need to search through the continuation for the nearest handler, which may be found in the topmost `try-cont` continuation. So in the specification of continuations we write

(apply-cont (raise1-cont *cont*) *val*)
= (apply-handler *val cont*)

where `apply-handler` is a procedure that finds the closest exception handler and applies it (figure 5.15).

To show how all this fits together, let us consider a calculation using a defined language implementation of `index`. Let exp_0 denote the expression

```
let index
    = proc (n)
        letrec inner (lst)
        = if null?(lst)
          then raise 99
          else if zero?(-(car(lst),n))
                then 0
                else -((inner cdr(lst)), -1)
        in proc (lst)
            try (inner lst)
            catch (x) -1
in ((index 5) list(2, 3))
```

apply-handler : *ExpVal* × *Cont* → *FinalAnswer*
```
(define apply-handler
  (lambda (val cont)
    (cases continuation cont
      (try-cont (var handler-exp saved-env saved-cont)
        (value-of/k handler-exp
          (extend-env var val saved-env)
          saved-cont))
      (end-cont ()
        (report-uncaught-exception))
      (diff1-cont (exp2 saved-env saved-cont)
        (apply-handler val saved-cont))
      (diff2-cont (val1 saved-cont)
        (apply-handler val saved-cont))
      ...)))
```

Figure 5.15 The procedure `apply-handler`

We start exp_0 in an arbitrary environment ρ_0 and an arbitrary continuation $cont_0$. We will show only the highlights of the calculation, with comments interspersed.

```
(value-of/k
  <<let index = ... in  ((index 5) list(2, 3))>>
  ρ0
  cont0)
= execute the body of the let
(value-of/k
  <<((index 5) list(2, 3))>>
  ((index                                         call this ρ1
      #(struct:proc-val
        #(struct:procedure n <<letrec ...>> ρ0)))
   (i #(struct:num-val 1))
   (v #(struct:num-val 5))
   (x #(struct:num-val 10)))
  #(struct:end-cont))
```

```
= eventually we evaluate the try
(value-of/k
  <<try (inner2 lst) catch (x) -1>>
  ((lst                                                    call this ρ_lst=(2 3)
     #(struct:list-val
         (#(struct:num-val 2) #(struct:num-val 3))))
   (inner2 ...)
   (n #(struct:num-val 5))
   ρ_0)
  #(struct:end-cont))
= evaluate the body of the try in a try-cont continuation
(value-of/k
  <<(inner2 lst)>>

  ρ_lst=(2 3)
  #(struct:try-cont x <<-1>> ρ_lst=(2 3)
     #(struct:end-cont)))
= evaluate the body of inner2 with lst bound to (2 3)
(value-of/k
  <<if null?(lst) ... >>

  ρ_lst=(2 3)
  #(struct:try-cont x <<-1>> ρ_lst=(2 3)
     #(struct:end-cont)))
= evaluate the conditional, getting to the recursion line
(value-of/k
  <<-((inner2 cdr(lst)), -1)>>

  ρ_lst=(2 3)
  #(struct:try-cont x <<-1>> ρ_lst=(2 3)
     #(struct:end-cont)))
= evaluate the first argument of the diff-exp
(value-of/k
  <<(inner2 cdr(lst))>>

  ρ_lst=(2 3)
  #(struct:diff1-cont <<-1>> ρ_lst=(2 3)
     #(struct:try-cont x <<-1>> ρ_lst=(2 3)
        #(struct:end-cont))))
= evaluate the body of inner2 with lst bound to (3)
(value-of/k
  <<if null?(lst) ...>>
  ((lst #(struct:list-val (#(struct:num-val 3)))) call this ρ_lst=(3)
   (inner2 ...)
   ρ_0)
  #(struct:diff1-cont <<-1>> ρ_lst=(2 3)
     #(struct:try-cont x <<-1>> ρ_lst=(2 3)
        #(struct:end-cont))))
```

= *evaluate the conditional, getting to the recursion line again*
```
(value-of/k
  <<-((inner2 cdr(lst)), -1)>>
  ρlst=(3)
  #(struct:diff1-cont <<-1>> ρlst=(2 3)
    #(struct:try-cont x <<-1>> ρlst=(2 3)
      #(struct:end-cont)))))
```
= *evaluate the first argument of the* diff-exp
```
(value-of/k
  <<(inner2 cdr(lst))>>
  ρlst=(3)
  #(struct:diff1-cont <<-1>> ρlst=(3)
    #(struct:diff1-cont <<-1>> ρlst=(2 3)
      #(struct:try-cont x <<-1>> ρlst=(2 3)
        #(struct:end-cont))))))
```
= *evaluate the body of* inner2 *with* lst *bound to* ()
```
(value-of/k
  <<if null?(lst) ... >>
  ((lst #(struct:list-val ()))              call this ρlst=()
   (inner2 ...)
   (n #(struct:num-val 5))
   ...)
  #(struct:diff1-cont <<-1>> ρlst=(3)
    #(struct:diff1-cont <<-1>> ρlst=(2 3)
      #(struct:try-cont x <<-1>> ρlst=(2 3)
        #(struct:end-cont)))))
```
= *evaluate the* raise *expression*
```
(value-of/k
  <<raise 99>>
  ρlst=(())
  #(struct:diff1-cont <<-1>> ρlst=(3)
    #(struct:diff1-cont <<-1>> ρlst=(2 3)
      #(struct:try-cont x <<-1>> ρlst=(2 3)
        #(struct:end-cont)))))
```
= *evaluate the argument of the* raise *expression*
```
(value-of/k
  <<99>>
  ρlst=(())
  #(struct:raise1-cont
    #(struct:diff1-cont <<-1>> ρlst=(3)
      #(struct:diff1-cont <<-1>> ρlst=(2 3)
        #(struct:try-cont x <<-1>> ρlst=(2 3)
          #(struct:end-cont))))))
```

```
=  use apply-handler to unwind the continuation until we find a handler
(apply-handler
  #(struct:num-val 99)
  #(struct:diff1-cont <<-1>> ρlst=(3)
      #(struct:diff1-cont <<-1>> ρlst=(2 3)
          #(struct:try-cont x <<-1>> ρlst=(2 3)
              #(struct:end-cont))))))
=
(apply-handler
  #(struct:num-val 99)
  #(struct:diff1-cont <<-1>> ρlst=(2 3)
      #(struct:try-cont x <<-1>> ρlst=(2 3)
          #(struct:end-cont))))
=
(apply-handler
  #(struct:num-val 99)
  #(struct:try-cont x <<-1>> ρlst=(2 3)
      #(struct:end-cont)))
=  Handler found; bind the value of the exception to x
(value-of/k
  #(struct:const-exp -1)
  ((x #(struct:num-val 99))
  ρlst=(2 3)...)
  #(struct:end-cont))
=
(apply-cont #(struct:end-cont) #(struct:num-val -1))
=
#(struct:num-val -1)
```

If the list had contained the desired element, then we would have called `apply-cont` instead of `apply-handler`, and we would have executed all the pending `diff`s in the continuation.

Exercise 5.35 [★★] This implementation is inefficient, because when an exception is raised, `apply-handler` must search linearly through the continuation to find a handler. Avoid this search by making the `try-cont` continuation available directly in each continuation.

Exercise 5.36 [★] An alternative design that also avoids the linear search in `apply-handler` is to use two continuations, a normal continuation and an exception continuation. Achieve this goal by modifying the interpreter of this section to take two continuations instead of one.

Exercise 5.37 [★] Modify the defined language to raise an exception when a procedure is called with the wrong number of arguments.

Exercise 5.38 [★] Modify the defined language to add a division expression. Raise an exception on division by zero.

Exercise 5.39 [★★] So far, an exception handler can propagate the exception by re-raising it, or it can return a value that becomes the value of the `try` expression. One might instead design the language to allow the computation to resume from the point at which the exception was raised. Modify the interpreter of this section to accomplish this by running the body of the handler with the continuation from the point at which the `raise` was invoked.

Exercise 5.40 [★★★] Give the exception handlers in the defined language the ability to either return or resume. Do this by passing the continuation from the `raise` exception as a second argument. This may require adding continuations as a new kind of expressed value. Devise suitable syntax for invoking a continuation on a value.

Exercise 5.41 [★★★] We have shown how to implement exceptions using a data-structure representation of continuations. We can't immediately apply the recipe of section 2.2.3 to get a procedural representation, because we now have two observers: `apply-handler` and `apply-cont`. Implement the continuations of this section as a pair of procedures: a one-argument procedure representing the action of the continuation under `apply-cont`, and a zero-argument procedure representing its action under `apply-handler`.

Exercise 5.42 [★★] The preceding exercise captures the continuation only when an exception is raised. Add to the language the ability to capture a continuation anywhere by adding the form `letcc` *Identifier* in *Expression* with the specification

```
(value-of/k (letcc var body)  ρ  cont)
= (value-of/k body (extend-env var cont ρ)  cont)
```

Such a captured continuation may be invoked with `throw`: the expression `throw` *Expression* to *Expression* evaluates the two subexpressions. The second expression should return a continuation, which is applied to the value of the first expression. The current continuation of the `throw` expression is ignored.

Exercise 5.43 [★★] Modify `letcc` as defined in the preceding exercise so that the captured continuation becomes a new kind of procedure, so instead of writing `throw` exp_1 to exp_2, one would write (exp_2 exp_1).

Exercise 5.44 [★★] An alternative to `letcc` and `throw` of the preceding exercises is to add a single procedure to the language. This procedure, which in Scheme is called `call-with-current-continuation`, takes a one-argument procedure, p, and passes to p a procedure that when invoked with one argument, passes that argument to the current continuation, `cont`. We could define `call-with-current-continuation` in terms of `letcc` and `throw` as follows:

```
let call-with-current-continuation
      = proc (p)
           letcc cont
           in (p proc (v) throw v to cont)
    in ...
```

Add `call-with-current-continuation` to the language. Then write a translator that takes the language with `letcc` and `throw` and translates it into the language without `letcc` and `throw`, but with `call-with-current-continuation`.

5.5   Threads

In many programming tasks, one may wish to have multiple computations proceeding at once. When these computations are run in the same address space as part of the same process, they are usually called *threads*. In this section, we will discover how to modify our interpreter to simulate the execution of multithreaded programs.

Rather than having a single thread of computation, our multithreaded interpreter will maintain several threads. Each thread consists of a computation in progress, like those shown earlier in this chapter. Threads communicate through a single shared memory, using assignment as in chapter 4.

In our system, the entire computation consists of a *pool* of threads. Each thread may be either *running*, *runnable*, or *blocked*. In our system, exactly one thread is running at a time. In a multi-CPU system, one might have several running threads. The runnable threads will be kept on a queue called the *ready queue*. There may be other threads that are not ready to be run, for one reason or another. We say that these threads are *blocked*. Blocked threads will be introduced later in this section.

Threads are scheduled for execution by a *scheduler*, which keeps the ready queue as part of its state. In addition, it keeps a timer, so that when a thread has completed a certain number of steps (its *time slice* or *quantum*), it is interrupted and put back on the ready queue, and a new thread is selected from the ready queue to run. This is called *pre-emptive scheduling*.

Our new language is based on IMPLICIT-REFS and is called THREADS. In THREADS, new threads are created by a construct called spawn. spawn takes one argument, which should evaluate to a procedure. A new thread is created, which, when run, passes an unspecified argument to that procedure. This thread is not run immediately, but is placed on the ready queue to be run when its turn arrives. spawn is executed for effect; in our system we have arbitrarily decided to have it return the number 73.

Let's look at two examples of programs in this language. Figure 5.16 defines a procedure noisy that takes a list, prints its first element and then recurs on the rest of the list. Here the main expression creates two threads, which compete to print out the lists [1,2,3,4,5] and [6,7,8,9,10]. The exact way in which the lists are interleaved depends on the scheduler; in this example each thread prints out two elements of its list before the scheduler interrupts it.

Figure 5.17 shows a producer and a consumer, connected by a buffer initialized to 0. The producer takes an argument n, goes around the wait loop

```
test: two-non-cooperating-threads

letrec
  noisy (l) = if null?(l)
               then 0
               else begin print(car(l)); (noisy cdr(l)) end
in
    begin
     spawn(proc (d) (noisy [1,2,3,4,5])) ;
     spawn(proc (d) (noisy [6,7,8,9,10])) ;
     print(100);
     33
    end

100
1
2
6
7
3
4
8
9
5
10
correct outcome: 33
actual outcome:  #(struct:num-val 33)
correct
```

Figure 5.16 Two threads showing interleaved computation

5 times, and then puts n in the buffer. Each time through the wait loop, it prints the countdown timer (expressed in 200s). The consumer takes an argument (which it ignores) and goes into a loop, waiting for the buffer to become non-zero. Each time through this loop, it prints a counter (expressed in 100s) to show how long it has waited for its result. The main thread puts the producer on the ready queue, prints 300, and starts the consumer in the main thread. So the first two items, 300 and 205, are printed by the main thread. As in the preceding example, the consumer thread and the producer thread each go around their loop about twice before being interrupted.

```
let buffer = 0
in let producer = proc (n)
        letrec
          wait(k) = if zero?(k)
                      then set buffer = n
                      else begin
                            print(-(k,-200));
                            (wait -(k,1))
                          end
        in (wait 5)
   in let consumer = proc (d)
          letrec busywait (k) = if zero?(buffer)
                                  then begin
                                        print(-(k,-100));
                                        (busywait -(k,-1))
                                      end
                                  else buffer
          in (busywait 0)
      in begin
          spawn(proc (d) (producer 44));
          print(300);
          (consumer 86)
        end
```

```
300
205
100
101
204
203
102
103
202
201
104
105
correct outcome: 44
actual outcome:  #(struct:num-val 44)
correct
```

Figure 5.17 A producer and consumer, linked by a buffer

The implementation starts with a continuation-passing interpreter for the language IMPLICIT-REFS. This is similar to the one in section 5.1, with the addition of a store like the one in IMPLICIT-REFS (of course!) and a `set-rhs-cont` continuation builder like the one in exercise 5.9.

To this interpreter we add a scheduler. The scheduler keeps a state consisting of four values and provides six procedures in its interface for manipulating those values. These are shown in figure 5.18.

Figure 5.19 shows the implementation of this interface. Here (`enqueue` *q val*) returns a queue like *q*, except that *val* has been placed at the end. (`dequeue` *q f*) takes the head of the queue and the rest of the queue and passes them to *f* as arguments.

We represent a thread as a Scheme procedure of no arguments that returns an expressed value:

Thread = () → *ExpVal*

If the ready queue is non-empty, then the procedure `run-next-thread` takes the first thread from the ready queue and runs it, giving it a new time slice of size `the-max-time-slice`. It also sets `the-ready-queue` so that it consists of the remaining threads, if any. If the ready queue is empty, then `run-next-thread` returns the contents of `the-final-answer`. This is how the computation eventually terminates.

We next turn to the interpreter. A `spawn` expression evaluates its argument in a continuation which, when executed, places a new thread on the ready queue and continues by returning 73 to the caller of the spawn. The new thread, when executed, passes an arbitrary value (here 28) to the procedure that was the value of the `spawn`'s argument. To accomplish this, we add to `value-of/k` the clause

```
(spawn-exp (exp)
  (value-of/k exp env
    (spawn-cont cont)))
```

and to `apply-cont` the clause

```
(spawn-cont (saved-cont)
  (let ((proc1 (expval->proc val)))
    (place-on-ready-queue!
      (lambda ()
        (apply-procedure/k proc1
          (num-val 28)
          (end-subthread-cont))))
    (apply-cont saved-cont (num-val 73))))
```

Internal State of the Scheduler

`the-ready-queue`	the ready queue
`the-final-answer`	the value of the main thread, if done
`the-max-time-slice`	the number of steps that each thread may run
`the-time-remaining`	the number of steps remaining for the currently running thread.

Scheduler Interface

initialize-scheduler!	$: Int \rightarrow Unspecified$
	initializes the scheduler state
place-on-ready-queue!	$: Thread \rightarrow Unspecified$
	places thread on the ready queue
run-next-thread	$: () \rightarrow FinalAnswer$
	runs next thread. If no ready threads, returns the final answer.
set-final-answer!	$: ExpVal \rightarrow Unspecified$
	sets the final answer
time-expired?	$: () \rightarrow Bool$
	tests whether timer is 0
decrement-timer!	$: () \rightarrow Unspecified$
	decrements `time-remaining`

Figure 5.18   State and interface of the scheduler

initialize-scheduler! : *Int* → *Unspecified*
```
(define initialize-scheduler!
  (lambda (ticks)
    (set! the-ready-queue (empty-queue))
    (set! the-final-answer 'uninitialized)
    (set! the-max-time-slice ticks)
    (set! the-time-remaining the-max-time-slice)))
```

place-on-ready-queue! : *Thread* → *Unspecified*
```
(define place-on-ready-queue!
  (lambda (th)
    (set! the-ready-queue
      (enqueue the-ready-queue th))))
```

run-next-thread : *()* → *FinalAnswer*
```
(define run-next-thread
  (lambda ()
    (if (empty? the-ready-queue)
      the-final-answer
      (dequeue the-ready-queue
        (lambda (first-ready-thread other-ready-threads)
          (set! the-ready-queue other-ready-threads)
          (set! the-time-remaining the-max-time-slice)
          (first-ready-thread))))))
```

set-final-answer! : *ExpVal* → *Unspecified*
```
(define set-final-answer!
  (lambda (val)
    (set! the-final-answer val)))
```

time-expired? : *()* → *Bool*
```
(define time-expired?
  (lambda ()
    (zero? the-time-remaining)))
```

decrement-timer! : *()* → *Unspecified*
```
(define decrement-timer!
  (lambda ()
    (set! the-time-remaining (- the-time-remaining 1))))
```

Figure 5.19 The scheduler

This is what the trampolined interpreter did when it created a snapshot: it packaged up a computation (here (lambda () (apply-procedure/k ...))) and passed it to another procedure for processing. In the trampoline example, we passed the thread to the trampoline, which simply ran it. Here we place the new thread on the ready queue and continue our own computation.

This leads us to the key question: what continuation should we run each thread in?

• The main thread should be run with a continuation that records the value of the main thread as the final answer, and then runs any remaining ready threads.

• When the subthread finishes, there is no way to report its value, so we run it in a continuation that ignores the value and simply runs any remaining ready threads.

This gives us two new continuations, whose behavior is implemented by the following lines in apply-cont:

```
(end-main-thread-cont ()
  (set-final-answer! val)
  (run-next-thread))

(end-subthread-cont ()
  (run-next-thread))
```

We start the entire system with value-of-program:

value-of-program : *Int × Program → FinalAnswer*
```
(define value-of-program
  (lambda (timeslice pgm)
    (initialize-store!)
    (initialize-scheduler! timeslice)
    (cases program pgm
      (a-program (exp1)
        (value-of/k
          exp1
          (init-env)
          (end-main-thread-cont))))))
```

Last, we modify apply-cont to decrement the timer each time it is called. If the timer has expired, then the current computation is suspended. We do this by putting on the ready queue a thread that will try the apply-cont again, with the timer restored by some call to run-next-thread.

```
let x = 0
in let incr_x = proc (id)
                  proc (dummy)
                    set x = -(x,-1)
in begin
     spawn((incr_x 100));
     spawn((incr_x 200));
     spawn((incr_x 300))
   end
```

Figure 5.20   An unsafe counter

apply-cont : *Cont* × *ExpVal* → *FinalAnswer*
```
(define apply-cont
  (lambda (cont val)
    (if (time-expired?)
      (begin
        (place-on-ready-queue!
          (lambda () (apply-cont cont val)))
        (run-next-thread))
      (begin
        (decrement-timer!)
        (cases continuation cont
          ...)))))
```

Shared variables are an unreliable method of communication because several threads may try to write to the same variable. For example, consider the program in figure 5.20. Here we create three threads, each of which tries to increment the same counter x. If one thread reads the counter, but is interrupted before it can update it, then both threads will change the counter to the same number. Hence the counter may become 2, or even 1, rather than 3.

We would like to be able to ensure that interferences like this do not occur. Similarly, we would like to be able to organize our program so that the consumer in figure 5.17 doesn't have to busy-wait. Instead, it should be able to put itself to sleep and be awakened when the producer has inserted a value in the shared buffer.

There are many ways to design such a synchronization facility. A simple one is the *mutex* (short for *mutual exclusion*) or *binary semaphore*.

A mutex may either be *open* or *closed*. It also contains a queue of threads that are *waiting* for the mutex to become open. There are three operations on mutexes:

- `mutex` is an operation that takes no arguments and creates an initially open mutex.

- `wait` is a unary operation by which a thread indicates that it wants access to a mutex. Its argument must be a mutex. Its behavior depends on the state of the mutex.

  - If the mutex is closed, then the current thread is placed on the mutex's wait queue, and is suspended. We say that the current thread is *blocked* waiting for this mutex.

  - If the mutex is open, it becomes closed and the current thread continues to run.

  A `wait` is executed for effect only; its return value is unspecified.

- `signal` is a unary operation by which a thread indicates that it is ready to release a mutex. Its argument must be a mutex.

  - If the mutex is closed, and there are no threads waiting on its wait queue, then mutex becomes open and the current thread proceeds.

  - If the mutex is closed and there are threads in its wait queue, then one of the threads from the wait queue is put on the scheduler's ready queue, and the mutex remains closed. The thread that executed the `signal` continues to compute.

  - If the mutex is open, then the thread leaves it open and proceeds.

  A `signal` is executed for effect only; its return value is unspecified. A `signal` operation always succeeds: the thread that executes it remains the running thread.

These properties guarantee that only one thread can execute between a successive pair of calls to `wait` and `signal`. This portion of the program is called a *critical region*. It is impossible for two different threads to be concurrently executing code in a critical region. For example, figure 5.21 shows

```
let x = 0
in let mut = mutex()
in let incr_x = proc (id)
                   proc (dummy)
                     begin
                       wait(mut);
                       set x = -(x,-1);
                       signal(mut)
                     end
in begin
     spawn((incr_x 100));
     spawn((incr_x 200));
     spawn((incr_x 300))
   end
```

Figure 5.21   A safe counter using a mutex

our previous example, with a mutex inserted around the critical line. In this program, only one thread can execute the set x = -(x,-1) at a time, so the counter is guaranteed to reach the final value of 3.

We model a mutex as two references: one to its state (either open or closed) and one to a list of threads waiting for this mutex. We also make mutexes expressed values.

```
(define-datatype mutex mutex?
  (a-mutex
    (ref-to-closed? reference?)
    (ref-to-wait-queue reference?)))
```

We add the appropriate line to value-of/k

```
(mutex-exp ()
  (apply-cont cont (mutex-val (new-mutex))))
```

where

new-mutex : () → *Mutex*
```
(define new-mutex
  (lambda ()
    (a-mutex
      (newref #f)
      (newref '()))))
```

wait and signal will be new unary operations, which simply call the procedures wait-for-mutex and signal-mutex. wait and signal both evaluate their single argument, so in apply-cont we write

```
(wait-cont (saved-cont)
  (wait-for-mutex
    (expval->mutex val)
    (lambda () (apply-cont saved-cont (num-val 52)))))

(signal-cont (saved-cont)
  (signal-mutex
    (expval->mutex val)
    (lambda () (apply-cont saved-cont (num-val 53)))))
```

Now we can write wait-for-mutex and signal-mutex. These procedures take two arguments: a mutex and a thread, and they work as described in the text above (figure 5.22).

Exercise 5.45 [⋆] Add to the language of this section a construct called yield. Whenever a thread executes a yield, it is placed on the ready queue, and the thread at the head of the ready queue is run. When the thread is resumed, it should appear as if the call to yield had returned the number 99.

Exercise 5.46 [⋆ ⋆] In the system of exercise 5.45, a thread may be placed on the ready queue either because its time slot has been exhausted or because it chose to yield. In the latter case, it will be restarted with a full time slice. Modify the system so that the ready queue keeps track of the remaining time slice (if any) of each thread, and restarts the thread only with the time it has remaining.

Exercise 5.47 [⋆] What happens if we are left with two subthreads, each waiting for a mutex held by the other subthread?

Exercise 5.48 [⋆] We have used a procedural representation of threads. Replace this by a data-structure representation.

Exercise 5.49 [⋆] Do exercise 5.15 (continuations as a stack of frames) for THREADS.

Exercise 5.50 [⋆ ⋆] Registerize the interpreter of this section. What is the set of mutually tail-recursive procedures that must be registerized?

Exercise 5.51 [⋆ ⋆ ⋆] We would like to be able to organize our program so that the consumer in figure 5.17 doesn't have to busy-wait. Instead, it should be able to put itself to sleep and be awakened when the producer has put a value in the buffer. Either write a program with mutexes to do this, or implement a synchronization operator that makes this possible.

Exercise 5.52 [⋆ ⋆ ⋆] Write a program using mutexes that will be like the program in figure 5.21, except that the main thread waits for all three of the subthreads to terminate, and then returns the value of x.

wait-for-mutex : *Mutex* × *Thread* → *FinalAnswer*
usage: waits for mutex to be open, then closes it.
```
(define wait-for-mutex
  (lambda (m th)
    (cases mutex m
      (a-mutex (ref-to-closed? ref-to-wait-queue)
        (cond
          ((deref ref-to-closed?)
           (setref! ref-to-wait-queue
             (enqueue (deref ref-to-wait-queue) th))
           (run-next-thread))
          (else
            (setref! ref-to-closed? #t)
            (th)))))))
```

signal-mutex : *Mutex* × *Thread* → *FinalAnswer*
```
(define signal-mutex
  (lambda (m th)
    (cases mutex m
      (a-mutex (ref-to-closed? ref-to-wait-queue)
        (let ((closed? (deref ref-to-closed?))
              (wait-queue (deref ref-to-wait-queue)))
          (if closed?
            (if (empty? wait-queue)
              (setref! ref-to-closed? #f)
              (dequeue wait-queue
                (lambda (first-waiting-th other-waiting-ths)
                  (place-on-ready-queue!
                    first-waiting-th)
                  (setref!
                    ref-to-wait-queue
                    other-waiting-ths)))))
          (th))))))
```

Figure 5.22   wait-for-mutex and signal-mutex

Exercise 5.53 [★★★] Modify the thread package to include *thread identifiers*. Each new thread is associated with a fresh thread identifier. When the child thread is spawned, it is passed its thread identifier as a value, rather than the arbitrary value 28 used in this section. The child's number is also returned to the parent as the value of the spawn expression. Instrument the interpreter to trace the creation of thread identifiers. Check to see that the ready queue contains at most one thread for each thread identifier. How can a child thread know its parent's identifier? What should be done about the thread identifier of the original program?

Exercise 5.54 [★★] Add to the interpreter of exercise 5.53 a `kill` facility. The `kill` construct, when given a thread number, finds the corresponding thread on the ready queue or any of the waiting queues and removes it. In addition, `kill` should return a true value if the target thread is found and false if the thread number is not found on any queue.

Exercise 5.55 [★★] Add to the interpreter of exercise 5.53 an interthread communication facility, in which each thread can send a value to another thread using its thread identifier. A thread can receive messages when it chooses, blocking if no message has been sent to it.

Exercise 5.56 [★★] Modify the interpreter of exercise 5.55 so that rather than sharing a store, each thread has its own store. In such a language, mutexes can almost always be avoided. Rewrite the example of this section in this language, without using mutexes.

Exercise 5.57 [★★★] There are lots of different synchronization mechanisms in your favorite OS book. Pick three and implement them in this framework.

Exercise 5.58 [definitely ★] Go off with your friends and have some pizza, but make sure only one person at a time grabs a piece!

6 *Continuation-Passing Style*

In chapter 5, we took an interpreter and rewrote it so that all of the major procedure calls were *tail calls*. By doing so, we guaranteed that the interpreter uses at most a bounded amount of control context at any one time, no matter how large or complex a program it is called upon to interpret. This property is called *iterative control behavior*.

We achieved this goal by passing an extra parameter, the *continuation*, to each procedure. This style of programming is called *continuation-passing style* or *CPS*, and it is not restricted to interpreters.

In this chapter we develop a systematic method for transforming any procedure into an equivalent procedure whose control behavior is iterative. This is accomplished by converting it into continuation-passing style.

6.1 Writing Programs in Continuation-Passing Style

We can use CPS for other things besides interpreters. Let's consider an old favorite, the factorial program:

```
(define fact
  (lambda (n)
    (if (zero? n) 1 (* n (fact (- n 1)))))))
```

A continuation-passing version of factorial would look something like

```
(define fact
  (lambda (n)
    (fact/k n (end-cont)))))

(define fact/k
  (lambda (n cont)
    (if (zero? n)
      (apply-cont cont 1)
      (fact/k (- n 1) (fact1-cont n cont)))))))
```

where

```
(apply-cont (end-cont) val) = val

(apply-cont (fact1-cont n cont) val)
= (apply-cont cont (* n val))
```

In this version, all the calls to fact/k and apply-cont are in tail position and therefore build up no control context.

We can implement these continuations as data structures by writing

```
(define-datatype continuation continuation?
  (end-cont)
  (fact1-cont
    (n integer?)
    (cont continuation?)))

(define apply-cont
  (lambda (cont val)
    (cases continuation cont
      (end-cont () val)
      (fact1-cont (saved-n saved-cont)
        (apply-cont saved-cont (* saved-n val))))))
```

We can transform this program in many ways. We could, for example, registerize it, as shown in figure 6.1.

We could even trampoline this version, as shown in figure 6.2. If we did this in an ordinary imperative language, we would of course replace the trampoline by a proper loop.

However, our primary concern in this chapter will be what happens when we use a procedural representation, as we did in figure 5.2. Recall that in the procedural representation, a continuation is represented by its action under apply-cont. The procedural representation looks like

```
(define end-cont
  (lambda ()
    (lambda (val) val)))

(define fact1-cont
  (lambda (n saved-cont)
    (lambda (val)
      (apply-cont saved-cont (* n val)))))

(define apply-cont
  (lambda (cont val)
    (cont val)))
```

```
(define n 'uninitialized)
(define cont 'uninitialized)
(define val 'uninitialized)

(define fact
  (lambda (arg-n)
    (set! cont (end-cont))
    (set! n arg-n)
    (fact/k)))

(define fact/k
  (lambda ()
    (if (zero? n)
      (begin
        (set! val 1)
        (apply-cont))
      (begin
        (set! cont (fact1-cont n cont))
        (set! n (- n 1))
        (fact/k)))))

(define apply-cont
  (lambda ()
    (cases continuation cont
      (end-cont () val)
      (fact1-cont (saved-n saved-cont)
        (set! cont saved-cont)
        (set! n saved-n)
        (apply-cont)))))
```

Figure 6.1 `fact/k` registerized

We can do even better by taking each call to a continuation-builder in the program and replacing it by its definition. This transformation is called *inlining*, because the definitions are expanded in-line. We also inline the calls to `apply-cont`, so instead of writing `(apply-cont cont val)`, we'll just write `(cont val)`.

```
(define n 'uninitialized)
(define cont 'uninitialized)
(define val 'uninitialized)
(define pc 'uninitialized)

(define fact
  (lambda (arg-n)
    (set! cont (end-cont))
    (set! n arg-n)
    (set! pc fact/k)
    (trampoline!)
    val))

(define trampoline!
  (lambda ()
    (if pc
      (begin
        (pc)
        (trampoline!)))))

(define fact/k
  (lambda ()
    (if (zero? n)
      (begin
        (set! val 1)
        (set! pc apply-cont))
      (begin
        (set! cont (fact1-cont n cont))
        (set! n (- n 1))
        (set! pc fact/k)))))

(define apply-cont
  (lambda ()
    (cases continuation cont
      (end-cont ()
        (set! pc #f))
      (fact1-cont (saved-n saved-cont)
        (set! cont saved-cont)
        (set! n saved-n)
        (set! pc apply-cont)))))
```

Figure 6.2 fact/k registerized and trampolined

If we inline all the uses of continuations in this way, we get

```
(define fact
  (lambda (n)
    (fact/k n (lambda (val) val))))

(define fact/k
  (lambda (n cont)
    (if (zero? n)
      (cont 1)
      (fact/k (- n 1) (lambda (val) (cont (* n val)))))))
```

We can read the definition of `fact/k` as:

If n is zero, send 1 to the continuation. Otherwise, evaluate `fact` *of* $n - 1$
in a continuation that calls the result `val`, *and then sends to the continuation*
the value `(* n val)`.

The procedure `fact/k` has the property that `(fact/k` n g`)` = $(g$ $n!)$.
This is easy to show by induction on n. For the base step, when $n = 0$, we
calculate

```
(fact/k 0 g) = (g 1) = (g (fact 0))
```

For the induction step, we assume that `(fact/k` n g`)` = $(g$ $n!)$, for some
value of n and try to show that `(fact/k` $(n+1)$ g`)` = $(g$ $(n+1)!)$. To do
this, we calculate:

```
(fact/k n+1 g)
= (fact/k n (lambda (val) (g (* n+1 val))))
= ((lambda (val) (g (* n+1 val)))        (by the induction hypothesis)
   (fact n))
= (g (* n+1 (fact n)))
= (g (fact n+1))
```

This completes the induction.

Here the g appears as a context argument, as in section 1.3, and the property that `(fact/k` n g`)` = $(g$ $n!)$ serves as the independent specification,
following our principle of *No Mysterious Auxiliaries*.

Now let's do the same thing for the Fibonacci sequence `fib`. We start with

```
(define fib
  (lambda (n)
    (if (< n 2)
      1
      (+
        (fib (- n 1))
        (fib (- n 2))))))
```

Here we have two recursive calls to `fib`, so we will need an `end-cont`
and two continuation-builders, one for each argument, just as we did for
difference expressions in section 5.1.

```
(define fib
  (lambda (n)
    (fib/k n (end-cont))))

(define fib/k
  (lambda (n cont)
    (if (< n 2)
      (apply-cont cont 1)
      (fib/k (- n 1) (fib1-cont n cont)))))
```

(apply-cont (end-cont) *val*) = *val*

(apply-cont (fib1-cont *n cont*) *val1*)
= (fib/k (- *n* 2) (fib2-cont *val1 cont*))

(apply-cont (fib2-cont *val1 cont*) *val2*)
= (apply-cont *cont* (+ *val1 val2*))

In the procedural representation we have

```
(define end-cont
  (lambda ()
    (lambda (val) val)))

(define fib1-cont
  (lambda (n cont)
    (lambda (val1)
      (fib/k (- n 2) (fib2-cont val1 cont)))))

(define fib2-cont
  (lambda (val1 cont)
    (lambda (val2)
      (apply-cont cont (+ val1 val2)))))

(define apply-cont
  (lambda (cont val)
    (cont val)))
```

If we inline all the uses of these procedures, we get

```
(define fib
  (lambda (n)
    (fib/k n (lambda (val) val))))

(define fib/k
  (lambda (n cont)
    (if (< n 2)
        (cont 1)
        (fib/k (- n 1)
          (lambda (val1)
            (fib/k (- n 2)
              (lambda (val2)
                (cont (+ val1 val2)))))))))
```

As we did for factorial, we can read this definition as

If n < 2, send 1 to the continuation. Otherwise, work on n − 1 in a continuation that calls the result val1 *and then works on n − 2 in a continuation that calls the result* val2 *and then sends* (+ val1 val2) *to the continuation.*

It is easy to see, by the same reasoning we used for fact, that for any *g*, (fib/k *n g*) = (*g* (fib *n*)). Here is an artificial example that extends these ideas.

```
(lambda (x)
  (cond
    ((zero? x) 17)
    ((= x 1) (f x))
    ((= x 2) (+ 22 (f x)))
    ((= x 3) (g 22 (f x)))
    ((= x 4) (+ (f x) 33 (g y)))
    (else (h (f x) (- 44 y) (g y)))))
```

becomes

```
(lambda (x cont)
  (cond
    ((zero? x) (cont 17))
    ((= x 1) (f x cont))
    ((= x 2) (f x (lambda (v1) (cont (+ 22 v1)))))
    ((= x 3) (f x (lambda (v1) (g 22 v1 cont))))
    ((= x 4) (f x (lambda (v1)
                    (g y (lambda (v2)
                           (cont (+ v1 33 v2)))))))
    (else (f x (lambda (v1)
                 (g y (lambda (v2)
                        (h v1 (- 44 y) v2 cont))))))))
```

where the procedures f, g, h, j, and p have been similarly transformed.

- In the (zero? x) line, we return 17 to the continuation.

- In the (= x 1) line, we call f tail-recursively.

- In the (= x 2) line, we call f in an operand position of an addition.

- In the (= x 3) line, we call f in an operand position of a procedure call.

- In the (= x 4) line, we have two procedure calls in operand positions in an addition.

- In the else line, we have two procedure calls in operand position inside another procedure call.

From these examples, we can see a pattern emerging.

The CPS Recipe

To convert a program to continuation-passing style

1. *Pass each procedure an extra parameter (typically* cont *or k).*

2. *Whenever the procedure returns a constant or variable, return that value to the continuation instead, as we did with* (cont 7) *above.*

3. *Whenever a procedure call occurs in a tail position, call the procedure with the same continuation* cont.

4. *Whenever a procedure call occurs in an operand position, evaluate the procedure call in a new continuation that gives a name to the result and continues with the computation.*

These rules are informal, but they illustrate the patterns.

Exercise 6.1 [⋆] Consider figure 6.2 without (set! pc fact/k) in the definition of fact/k and without (set! pc apply-cont) in the definition of apply-cont. Why does the program still work?

Exercise 6.2 [⋆] Prove by induction on n that for any g, (fib/k n g) = (g (fib n)).

Exercise 6.3 [⋆] Rewrite each of the following Scheme expressions in continuation-passing style. Assume that any unknown functions have also been rewritten in CPS.

1. `(lambda (x y) (p (+ 8 x) (q y)))`
2. `(lambda (x y u v) (+ 1 (f (g x y) (+ u v))))`
3. `(+ 1 (f (g x y) (+ u (h v))))`
4. `(zero? (if a (p x) (p y)))`
5. `(zero? (if (f a) (p x) (p y)))`
6. `(let ((x (let ((y 8)) (p y)))) x)`
7. `(let ((x (if a (p x) (p y)))) x)`

Exercise 6.4 [⋆⋆] Rewrite each of the following procedures in continuation-passing style. For each procedure, do this first using a data-structure representation of continuations, then with a procedural representation, and then with the inlined procedural representation. Last, write the registerized version. For each of these four versions, test to see that your implementation is tail-recursive by defining end-cont by

```
(apply-cont (end-cont) val)
= (begin
    (eopl:printf "End of computation.~%")
    (eopl:printf "This sentence should appear only once.~%")
    val)
```

as we did in chapter 5.

1. `remove-first` (section 1.2.3).
2. `list-sum` (section 1.3).
3. `occurs-free?` (section 1.2.4).
4. `subst` (section 1.2.5).

Exercise 6.5 [⋆] When we rewrite an expression in CPS, we choose an evaluation order for the procedure calls in the expression. Rewrite each of the preceding examples in CPS so that all the procedure calls are evaluated from right to left.

Exercise 6.6 [⋆] How many different evaluation orders are possible for the procedure calls in `(lambda (x y) (+ (f (g x)) (h (j y))))`? For each evaluation order, write a CPS expression that calls the procedures in that order.

Exercise 6.7 [⋆⋆] Write out the procedural and the inlined representations for the interpreter in figures 5.4, 5.5, and 5.6.

Exercise 6.8 [★★★] Rewrite the interpreter of section 5.4 using a procedural and inlined representation. This is challenging because we effectively have two observers, `apply-cont` and `apply-handler`. As a hint, consider modifying the recipe on page 6.1 so that we add to each procedure two extra arguments, one representing the behavior of the continuation under `apply-cont` and one representing its behavior under `apply-handler`.

Sometimes we can find clever representations of continuations. Let's reconsider the version of `fact` with the procedural representation of continuations. There we had two continuation builders, which we wrote as

```
(define end-cont
  (lambda ()
    (lambda (val) val)))

(define fact1-cont
  (lambda (n cont)
    (lambda (val) (cont (* n val)))))

(define apply-cont
  (lambda (cont val)
    (cont val)))
```

In this system, all a continuation does is multiply its argument by some number. `(end-cont)` multiplies its argument by 1, and if *cont* multiplies its value by k, then `(fact1` *n cont*`)` multiplies its value by $k * n$.

So every continuation is of the form `(lambda (val) (* ` k ` val))`. This means we could represent such a continuation simply by its lone free variable, the number k. In this representation we would have

```
(define end-cont
  (lambda ()
    1))

(define fact1-cont
  (lambda (n cont)
    (* cont n)))

(define apply-cont
  (lambda (cont val)
    (* cont val)))
```

If we inline these definitions into our original definition of `fact/k`, and use the property that $(* \; cont \; 1) = cont$, we get

```
(define fact
  (lambda (n)
    (fact/k n 1)))

(define fact/k
  (lambda (n cont)
    (if (zero? n)
        cont
        (fact/k (- n 1) (* cont n))))))
```

But this is just the same as `fact-iter` (page 139)! So we see that an accumulator is often just a representation of a continuation. This is impressive. Quite a few classic program optimizations turn out to be instances of this idea.

Exercise 6.9 [⋆] What property of multiplication makes this program optimization possible?

Exercise 6.10 [⋆] For `list-sum`, formulate a succinct representation of the continuations, like the one for `fact/k` above.

6.2   Tail Form

In order to write down a program for converting to continuation-passing style, we need to identify the input and output languages. For our input language, we choose the language LETREC, augmented by having multiargument procedures and multideclaration `letrec` expressions. Its grammar is shown in figure 6.3. We call this language CPS-IN. To distinguish the expressions of this language from those of our output language, we call these *input expressions*.

To define the class of possible outputs from our CPS conversion algorithm, we need to identify a subset of CPS-IN in which procedure calls never build any control context.

Recall our principle from chapter 5:

> **It is evaluation of operands, not the calling of procedures, that makes the control context grow.**

Program ::= *InpExp*
                `a-program (exp1)`

InpExp   ::= *Number*
                `const-exp (num)`

InpExp   ::= `-` `(`*InpExp*`,` *InpExp*`)`
                `diff-exp (exp1 exp2)`

InpExp   ::= `zero?` `(`*InpExp*`)`
                `zero?-exp (exp1)`

InpExp   ::= `if` *InpExp* `then` *InpExp* `else` *InpExp*
                `if-exp (exp1 exp2 exp3)`

InpExp   ::= *Identifier*
                `var-exp (var)`

InpExp   ::= `let` *Identifier* `=` *InpExp* `in` *InpExp*
                `let-exp (var exp1 body)`

InpExp   ::= `letrec` {*Identifier* `(`{*Identifier*}$^{*(,)}$`)` `=` *InpExp*}* `in` *InpExp*
                `letrec-exp (p-names b-varss p-bodies letrec-body)`

InpExp   ::= `proc` `(`{*Identifier*}$^{*(,)}$`)` *InpExp*
                `proc-exp (vars body)`

InpExp   ::= `(`*InpExp* {*InpExp*}*`)`
                `call-exp (rator rands)`

Figure 6.3   Grammar for CPS-IN

Thus in

```
(define fact
  (lambda (n)
    (if (zero? n) 1 (* n (fact (- n 1))))))
```

it is the position of the call to `fact` *as an operand* that requires the creation of a control context. By contrast, in

```
(define fact-iter
  (lambda (n)
    (fact-iter-acc n 1)))

(define fact-iter-acc
  (lambda (n a)
    (if (zero? n) a (fact-iter-acc (- n 1) (* n a)))))
```

none of the procedure calls is in operand position. We say these calls are in *tail position* because their value is the result of the whole call. We refer to them as *tail calls*.

We can also recall the Tail Calls Don't Grow Control Context principle:

Tail Calls Don't Grow Control Context

If the value of exp_1 is returned as the value of exp_2, then exp_1 and exp_2 should run in the same continuation.

We say that an expression is in *tail form* if every procedure call, and every expression containing a procedure call, is in tail position. This condition implies that no procedure call builds control context.

Hence in Scheme

```
(if (zero? x) (f y) (g z))
```

is in tail form, as is

```
(if b
  (if (zero? x) (f y) (g z))
  (h u))
```

but

```
(+
  (if (zero? x) (f y) (g z))
  37)
```

is not in tail form, since the `if` expression, which contains a procedure call, is not in tail position.

In general, we must understand the meaning of a language in order to determine its tail positions. A subexpression in tail position has the property that if it is evaluated, its value immediately becomes the value of the entire

---

```
zero? (O)
- (O, O)
if O then T else T
let Var = O in T
letrec {Var ({Var}*⁽ʼ⁾) = T}* in T
proc ({Var}*⁽ʼ⁾) T
(O O ... O )
```

Figure 6.4 Tail and operand positions in CPS-IN. Tail positions are marked with T. Operand positions are marked with O.

---

expression. An expression may have more than one tail position. For example, an `if` expression may choose either the true or the false branch. For a subexpression in tail position, no information need be saved, and therefore no control context need be built.

The tail positions for CPS-IN are shown in figure 6.4. The value of each subexpression in tail position could become the value of the entire expression. In the continuation-passing interpreter, the subexpressions in operand positions are the ones that require building new continuations. The subexpressions in tail position are evaluated in the same continuation as the original expression, as illustrated on page 152.

We use this distinction to design a target language CPS-OUT for our CPS conversion algorithm. The grammar for this language is shown in figure 6.5. This grammar defines a subset of CPS-IN, but with a different grammar. Its production names always begin with `cps-`, so they will not be confused with the production names in CPS-IN.

The new grammar has two nonterminals, *SimpleExp* and *TfExp*. It is designed so that expressions in *SimpleExp* are guaranteed never to contain any procedure calls, and so that expressions in *TfExp* are guaranteed to be in tail form.

Expressions in *SimpleExp* are guaranteed to never contain any procedure calls, so they correspond roughly to simple straight-line code, and for our purposes we consider them too simple to require any use of the control stack. Simple expressions include `proc` expressions, since a `proc` expression returns immediately with a procedure value, but the body of that procedure must be in tail form.

A continuation-passing interpreter for tail-form expressions is shown in figure 6.6. Since procedures in this language take multiple arguments, we use `extend-env*` from exercise 2.10 to create multiple bindings, and we similarly extend `extend-env-rec` to get `extend-env-rec*`.

In this interpreter, all the recursive calls are in tail position (in Scheme), so running the interpreter builds no control context in Scheme. (This isn't quite true: the procedure `value-of-simple-exp` (exercise 6.11) builds control context in Scheme, but that can be fixed (see exercise 6.18).)

More importantly, the interpreter creates no new continuations. The procedure `value-of/k` takes one continuation argument and passes it unchanged in every recursive call. So we could easily have removed the continuation argument entirely.

Of course, there is no completely general way of determining whether the control behavior of a procedure is iterative or not. Consider

```
(lambda (n)
  (if (strange-predicate? n)
    (fact n)
    (fact-iter n)))
```

This procedure is iterative only if `strange-predicate?` returns false for all sufficiently large values of n. But it is not always possible to determine the truth or falsity of this condition, even if it is possible to examine the code of `strange-predicate?`. Therefore the best we can hope for is to make sure that no procedure call in the program will build up control context, whether or not it is actually executed.

Exercise 6.11 [⋆] Complete the interpreter of figure 6.6 by writing `value-of-simple-exp`.

Exercise 6.12 [⋆] Determine whether each of the following expressions is simple.

1. `-((f -(x,1)),1)`
2. `(f -(-(x,y),1))`
3. `if zero?(x) then -(x,y) else -(-(x,y),1)`
4. `let x = proc (y) (y x) in -(x,3)`
5. `let f = proc (x) x in (f 3)`

Program   ::= *TfExp*
> a-program (exp1)

SimpleExp ::= *Number*
> const-exp (num)

SimpleExp ::= *Identifier*
> var-exp (var)

SimpleExp ::= -(*SimpleExp* , *SimpleExp*)
> cps-diff-exp (simple1 simple2)

SimpleExp ::= zero?(*SimpleExp*)
> cps-zero?-exp (simple1)

SimpleExp ::= proc ({*Identifier*}*) *TfExp*
> cps-proc-exp (vars body)

TfExp   ::= *SimpleExp*
> simple-exp->exp (simple-exp1)

TfExp   ::= let *Identifier* = *SimpleExp* in *TfExp*
> cps-let-exp (var simple1 body)

TfExp   ::= letrec {*Identifier* ({*Identifier*}*$^{(,)}$) = *TfExp*}* in *TfExp*
> cps-letrec-exp (p-names b-varss p-bodies body)

TfExp   ::= if *SimpleExp* then *TfExp* else *TfExp*
> cps-if-exp (simple1 body1 body2)

TfExp   ::= (*SimpleExp* {*SimpleExp*}*)
> cps-call-exp (rator rands)

Figure 6.5   Grammar for CPS-OUT

value-of/k : *TfExp* × *Env* × *Cont* → *FinalAnswer*

```
(define value-of/k
  (lambda (exp env cont)
    (cases tfexp exp
      (simple-exp->exp (simple)
        (apply-cont cont
          (value-of-simple-exp simple env)))
      (let-exp (var rhs body)
        (let ((val (value-of-simple-exp rhs env)))
          (value-of/k body
            (extend-env (list var) (list val) env)
            cont)))
      (letrec-exp (p-names b-varss p-bodies letrec-body)
        (value-of/k letrec-body
          (extend-env-rec** p-names b-varss p-bodies env)
          cont))
      (if-exp (simple1 body1 body2)
        (if (expval->bool (value-of-simple-exp simple1 env))
          (value-of/k body1 env cont)
          (value-of/k body2 env cont)))
      (call-exp (rator rands)
        (let ((rator-proc
               (expval->proc
                 (value-of-simple-exp rator env)))
              (rand-vals
               (map
                 (lambda (simple)
                   (value-of-simple-exp simple env))
                 rands)))
          (apply-procedure/k rator-proc rand-vals cont))))))
```

apply-procedure : *Proc* × *ExpVal* → *ExpVal*

```
(define apply-procedure/k
  (lambda (proc1 args cont)
    (cases proc proc1
      (procedure (vars body saved-env)
        (value-of/k body
          (extend-env* vars args saved-env)
          cont)))))
```

Figure 6.6   Interpreter for tail-form expressions in CPS-OUT.

Exercise 6.13 [*] Translate each of these expressions in CPS-IN into continuation-passing style using the CPS recipe on page 200 above. Test your transformed programs by running them using the interpreter of figure 6.6. Be sure that the original and transformed versions give the same answer on each input.

1. `removeall`.

```
letrec
 removeall(n,s) =
  if null?(s)
  then emptylist
  else if number?(car(s))
        then if equal?(n,car(s))
              then (removeall n cdr(s))
              else cons(car(s),
                        (removeall n cdr(s)))
        else cons((removeall n car(s)),
                  (removeall n cdr(s)))
```

2. `occurs-in?`.

```
letrec
 occurs-in?(n,s) =
  if null?(s)
  then 0
  else if number?(car(s))
        then if equal?(n,car(s))
              then 1
              else (occurs-in? n cdr(s))
        else if (occurs-in? n car(s))
              then 1
              else (occurs-in? n cdr(s))
```

3. `remfirst`. This uses `occurs-in?` from the preceding example.

```
letrec
 remfirst(n,s) =
  letrec
   loop(s) =
    if null?(s)
    then emptylist
    else if number?(car(s))
          then if equal?(n,car(s))
                then cdr(s)
                else cons(car(s),(loop cdr(s)))
          else if (occurs-in? n car(s))
                then cons((remfirst n car(s)),
                          cdr(s))
                else cons(car(s),
                          (remfirst n cdr(s)))
   in (loop s)
```

4. depth.

```
letrec
 depth(s) =
  if null?(s)
  then 1
  else if number?(car(s))
       then (depth cdr(s))
       else if less?(add1((depth car(s))),
                     (depth cdr(s)))
            then (depth cdr(s))
            else add1((depth car(s)))
```

5. depth-with-let.

```
letrec
 depth(s) =
  if null?(s)
  then 1
  else if number?(car(s))
       then (depth cdr(s))
       else let dfirst = add1((depth car(s)))
                drest = (depth cdr(s))
            in if less?(dfirst,drest)
               then drest
               else dfirst
```

6. map.

```
letrec
 map(f, l) = if null?(l)
             then emptylist
             else cons((f car(l)),
                       (map f cdr(l)))
 square(n) = *(n,n)
in (map square list(1,2,3,4,5))
```

7. fnlrgtn. This procedure takes an n-list, like an s-list (page 9), but with numbers instead of symbols, and a number n and returns the first number in the list (in left-to-right order) that is greater than n. Once the result is found, no further elements in the list are examined. For example,

```
(fnlrgtn list(1,list(3,list(2),7,list(9)))
 6)
```

finds 7.

8. `every`. This procedure takes a predicate and a list and returns a true value if and only if the predicate holds for each list element.

```
letrec
 every(pred, l) =
  if null?(l)
  then 1
  else if (pred car(l))
        then (every pred cdr(l))
        else 0
in (every proc(n)greater?(n,5) list(6,7,8,9))
```

Exercise 6.14 [*] Complete the interpreter of figure 6.6 by supplying definitions for `value-of-program` and `apply-cont`.

Exercise 6.15 [*] Observe that in the interpreter of the preceding exercise, there is only one possible value for `cont`. Use this observation to remove the `cont` argument entirely.

Exercise 6.16 [*] Registerize the interpreter of figure 6.6.

Exercise 6.17 [*] Trampoline the interpreter of figure 6.6.

Exercise 6.18 [* *] Modify the grammar of CPS-OUT so that a simple `diff-exp` or `zero?-exp` can have only a constant or variable as an argument. Thus in the resulting language `value-of-simple-exp` can be made nonrecursive.

Exercise 6.19 [* *] Write a Scheme procedure `tail-form?` that takes the syntax tree of a program in CPS-IN, expressed in the grammar of figure 6.3, and determines whether the same string would be in tail form according to the grammar of figure 6.5.

6.3   Converting to Continuation-Passing Style

In this section we develop an algorithm for transforming any program in CPS-IN to CPS-OUT.

Like the continuation-passing interpreter, our translator will *Follow the Grammar*. Also like the continuation-passing interpreter, our translator will take an additional argument that represents a continuation. This additional argument will be a simple expression that represents the continuation.

As we have done in the past, we will proceed from examples to a specification, and from a specification to a program. Figure 6.7 shows a somewhat more detailed version of the motivating examples, written in Scheme so that they will be similar to those of the preceding section.

```
(lambda (x)
  (cond
    ((zero? x) 17)
    ((= x 1) (f (- x 13) 7))
    ((= x 2) (+ 22 (- x 3) x))
    ((= x 3) (+ 22 (f x) 37))
    ((= x 4) (g 22 (f x)))
    ((= x 5) (+ 22 (f x) 33 (g y)))
    (else (h (f x) (- 44 y) (g y)))))))
```

becomes

```
(lambda (x k)
  (cond
    ((zero? x) (k 17))
    ((= x 1) (f (- x 13) 7 k))
    ((= x 2) (k (+ 22 (- x 3) x)))
    ((= x 3) (f x (lambda (v1) (k (+ 22 v1 37)))))
    ((= x 4) (f x (lambda (v1) (g 22 v1 k))))
    ((= x 5) (f x (lambda (v1)
                    (g y (lambda (v2)
                           (k (+ 22 v1 33 v2)))))))
    (else (f x (lambda (v1)
                 (g y (lambda (v2)
                        (h v1 (- 44 y) v2 k))))))))))
```

Figure 6.7   Motivating examples for CPS conversion (in Scheme)

The first case is that of a constant. Constants are just sent to the continuation, as in the (zero? x) line above.

```
(cps-of-exp n K) = (K n)
```

Here *K* is some simple-exp that denotes a continuation.
Similarly, variables are just sent to the continuation.

```
(cps-of-exp var K) = (K var)
```

Of course, the input and output of our algorithm will be abstract syntax trees, so we should have written the builders for the abstract syntax instead of the concrete syntax, like

```
(cps-of-exp (const-exp n) K)
= (make-send-to-cont K (cps-const-exp n))

(cps-of-exp (var-exp var) K)
= (make-send-to-cont K (cps-var-exp var))
```

where

make-send-to-cont : *SimpleExp* × *SimpleExp* → *TfExp*
```
(define make-send-to-cont
  (lambda (k-exp simple-exp)
    (cps-call-exp k-exp (list simple-exp))))
```

We need the `list` since in CPS-OUT every call expression takes a list of operands.

We will, however, continue to use concrete syntax in our specifications because the concrete syntax is generally easier to read.

What about procedures? We convert a procedure, like the `(lambda (x) ...)` in figure 6.7, by adding an additional parameter `k` and converting the body to send its value to the continuation `k`. This is just what we did in figure 6.7. So

```
proc (var₁, ..., varₙ) exp
```

becomes

```
proc (var₁, ..., varₙ, k) (cps-of-exp exp k)
```

as in the figure. However, this doesn't quite finish the job. Our goal was to produce code that would evaluate the `proc` expression and send the result to the continuation *K*. So the entire specification for a `proc` expression is

```
(cps-of-exp <<proc (var₁, ..., varₙ) exp>> K)
= (K <<proc (var₁, ..., varₙ, k) (cps-of-exp exp k)>>)
```

Here `k` is a fresh variable, and *K* is an arbitrary simple expression that denotes a continuation.

What about expressions that have operands? Let us add, for the moment, a sum expression to our language, with arbitrarily many operands. To do this, we add to the grammar of CPS-IN the production

$$Expression ::= + (\{InpExp\}^{*(\,\prime\,)})$$

$$\boxed{\texttt{sum-exp (exps)}}$$

and to the grammar of CPS-OUT the production

$$SimpleExp ::= + (\{SimpleExp\}^{*(\,\prime\,)})$$

$$\boxed{\texttt{cps-sum-exp (simple-exps)}}$$

This new production preserves the property that no procedure call ever appears inside a simple expression.

What are the possibilities for $(\texttt{cps-of-exp} \ll + (exp_1, \ldots, exp_n) \gg K)$? It could be that all of $exp_1, \ldots, exp_n$ are simple, as in the $(=\ \texttt{x}\ 2)$ case in figure 6.7. Then the entire sum expression is simple, and we can just pass it to the continuation. We let *simp* denote a simple expression. In this case we can say

```
(cps-of-exp <<+ (simp₁, ..., simpₙ) >> K)
= (K + (simp₁, ..., simpₙ))
```

What if one of the operands is nonsimple? Then we need to evaluate it in a continuation that gives a name to its value and proceeds with the sum, as in the $(=\ \texttt{x}\ 3)$ case above. There the second operand is the first nonsimple one. Then our CPS converter should have the property that

```
(cps-of-exp <<+ (simp₁, exp₂, simp₃, ..., simpₙ) >> K)
= (cps-of-exp exp₂
      <<proc (var₂) (K + (simp₁, var₂, simp₃, ..., simpₙ)) >>
```

If exp_2 is just a procedure call, then the output will look like the one in the figure. But exp_2 might be more complicated, so we recur, calling `cps-of-exp` on exp_2 and the larger continuation

```
proc (var₂) (K + (simp₁, var₂, simp₃, ..., simpₙ))
```

There might, however, be other nonsimple operands in the sum expression, as there are in the (= x 5) case. So instead of simply using the continuation

$$\texttt{proc}\ (\mathit{var}_2)\ (K\ \texttt{+}(\mathit{simp}_1,\ \mathit{var}_2,\ \mathit{simp}_3,\ \ldots,\ \mathit{simp}_n))$$

we need to recur on the later arguments as well. We can summarize this rule as

```
(cps-of-exp <<+(simp₁, exp₂, exp₃, ..., expₙ)>> K)
= (cps-of-exp exp₂
    <<proc (var₂)
        (cps-of-exp <<+(simp₁, var₂, exp₃, ..., expₙ)>> K))
```

Each of the recursive calls to cps-of-exp is guaranteed to terminate. The first call terminates because exp_2 is smaller than the original expression. The second call terminates because its argument is also smaller than the original: var_2 is always smaller than exp_2.

For example, looking at the (= x 5) line and using the syntax of CPS-IN, we have

```
(cps-of-exp <<+((f x), 33, (g y))>> K)
= (cps-of-exp <<(f x)>>
    <<proc (v1)
        (cps-of-exp +(v1, 33, (g y)) K)>>)
= (cps-of-exp <<(f x)>>
    <<proc (v1)
        (cps-of-exp <<(g y)>>
            <<proc (v2)
                (cps-of-exp <<+(v1, 33, v2)>> K)))
= (cps-of-exp <<(f x)>>
    <<proc (v1)
        (cps-of-exp <<(g y)>>
            <<proc (v2)
                (K <<+(v1, 33, v2)>>)))
= (f x
    proc (v1)
    (g y
     proc (v2)
      (K +(v1, 33, v2)))))
```

Procedure calls work the same way. If both the operator and all the operands are simple, then we just call the procedure with a continuation argument, as in the $(=\ x\ 2)$ line.

```
(cps-of-exp << (simp₀ simp₁ ... simpₙ) >> K)
= (simp₀ simp₁ ... simpₙ K)
```

If, on the other hand, one of the operands is nonsimple, then we must cause it to be evaluated first, as in the $(=\ x\ 4)$ line.

```
(cps-of-exp << (simp₀ simp₁ exp₂ exp₃ ... expₙ) >> K)
= (cps-of-exp exp₂
     <<proc (var₂)
         (cps-of-exp << (simp₀ simp₁ var₂ exp₃ ... expₙ) >> K) >>)
```

And, as before, the second call to cps-of-exp will recur down the procedure call, calling cps-of-exp for each of the nonsimple arguments, until there are only simple arguments left.

Here is how these rules handle the $(=\ x\ 5)$ example, written in CPS-IN.

```
(cps-of-exp << (h (f x) -(44,y) (g y)) >> K)
= (cps-of-exp << (f x) >>
    <<proc (v1)
        (cps-of-exp << (h v1 -(44,y) (g y)) >> K) >>)
= (f x
   proc (v1)
     (cps-of-exp << (h v1 -(44,y) (g y)) >> K) >>)
= (f x
   proc (v1)
     (cps-of-exp << (g y) >>
      <<proc (v2)
          (cps-of-exp << (h v1 -(44,y) v2) >> K)))
= (f x
   proc (v1)
     (g y
      proc (v2)
        (cps-of-exp << (h v1 -(44,y) v2) >> K)))
= (f x
   proc (v1)
     (g y
      proc (v2)
        (h v1 -(44,y) v2 K)))
```

The specifications for sum expressions and procedure calls follow a similar pattern: they find the first nonsimple operand and recur on that operand

and on the modified list of operands. This works for any expression that evaluates its operands. If `complex-exp` is some CPS-IN expression that evaluates its operands, then we should have

```
(cps-of-exp (complex-exp simp₀ simp₁ exp₂ exp₃ ... expₙ) K)
= (cps-of-exp exp₂
    <<proc (var₂)
      (cps-of-exp
        (complex-exp simp₀ simp₁ var₂ exp₃ ... expₙ)
        K)>>)
```

where var_2 is a fresh variable.

The only time that the treatment of sum expressions and procedure calls differs is when the arguments are all simple. In that case, we need to convert each of the arguments to a CPS-OUT `simple-exp` and produce a tail-form expression with the results.

We can encapsulate this behavior into the procedure `cps-of-exps`, shown in figure 6.8. Its arguments are a list of input expressions and a procedure `builder`. It finds the position of the first nonsimple expression in the list, using the procedure `list-index` from exercise 1.23. If there is such a nonsimple expression, then it is converted in a continuation that gives the value a name (the identifier bound to `var`) and recurs down the modified list of expressions.

If there are no nonsimple expressions, then we would like to apply `builder` to the list of expressions. However, although these expressions are simple, they are still in the grammar of CPS-IN. Therefore we convert each expression to the grammar of CPS-OUT using the procedure `cps-of-simple-exp`. We then send the list of *SimpleExp*s to `builder`. (`list-set` is described in exercise 1.19.)

The procedure `inp-exp-simple?` takes an expression in CPS-IN and determines whether its string would be parseable as a *SimpleExp*. It uses the procedure `every?` from exercise 1.24. The expression (`every?` *pred lst*) returns #t if every element of *lst* satisfies *pred*, and returns #f otherwise.

The code for `cps-of-simple-exp` is straightforward and is shown in figure 6.9. It also translates the body of a `proc-exp` into CPS, which is necessary for the output to be a *SimpleExp*.

We can generate tail-form expressions for sum expressions and procedure calls using `cps-of-exps`.

cps-of-exps : *Listof(InpExp)* × (*Listof(InpExp)* → *TfExp*) → *TfExp*
```
(define cps-of-exps
  (lambda (exps builder)
    (let cps-of-rest ((exps exps))
```
  cps-of-rest : *Listof(InpExp)* → *TfExp*
```
      (let ((pos (list-index
                   (lambda (exp)
                     (not (inp-exp-simple? exp)))
                   exps)))
        (if (not pos)
          (builder (map cps-of-simple-exp exps))
          (let ((var (fresh-identifier 'var)))
            (cps-of-exp
              (list-ref exps pos)
              (cps-proc-exp (list var)
                (cps-of-rest
                  (list-set exps pos (var-exp var)))))))))))
```

inp-exp-simple? : *InpExp* → *Bool*
```
(define inp-exp-simple?
  (lambda (exp)
    (cases expression exp
      (const-exp (num) #t)
      (var-exp (var) #t)
      (diff-exp (exp1 exp2)
        (and (inp-exp-simple? exp1) (inp-exp-simple? exp2)))
      (zero?-exp (exp1) (inp-exp-simple? exp1))
      (proc-exp (ids exp) #t)
      (sum-exp (exps) (every? inp-exp-simple? exps))
      (else #f))))
```

Figure 6.8   `cps-of-exps`

---

cps-of-diff-exp : *Listof(InpExp)* × *SimpleExp* → *TfExp*
```
(define cps-of-sum-exp
  (lambda (exps k-exp)
    (cps-of-exps exps
      (lambda (simples)
        (make-send-to-cont
          k-exp
          (cps-sum-exp simples))))))
```

```
cps-of-simple-exp  : InpExp  →  SimpleExp
usage:  assumes (inp-exp-simple? exp).
(define cps-of-simple-exp
  (lambda (exp)
    (cases expression exp
      (const-exp (num) (cps-const-exp num))
      (var-exp (var) (cps-var-exp var))
      (diff-exp (exp1 exp2)
        (cps-diff-exp
          (cps-of-simple-exp exp1)
          (cps-of-simple-exp exp2)))
      (zero?-exp (exp1)
        (cps-zero?-exp (cps-of-simple-exp exp1)))
      (proc-exp (ids exp)
        (cps-proc-exp (append ids (list 'k%00))
          (cps-of-exp exp (cps-var-exp 'k%00))))
      (sum-exp (exps)
        (cps-sum-exp (map cps-of-simple-exp exps)))
      (else
        (report-invalid-exp-to-cps-of-simple-exp exp)))))
```

Figure 6.9 cps-of-simple-exp

cps-of-call-exp : InpExp × Listof(InpExp) × SimpleExp → TfExp
```
(define cps-of-call-exp
  (lambda (rator rands k-exp)
    (cps-of-exps (cons rator rands)
      (lambda (simples)
        (cps-call-exp
          (car simples)
          (append (cdr simples) (list k-exp)))))))
```

We can now write the rest of our CPS translator (figures 6.10–6.12). It *Follows the Grammar*. When the expression is always simple, as for constants, variables, and procedures, we generate the code immediately using make-send-to-cont. Otherwise, we call an auxiliary procedure. Each auxiliary procedure calls cps-of-exps to evaluate its subexpressions, supplying an appropriate builder to construct the innermost portion of the CPS output. The one exception is cps-of-letrec-exp, which has no immediate subexpressions, so it generates the CPS output directly. Finally, we translate a program by calling cps-of-exps on the whole program, with a builder that just returns the value of the simple.

For the following exercises, make sure that your output expressions are in tail form by running them using the grammar and interpreter for CPS-OUT.

Exercise 6.20 [⋆] Our procedure `cps-of-exps` causes subexpressions to be evaluated from left to right. Modify `cps-of-exps` so that subexpressions are evaluated from right to left.

Exercise 6.21 [⋆] Modify `cps-of-call-exp` so that the operands are evaluated from left to right, followed by the operator.

Exercise 6.22 [⋆] Sometimes, when we generate (K *simp*), K is already a `proc-exp`. So instead of generating

```
(proc (var₁) ... simp)
```

we could generate

```
let var₁ = simp
in ...
```

This leads to CPS code with the property that it never contains a subexpression of the form

```
(proc (var) exp₁
 simp)
```

unless that subexpression was in the original expression.

Modify `make-send-to-cont` to generate this better code. When does the new rule apply?

Exercise 6.23 [⋆ ⋆] Observe that our rule for `if` makes two copies of the continuation K, so in a nested `if` the size of the transformed program can grow exponentially. Run an example to confirm this observation. Then show how this may be avoided by changing the transformation to bind a fresh variable to K.

Exercise 6.24 [⋆ ⋆] Add lists to the language (exercise 3.10). Remember that the arguments to a list are not in tail position.

Exercise 6.25 [⋆ ⋆] Extend CPS-IN so that a `let` expression can declare an arbitrary number of variables (exercise 3.16).

Exercise 6.26 [⋆ ⋆] A continuation variable introduced by `cps-of-exps` will only occur once in the continuation. Modify `make-send-to-cont` so that instead of generating

```
let var₁ = simp₁
in T
```

as in exercise 6.22, it generates $T[simp_1/var_1]$, where the notation $E_1[E_2/var]$ means expression E_1 with every free occurrence of the variable *var* replaced by E_2.

cps-of-exp : *InpExp* × *SimpleExp* → *TfExp*
```
(define cps-of-exp
  (lambda (exp k-exp)
    (cases expression exp
      (const-exp (num)
        (make-send-to-cont k-exp (cps-const-exp num)))
      (var-exp (var)
        (make-send-to-cont k-exp (cps-var-exp var)))
      (proc-exp (vars body)
        (make-send-to-cont k-exp
          (cps-proc-exp (append vars (list 'k%00))
            (cps-of-exp body (cps-var-exp 'k%00)))))
      (zero?-exp (exp1)
        (cps-of-zero?-exp exp1 k-exp))
      (diff-exp (exp1 exp2)
        (cps-of-diff-exp exp1 exp2 k-exp))
      (sum-exp (exps)
        (cps-of-sum-exp exps k-exp))
      (if-exp (exp1 exp2 exp3)
        (cps-of-if-exp exp1 exp2 exp3 k-exp))
      (let-exp (var exp1 body)
        (cps-of-let-exp var exp1 body k-exp))
      (letrec-exp (p-names b-varss p-bodies letrec-body)
        (cps-of-letrec-exp
          p-names b-varss p-bodies letrec-body k-exp))
      (call-exp (rator rands)
        (cps-of-call-exp rator rands k-exp)))))
```

cps-of-zero?-exp : *InpExp* × *SimpleExp* → *TfExp*
```
(define cps-of-zero?-exp
  (lambda (exp1 k-exp)
    (cps-of-exps (list exp1)
      (lambda (simples)
        (make-send-to-cont
          k-exp
          (cps-zero?-exp
            (car simples)))))))
```

Figure 6.10 cps-of-exp, part 1

cps-of-diff-exp : *InpExp* × *InpExp* × *SimpleExp* → *TfExp*
```
(define cps-of-diff-exp
  (lambda (exp1 exp2 k-exp)
    (cps-of-exps
      (list exp1 exp2)
      (lambda (simples)
        (make-send-to-cont
          k-exp
          (cps-diff-exp
            (car simples)
            (cadr simples)))))))
```

cps-of-if-exp : *InpExp* × *InpExp* × *InpExp* × *SimpleExp* → *TfExp*
```
(define cps-of-if-exp
  (lambda (exp1 exp2 exp3 k-exp)
    (cps-of-exps (list exp1)
      (lambda (simples)
        (cps-if-exp (car simples)
          (cps-of-exp exp2 k-exp)
          (cps-of-exp exp3 k-exp))))))
```

cps-of-let-exp : *Var* × *InpExp* × *InpExp* × *SimpleExp* → *TfExp*
```
(define cps-of-let-exp
  (lambda (id rhs body k-exp)
    (cps-of-exps (list rhs)
      (lambda (simples)
        (cps-let-exp id
          (car simples)
          (cps-of-exp body k-exp))))))
```

cps-of-letrec-exp :
Listof(Var) × *Listof(Listof(Var))* × *Listof(InpExp)* × *SimpleExp* → *TfExp*
```
(define cps-of-letrec-exp
  (lambda (p-names b-varss p-bodies letrec-body k-exp)
    (cps-letrec-exp
      p-names
      (map
        (lambda (b-vars) (append b-vars (list 'k%00)))
        b-varss)
      (map
        (lambda (p-body)
          (cps-of-exp p-body (cps-var-exp 'k%00)))
        p-bodies)
      (cps-of-exp letrec-body k-exp))))
```

Figure 6.11   `cps-of-exp`, part 2

```
cps-of-program : InpExp → TfExp
(define cps-of-program
  (lambda (pgm)
    (cases program pgm
      (a-program (exp1)
        (cps-a-program
          (cps-of-exps (list exp1)
            (lambda (new-args)
              (simple-exp->exp (car new-args)))))))))
```

Figure 6.12   cps-of-program

Exercise 6.27 [★★] As it stands, `cps-of-let-exp` will generate a useless `let` expression. (Why?) Modify this procedure so that the continuation variable is the same as the `let` variable. Then if exp_1 is nonsimple,

```
(cps-of-exp <<let var₁ = exp₁ in exp₂>> K)
= (cps-of-exp exp₁ <<proc (var₁) (cps-of-exp exp₂ K)>>
```

Exercise 6.28 [★] Food for thought: imagine a CPS transformer for Scheme programs, and imagine that you apply it to the first interpreter from chapter 3. What would the result look like?

Exercise 6.29 [★★] Consider this variant of `cps-of-exps`.

```
(define cps-of-exps
  (lambda (exps builder)
    (let cps-of-rest ((exps exps) (acc '()))
      cps-of-rest : Listof(InpExp) × Listof(SimpleExp) → TfExp
      (cond
        ((null? exps) (builder (reverse acc)))
        ((inp-exp-simple? (car exps))
         (cps-of-rest (cdr exps)
           (cons
             (cps-of-simple-exp (car exps))
             acc)))
        (else
         (let ((var (fresh-identifier 'var)))
           (cps-of-exp (car exps)
             (cps-proc-exp (list var)
               (cps-of-rest (cdr exps)
                 (cons
                   (cps-of-simple-exp (var-exp var))
                   acc)))))))))))
```

Why is this variant of `cps-of-exp` more efficient than the one in figure 6.8?

Exercise 6.30 [⋆⋆] A call to `cps-of-exps` with a list of expressions of length one can be simplified as follows:

```
(cps-of-exps (list exp) builder)
= (cps-of-exp/ctx exp (lambda (simp) (builder (list simp))))
```

where

```
cps-of-exp/ctx : InpExp × (SimpleExp → TfExp) → TfExp
(define cps-of-exp/ctx
  (lambda (exp context)
    (if (inp-exp-simple? exp)
      (context (cps-of-simple-exp exp))
      (let ((var (fresh-identifier 'var)))
        (cps-of-exp exp
          (cps-proc-exp (list var)
            (context (cps-var-exp var)))))))))
```

Thus, we can simplify occurrences of `(cps-of-exps (list ...))`, since the number of arguments to list is known. Therefore the definition of, for example, `cps-of-diff-exp` could be defined with `cps-of-exp/ctx` instead of with `cps-of-exps`.

```
(define cps-of-diff-exp
  (lambda (exp1 exp2 k-exp)
    (cps-of-exp/ctx exp1
      (lambda (simp1)
        (cps-of-exp/ctx exp2
          (lambda (simp2)
            (make-send-to-cont k-exp
              (cps-diff-exp simp1 simp2))))))))
```

For the use of `cps-of-exps` in `cps-of-call-exp`, we can use `cps-of-exp/ctx` on the `rator`, but we still need `cps-of-exps` for the `rands`. Remove all other occurrences of `cps-of-exps` from the translator.

Exercise 6.31 [⋆⋆⋆] Write a translator that takes the output of `cps-of-program` and produces an equivalent program in which all the continuations are represented by data structures, as in chapter 5. Represent data structures like those constructed using `define-datatype` as lists. Since our language does not have symbols, you can use an integer tag in the car position to distinguish the variants of a data type.

Exercise 6.32 [⋆⋆⋆] Write a translator like the one in exercise 6.31, except that it represents all procedures by data structures.

Exercise 6.33 [⋆⋆⋆] Write a translator that takes the output from exercise 6.32 and converts it to a register program like the one in figure 6.1.

Exercise 6.34 [★★] When we convert a program to CPS, we do more than produce a program in which the control contexts become explicit. We also choose the exact order in which the operations are done, and choose names for each intermediate result. The latter is called *sequentialization*. If we don't care about obtaining iterative behavior, we can sequentialize a program by converting it to *A-normal form* or *ANF*. Here's an example of a program in ANF.

```
(define fib/anf
  (lambda (n)
    (if (< n 2)
      1
      (let ((val1 (fib/anf (- n 1))))
        (let ((val2 (fib/anf (- n 2))))
          (+ val1 val2))))))
```

Whereas a program in CPS sequentializes computation by passing continuations that name intermediate results, a program in ANF sequentializes computation by using `let` expressions that name all of the intermediate results.

Retarget `cps-of-exp` so that it generates programs in ANF instead of CPS. (For conditional expressions occurring in nontail position, use the ideas in exercise 6.23.) Then, show that applying the revised `cps-of-exp` to, e.g., the definition of `fib` yields the definition of `fib/anf`. Finally, show that given an input program which is already in ANF, your translator produces the same program except for the names of bound variables.

Exercise 6.35 [★] Verify on a few examples that if the optimization of exercise 6.27 is installed, CPS-transforming the output of your ANF transformer (exercise 6.34) on a program yields the same result as CPS-transforming the program.

6.4 Modeling Computational Effects

Another important use of CPS is to provide a model in which computational effects can be made explicit. A computational effect is an effect like printing or assigning to a variable, which is difficult to model using equational reasoning of the sort used in chapter 3. By transforming to CPS, we can make these effects explicit, just as we did with nonlocal control flow in chapter 5.

In using CPS to model effects, our basic principle is that a simple expression should have no effects. This principle underlies our rule that a simple expression should have no procedure calls, since a procedure call could fail to terminate (which is certainly an effect!).

In this section we study three effects: printing, a store (using the explicit-reference model), and nonstandard control flow.

Let us first consider printing. Printing certainly has an effect:

```
(f print(3) print(4))
```

and

```
(f 1 1)
```

have different effects, even though they return the same answer. The effect also depends on the order of evaluation of arguments; up to now our languages have always evaluated their arguments from left to right, but other languages might not do so.

We can model these considerations by modifying our CPS transformation in the following ways:

- We add to CPS-IN a print expression

$$InpExp ::= \texttt{print} \quad (InpExp)$$
$$\boxed{\texttt{print-exp (exp1)}}$$

  We have not written an interpreter for CPS-IN, but the interpreter would have to be extended so that a print-exp prints the value of its argument and returns some value (which we arbitrarily choose to be 38).

- We add to CPS-OUT a printk expression

$$TfExp ::= \texttt{printk} \quad (SimpleExp) \quad ; \quad TfExp$$
$$\boxed{\texttt{cps-printk-exp (simple-exp1 body)}}$$

  The expression printk (*simp*) ; *exp* has an effect: it prints. Therefore it must be a *TfExp*, not a *SimpleExp*, and can appear only in tail position. The value of *exp* becomes the value of the entire printk expression, so *exp* is itself in tail position and can be a tfexp. Thus we might write bits of code like

```
proc (v1)
 printk(-(v1,1));
 (f v1 K)
```

To implement this, we add to the interpreter for CPS-OUT the line

```
(printk-exp (simple body)
  (begin
    (eopl:printf "~s~%"
      (value-of-simple-exp simple env))
    (value-of/k body env cont)))
```

- We add to cps-of-exp a line that translates from a print expression to
  a printk expression. We have arbitrarily decided to have print expression return the value 38. So our translation should be

$$(\text{cps-of-exp } \langle\langle\text{print}\,(simp_1)\rangle\rangle\ K)\ =\ \text{printk}\,(simp_1);\ (K\ 38))$$

and we use cps-of-exps to take care of the possibility that the argument
to print is nonsimple. This gets us to a new line in cps-of-exp that
says:

```
(print-exp (rator)
  (cps-of-exps (list rator)
    (lambda (simples)
      (cps-printk-exp
        (car simples)
        (make-send-to-cont k-exp
          (cps-const-exp 38))))))
```

Let us watch this work on a larger example.

```
(cps-of-exp <<(f print((g x)) print(4))>> K)
= (cps-of-exp <<print((g x))>>
    <<proc (v1)
        (cps-of-exp <<(f v1 print(4))>> K)>>)
= (cps-of-exp <<(g x)>>
    <<proc (v2)
        (cps-of-exp <<(print v2)>>
          <<proc (v1)
              (cps-of-exp <<(f v1 print(4))>> K)>>)>>)
= (g x
    proc (v2)
     (cps-of-exp <<(print v2)>>
       <<proc (v1)
           (cps-of-exp <<(f v1 print(4))>> K)))
= (g x
    proc (v2)
     printk(v2);
     let v1 = 38
     in (cps-of-exp <<(f v1 print(4)>> K)))
```

```
= (g x
   proc (v2)
   printk(v2);
   let v1 = 38
   in (cps-of-exp <<print(4)>>
            <<proc (v3)
                (cps-of-exp <<(f v1 v3)>> K)>>))
= (g x
   proc (v2)
   printk(v2);
   let v1 = 38
   in printk(4);
      let v3 = 38
      in (cps-of-exp <<(f v1 v3)>> K))
= (g x
   proc (v2)
   printk(v2);
   let v1 = 38
   in printk(4);
      let v3 = 38
      in (f v1 v3 K))
```

Here, we call g in a continuation that names the result v2. The continuation prints the value of v2 and sends 38 to the next continuation, which binds v1 to its argument 38, prints 4 and then calls the next continuation, which binds v3 to its argument (also 38) and then calls f with v1, v3, and *K*. In this way the sequencing of the different printing actions becomes explicit.

To model explicit references (section 4.2), we go through the same steps: we add new syntax to CPS-IN and CPS-OUT, write new interpreter lines to interpret the new syntax in CPS-OUT, and add new lines to cps-of-exp to translate the new syntax from CPS-IN to CPS-OUT. For explicit references, we will need to add syntax for reference creation, dereference, and assignment.

- We add to CPS-IN the syntax

$$InpExp ::= \texttt{newref} \ (InpExp)$$
$$\boxed{\texttt{newref-exp (exp1)}}$$

$$InpExp ::= \texttt{deref} \ (InpExp)$$
$$\boxed{\texttt{deref-exp (exp1)}}$$

$$InpExp ::= \texttt{setref} \ (InpExp \ , \ InpExp)$$
$$\boxed{\texttt{setref-exp (exp1 exp2)}}$$

- We add to CPS-OUT the syntax

$$TfExp ::= \mathtt{newrefk} \ (simple\text{-}exp \ , \ simple\text{-}exp)$$
> ```
> cps-newrefk-exp (simple1 simple2)
> ```

$$TfExp ::= \mathtt{derefk} \ (simple\text{-}exp \ , \ simple\text{-}exp)$$
> ```
> cps-derefk-exp (simple1 simple2)
> ```

$$TfExp ::= \mathtt{setrefk} \ (simple\text{-}exp \ , \ simple\text{-}exp) \ ; \ TfExp$$
> ```
> cps-setrefk-exp (simple1 simple2 body)
> ```

A `newrefk` expression takes two arguments: the value to be placed in the newly allocated cell, and a continuation to receive a reference to the new location. `derefk` behaves similarly. Since `setref` is normally executed for effect only, the design of `setrefk` follows that of `printk`. It assigns the value of the second argument to the value of the first argument, which should be a reference, and then executes the third argument tail-recursively.

In this language we would write

```
newrefk(33, proc (loc1)
            newrefk(44, proc (loc2)
                        setrefk(loc1,22);
                        derefk(loc1, proc (val)
                                     -(val,1)))))
```

This program allocates a new location containing 33, and binds `loc1` to that location. It then allocates a new location containing 44, and binds `loc2` to that location. It then sets the contents of location `loc1` to 22. Finally, it dereferences `loc1`, binds the result (which should be 22) to `val`, and returns the value of `-(val,1)`, yielding 21.

To get this behavior, we add these lines to the interpreter for CPS-OUT.

```
(cps-newrefk-exp (simple1 simple2)
  (let ((val1 (value-of-simple-exp simple1 env))
        (val2 (value-of-simple-exp simple2 env)))
    (let ((newval (ref-val (newref val1))))
      (apply-procedure
        (expval->proc val2)
        (list newval)
        k-exp))))
```

```
(cps-derefk-exp (simple1 simple2)
  (apply-procedure
    (expval->proc (value-of-simple-exp simple2 env))
    (list
      (deref
        (expval->ref
          (value-of-simple-exp simple1 env))))
    k-exp))

(cps-setrefk-exp (simple1 simple2 body)
  (let ((ref (expval->ref
                (value-of-simple-exp simple1 env)))
        (val (value-of-simple-exp simple2 env)))
    (begin
      (setref! ref val)
      (value-of/k body env k-exp))))
```

- Finally, we add these lines to `cps-of-exp` to implement the translation.

```
(newref-exp (exp1)
  (cps-of-exps (list exp1)
    (lambda (simples)
      (cps-newrefk-exp (car simples) k-exp))))

(deref-exp (exp1)
  (cps-of-exps (list exp1)
    (lambda (simples)
      (cps-derefk-exp (car simples) k-exp))))

(setref-exp (exp1 exp2)
  (cps-of-exps (list exp1 exp2)
    (lambda (simples)
      (cps-setrefk-exp
        (car simples)
        (cadr simples)
        (make-send-to-cont k-exp
          (cps-const-exp 23))))))
```

In the last line, we make it appear that a `setref` returns the value of 23, just like in EXPLICIT-REFS.

Exercise 6.36 [★★] Add a `begin` expression (exercise 4.4) to CPS-IN. You should not need to add anything to CPS-OUT.

Exercise 6.37 [★★★] Add implicit references (section 4.3) to CPS-IN. Use the same version of CPS-OUT, with explicit references, and make sure your translator inserts allocation and dereference where necessary. As a hint, recall that in the presence of implicit references, a `var-exp` is no longer simple, since it reads from the store.

Exercise 6.38 [★ ★ ★] If a variable never appears on the left-hand side of a set expression, then it is immutable, and could be treated as simple. Extend your solution to the preceding exercise so that all such variables are treated as simple.

Finally, we come to nonlocal control flow. Let's consider letcc from exercise 5.42. A letcc expression letcc *var* in *body* binds the current continuation to the variable *var*. This binding is in scope in *body*. The only operation on continuations is throw. We use the syntax throw *Expression* to *Expression*, which evaluates the two subexpressions. The second expression should return a continuation, which is applied to the value of the first expression. The current continuation of the throw expression is ignored.

We first analyze these expressions according to the paradigm of this chapter. These expressions are never simple. The body part of a letcc is a tail position, since its value is the value of the entire expression. Since both positions in a throw are evaluated, and neither is the value of the throw (indeed, the throw has no value, since it never returns to its immediate continuation), they are both operand positions.

We can now sketch the rules for converting these two expressions.

```
(cps-of-exp <<letcc var in body>> K)
= let var = K
  in (cps-of-exp body var)

(cps-of-exp <<throw simp₁ to simp₂>> K)
= (simp₂ simp₁)
```

We will use cps-of-exps, as usual, to deal with the possibility that the arguments to throw are nonsimple. Here *K* is ignored, as desired.

For this example we do not have to add any syntax to CPS-OUT, since we are just manipulating control structure.

Exercise 6.39 [★] Implement letcc and throw in the CPS translator.

Exercise 6.40 [★ ★] Implement try/catch and throw from section 5.4 by adding them to the CPS translator. You should not need to add anything to CPS-OUT. Instead, modify cps-of-exp to take two continuations: a success continuation and an error continuation.

7 *Types*

We've seen how we can use interpreters to model the run-time behavior of programs. Now we'd like to use the same technology to *analyze* or *predict* the behavior of programs without running them.

We've already seen some of this: our lexical-address translator predicts at analysis time where in the environment each variable will be found at run time. Further, the actual translator looked like an interpreter, except that instead of passing around an environment, we passed around a static environment.

Our goal is to analyze a program to predict whether evaluation of a program is *safe*, that is, whether the evaluation will proceed without certain kinds of errors. Exactly what is meant by safety, however, may vary from language to language. If we can guarantee that evaluation is safe, we will be sure that the program satisfies its contract.

In this chapter, we will consider languages that are similar to LETREC in chapter 3. For these languages we say that an evaluation is *safe* if and only if:

1. For every evaluation of a variable *var*, the variable is bound.

2. For every evaluation of a difference expression (diff-exp exp_1 exp_2), the values of exp_1 and exp_2 are both num-vals.

3. For every evaluation of an expression of the form (zero?-exp exp_1), the value of exp_1 is a num-val.

4. For every evaluation of a conditional expression (if-exp exp_1 exp_2 exp_3), the value of exp_1 is a bool-val.

5. For every evaluation of a procedure call (call-exp *rator rand*), the value of *rator* is a proc-val.

These conditions assert that each operator is performed only on operands of the correct type. We therefore call violations of these conditions *type errors*.

A safe evaluation may still fail for other reasons: division by zero, taking the `car` of an empty list, etc. We do not include these as part of our definition of safety because predicting safety for these conditions is much harder than guaranteeing the conditions listed above. Similarly, a safe evaluation may run infinitely. We do not include nontermination as part of safety because checking for termination is also very difficult (indeed, it is undecidable in general). Some languages have type systems that guarantee conditions stronger than the ones above, but those are more complex than the ones we consider here.

Our goal is to write a procedure that looks at the program text and either accepts or rejects it. Furthermore, we would like our analysis procedure to be conservative: if the analysis accepts the program, then we can be sure evaluation of the program will be safe. If the analysis cannot be sure that evaluation will be safe, it must reject the program. In this case, we say that the analysis is *sound*.

An analysis that rejected every program would still be sound, so we also want our analysis to accept a large set of programs. The analyses in this chapter will accept enough programs to be useful.

Here are some examples of programs that should be rejected or accepted by our analysis:

```
if 3 then 88 else 99          reject: non-boolean test
proc (x) (3 x)                reject: non-proc-val rator
proc (x) (x 3)                accept
proc (f) proc (x) (f x)       accept
let x = 4 in (x 3)            reject: non-proc-val rator

(proc (x) (x 3)               reject: same as preceding example
 4)

let x = zero?(0)              reject: non-integer argument to a diff-exp
in -(3, x)

(proc (x) -(3,x)              reject: same as preceding example
 zero?(0))

let f = 3
in proc (x) (f x)             reject: non-proc-val rator

(proc (f) proc (x) (f x)      reject: same as preceding example
 3)

letrec f(x) = (f -(x,-1))     accept nonterminating but safe
in (f 1)
```

Although the evaluation of the last example does not terminate, the evaluation is safe by the definition given above, so our analysis is permitted to accept it. As it turns out, our analysis will accept it, because the analysis is not fine enough to determine that this program does not halt.

7.1 Values and Their Types

Since the safety conditions talk only about num-val, bool-val, and proc-val, one might think that it would be enough to keep track of these three types. But that is not enough: if all we know is that f is bound to a proc-val, then we can not draw any conclusions whatsoever about the value of (f 1). From this argument, we learn that we need to keep track of finer information about procedures. This finer information is called the *type structure* of the language.

Our languages will have a very simple type structure. For the moment, consider the expressed values of LETREC. These values include only one-argument procedures, but dealing with multiargument procedures, as in exercise 3.33, is straightforward: it requires some additional work but does not require any new ideas.

Grammar for Types

Type ::= int

$\quad$ int-type ()

Type ::= bool

$\quad$ bool-type ()

Type ::= (*Type* -> *Type*)

$\quad$ proc-type (arg-type result-type)

To see how this type system works, let's look at some examples.

Examples of values and their types

The value of 3 has type `int`.

The value of `-(33,22)` has type `int`.

The value of `zero?(11)` has type `bool`.

The value of `proc (x) -(x,11)` has type `(int -> int)` since, when given an integer, it returns an integer.

The value of `proc (x) let y = -(x,11) in -(x,y)`
has type `(int -> int)`, since when given an integer, it returns an integer.

The value of `proc (x) if x then 11 else 22`
has type `(bool -> int)`, since when given a boolean, it returns an integer.

The value of `proc (x) if x then 11 else zero?(11)` has no type in our type system, since when given a boolean it might return either an integer or a boolean, and we have no type that describes this behavior.

The value of `proc (x) proc (y) if y then x else 11`
has type `(int -> (bool -> int))`, since when given a boolean, it returns a procedure from booleans to integers.

The value of `proc (f) if (f 3) then 11 else 22`
has type `((int -> bool) -> int)`, since when given a procedure from integers to booleans, it returns an integer.

The value of `proc (f) (f 3)` has type `((int -> $t$) -> $t$)` for any type t, since when given a procedure of type `(int -> $t$)`, it returns a value of type t.

The value of `proc (f) proc (x) (f (f x))` has type `(($t$ -> $t$) -> ($t$ -> $t$))` for any type t, since when given a procedure of type `($t$ -> $t$)`, it returns another procedure that, when given an argument of type t, returns a value of type t.

We can explain these examples by the following definition.

Definition 7.1.1 *The property of an expressed value v being of type t is defined by induction on t:*

- *An expressed value is of type* int *if and only if it is a* num-val.

- *It is of type* bool *if and only if it is a* bool-val.

- *It is of type* $(t_1 \rightarrow t_2)$ *if and only if it is a* proc-val *with the property that if it is given an argument of type t_1, then one of the following things happens:*

   1. *it returns a value of type t_2*

   2. *it fails to terminate*

   3. *it fails with an error other than a type error.*

We occasionally say "v has type t" instead of "v is of type t."

This is a definition by induction on t. It depends, however, on the set of type errors being defined independently, as we did above.

In this system, a value v can be of more than one type. For example, the value of proc (x) x is of type $(t \rightarrow t)$ for any type t. Some values may have no type, like the value of proc (x) if x then 11 else zero?(11).

Exercise 7.1 [⋆] Below is a list of closed expressions. Consider the value of each expression. For each value, what type or types does it have? Some of the values may have no type that is describable in our type language.

1. proc (x) -(x,3)
2. proc (f) proc (x) -((f x), 1)
3. proc (x) x
4. proc (x) proc (y) (x y).
5. proc (x) (x 3)
6. proc (x) (x x)
7. proc (x) if x then 88 else 99
8. proc (x) proc (y) if x then y else 99
9. (proc (p) if p then 88 else 99
      33)
10. (proc (p) if p then 88 else 99
      proc (z) z)
11. proc (f)
      proc (g)
       proc (p)
        proc (x) if (p (f x)) then (g 1) else -((f x),1)

```
12. proc (x)
      proc(p)
       proc (f)
         if (p x) then -(x,1) else (f p)
13. proc (f)
      let d = proc (x)
                proc (z) ((f (x x)) z)
      in proc (n) ((f (d d)) n)
```

Exercise 7.2 [★★] Are there any expressed values that have exactly two types according to definition 7.1.1?

Exercise 7.3 [★★] For the language LETREC, is it decidable whether an expressed value *val* is of type *t*?

7.2   Assigning a Type to an Expression

So far, we've dealt only with the types of expressed values. In order to analyze programs, we need to write a procedure that takes an expression and predicts the type of its value.

More precisely, our goal is to write a procedure type-of which, given an expression (call it *exp*) and a *type environment* (call it *tenv*) mapping each variable to a type, assigns to *exp* a type *t* with the property that

Specification of type-of

Whenever *exp* is evaluated in an environment in which each variable has a value of the type specified for it by *tenv*, one of the following happens:

- the resulting value has type *t*,

- the evaluation does not terminate, or

- the evaluation fails on an error other than a type error.

If we can assign an expression to a type, we say that the expression is *well-typed*; otherwise we say it is *ill-typed* or *has no type*.

Our analysis will be based on the principle that if we can predict the types of the values of each of the subexpressions in an expression, we can predict the type of the value of the expression.

We'll use this idea to write down a set of rules that `type-of` should follow. Assume that *tenv* is a *type environment* mapping each variable to its type. Then we should have:

Simple typing rules

(type-of (const-exp *num*) *tenv*) = int

(type-of (var-exp *var*) *tenv*) = *tenv*(*var*)

$$\frac{\text{(type-of } exp_1 \; tenv) \; = \; \text{int}}{\text{(type-of (zero?-exp } exp_1) \; tenv) \; = \; \text{bool}}$$

$$\frac{\text{(type-of } exp_1 \; tenv) \; = \; \text{int} \qquad \text{(type-of } exp_2 \; tenv) \; = \; \text{int}}{\text{(type-of (diff-exp } exp_1 \; exp_2) \; tenv) \; = \; \text{int}}$$

$$\frac{\text{(type-of } exp_1 \; tenv) \; = \; t_1 \qquad \text{(type-of } body \; [var=t_1] \, tenv) \; = \; t_2}{\text{(type-of (let-exp } var \; exp_1 \; body) \; tenv) \; = \; t_2}$$

$$\frac{\begin{array}{c}\text{(type-of } exp_1 \; tenv) \; = \; \text{bool} \\ \text{(type-of } exp_2 \; tenv) \; = \; t \\ \text{(type-of } exp_3 \; tenv) \; = \; t\end{array}}{\text{(type-of (if-exp } exp_1 \; exp_2 \; exp_3) \; tenv) \; = \; t}$$

$$\frac{\text{(type-of } rator \; tenv) \; = \; (t_1 \rightarrow t_2) \qquad \text{(type-of } rand \; tenv) \; = \; t_1}{\text{(type-of (call-exp } rator \; rand) \; tenv) \; = \; t_2}$$

If we evaluate an expression *exp* of type *t* in a suitable environment, we know not only that its value is of type *t*, but we also know something about the history of that value. Because the evaluation of *exp* is guaranteed to be safe, we know that the value of *exp* was constructed only by operators that are legal for type *t*. This point of view will be helpful when we consider data abstraction in more detail in chapter 8.

What about procedures? If proc (var) $body$ has type $(t_1 \rightarrow t_2)$, then it is intended to be called on an argument of type t_1. When $body$ is evaluated, the variable var will be bound to a value of type t_1.

This suggests the following rule:

$$\frac{(\text{type-of } body \ [var{=}t_1] \ tenv) \ = \ t_2}{(\text{type-of } (\text{proc-exp } var \ body) \ tenv) \ = \ (t_1 \rightarrow t_2)}$$

This rule is sound: if type-of makes correct predictions about $body$, then it makes correct predictions about (proc-exp var $body$).

There's only one problem: if we are trying to compute the type of a proc expression, how are we going to find the type t_1 for the bound variable? It is nowhere to be found.

There are two standard designs for rectifying this situation:

- *Type Checking*: In this approach the programmer is required to supply the missing information about the types of bound variables, and the type-checker deduces the types of the other expressions and checks them for consistency.

- *Type Inference*: In this approach the type-checker attempts to *infer* the types of the bound variables based on how the variables are used in the program. If the language is carefully designed, the type-checker can infer most or all of these types.

We will study each of these in turn.

Exercise 7.4 [⋆] Using the rules of this section, write derivations, like the one on page 5, that assign types for proc (x) x and proc (x) proc (y) (x y). Use the rules to assign at least two types for each of these terms. Do the values of these expressions have the same types?

7.3   CHECKED: A Type-Checked Language

Our new language will be the same as LETREC, except that we require the programmer to include the types of all bound variables. For letrec-bound variables, we also require the programmer to specify the result type of the procedure as well.

Here are some example programs in CHECKED.

```
proc (x : int) -(x,1)

letrec
 int double (x : int) = if zero?(x)
                        then 0
                        else -((double -(x,1)), -2)
in double

proc (f : (bool -> int)) proc (n : int) (f zero?(n))
```

The result type of `double` is `int`, but the type of `double` itself is `(int
-> int)`, since it is a procedure that takes an integer and returns an integer.

To define the syntax of this language, we change the productions for `proc`
and `letrec` expressions.

Changed productions for CHECKED

Expression ::= `proc` (*Identifier* : *Type*) *Expression*

> `proc-exp (var ty body)`

Expression ::= `letrec`
> *Type Identifier* (*Identifier* : *Type*) = *Expression*
> `in` *Expression*

```
letrec-exp
   (p-result-type p-name b-var b-var-type
    p-body
    letrec-body)
```

For a `proc` expression with the type of its bound variable specified, the
rule becomes

$$\frac{(\texttt{type-of}\ body\ [var{=}t_{var}]\ tenv)\ =\ t_{res}}{(\texttt{type-of}\ (\texttt{proc-exp}\ var\ t_{var}\ body)\ tenv)\ =\ (t_{var}\ \rightarrow\ t_{res})}$$

What about `letrec`? A typical `letrec` looks like

$$\begin{aligned}
&\texttt{letrec}\\
&\quad t_{res}\ p\ (var : t_{var})\ =\ e_{proc\text{-}body}\\
&\texttt{in}\ e_{letrec\text{-}body}
\end{aligned}$$

This expression declares a procedure named p, with formal parameter *var* of type t_{var} and body $e_{proc\text{-}body}$. Hence the type of p should be $t_{var} \rightarrow t_{res}$.

Each of the expressions in the `letrec`, $e_{proc\text{-}body}$ and $e_{letrec\text{-}body}$, must be checked in a type environment where each variable is given its correct type. We can use our scoping rules to determine what variables are in scope, and hence what types should be associated with them.

In $e_{letrec\text{-}body}$, the procedure name p is in scope. As suggested above, p is declared to have type $t_{var} \rightarrow t_{res}$. Hence $e_{letrec\text{-}body}$ should be checked in the type environment

$$tenv_{letrec\text{-}body} = [p = (t_{var} \rightarrow t_{res})]tenv$$

What about $e_{proc\text{-}body}$? In $e_{proc\text{-}body}$, the variable p is in scope, with type $t_{var} \rightarrow t_{res}$, and the variable *var* is in scope, with type t_{var}. Hence the type environment for $e_{proc\text{-}body}$ should be

$$tenv_{proc\text{-}body} = [var = t_{var}]tenv_{letrec\text{-}body}$$

Furthermore, in this type environment, $e_{proc\text{-}body}$ should have result type t_{res}.

Writing this down as a rule, we get:

$$\frac{\texttt{(type-of } e_{proc\text{-}body} \; \texttt{[}var{=}t_{var}\texttt{] [}p = (t_{var} \; \rightarrow \; t_{res})\texttt{]} tenv\texttt{)} \; = \; t_{res} \qquad \texttt{(type-of } e_{letrec\text{-}body} \; \texttt{[}p = (t_{var} \; \rightarrow \; t_{res})\texttt{]} tenv\texttt{)} \; = \; t}{\texttt{(type-of letrec } t_{res} \; p \, (var : t_{var}) = e_{proc\text{-}body} \; \texttt{in} \; e_{letrec\text{-}body} \; tenv\texttt{)} \; = \; t}$$

Now we have written down all the rules, so we are ready to implement a type checker for this language.

7.3.1   The Checker

We will need to compare types for equality. We do this with the procedure `check-equal-type!`, which compares two types and reports an error unless they are equal. `check-equal-type!` takes a third argument, which is the expression that we will blame if the types are unequal.

check-equal-type! : *Type* × *Type* × *Exp* → *Unspecified*
```
(define check-equal-type!
  (lambda (ty1 ty2 exp)
    (if (not (equal? ty1 ty2))
      (report-unequal-types ty1 ty2 exp))))
```

report-unequal-types : *Type* × *Type* × *Exp* → *Unspecified*
```
(define report-unequal-types
  (lambda (ty1 ty2 exp)
    (eopl:error 'check-equal-type!
      "Types didn't match: ~s != ~a in~%~a"
      (type-to-external-form ty1)
      (type-to-external-form ty2)
      exp)))
```

We never use the value of a call to check-equal-type!; thus a call to check-equal-type! is executed for effect only, like the setref expressions in section 4.2.2.

The procedure report-unequal-types uses type-to-external-form, which converts a type back into a list that is easy to read.

type-to-external-form : *Type* → *List*
```
(define type-to-external-form
  (lambda (ty)
    (cases type ty
      (int-type () 'int)
      (bool-type () 'bool)
      (proc-type (arg-type result-type)
        (list
          (type-to-external-form arg-type)
          '->
          (type-to-external-form result-type))))))
```

Now we can transcribe the rules into a program, just as we did for interpreters in chapter 3. The result is shown in figures 7.1–7.3.

Exercise 7.5 [★★] Extend the checker to handle multiple let declarations, multiargument procedures, and multiple letrec declarations. You will need to add types of the form $(t_1 * t_2 * \ldots * t_n \rightarrow t)$ to handle multiargument procedures.

Exercise 7.6 [★] Extend the checker to handle assignments (section 4.3).

Exercise 7.7 [★] Change the code for checking an if-exp so that if the test expression is not a boolean, the other expressions are not checked. Give an expression for which the new version of the checker behaves differently from the old version.

Exercise 7.8 [★★] Add pairof types to the language. Say that a value is of type pairof $t_1 * t_2$ if and only if it is a pair consisting of a value of type t_1 and a value of type t_2. Add to the language the following productions:

Tenv = Var → Type

type-of-program : *Program → Type*
```
(define type-of-program
  (lambda (pgm)
    (cases program pgm
      (a-program (exp1) (type-of exp1 (init-tenv)))))))
```
type-of : *Exp × Tenv → Type*
```
(define type-of
  (lambda (exp tenv)
    (cases expression exp
```

$$\boxed{(\text{type-of } \textit{num} \textit{ tenv}) = \text{int}}$$
```
      (const-exp (num) (int-type))
```

$$\boxed{(\text{type-of } \textit{var} \textit{ tenv}) = \textit{tenv}(\textit{var})}$$
```
      (var-exp (var) (apply-tenv tenv var))
```

$$\boxed{\dfrac{(\text{type-of } e_1 \textit{ tenv}) = \text{int} \qquad (\text{type-of } e_2 \textit{ tenv}) = \text{int}}{(\text{type-of } (\text{diff-exp } e_1\ e_2)\textit{ tenv}) = \text{int}}}$$
```
      (diff-exp (exp1 exp2)
        (let ((ty1 (type-of exp1 tenv))
              (ty2 (type-of exp2 tenv)))
          (check-equal-type! ty1 (int-type) exp1)
          (check-equal-type! ty2 (int-type) exp2)
          (int-type)))
```

$$\boxed{\dfrac{(\text{type-of } e_1 \textit{ tenv}) = \text{int}}{(\text{type-of } (\text{zero?-exp } e_1)\textit{ tenv}) = \text{bool}}}$$
```
      (zero?-exp (exp1)
        (let ((ty1 (type-of exp1 tenv)))
          (check-equal-type! ty1 (int-type) exp1)
          (bool-type)))
```

$$\boxed{\dfrac{\begin{array}{c}(\text{type-of } e_1 \textit{ tenv}) = \text{bool} \\ (\text{type-of } e_2 \textit{ tenv}) = t \\ (\text{type-of } e_3 \textit{ tenv}) = t\end{array}}{(\text{type-of } (\text{if-exp } e_1\ e_2\ e_3)\textit{ tenv}) = t}}$$
```
      (if-exp (exp1 exp2 exp3)
        (let ((ty1 (type-of exp1 tenv))
              (ty2 (type-of exp2 tenv))
              (ty3 (type-of exp3 tenv)))
          (check-equal-type! ty1 (bool-type) exp1)
          (check-equal-type! ty2 ty3 exp)
          ty2))
```

Figure 7.1 `type-of` for CHECKED

$$\frac{(\texttt{type-of } e_1 \ tenv) \ = \ t_1 \qquad (\texttt{type-of } body \ [var=t_1] \ tenv) \ = \ t_2}{(\texttt{type-of } (\texttt{let-exp } var \ e_1 \ body) \ tenv) \ = \ t_2}$$

```
(let-exp (var exp1 body)
  (let ((exp1-type (type-of exp1 tenv)))
    (type-of body
      (extend-tenv var exp1-type tenv))))
```

$$\frac{(\texttt{type-of } body \ [var=t_{var}] \ tenv) \ = \ t_{res}}{(\texttt{type-of } (\texttt{proc-exp } var \ t_{var} \ body) \ tenv) \ = \ (t_{var} \ \rightarrow \ t_{res})}$$

```
(proc-exp (var var-type body)
  (let ((result-type
          (type-of body
            (extend-tenv var var-type tenv))))
    (proc-type var-type result-type)))
```

$$\frac{(\texttt{type-of } rator \ tenv) \ = \ (t_1 \ \rightarrow \ t_2) \qquad (\texttt{type-of } rand \ tenv) \ = \ t_1}{(\texttt{type-of } (\texttt{call-exp } rator \ rand) \ tenv) \ = \ t_2}$$

```
(call-exp (rator rand)
  (let ((rator-type (type-of rator tenv))
        (rand-type  (type-of rand tenv)))
    (cases type rator-type
      (proc-type (arg-type result-type)
        (begin
          (check-equal-type! arg-type rand-type rand)
          result-type))
      (else
        (report-rator-not-a-proc-type
          rator-type rator)))))
```

Figure 7.2 type-of for CHECKED, cont'd.

Type ::= pairof *Type* ∗ *Type*

> pair-type (ty1 ty2)

Expression ::= newpair (*Expression* , *Expression*)

> pair-exp (exp1 exp2)

Expression ::= unpair *Identifier Identifier* = *Expression*
    in *Expression*

> unpair-exp (var1 var2 exp body)

$$(\text{type-of } e_{proc\text{-}body} \ [var=t_{var}] \ [p=(t_{var} \rightarrow t_{res})] \ tenv) = t_{res}$$
$$(\text{type-of } e_{letrec\text{-}body} \ [p=(t_{var} \rightarrow t_{res})] \ tenv) = t$$
$$\overline{(\text{type-of } letrec \ t_{res} \ p \ (var : t_{var}) = e_{proc\text{-}body} \ \text{in } e_{letrec\text{-}body} \ tenv) = t}$$

```
(letrec-exp (p-result-type p-name b-var b-var-type
                p-body letrec-body)
  (let ((tenv-for-letrec-body
          (extend-tenv p-name
            (proc-type b-var-type p-result-type)
            tenv)))
    (let ((p-body-type
            (type-of p-body
              (extend-tenv b-var b-var-type
                tenv-for-letrec-body))))
      (check-equal-type!
        p-body-type p-result-type p-body)
      (type-of letrec-body tenv-for-letrec-body)))))))))
```

Figure 7.3　type-of for CHECKED, cont'd.

A pair expression creates a pair; an unpair expression (like exercise 3.18) binds its two variables to the two parts of the expression; the scope of these variables is body. The typing rules for pair and unpair are:

$$(\text{type-of } e_1 \ tenv) = t_1$$
$$(\text{type-of } e_2 \ tenv) = t_2$$
$$\overline{(\text{type-of } (pair\text{-}exp \ e_1 \ e_2) \ tenv) = pairof \ t_1 * t_2}$$

$$(\text{type-of } e_{pair} \ tenv) = (pairof \ t_1 \ t_2)$$
$$(\text{type-of } e_{body} \ [var_1=t_1] \ [var_2=t_2] \ tenv) = t_{body}$$
$$\overline{(\text{type-of } (unpair\text{-}exp \ var_1 \ var_2 \ e_1 \ e_{body}) \ tenv) = t_{body}}$$

Extend CHECKED to implement these rules. In type-to-external-form, produce the list (pairof t_1 t_2) for a pair type.

Exercise 7.9 [⋆ ⋆] Add `listof` types to the language, with operations similar to those of exercise 3.9. A value is of type `listof` t if and only if it is a list and all of its elements are of type t. Extend the language with the productions

$$Type \quad ::= \text{listof } Type$$
$$\boxed{\texttt{list-type (ty)}}$$

$$Expression ::= \text{list } (Expression \; \{, Expression\}^* \;)$$
$$\boxed{\texttt{list-exp (exp1 exps)}}$$

$$Expression ::= \text{cons } (Expression \; , \; Expression)$$
$$\boxed{\texttt{cons-exp (exp1 exp2)}}$$

$$Expression ::= \text{null? } (Expression)$$
$$\boxed{\texttt{null-exp (exp1)}}$$

$$Expression ::= \text{emptylist\_} Type$$
$$\boxed{\texttt{emptylist-exp (ty)}}$$

with types given by the following four rules:

$$
\frac{\begin{array}{c}
(\texttt{type-of } e_1 \; tenv) \; = \; t \\
(\texttt{type-of } e_2 \; tenv) \; = \; t \\
\vdots \\
(\texttt{type-of } e_n \; tenv) \; = \; t
\end{array}}{(\texttt{type-of } (\texttt{list-exp } e_1 \; (e_2 \; \ldots \; e_n)) \; tenv) \; = \; \texttt{listof } t}
$$

$$
\frac{\begin{array}{c}
(\texttt{type-of } e_1 \; tenv) \; = \; t \\
(\texttt{type-of } e_2 \; tenv) \; = \; \texttt{listof } t
\end{array}}{(\texttt{type-of } \texttt{cons}(e_1, e_2) \; tenv) \; = \; \texttt{listof } t}
$$

$$
\frac{(\texttt{type-of } e_1 \; tenv) \; = \; \texttt{listof } t}{(\texttt{type-of } \texttt{null?}(e_1) \; tenv) \; = \; \texttt{bool}}
$$

$$(\texttt{type-of } \texttt{emptylist}[t] \; tenv) \; = \; \texttt{listof } t$$

Although `cons` is similar to `pair`, it has a very different typing rule.

Write similar rules for `car` and `cdr`, and extend the checker to handle these as well as the other expressions. Use a trick similar to the one in exercise 7.8 to avoid conflict with `proc-type-exp`. These rules should guarantee that `car` and `cdr` are applied to lists, but they should not guarantee that the lists be non-empty. Why would it be unreasonable for the rules to guarantee that the lists be non-empty? Why is the type parameter in `emptylist` necessary?

Exercise 7.10 [⋆ ⋆] Extend the checker to handle EXPLICIT-REFS. You will need to do the following:

- Add to the type system the types refto t, where t is any type. This is the type of references to locations containing a value of type t. Thus, if e is of type t, (newref e) is of type refto t.

- Add to the type system the type void. This is the type of the value returned by setref. You can't apply any operation to a value of type void, so it doesn't matter what value setref returns. This is an example of types serving as an information-hiding mechanism.

- Write down typing rules for newref, deref, and setref.

- Implement these rules in the checker.

Exercise 7.11 [⋆ ⋆] Extend the checker to handle MUTABLE-PAIRS.

7.4   INFERRED: A Language with Type Inference

Writing down the types in the program may be helpful for design and documentation, but it can be time-consuming. Another design is to have the compiler figure out the types of all the variables, based on observing how they are used, and utilizing any hints the programmer might give. Surprisingly, for a carefully designed language, the compiler can *always* infer the types of the variables. This strategy is called *type inference*. We can do it for languages like LETREC, and it scales up to reasonably-sized languages.

For our case study in type inference, we start with the language of CHECKED. We then change the language so that all the type expressions are optional. In place of a missing type expression, we use the marker ?. Hence a typical program looks like

```
letrec
 ? foo (x : ?) = if zero?(x)
                 then 1
                 else -(x, (foo -(x,1)))
in foo
```

Each question mark (except, of course, for the one at the end of zero?) indicates a place where a type expression must be inferred.

Since the type expressions are optional, we may fill in some of the ?'s with types, as in

```
letrec
 ? even (x : int) = if zero?(x) then 1 else (odd -(x,1))
 bool odd (x : ?) = if zero?(x) then 0 else (even -(x,1))
in (odd 13)
```

To specify this syntax, we add a new nonterminal, *Optional-type*, and we modify the productions for `proc` and `letrec` to use optional types instead of types.

Optional-type ::= ?

> `no-type ()`

Optional-type ::= *Type*

> `a-type (ty)`

Expression ::= proc (*Identifier* : *Optional-type*) *Expression*

> `proc-exp (var otype body)`

Expression ::= letrec
> *Optional-type* *Identifier* (*Identifier* : *Optional-type*) = *Expression*
> in *Expression*

```
letrec-exp
  (p-result-otype p-name
   b-var b-var-otype p-body
   letrec-body)
```

The omitted types will be treated as unknowns that we need to find. We do this by traversing the abstract syntax tree and generating equations between these types, possibly including these unknowns. We then solve the equations for the unknown types.

To see how this works, we need names for the unknown types. For each expression *e* or bound variable *var*, let t_e or t_{var} denote the type of the expression or bound variable.

For each node in the abstract syntax tree of the expression, the type rules dictate some equations that must hold between these types. For our PROC language, the equations would be:

$$(\texttt{diff-exp } e_1 \ e_2) \ : \ t_{e_1} = \texttt{int}$$
$$t_{e_2} = \texttt{int}$$
$$t_{(\texttt{diff-exp } e_1 \ e_2)} = \texttt{int}$$

$$(\texttt{zero?-exp } e_1) \ : \ t_{e_1} = \texttt{int}$$
$$t_{(\texttt{zero?-exp } e_1)} = \texttt{bool}$$

$$(\texttt{if-exp } e_1 \ e_2 \ e_3) \ : \ t_{e_1} = \texttt{bool}$$
$$t_{e_2} = t_{(\texttt{if-exp } e_1 \ e_2 \ e_3)}$$
$$t_{e_3} = t_{(\texttt{if-exp } e_1 \ e_2 \ e_3)}$$

$$(\texttt{proc-exp } var \; body) \quad : \; t_{(\texttt{proc-exp } var \; body)} = (t_{var} \rightarrow t_{body})$$

$$(\texttt{call-exp } rator \; rand) \; : \; t_{rator} = (t_{rand} \rightarrow t_{(\texttt{call-exp } rator \; rand)})$$

- The first rule says that the arguments and the result of a `diff-exp` must all be of type `int`.

- The second rule says that the argument of a `zero?-exp` must be an `int`, and its result is a `bool`.

- The third rule says that in an `if` expression, the test must be of type `bool`, and that the types of the two alternatives must be the same as the type of the entire `if` expression.

- The fourth rule says that the type of a `proc` expression is that of a procedure whose argument type is given by the type of its bound variable, and whose result type is given by the type of its body.

- The fifth rule says that in a procedure call, the operator must have the type of a procedure that accepts arguments of the same type as that of the operand, and that produces results of the same type as that of the calling expression.

To infer the type of an expression, we'll introduce a type variable for every subexpression and every bound variable, generate the constraints for each subexpression, and then solve the resulting equations. To see how this works, we will infer the types of several sample expressions.

Let us start with the expression `proc (f) proc(x) -((f 3),(f x))`. We begin by making a table of all the bound variables, `proc` expressions, `if` expressions, and procedure calls in this expression, and assigning a type variable to each one.

Expression	Type Variable
`f`	t_f
`x`	t_x
`proc(f)proc(x)-((f 3),(f x))`	t_0
`proc(x)-((f 3),(f x))`	t_1
`-((f 3),(f x))`	t_2
`(f 3)`	t_3
`(f x)`	t_4

Now, for each compound expression, we can write down a type equation according to the rules above.

Expression	Equations	
`proc(f)proc(x)-((f 3),(f x))`	1.	$t_0 = t_f \rightarrow t_1$
`proc(x)-((f 3),(f x))`	2.	$t_1 = t_x \rightarrow t_2$
`-((f 3),(f x))`	3.	$t_3 = \texttt{int}$
	4.	$t_4 = \texttt{int}$
	5.	$t_2 = \texttt{int}$
`(f 3)`	6.	$t_f = \texttt{int} \rightarrow t_3$
`(f x)`	7.	$t_f = t_x \rightarrow t_4$

- Equation 1 says that the entire expression produces a procedure that takes an argument of type t_f and produces a value of the same type as that of `proc(x)-((f 3),(f x))`.

- Equation 2 says that `proc(x)-((f 3),(f x))` produces a procedure that takes an argument of type t_x and produces a value of the same type as that of `-((f 3),(f x))`.

- Equations 3–5 say that the arguments and the result of the subtraction in `-((f 3),(f x))` are all integers.

- Equation 6 says that `f` expects an argument of type `int` and returns a value of the same type as that of `(f 3)`.

- Similarly equation 7 says that `f` expects an argument of the same type as that of `x` and returns a value of the same type as that of `(f x)`.

We can fill in t_f, t_x, t_0, t_1, t_2, t_3, and t_4 in any way we like, so long as they satisfy the equations

$$t_0 = t_f \rightarrow t_1$$
$$t_1 = t_x \rightarrow t_2$$
$$t_3 = \texttt{int}$$
$$t_4 = \texttt{int}$$
$$t_2 = \texttt{int}$$
$$t_f = \texttt{int} \rightarrow t_3$$
$$t_f = t_x \rightarrow t_4$$

Our goal is to find values for the variables that make all the equations true. We can express such a solution as a set of equations where the left-hand sides are all variables. We call such a set of equations a *substitution*. The variables that occur on the left-hand side of some equation in the substitution are said to be *bound* in the substitution.

We can solve such equations systematically. This process is called *unification*.

We separate the state of our calculation into the set of equations still to be solved and the substitution found so far. Initially, all of the equations are to be solved, and the substitution found is empty.

Equations	**Substitution**
$t_0 = t_f \rightarrow t_1$	
$t_1 = t_x \rightarrow t_2$	
$t_3 = \text{int}$	
$t_4 = \text{int}$	
$t_2 = \text{int}$	
$t_f = \text{int} \rightarrow t_3$	
$t_f = t_x \rightarrow t_4$	

We consider each equation in turn. If the equation's left-hand side is a variable, we move it to the substitution.

Equations	**Substitution**
$t_1 = t_x \rightarrow t_2$	$t_0 = t_f \rightarrow t_1$
$t_3 = \text{int}$	
$t_4 = \text{int}$	
$t_2 = \text{int}$	
$t_f = \text{int} \rightarrow t_3$	
$t_f = t_x \rightarrow t_4$	

However, doing this may change the substitution. For example, our next equation gives a value for t_1. We need to propagate that information into the value for t_0, which contains t_1 on its right-hand side. So we substitute the right-hand side for each occurrence of t_1 in the substitution. This gets us:

Equations	**Substitution**
$t_3 = \text{int}$	$t_0 = t_f \rightarrow (t_x \rightarrow t_2)$
$t_4 = \text{int}$	$t_1 = t_x \rightarrow t_2$
$t_2 = \text{int}$	
$t_f = \text{int} \rightarrow t_3$	
$t_f = t_x \rightarrow t_4$	

If the right-hand side were a variable, we'd switch the sides and do the same thing. We can continue in this manner for the next three equations.

Equations	**Substitution**
$t_4 = \mathtt{int}$	$t_0 = t_f \rightarrow (t_x \rightarrow t_2)$
$t_2 = \mathtt{int}$	$t_1 = t_x \rightarrow t_2$
$t_f = \mathtt{int} \rightarrow t_3$	$t_3 = \mathtt{int}$
$t_f = t_x \rightarrow t_4$	

Equations	**Substitution**
$t_2 = \mathtt{int}$	$t_0 = t_f \rightarrow (t_x \rightarrow t_2)$
$t_f = \mathtt{int} \rightarrow t_3$	$t_1 = t_x \rightarrow t_2$
$t_f = t_x \rightarrow t_4$	$t_3 = \mathtt{int}$
	$t_4 = \mathtt{int}$

Equations	**Substitution**
$t_f = \mathtt{int} \rightarrow t_3$	$t_0 = t_f \rightarrow (t_x \rightarrow \mathtt{int})$
$t_f = t_x \rightarrow t_4$	$t_1 = t_x \rightarrow \mathtt{int}$
	$t_3 = \mathtt{int}$
	$t_4 = \mathtt{int}$
	$t_2 = \mathtt{int}$

Now, the next equation to be considered contains t_3, which is already bound to $\mathtt{int}$ in the substitution. So we substitute $\mathtt{int}$ for t_3 in the equation. We would do the same thing for any other type variables in the equation. We call this *applying* the substitution to the equation.

Equations	**Substitution**
$t_f = \mathtt{int} \rightarrow \mathtt{int}$	$t_0 = t_f \rightarrow (t_x \rightarrow \mathtt{int})$
$t_f = t_x \rightarrow t_4$	$t_1 = t_x \rightarrow \mathtt{int}$
	$t_3 = \mathtt{int}$
	$t_4 = \mathtt{int}$
	$t_2 = \mathtt{int}$

We move the resulting equation into the substitution and update the substitution as necessary.

Equations	**Substitution**
$t_f = t_x \rightarrow t_4$	$t_0 = (\mathtt{int} \rightarrow \mathtt{int}) \rightarrow (t_x \rightarrow \mathtt{int})$
	$t_1 = t_x \rightarrow \mathtt{int}$
	$t_3 = \mathtt{int}$
	$t_4 = \mathtt{int}$
	$t_2 = \mathtt{int}$
	$t_f = \mathtt{int} \rightarrow \mathtt{int}$

The next equation, $t_f = t_x \rightarrow t_4$, contains t_f and t_4, which are bound in the substitution, so we apply the substitution to this equation. This gets

Equations	Substitution
$\texttt{int} \rightarrow \texttt{int} = t_x \rightarrow \texttt{int}$	$t_0 = (\texttt{int} \rightarrow \texttt{int}) \rightarrow (t_x \rightarrow \texttt{int})$
	$t_1 = t_x \rightarrow \texttt{int}$
	$t_3 = \texttt{int}$
	$t_4 = \texttt{int}$
	$t_2 = \texttt{int}$
	$t_f = \texttt{int} \rightarrow \texttt{int}$

If neither side of the equation is a variable, we can simplify, yielding two new equations.

Equations	Substitution
$\texttt{int} = t_x$	$t_0 = (\texttt{int} \rightarrow \texttt{int}) \rightarrow (t_x \rightarrow \texttt{int})$
$\texttt{int} = \texttt{int}$	$t_1 = t_x \rightarrow \texttt{int}$
	$t_3 = \texttt{int}$
	$t_4 = \texttt{int}$
	$t_2 = \texttt{int}$
	$t_f = \texttt{int} \rightarrow \texttt{int}$

We can process these as usual: we switch the sides of the first equation, add it to the substitution, and update the substitution, as we did before.

Equations	Substitution
$\texttt{int} = \texttt{int}$	$t_0 = (\texttt{int} \rightarrow \texttt{int}) \rightarrow (\texttt{int} \rightarrow \texttt{int})$
	$t_1 = \texttt{int} \rightarrow \texttt{int}$
	$t_3 = \texttt{int}$
	$t_4 = \texttt{int}$
	$t_2 = \texttt{int}$
	$t_f = \texttt{int} \rightarrow \texttt{int}$
	$t_x = \texttt{int}$

The final equation, $\texttt{int} = \texttt{int}$, is always true, so we can discard it.

Equations	Substitution
	$t_0 = (\texttt{int} \rightarrow \texttt{int}) \rightarrow (\texttt{int} \rightarrow \texttt{int})$
	$t_1 = \texttt{int} \rightarrow \texttt{int}$
	$t_3 = \texttt{int}$
	$t_4 = \texttt{int}$
	$t_2 = \texttt{int}$
	$t_f = \texttt{int} \rightarrow \texttt{int}$
	$t_x = \texttt{int}$

We have no more equations, so we are done. We conclude from this calculation that our original expression `proc (f) proc (x) -((f 3),(f x))` should be assigned the type

$$((\text{int} \rightarrow \text{int}) \rightarrow (\text{int} \rightarrow \text{int}))$$

This is reasonable: The first argument `f` must take an `int` argument because it is given `3` as an argument. It must produce an `int`, because its value is used as an argument to the subtraction operator. And `x` must be an `int`, because it is also supplied as an argument to `f`.

Let us consider another example: `proc(f) (f 11)`. Again, we start by assigning type variables:

Expression	Type Variable
`f`	t_f
`proc(f)(f 11)`	t_0
`(f 11)`	t_1

Next we write down the equations

Expression	Equations
`proc(f)(f 11)`	$t_0 = t_f \rightarrow t_1$
`(f 11)`	$t_f = \text{int} \rightarrow t_1$

And next we solve:

Equations	Substitution
$t_0 = t_f \rightarrow t_1$	
$t_f = \text{int} \rightarrow t_1$	

Equations	Substitution
$t_f = \text{int} \rightarrow t_1$	$t_0 = t_f \rightarrow t_1$

Equations	Substitution
	$t_0 = (\text{int} \rightarrow t_1) \rightarrow t_1$
	$t_f = \text{int} \rightarrow t_1$

This means that we can assign `proc (f) (f 11)` the type $(\text{int} \rightarrow t_1) \rightarrow t_1$, for any choice of t_1. Again, this is reasonable: we can infer that `f` must be able to take an `int` argument, but we have no information about the result type of `f`, and indeed for any t_1, this code will work for any `f` that takes an `int` argument and returns a value of type t_1. We say it is *polymorphic* in t_1.

Let's try a third example. Consider `if x then -(x,1) else 0`. Again, let's assign type variables to each subexpression that is not a constant.

Expression	Type Variable
x	t_x
if x then -(x,1) else 0	t_0
-(x,1)	t_1

We then generate the equations

Expression	Equations
if x then -(x,1) else 0	t_x = bool
	t_1 = t_0
	int = t_0
-(x,1)	t_x = int
	t_1 = int

Processing these equations as we did before, we get

Equations	Substitution
$t_x = $ bool	
$t_1 = t_0$	
int $= t_0$	
$t_x = $ int	
$t_1 = $ int	

Equations	Substitution
$t_1 = t_0$	$t_x = $ bool
int $= t_0$	
$t_x = $ int	
$t_1 = $ int	

Equations	Substitution
int $= t_0$	$t_x = $ bool
$t_x = $ int	$t_1 = t_0$
$t_1 = $ int	

Equations	Substitution
$t_0 = $ int	$t_x = $ bool
$t_x = $ int	$t_1 = t_0$
$t_1 = $ int	

Equations	Substitution
$t_x = $ int	$t_x = $ bool
$t_1 = $ int	$t_1 = $ int
	$t_0 = $ int

Since t_x is already bound in the substitution, we apply the current substitution to the next equation, getting

Equations	Substitution
$\texttt{bool} = \texttt{int}$	$t_x = \texttt{bool}$
$t_1 = \texttt{int}$	$t_1 = \texttt{int}$
	$t_0 = \texttt{int}$

What has happened here? We have inferred from these equations that $\texttt{bool} = \texttt{int}$. So in any solution of these equations, $\texttt{bool} = \texttt{int}$. But $\texttt{bool}$ and $\texttt{int}$ cannot be equal. Therefore there is no solution to these equations. Therefore it is impossible to assign a type to this expression. This is reasonable, since the expression `if x then -(x,1) else 0` uses x as both a boolean and an integer, which is illegal in our type system.

Let us do one more example. Consider `proc (f) zero?((f f))`. We proceed as before.

Expression	Type Variable
`proc (f) zero?((f f))`	t_0
`f`	t_f
`zero?((f f))`	t_1
`(f f)`	t_2

Expression	Equations
`proc (f) zero?((f f))`	$t_0 \ = \ t_f \ \rightarrow \ t_1$
`zero?((f f))`	$t_1 \ = \ \texttt{bool}$
	$t_2 \ = \ \texttt{int}$
`(f f)`	$t_f \ = \ t_f \ \rightarrow \ t_2$

And we solve as usual:

Equations	Substitution
$t_0 = t_f \rightarrow t_1$	
$t_1 = \texttt{bool}$	
$t_2 = \texttt{int}$	
$t_f = t_f \rightarrow t_2$	

Equations	Substitution
$t_1 = \texttt{bool}$	$t_0 = t_f \rightarrow t_1$
$t_2 = \texttt{int}$	
$t_f = t_f \rightarrow t_2$	

Equations	**Substitution**
$t_2 = \texttt{int}$	$t_0 = t_f \rightarrow \texttt{bool}$
$t_f = t_f \rightarrow t_2$	$t_1 = \texttt{bool}$

Equations	**Substitution**
$t_f = t_f \rightarrow t_2$	$t_0 = t_f \rightarrow \texttt{bool}$
	$t_1 = \texttt{bool}$
	$t_2 = \texttt{int}$

Equations	**Substitution**
$t_f = t_f \rightarrow \texttt{int}$	$t_0 = t_f \rightarrow \texttt{bool}$
	$t_1 = \texttt{bool}$
	$t_2 = \texttt{int}$

Now we have a problem. We've now inferred that $t_f = t_f \rightarrow Int$. But there is no type with this property, because the right-hand side of this equation is always larger than the left: If the syntax tree for t_f contains k nodes, then the right-hand side will always contain $k + 2$ nodes.

So if we ever deduce an equation of the form $tv = t$ where the type variable tv occurs in the type t, we must again conclude that there is no solution to the original equations. This extra condition is called the *occurrence check*.

This condition also means that the substitutions we build will satisfy the following invariant:

The no-occurrence invariant

No variable bound in the substitution occurs in any of the right-hand sides of the substitution.

Our code for solving equations will depend critically on this invariant.

Exercise 7.12 [⋆] Using the methods in this section, derive types for each of the expressions in exercise 7.1, or determine that no such type exists. As in the other examples of this section, assume there is a ? attached to each bound variable.

Exercise 7.13 [⋆] Write down a rule for doing type inference for `let` expressions. Using your rule, derive types for each of the following expressions, or determine that no such type exists.

1. `let x = 4 in (x 3)`
2. `let f = proc (z) z in proc (x) -((f x), 1)`
3. `let p = zero?(1) in if p then 88 else 99`
4. `let p = proc (z) z in if p then 88 else 99`

Exercise 7.14 [⋆] What is wrong with this expression?

```
letrec
 ? even(odd : ?) =
    proc (x : ?)
      if zero?(x) then 1 else (odd -(x,1))
in letrec
    ? odd(x : bool) =
       if zero?(x) then 0 else ((even odd) -(x,1))
   in (odd 13)
```

Exercise 7.15 [⋆ ⋆] Write down a rule for doing type inference for a `letrec` expression. Your rule should handle multiple declarations in a `letrec`. Using your rule, derive types for each of the following expressions, or determine that no such type exists:

1.
```
letrec ? f (x : ?)
           = if zero?(x) then 0 else -((f -(x,1)), -2)
in f
```

2.
```
letrec ? even (x : ?)
            = if zero?(x) then 1 else (odd -(x,1))
         ? odd (x : ?)
            = if zero?(x) then 0 else (even -(x,1))
in (odd 13)
```

3.
```
letrec ? even (odd : ?)
           = proc (x) if zero?(x)
                      then 1
                      else (odd -(x,1))
in letrec ? odd (x : ?) =
             if zero?(x)
             then 0
             else ((even odd) -(x,1))
   in (odd 13)
```

Exercise 7.16 [⋆ ⋆ ⋆] Modify the grammar of INFERRED so that missing types are simply omitted, rather than marked with ?.

7.4.1   Substitutions

We will build the implementation in a bottom-up fashion. We first consider substitutions.

We represent type variables as an additional variant of the type data type. We do this using the same technique that we used for lexical addresses in section 3.7. We add to the grammar the production

$$\textit{Type} ::= \texttt{\%tvar-type } \textit{Number}$$
$$\boxed{\texttt{tvar-type (serial-number)}}$$

We call these extended types *type expressions*. A basic operation on type expressions is substitution of a type for a type variable, defined by apply-one-subst. (apply-one-subst t_0 tv t_1) returns the type obtained by substituting t_1 for every occurrence of tv in t_0. This is sometimes written $t_0[tv = t_1]$.

apply-one-subst : *Type* $\times$ *Tvar* $\times$ *Type* $\rightarrow$ *Type*
```
(define apply-one-subst
  (lambda (ty0 tvar ty1)
    (cases type ty0
      (int-type () (int-type))
      (bool-type () (bool-type))
      (proc-type (arg-type result-type)
        (proc-type
          (apply-one-subst arg-type tvar ty1)
          (apply-one-subst result-type tvar ty1)))
      (tvar-type (sn)
        (if (equal? ty0 tvar) ty1 ty0)))))
```

This procedure deals with substituting for a single type variable. It doesn't deal with full-fledged substitutions like those we had in the preceding section.

A substitution is a list of equations between type variables and types. Equivalently, we can think of this list as a function from type variables to types. We say a type variable is *bound* in the substitution if and only if it occurs on the left-hand side of one of the equations in the substitution.

We represent a substitution as a list of pairs (type variable . type). The basic observer for substitutions is apply-subst-to-type. This walks through the type t, replacing each type variable by its binding in the substitution σ. If a variable is not bound in the substitution, then it is left unchanged. We write $t\sigma$ for the resulting type.

The implementation uses the Scheme procedure `assoc` to look up the type variable in the substitution. `assoc` returns either the matching (type variable, type) pair or `#f` if the given type variable is not the `car` of any pair in the list. We write

apply-subst-to-type : *Type* × *Subst* → *Type*
```
(define apply-subst-to-type
  (lambda (ty subst)
    (cases type ty
      (int-type () (int-type))
      (bool-type () (bool-type))
      (proc-type (t1 t2)
        (proc-type
          (apply-subst-to-type t1 subst)
          (apply-subst-to-type t2 subst)))
      (tvar-type (sn)
        (let ((tmp (assoc ty subst)))
          (if tmp
            (cdr tmp)
            ty))))))) 
```

The constructors for substitutions are `empty-subst` and `extend-subst`. `(empty-subst)` produces a representation of the empty substitution. `(extend-subst σ tv t)` takes the substitution σ and adds the equation $tv = t$ to it, as we did in the preceding section. We write $\sigma[tv = t]$ for the resulting substitution. This was a two-step operation: first we substituted t for tv in each of the right-hand sides of the equations in the substitution, and then we added the equation $tv = t$ to the list. Pictorially,

$$\begin{pmatrix} tv_1 = t_1 \\ \vdots \\ tv_n = t_n \end{pmatrix} [tv = t] \;=\; \begin{pmatrix} tv \;= t \\ tv_1 = t_1[tv = t] \\ \vdots \\ tv_n = t_n[tv = t] \end{pmatrix}$$

This definition has the property that for any type t,

$$(t\sigma)[tv = t'] = t(\sigma[tv = t'])$$

The implementation of `extend-subst` follows the picture above. It substitutes t_0 for tv_0 in all of the existing bindings in σ_0, and then adds the binding for t_0.

empty-subst : () → *Subst*
```
(define empty-subst (lambda () '()))
```

extend-subst : *Subst* × *Tvar* × *Type* → *Subst*
usage: tvar not already bound in subst.
```
(define extend-subst
  (lambda (subst tvar ty)
    (cons
      (cons tvar ty)
      (map
        (lambda (p)
          (let ((oldlhs (car p))
                (oldrhs (cdr p)))
            (cons
              oldlhs
              (apply-one-subst oldrhs tvar ty))))
        subst)))))
```

This implementation preserves the no-occurrence invariant, but it does not depend on, nor does it attempt to enforce it. That is the job of the unifier, in the next section.

Exercise 7.17 [★ ★] In our representation, extend-subst may do a lot of work if σ is large. Implement an alternate representation in which extend-subst is implemented as

```
(define extend-subst
  (lambda (subst tvar ty)
    (cons (cons tvar ty) subst)))
```

and the extra work is shifted to apply-subst-to-type, so that the property $t(\sigma[tv = t']) = (t\sigma)[tv = t']$ is still satisfied. For this definition of extend-subst, is the no-occurrence invariant needed?

Exercise 7.18 [★ ★] Modify the implementation in the preceding exercise so that apply-subst-to-type computes the substitution for any type variable at most once.

7.4.2   The Unifier

The main procedure of the unifier is unifier. The unifier performs one step of the inference procedure outlined above: It takes two types, t_1 and t_2, a substitution σ that satisfies the no-occurrence invariant, and an expression *exp*. It returns the substitution that results from adding t_1 = t_2 to σ. This will be the smallest extension of σ that unifies $t_1\sigma$ and $t_2\sigma$. This substitution will still satisfy the no-occurrence invariant. If adding $t_1 = t_2$ yields an inconsistency or violates the no-occurrence invariant, then the unifier reports an error, and blames the expression exp. This is typically the expression that gave rise to the equation $t_1 = t_2$.

This is an algorithm for which cases gives awkward code, so we use simple predicates and extractors on types instead. The algorithm is shown in figure 7.4, and it works as follows:

- First, as we did above, we apply the substitution to each of the types t_1 and t_2.

- If the resulting types are the same, we return immediately. This corresponds to the step of deleting a trivial equation above.

- If ty1 is an unknown type, then the no-occurrence invariant tells us that it is not bound in the substitution. Hence it must be unbound, so we propose to add $t_1 = t_2$ to the substitution. But we need to perform the occurrence check, so that the no-occurrence invariant is preserved. The call (no-occurrence? *tv t*) returns #t if and only if there is no occurrence of the type variable *tv* in *t* (figure 7.5).

- If t_2 is an unknown type, we do the same thing, reversing the roles of t_1 and t_2.

- If neither t_1 nor t_2 is a type variable, then we can analyze further.

   If they are both proc types, then we simplify by equating the argument types, and then equating the result types in the resulting substitution.

   Otherwise, either one of t_1 and t_2 is int and the other is bool, or one is a proc type and the other is int or bool. In any of these cases, there is no solution to the equation, so an error is reported.

Here is another way of thinking about all this that is sometimes useful. The substitution is a *store*, and an unknown type is a *reference* into that store. unifier produces the new store that is obtained by adding ty1 = ty2 to the store.

Last, we must implement the occurrence check. This is a straightforward recursion on the type, and is shown in figure 7.5.

Exercise 7.19 [⋆] We wrote: "If ty1 is an unknown type, then the no-occurrence invariant tells us that it is not bound in the substitution." Explain in detail why this is so.

unifier : *Type* × *Type* × *Subst* × *Exp* → *Subst*
```
(define unifier
  (lambda (ty1 ty2 subst exp)
    (let ((ty1 (apply-subst-to-type ty1 subst))
          (ty2 (apply-subst-to-type ty2 subst)))
      (cond
        ((equal? ty1 ty2) subst)
        ((tvar-type? ty1)
         (if (no-occurrence? ty1 ty2)
           (extend-subst subst ty1 ty2)
           (report-no-occurrence-violation ty1 ty2 exp)))
        ((tvar-type? ty2)
         (if (no-occurrence? ty2 ty1)
           (extend-subst subst ty2 ty1)
           (report-no-occurrence-violation ty2 ty1 exp)))
        ((and (proc-type? ty1) (proc-type? ty2))
         (let ((subst (unifier
                        (proc-type->arg-type ty1)
                        (proc-type->arg-type ty2)
                        subst exp)))
           (let ((subst (unifier
                          (proc-type->result-type ty1)
                          (proc-type->result-type ty2)
                          subst exp)))
             subst)))
        (else (report-unification-failure ty1 ty2 exp)))))))
```

Figure 7.4   The unifier

Exercise 7.20 [★★] Modify the unifier so that it calls `apply-subst-to-type` only on type variables, rather than on its arguments.

Exercise 7.21 [★★] We said the substitution is like a store. Implement the unifier, using the representation of substitutions from exercise 7.17, and keeping the substitution in a global Scheme variable, as we did in figures 4.1 and 4.2.

Exercise 7.22 [★★] Refine the implementation of the preceding exercise so that the binding of each type variable can be obtained in constant time.

```
no-occurrence? : Tvar × Type → Bool
(define no-occurrence?
  (lambda (tvar ty)
    (cases type ty
      (int-type () #t)
      (bool-type () #t)
      (proc-type (arg-type result-type)
        (and
          (no-occurrence? tvar arg-type)
          (no-occurrence? tvar result-type)))
      (tvar-type (serial-number) (not (equal? tvar ty)))))))
```

Figure 7.5 The occurrence check

7.4.3 Finding the Type of an Expression

We convert optional types to types with unknowns by defining a fresh type variable for each ?, using `otype->type`.

```
otype->type : OptionalType → Type
(define otype->type
  (lambda (otype)
    (cases optional-type otype
      (no-type () (fresh-tvar-type))
      (a-type (ty) ty))))
```

```
fresh-tvar-type : () → Type
(define fresh-tvar-type
  (let ((sn 0))
    (lambda ()
      (set! sn (+ sn 1))
      (tvar-type sn))))
```

When we convert to external form, we represent a type variable by a symbol containing its serial number.

type-to-external-form : *Type* → *List*
```
(define type-to-external-form
  (lambda (ty)
    (cases type ty
      (int-type () 'int)
      (bool-type () 'bool)
      (proc-type (arg-type result-type)
        (list
          (type-to-external-form arg-type)
          '->
          (type-to-external-form result-type)))
      (tvar-type (serial-number)
        (string->symbol
          (string-append
            "ty"
            (number->string serial-number)))))))
```

Now we can write `type-of`. It takes an expression, a type environment mapping program variables to type expressions, and a substitution satisfying the no-occurrence invariant, and it returns a type and a new no-occurrence substitution.

The type environment associates a type expression with each program variable. The substitution explains the meaning of each type variable in the type expressions. We use the metaphor of a substitution as a *store*, and a type variable as *reference* into that store. Therefore, `type-of` returns two values: a type expression, and a substitution in which to interpret the type variables in that expression. We implement this as we did in exercise 4.12, by defining a new data type that contains the two values, and using that as the return value.

The definition of `type-of` is shown in figures 7.6–7.8. For each kind of expression, we recur on the subexpressions, passing along the solution so far in the substitution argument. Then we generate the equations for the current expression, according to the specification, and record these in the substitution by calling `unifier`.

Testing the inferencer is somewhat more subtle than testing our previous interpreters, because of the possibility of polymorphism. For example, if the inferencer is given `proc (x) x`, it might generate any of the external forms `(tvar1 -> tvar1)` or `(tvar2 -> tvar2)` or `(tvar3 -> tvar3)`, and so on. These may be different every time through the inferencer, so we won't

---

Answer = Type × Subst

```
(define-datatype answer answer?
  (an-answer
    (ty type?)
    (subst substitution?)))
```

type-of-program : *Program* → *Type*
```
(define type-of-program
  (lambda (pgm)
    (cases program pgm
      (a-program (exp1)
        (cases answer (type-of exp1
                        (init-tenv) (empty-subst))
          (an-answer (ty subst)
            (apply-subst-to-type ty subst)))))))
```

type-of : *Exp* × *Tenv* × *Subst* → *Answer*
```
(define type-of
  (lambda (exp tenv subst)
    (cases expression exp

      (const-exp (num) (an-answer (int-type) subst))
```

```
┌─────────────────────────────────────────────────┐
│ (zero?-exp e₁)    :    t_{e_1} = int             │
│                       t_{(zero?-exp e_1)} = bool │
└─────────────────────────────────────────────────┘
```

$$(\texttt{zero?-exp } e_1) \quad : \quad t_{e_1} = \texttt{int}$$
$$t_{(\texttt{zero?-exp } e_1)} = \texttt{bool}$$

```
      (zero?-exp (exp1)
        (cases answer (type-of exp1 tenv subst)
          (an-answer (ty1 subst1)
            (let ((subst2
                    (unifier ty1 (int-type) subst1 exp)))
              (an-answer (bool-type) subst2)))))
```

Figure 7.6 `type-of` for INFERRED, part 1

$$
\boxed{
\begin{array}{ll}
(\texttt{diff-exp } e_1\ e_2) \quad : & t_{e_1} = \texttt{int} \\
& t_{e_2} = \texttt{int} \\
& t_{(\texttt{diff-exp } e_1\ e_2)} = \texttt{int}
\end{array}
}
$$

```
(diff-exp (exp1 exp2)
  (cases answer (type-of exp1 tenv subst)
    (an-answer (ty1 subst1)
      (let ((subst1
              (unifier ty1 (int-type) subst1 exp1)))
        (cases answer (type-of exp2 tenv subst1)
          (an-answer (ty2 subst2)
            (let ((subst2
                    (unifier ty2 (int-type)
                      subst2 exp2)))
              (an-answer (int-type) subst2)))))))))
```

$$
\boxed{
\begin{array}{ll}
(\texttt{if-exp } e_1\ e_2\ e_3) \quad : & t_{e_1} = \texttt{bool} \\
& t_{e_2} = t_{(\texttt{if-exp } e_1\ e_2\ e_3)} \\
& t_{e_3} = t_{(\texttt{if-exp } e_1\ e_2\ e_3)}
\end{array}
}
$$

```
(if-exp (exp1 exp2 exp3)
  (cases answer (type-of exp1 tenv subst)
    (an-answer (ty1 subst)
      (let ((subst
              (unifier ty1 (bool-type) subst exp1)))
        (cases answer (type-of exp2 tenv subst)
          (an-answer (ty2 subst)
            (cases answer (type-of exp3 tenv subst)
              (an-answer (ty3 subst)
                (let ((subst
                        (unifier ty2 ty3 subst exp)))
                  (an-answer ty2 subst)))))))))))

(var-exp (var)
  (an-answer (apply-tenv tenv var) subst))

(let-exp (var exp1 body)
  (cases answer (type-of exp1 tenv subst)
    (an-answer (exp1-type subst)
      (type-of body
        (extend-tenv var exp1-type tenv)
        subst))))
```

Figure 7.7 `type-of` for INFERRED, part 2

$$\boxed{\texttt{(proc-exp } \textit{var body)} \quad : \quad t_{\texttt{(proc-exp } \textit{var body})} = (t_{\textit{var}} \;\rightarrow\; t_{\textit{body}})}$$

```
(proc-exp (var otype body)
  (let ((var-type (otype->type otype)))
    (cases answer (type-of body
                      (extend-tenv var var-type tenv)
                      subst)
      (an-answer (body-type subst)
        (an-answer
          (proc-type var-type body-type)
          subst)))))
```

$$\boxed{\texttt{(call-exp } \textit{rator rand)} \quad : \quad t_{\textit{rator}} = (t_{\textit{rand}} \;\rightarrow\; t_{\texttt{(call-exp } \textit{rator rand})})}$$

```
(call-exp (rator rand)
  (let ((result-type (fresh-tvar-type)))
    (cases answer (type-of rator tenv subst)
      (an-answer (rator-type subst)
        (cases answer (type-of rand tenv subst)
          (an-answer (rand-type subst)
            (let ((subst
                    (unifier
                      rator-type
                      (proc-type
                        rand-type result-type)
                      subst
                      exp)))
              (an-answer result-type subst)))))))))
```

Figure 7.8 `type-of` for INFERRED, part 3

be able to anticipate them when we write our test items. So when we compare the produced type to the correct type, we'll fail. We need to accept all of the alternatives above, but reject (tvar3 -> tvar4) or (int -> tvar17).

To compare two types in external form, we standardize the names of the unknown types, by walking through each external form, renumbering all the type variables so that they are numbered starting with ty1. We can then compare the renumbered types with equal? (figures 7.10–7.11).

To systematically rename each unknown type, we construct a substitution with canonical-subst. This is a straightforward recursion, with table

$$\texttt{letrec}\ t_{proc-result}\ p\ (var\ :\ t_{var}) = e_{proc\text{-}body}\ \texttt{in}\ e_{letrec\text{-}body} \quad :$$
$$t_p = t_{var} \rightarrow t_{e_{proc\text{-}body}}$$
$$t_{e_{letrec\text{-}body}} = t_{\texttt{letrec}\ t_{proc-result}\ p\ (var\ :\ t_{var}) = e_{proc\text{-}body}\ \texttt{in}\ e_{letrec\text{-}body}}$$

```
(letrec-exp (p-result-otype p-name b-var b-var-otype
             p-body letrec-body)
  (let ((p-result-type (otype->type p-result-otype))
        (p-var-type (otype->type b-var-otype)))
    (let ((tenv-for-letrec-body
           (extend-tenv p-name
             (proc-type p-var-type p-result-type)
             tenv)))
      (cases answer (type-of p-body
                      (extend-tenv b-var p-var-type
                        tenv-for-letrec-body)
                      subst)
        (an-answer (p-body-type subst)
          (let ((subst
                  (unifier p-body-type p-result-type
                    subst p-body)))
            (type-of letrec-body
              tenv-for-letrec-body
              subst))))))))))))
```

Figure 7.9 `type-of` for INFERRED, part 4

playing the role of an accumulator. The length of `table` tells us how many distinct unknown types we have found, so we can use its length to give the number of the "next" `ty` symbol. This is similar to the way we used `length` in figure 4.1.

Exercise 7.23 [$\star\star$] Extend the inferencer to handle pair types, as in exercise 7.8.

Exercise 7.24 [$\star\star$] Extend the inferencer to handle multiple `let` declarations, multi-argument procedures, and multiple `letrec` declarations.

TvarTypeSym = a symbol ending with a digit

A-list = *Listof*(*Pair*(*TvarTypeSym*, *TvarTypeSym*))

equal-up-to-gensyms? : *S-exp* × *S-exp* → *Bool*
```
(define equal-up-to-gensyms?
  (lambda (sexp1 sexp2)
    (equal?
      (apply-subst-to-sexp (canonical-subst sexp1) sexp1)
      (apply-subst-to-sexp (canonical-subst sexp2) sexp2))))
```

canonical-subst : *S-exp* → *A-list*
```
(define canonical-subst
  (lambda (sexp)
```
      loop : *S-exp* × *A-list* → *A-list*
```
    (let loop ((sexp sexp) (table '()))
      (cond
        ((null? sexp) table)
        ((tvar-type-sym? sexp)
         (cond
           ((assq sexp table) table)
           (else
             (cons
               (cons sexp (ctr->ty (length table)))
               table))))
        ((pair? sexp)
         (loop (cdr sexp)
           (loop (car sexp) table)))
        (else table)))))
```

Figure 7.10   equal-up-to-gensyms?, part 1

Exercise 7.25 [⋆⋆] Extend the inferencer to handle list types, as in exercise 7.9. Modify the language to use the production

$$Expression ::= \texttt{emptylist}$$

instead of

$$Expression ::= \texttt{emptylist\_}Type$$

As a hint, consider creating a type variable in place of the missing _t.

tvar-type-sym? : *Sym* → *Bool*
```
(define tvar-type-sym?
  (lambda (sym)
    (and (symbol? sym)
      (char-numeric? (car (reverse (symbol->list sym)))))))
```

symbol->list : *Sym* → *List*
```
(define symbol->list
  (lambda (x)
    (string->list (symbol->string x))))
```

apply-subst-to-sexp : *A-list* × *S-exp* → *S-exp*
```
(define apply-subst-to-sexp
  (lambda (subst sexp)
    (cond
      ((null? sexp) sexp)
      ((tvar-type-sym? sexp)
       (cdr (assq sexp subst)))
      ((pair? sexp)
       (cons
         (apply-subst-to-sexp subst (car sexp))
         (apply-subst-to-sexp subst (cdr sexp))))
      (else sexp))))
```

ctr->ty : *N* → *Sym*
```
(define ctr->ty
  (lambda (n)
    (string->symbol
      (string-append "tvar" (number->string n)))))
```

Figure 7.11   equal-up-to-gensyms?, part 2

Exercise 7.26 [★★] Extend the inferencer to handle EXPLICIT-REFS, as in exercise 7.10.

Exercise 7.27 [★★] Rewrite the inferencer so that it works in two phases. In the first phase it should generate a set of equations, and in the second phase, it should repeatedly call unify to solve them.

Exercise 7.28 [★★] Our inferencer is very useful, but it is not powerful enough to allow the programmer to define procedures that are polymorphic, like the polymorphic primitives `pair` or `cons`, which can be used at many types. For example, our inferencer would reject the program

```
let f = proc (x : ?) x
in if (f zero?(0))
   then (f 11)
   else (f 22)
```

even though its execution is safe, because f is used both at type (bool→ bool) and at type (int→ int). Since the inferencer of this section is allowed to find at most one type for f, it will reject this program.

For a more realistic example, one would like to write programs like

```
let
 ? map (f : ?) =
    letrec
     ? foo (x : ?) = if null?(x)
                       then emptylist
                       else cons((f car(x)),
                                 ((foo f) cdr(x)))
        in foo
 in letrec
     ? even (y : ?) = if zero?(y)
                        then zero?(0)
                        else if zero?(-(y,1))
                               then zero?(1)
                               else (even -(y,2))
     in pair(((map proc(x : int)-(x,1))
              cons(3,cons(5,emptylist))),
             ((map even)
              cons(3,cons(5,emptylist)))))
```

This expression uses map twice, once producing a list of ints and once producing a list of bools. Therefore it needs two different types for the two uses. Since the inferencer of this section will find at most one type for map, it will detect the clash between int and bool and reject the program.

One way to avoid this problem is to allow polymorphic values to be introduced only by let, and then to treat (let-exp *var* e_1 e_2) differently from (call-exp (proc-exp *var* e_2) e_1) for type-checking purposes.

Add polymorphic bindings to the inferencer by treating (let-exp *var* e_1 e_2) like the expression obtained by substituting e_1 for each free occurrence of *var* in e_2. Then, from the point of view of the inferencer, there are many different copies of e_1 in the body of the let, so they can have different types, and the programs above will be accepted.

Exercise 7.29 [★ ★ ★] The type inference algorithm suggested in the preceding exercise will analyze e_1 many times, once for each of its occurrences in e_2. Implement Milner's Algorithm W, which analyzes e_1 only once.

Exercise 7.30 [★ ★ ★] The interaction between polymorphism and effects is subtle. Consider a program starting

```
let p = newref(proc (x : ?) x)
in ...
```

1. Finish this program to produce a program that passes the polymorphic inferencer, but whose evaluation is not safe according to the definition at the beginning of the chapter.

2. Avoid this difficulty by restricting the right-hand side of a `let` to have no effect on the store. This is called the *value restriction*.

8 *Modules*

The language features we have introduced so far are very powerful for building systems of a few hundred lines of code. If we are to build larger systems, with thousands of lines of code, we will need some more ingredients.

1. We will need a good way to separate the system into relatively self-contained parts, and to document the dependencies between those parts.

2. We will need a better way to control the scope and binding of names. Lexical scoping is a powerful tool for name control, but it is not sufficient when programs may be large or split up over multiple sources.

3. We will need a way to enforce abstraction boundaries. In chapter 2, we introduced the idea of an abstract data type. Inside the implementation of the type, we can manipulate the values arbitrarily, but outside the implementation, the values of the type are to be created and manipulated only by the procedures in the interface of that type. We call this an *abstraction boundary*. If a program respects this boundary, we can change the implementation of the data type. If, however, some piece of code breaks the abstraction by relying on the details of the implementation, then we can no longer change the implementation freely without breaking other code.

4. Last, we need a way to combine these parts flexibly, so that a single part may be reused in different contexts.

In this chapter, we introduce *modules* as a way of satisfying these needs. In particular, we show how we can use the type system to create and enforce abstraction boundaries.

A program in our module language consists of a sequence of *module definitions* followed by an expression to be evaluated. Each module definition binds a name to a *module*. A created module is either a *simple module*, which is a set of bindings, much like an environment, or a *module procedure* that takes a module and produces another module.

Each module will have an *interface*. A module that is a set of bindings will have a *simple interface*, which lists the bindings offered by the module, and their types. A module procedure will have an interface that specifies the interfaces of the argument and result modules of the procedure, much as a procedure has a type that specifies the types of its argument and result.

These interfaces, like types, determine the ways in which modules can be combined. We therefore emphasize the types of our examples, since evaluation of these programs is straightforward. As we have seen before, understanding the scoping and binding rules of the language will be the key to both analyzing and evaluating programs in the language.

8.1   The Simple Module System

Our first language, SIMPLE-MODULES, has only simple modules. It does not have module procedures, and it creates only very simple abstraction boundaries. This module system is similar to that used in several popular languages.

8.1.1   Examples

Imagine a software project involving three developers: Alice, Bob, and Charlie. Alice, Bob, and Charlie are developing largely independent pieces of the project. These developers are geographically dispersed, perhaps in different time zones. Each piece of the project is to implement an interface, like those in section 2.1, but the implementation of that interface may involve a large number of additional procedures. Furthermore, each of the developers needs to make sure that there are no name conflicts that would interfere with the other portions of the project when the pieces are integrated.

To accomplish this goal, each of the developers needs to publish an interface, listing the names for each of their procedures that they expect others to use. It will be the job of the module system to ensure that these names are public, but any other names they use are private and will not be overridden by any other piece of code in the project.

We could use the scoping techniques of chapter 3, but these do not scale to larger projects. Instead, we will use a module system. Each of our developers will produce a module consisting of a public interface and a private implementation. Each developer can see the interface and implementation of his or her own module, but Alice can see only the interfaces of the other modules. Nothing she can do can interfere with the implementations of the other modules, nor can their module implementations interfere with hers. (See figure 8.1.)

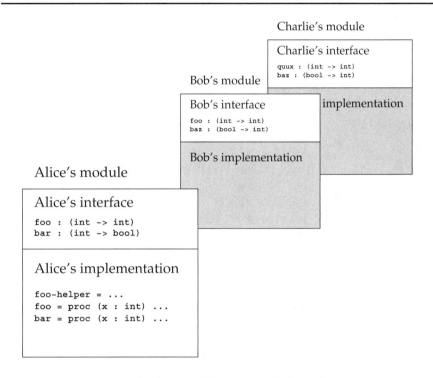

Figure 8.1   Alice's view of the three modules in the project

Here is a short example in SIMPLE-MODULES.

Example 8.1

```
module m1
  interface
   [a : int
    b : int
    c : int]
  body
   [a = 33
    x = -(a,1)    % = 32
    b = -(a,x)    % =  1
    c = -(x,b)]   % = 31
let a = 10
in -(-(from m1 take a,
       from m1 take b),
     a)
```

has type int and value $((33 - 1) - 10) = 22$.

This program begins with the definition of a module named m1. Like all modules, it has an *interface* and a *body*. The body *implements* the interface. The interface *declares* the variables a, b, and c. The body *defines* bindings for a, x, b, and c.

When we evaluate the program, the expressions in m1's body are evaluated. The appropriate values are bound to the variables from m1 take a, from m1 take b, and from m1 take c, which are in scope after the module definition. from m1 take x is not in scope after the module definition, since it has not been declared in the interface.

These new variables are called *qualified variables* to distinguish them from our previous *simple variables*. In conventional languages, qualified variables might be written m1.a or m1:a or m1::a. The notation m1.a is often used for something different in object-oriented languages, which we study in chapter 9.

We say that the interface *offers* (or *advertises* or *promises*) three integer values, and that the body *supplies* (or *provides* or *exports*) these values. A module body *satisfies* an interface when it supplies a value of the advertised type for each of the variables that are named in the interface.

In the body, definitions have let* scoping, so that a is in scope in the definitions of x, b, and c. Some of the scopes are pictured in figure 8.2.

In this example, the expression, starting with let a = 10, is the *program body*. Its value will become the value of the program.

Each module establishes an abstraction boundary between the module body and the rest of the program. The expressions in the module body are *inside* the abstraction boundary, and everything else is *outside* the abstraction boundary. A module body may supply bindings for names that are not in the interface, but those bindings are not visible in the program body or in other modules, as suggested in figure 8.1. In our example, from m1 take x is not in scope. Had we written -(from m1 take a, from m1 take x), the resulting program would have been ill-typed.

Example 8.2 The program

```
module m1
 interface
  [u : bool]
 body
  [u = 33]

44
```

is not well-typed. The body of the module must associate each name in the interface with a value of the appropriate type, even if those values are not used elsewhere in the program.

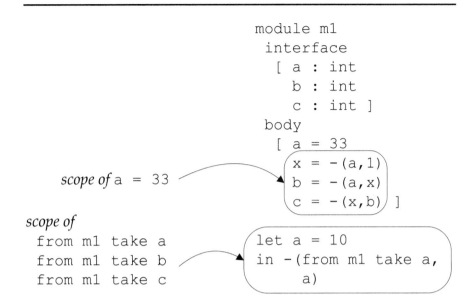

Figure 8.2   Some of the scopes for a simple module

Example 8.3 The module body must supply bindings for all the declarations in the interface. For example,

```
module m1
  interface
   [u : int
    v : int]
  body
   [u = 33]

  44
```

is not well-typed, because the body of m1 does not provide all of the values that its interface advertises.

Example 8.4 To keep the implementation simple, our language requires that the module body produce the values in the same order as the interface. Hence

```
module m1
 interface
  [u : int
   v : int]
 body
  [v = 33
   u = 44]

from m1 take u
```

is not well-typed. This can be fixed (exercises 8.8, 8.17).

Example 8.5 In our language, modules have let* scoping (exercise 3.17). For example,

```
module m1
 interface
  [u : int]
 body
  [u = 44]

module m2
 interface
  [v : int]
 body
  [v = -(from m1 take u,11)]

-(from m1 take u, from m2 take v)
```

has type int. But if we reverse the order of the definitions, we get

```
module m2
 interface
  [v : int]
 body
  [v = -(from m1 take u,11)]

module m1
 interface
  [u : int]
 body
  [u = 44]

-(from m1 take u, from m2 take v)
```

which is not well-typed, since from m1 take u is not in scope where it is used in the body of m2.

8.1.2 Implementing the Simple Module System

Syntax

A program in SIMPLE-MODULES consists of a sequence of module definitions, followed by an expression.

$$program ::= \{ModuleDefn\}^* \; Expression$$
```
a-program (m-defs body)
```

A module definition consists of its name, its interface, and its body.

$$ModuleDefn ::= \texttt{module} \; Identifier \; \texttt{interface} \; Iface \; \texttt{body} \; ModuleBody$$
```
a-module-definition (m-name expected-iface m-body)
```

An interface for a simple module consists of an arbitrary number of declarations. Each declaration declares a program variable and its type. We call these *value declarations*, since the variable being declared will denote a value. In later sections, we introduce other kinds of interfaces and declarations.

$$Iface ::= \texttt{[} \; \{Decl\}^* \; \texttt{]}$$
```
simple-iface (decls)
```

$$Decl ::= Identifier \; \texttt{:} \; Type$$
```
val-decl (var-name ty)
```

A module body consists of an arbitrary number of definitions. Each definition associates a variable with the value of an expression.

$$ModuleBody ::= \texttt{[} \; \{Defn\}^* \; \texttt{]}$$
```
defns-module-body (defns)
```

$$Defn ::= Identifier \; \texttt{=} \; Expression$$
```
val-defn (var-name exp)
```

Our expressions are those of CHECKED (section 7.3), but we modify the grammar to add a new kind of expression for a reference to a qualified variable.

$$Expression ::= \texttt{from} \; Identifier \; \texttt{take} \; Identifier$$
```
qualified-var-exp (m-name var-name)
```

The Interpreter

Evaluation of a module body will produce a *module*. In our simple module language, a module will be an environment consisting of all the bindings exported by the module. We represent these with the data type `typed-module`.

```
(define-datatype typed-module typed-module?
  (simple-module
    (bindings environment?)))
```

We bind module names in the environment, using a new kind of binding:

```
(define-datatype environment environment?
  (empty-env)
  (extend-env ...as before...)
  (extend-env-rec ...as before...)
  (extend-env-with-module
    (m-name symbol?)
    (m-val typed-module?)
    (saved-env environment?)))
```

For example, if our program is

```
module m1
 interface
  [a : int
   b : int
   c : int]
 body
  [a = 33
   b = 44
   c = 55]
module m2
 interface
  [a : int
   b : int]
 body
  [a = 66
   b = 77]
let z = 99
in -(z, -(from m1 take a, from m2 take a))
```

then the environment after the declaration of z is

```
#(struct:extend-env
   z #(struct:num-val 99)
  #(struct:extend-env-with-module
     m2 #(struct:simple-module
           #(struct:extend-env
              a #(struct:num-val 66)
              #(struct:extend-env
                 b #(struct:num-val 77)
                 #(struct:empty-env))))
  #(struct:extend-env-with-module
     m1 #(struct:simple-module
           #(struct:extend-env
              a #(struct:num-val 33)
              #(struct:extend-env
                 b #(struct:num-val 44)
                 #(struct:extend-env
                    c #(struct:num-val 55)
                    #(struct:empty-env)))))
  #(struct:empty-env))))
```

In this environment, both m1 and m2 are bound to simple modules, which contain a small environment.

To evaluate a reference to a qualified variable from *m* take *var*, we use lookup-qualified-var-in-env. This first looks up the module *m* in the current environment, and then looks up *var* in the resulting environment.

lookup-qualified-var-in-env : *Sym* × *Sym* × *Env* → *ExpVal*
```
(define lookup-qualified-var-in-env
  (lambda (m-name var-name env)
    (let ((m-val (lookup-module-name-in-env m-name env)))
      (cases typed-module m-val
        (simple-module (bindings)
          (apply-env bindings var-name))))))
```

To evaluate a program, we evaluate its body in an initial environment built by adding all the module definitions to the environment. The procedure add-module-defns-to-env loops through the module definitions. For each module definition, the body is evaluated, and the resulting module is added to the environment. See figure 8.3.

Last, to evaluate a module body, we build an environment, evaluating each expression in the appropriate environment to get let* scoping. The procedure defns-to-env produces an environment containing only the bindings produced by the definitions defns (figure 8.4).

```
value-of-program : Program → ExpVal
(define value-of-program
  (lambda (pgm)
    (cases program pgm
      (a-program (m-defns body)
        (value-of body
          (add-module-defns-to-env m-defns (empty-env))))))))

add-module-defns-to-env : Listof(Defn) × Env → Env
(define add-module-defns-to-env
  (lambda (defns env)
    (if (null? defns)
      env
      (cases module-definition (car defns)
        (a-module-definition (m-name iface m-body)
          (add-module-defns-to-env
            (cdr defns)
            (extend-env-with-module
              m-name
              (value-of-module-body m-body env)
              env)))))))))
```

Figure 8.3   Interpreter for SIMPLE-MODULES, part 1

The Checker

The job of the checker is to make sure that each module body satisfies its
interface, and that each variable is used consistently with its type.

The scoping rules of our language are fairly simple: Modules follow
`let*` scoping, putting into scope qualified variables for each of the bindings exported by the module. The interface tells us the type of each qualified
variable. Declarations and definitions both follow `let*` scoping as well (see
figure 8.2).

As we did with the checker in chapter 7, we use the type environment to
keep track of information about each name that is in scope. Since we now
have module names, we bind module names in the type environment. Each
module name will be bound to its interface, which plays the role of a type.

```
value-of-module-body : ModuleBody × Env → TypedModule
(define value-of-module-body
  (lambda (m-body env)
    (cases module-body m-body
      (defns-module-body (defns)
        (simple-module
          (defns-to-env defns env))))))
```

```
defns-to-env : Listof(Defn) × Env → Env
(define defns-to-env
  (lambda (defns env)
    (if (null? defns)
      (empty-env)
      (cases definition (car defns)
        (val-defn (var exp)
          (let ((val (value-of exp env)))
            (let ((new-env (extend-env var val env)))
              (extend-env var val
                (defns-to-env
                  (cdr defns) new-env)))))))))
```

Figure 8.4   Interpreter for SIMPLE-MODULES, part 2

```
(define-datatype type-environment type-environment?
  (empty-tenv)
  (extend-tenv ...as before...)
  (extend-tenv-with-module
    (name symbol?)
    (interface interface?)
    (saved-tenv type-environment?)))
```

We find the type of a qualified variable from *m* take *var* by first look-ing up *m* in the type environment, and then looking up the type of *var* in the resulting interface.

```
lookup-qualified-var-in-tenv : Sym × Sym × Tenv → Type
(define lookup-qualified-var-in-tenv
  (lambda (m-name var-name tenv)
    (let ((iface (lookup-module-name-in-tenv tenv m-name)))
      (cases interface iface
        (simple-iface (decls)
          (lookup-variable-name-in-decls var-name decls))))))
```

---

type-of-program : *Program → Type*

```
(define type-of-program
  (lambda (pgm)
    (cases program pgm
      (a-program (module-defns body)
        (type-of body
          (add-module-defns-to-tenv module-defns
            (empty-tenv)))))))
```

add-module-defns-to-tenv : *Listof(ModuleDefn) × Tenv → Tenv*

```
(define add-module-defns-to-tenv
  (lambda (defns tenv)
    (if (null? defns)
      tenv
      (cases module-definition (car defns)
        (a-module-definition (m-name expected-iface m-body)
          (let ((actual-iface (interface-of m-body tenv)))
            (if (<:-iface actual-iface expected-iface tenv)
              (let ((new-tenv
                      (extend-tenv-with-module
                        m-name
                        expected-iface
                        tenv)))
                (add-module-defns-to-tenv
                  (cdr defns) new-tenv))
              (report-module-doesnt-satisfy-iface
                m-name expected-iface actual-iface))))))))
```

Figure 8.5   Checker for SIMPLE-MODULES, part 1

Just as in chapter 7, the process of typechecking a program mimics the evaluation of the program, except that instead of keeping track of values, we keep track of types. Instead of `value-of-program`, we have `type-of-program`, and instead of `add-module-defns-to-env`, we have `add-module-defns-to-tenv`. The procedure `add-module-defns-to-tenv` checks each module to see whether the interface produced by the module body matches the advertised interface, using the procedure `<:-iface`. If it does, the module is added to the type environment. Otherwise, an error is reported.

The interface of a module body associates each variable defined in the body with the type of its definition. For example, if we looked at the body from our first example,

```
[a = 33
 x = -(a,1)
 b = -(a,x)
 c = -(x,b)]
```

we should get

```
[a : int
 x : int
 b : int
 c : int]
```

Once we build an interface describing all the bindings exported by the module body, we can compare it to the interface that the module advertises.

Recall that a simple interface contains a list of declarations. The procedure `defns-to-decls` creates such a list, calling `type-of` to find the type of each definition. At every step it also extends the local type environment, to follow the correct `let*` scoping. (See figure 8.6.)

All that's left is to compare the actual and expected types of each module, using the procedure `<:-iface`. We intend to define `<:` so that if $i_1 <: i_2$, then any module that satisfies interface i_1 also satisfies interface i_2. For example

```
[u : int          [u : int
 v : bool   <:     z : int]
 z : int]
```

since any module that satisfies the interface [u : int v : bool z : int] provides all the values that are advertised by the interface [u : int z : int].

For our simple module language, `<:-iface` just calls `<:-decls`, which compares declarations. These procedures take a `tenv` argument that is not used for the simple module system, but will be needed in section 8.2. See figure 8.7.

The procedure `<:-decls` does the main work of comparing two sets of declarations. If *decls*$_1$ and *decls*$_2$ are two sets of declarations, we say *decls*$_1$ <: *decls*$_2$ if and only if any module that supplies bindings for the declarations in *decls*$_1$ also supplies bindings for the declarations in *decls*$_2$. This can be assured

```
interface-of  :  ModuleBody  ×  Tenv  →  Iface
(define interface-of
  (lambda (m-body tenv)
    (cases module-body m-body
      (defns-module-body (defns)
        (simple-iface
          (defns-to-decls defns tenv))))))

defns-to-decls  :  Listof(Defn)  ×  Tenv  →  Listof(Decl)
(define defns-to-decls
  (lambda (defns tenv)
    (if (null? defns)
      '()
      (cases definition (car defns)
        (val-defn (var-name exp)
          (let ((ty (type-of exp tenv)))
            (cons
              (val-decl var-name ty)
              (defns-to-decls
                (cdr defns)
                (extend-tenv var-name ty tenv)))))))))
```

Figure 8.6 Checker for SIMPLE-MODULES, part 2

if *decls*$_1$ contains a matching declaration for every declaration in *decls*$_2$, as in the example above.

The procedure <:-decls first checks decls1 and decls2. If decls2 is empty, then it makes no demands on decls1, so the answer is #t. If decls2 is non-empty, but decls1 is empty, then decls2 requires something, but decls1 has nothing. So the answer is #f. Otherwise, we compare the names of the first variables declared by decls1 and decls2. If they are the same, then their types must match, and we recur on the rest of both lists of declarations. If they are not the same, then we recur on the cdr of decls1 to look for something that matches the first declaration of decls2.

This completes the simple module system.

```
<:-iface : Iface × Iface × Tenv → Bool
(define <:-iface
  (lambda (iface1 iface2 tenv)
    (cases interface iface1
      (simple-iface (decls1)
        (cases interface iface2
          (simple-iface (decls2)
            (<:-decls decls1 decls2 tenv)))))))

<:-decls : Listof(Decl) × Listof(Decl) × Tenv → Bool
(define <:-decls
  (lambda (decls1 decls2 tenv)
    (cond
      ((null? decls2) #t)
      ((null? decls1) #f)
      (else
        (let ((name1 (decl->name (car decls1)))
              (name2 (decl->name (car decls2))))
          (if (eqv? name1 name2)
            (and
              (equal?
                (decl->type (car decls1))
                (decl->type (car decls2)))
              (<:-decls (cdr decls1) (cdr decls2) tenv))
            (<:-decls (cdr decls1) decls2 tenv)))))))
```

Figure 8.7   Comparing interfaces for SIMPLE-MODULES

Exercise 8.1 [⋆] Modify the checker to detect and reject any program that defines two modules with the same name.

Exercise 8.2 [⋆] The procedure `add-module-defn-to-env` is not quite right, because it adds all the values defined by the module, not just the ones in the interface. Modify `add-module-defn-to-env` so that it adds to the environment only the values declared in the interface. Does `add-module-defn-to-tenv` suffer from the same problem?

Exercise 8.3 [⋆] Change the syntax of the language so that a qualified variable reference appears as `m.v`, rather than `from m take v`.

Exercise 8.4 [⋆] Change the expression language to include multiple `let` declarations, multiargument procedures, and multiple `letrec` declarations, as in exercise 7.24.

Exercise 8.5 [⋆] Allow `let` and `letrec` declarations to be used in module bodies. For example, one should be able to write

```
module even-odd
  interface
  [even : int -> bool
   odd  : int -> bool]
  body
   letrec
    bool local-odd (x : int)  = ... (local-even -(x,1)) ...
    bool local-even (x : int) = ... (local-odd -(x,1)) ...
   in [even = local-even
       odd  = local-odd]
```

Exercise 8.6 [⋆⋆] Allow local module definitions to appear in module bodies. For example, one should be able to write

```
module m1
  interface
  [u : int
   v : int]
  body
   module m2
    interface [v : int]
    body [v = 33]
   [u = 44
    v = -(from m2 take v, 1)]
```

Exercise 8.7 [⋆⋆] Extend your solution to the preceding exercise to allow modules to export other modules as components. For example, one should be able to write

```
module m1
  interface
  [u : int
   n : [v : int]]
  body
   module m2
    interface [v : int]
    body [v = 33]
   [u = 44
    n = m2]


from m1 take n take v
```

Exercise 8.8 [⋆⋆] In our language, the module must produce the values in the same order as the interface, but that could easily be fixed. Fix it.

Exercise 8.9 [⋆⋆] We said that our module system should document the dependencies between modules. Add this capability to SIMPLE-MODULES by requiring a

depends-on clause in each module body and in the program body. Rather than
having all preceding modules in scope in a module m, a preceding module is in scope
only if it is listed in m's depends-on clause. For example, consider the program

```
module m1 ...
module m2 ...
module m3 ...
module m4 ...
module m5
 interface [...]
 body
  depends-on m1, m3
  [...]
```

In the body of m5, qualified variables would be in scope only if they came from m1 or
m3. A reference to from m4 take x would be ill-typed, even if m4 exported a value
for x.

Exercise 8.10 [★ ★ ★] We could also use a feature like depends-on to control when
module bodies are evaluated. Add this capability to SIMPLE-MODULES by requiring an imports clause to each module body and program body. imports is like
depends-on, but has the additional property that the body of a module is evaluated
only when it is imported by some other module (using an imports clause).

Thus if our language had print expressions, the program

```
module m1
 interface [] body [x = print(1)]
module m2
 interface [] body [x = print(2)]
module m3
 interface []
 body
  import m2
  [x = print(3)]
import m3, m1
33
```

would print 2, 3, and 1 before returning 33. Here the modules have empty interfaces,
because we are only concerned with the order in which the bodies are evaluated.

Exercise 8.11 [★ ★ ★] Modify the checker to use INFERRED as the language of expressions. For this exercise you will need to modify <:-decls to use something other
than equal? to compare types. For example, in

```
module m
 interface [f : (int -> int)]
 body [f = proc (x : ?) x]
```

the actual type for f reported by the type inference engine will be something like
(tvar07 -> tvar07), and this should be accepted. On the other hand, we should
reject the module

```
module m
  interface [f : (int -> bool)]
  body [f = proc (x : ?) x]
```

even though the type inference engine will report the same type (tvar07 ->
tvar07) for f.

8.2 Modules That Declare Types

So far, our interfaces have declared only ordinary variables and their types.
In the next module language, OPAQUE-TYPES, we allow interfaces to
declare types as well. For example, in the definition

```
module m1
  interface
   [opaque t
    zero : t
    succ : (t -> t)
    pred : (t -> t)
    is-zero : (t -> bool)]
  body
    ...
```

the interface declares a type t, and some operations zero, succ, pred, and
is-zero that operate on values of that type. This is the interface that might
be associated with an implementation of arithmetic, as in section 2.1. Here
t is declared to be an *opaque type*, meaning that code outside the module
boundary does not know how values of this type are represented. All the
outside code knows is that it can manipulate values of type from m1 take
t with the procedures from m1 take zero, from m1 take succ, etc.
Thus from m1 take t behaves like a primitive type such as int or bool.

We will introduce two kinds of type declarations: *transparent* and *opaque*.
Both are necessary for a good module system.

8.2.1   Examples

To motivate this, consider our developers again. Alice has been using a data structure consisting of a pair of integers, representing the x- and y-coordinates of a point. She is using a language with types like those of exercise 7.8, so her module, named `Alices-points`, has an interface with declarations like

```
initial-point : (int -> pairof int * int)
increment-x   : (pairof int * int -> pairof int * int)
```

Bob and Charlie complain about this. They don't want to have to write `pairof int * int` over and over again. Alice therefore rewrites her interface to use transparent type declarations. This allows her to write

```
module Alices-points
  interface
   [transparent point = pairof int * int
    initial-point : (int -> point)
    increment-x   : (point -> point)
    get-x         : (point -> int)
    ...]
```

This simplifies her task, since she has less writing to do, and it makes her collaborators' tasks simpler, because in their implementations they can write definitions like

```
[transparent point = from Alices-points take point
 foo = proc (p1 : point)
         proc (p2 : point) ...
 ...]
```

For some projects, this would do nicely. On the other hand, the points in Alice's project happen to represent points on a metal track with a fixed geometry, so the x- and y-coordinates are not independent. Alice's implementation of `increment-x` carefully updates the y-coordinate to match the change in the x-coordinate. But Bob doesn't know this, and so he writes his own procedure

```
increment-y = proc (p : point)
                unpair x y = p
                in newpair(x, -(y,-1))
```

Because Bob's code changes the y-coordinate without changing the x-coordinate correspondingly, Alice's code no longer works correctly.

Worse yet, what if Alice decides to change the representation of points so that the y-coordinate is in the first component? She can change her code to match this new representation. But then Bob's code would be broken, because his `increment-y` procedure now changes the wrong component of the pair.

Alice can solve her problem by making `point` an *opaque* data type. She rewrites her interface to say

```
opaque point
initial-point : (int -> point)
increment-x   : (point -> point)
get-x         : (point -> int)
```

Now Bob can create new points using the procedure `initial-point`, and he can manipulate points using `from Alices-points take get-x` and `from Alices-points take increment-x`, but he can no longer manipulate points using any procedures other than the ones in Alice's interface. In particular, he can no longer write the `increment-y` procedure, since it manipulates a point using something other than the procedures in Alice's interface.

In the remainder of this section, we explore further examples of these facilities.

Transparent Types

We begin by discussing *transparent* type declarations. These are sometimes called *concrete* type declarations or *type abbreviations*.

Example 8.6 The program

```
module m1
  interface
   [transparent t = int
    z : t
    s : (t -> t)
    is-z? : (t -> bool)]
  body
   [type t = int
    z = 33
    s = proc (x : t) -(x,-1)
    is-z? = proc (x : t) zero?(-(x,z))]

  proc (x : from m1 take t)
   (from m1 take is-z? -(x,0))
```

has type `(int -> bool)`.

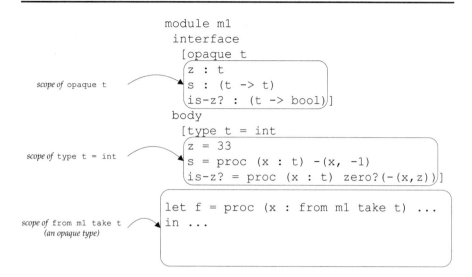

scope of `opaque t`

scope of `type t = int`

scope of `from m1 take t`
(an opaque type)

Figure 8.8   Scopes for a module that declares types

The declaration `transparent t = int` in the interface binds `t` to the type `int` in the rest of the interface, so we can write `z : t`. More importantly, it also binds `from m1 take t` to `int` in the rest of the program. We call this a *qualified type*. Here we have used it to declare the type of the bound variable `z`. The scope of a declaration is the rest of the interface and the rest of the program after the module definition.

The definition `type t = int` in the body binds `t` to the type `int` in the rest of the module body, so we could write `s = proc (x : t)`.... As before, the scope of a definition is the rest of the body (see figure 8.8).

Of course, we can use any name we like for the type, and we can declare more than one type. The type declarations can appear anywhere in the interface, so long as each declaration precedes all of its uses.

Opaque Types

A module can also export *opaque* types by using an `opaque-type` declaration. Opaque types are sometimes called *abstract* types.

Example 8.7 Let's take the program in example 8.6 and replace the transparent type declaration by an opaque one. The resulting program is

```
module m1
  interface
   [opaque t
    z : t
    s : (t -> t)
    is-z? : (t -> bool)]
  body
   [type t = int
    z = 33
    s = proc (x : t) -(x,-1)
    is-z? = proc (x : t) zero?(-(x,z))]

  proc (x : from m1 take t)
   (from m1 take is-z? -(x,0))
```

The declaration `opaque t` in the interface declares `t` to be the name of a new opaque type. An opaque type behaves like a new primitive type, such as `int` or `bool`. The named type `t` is bound to this opaque type in the rest of the interface, and the qualified type `from m1 take t` is bound to the same opaque type in the rest of the program. All the rest of the program knows about the type `from m1 take t` is that `from m1 take z` is bound to a value of that type, and that `from m1 take s` and `from m1 take is-z?` are bound to procedures that can manipulate values of that type. This is the abstraction boundary. The type checker guarantees that the evaluation of an expression that has type `from m1 take t` is safe, so that the value of the expression has been constructed only by these operators, as discussed on page 239.

The corresponding definition `type t = int` defines `t` to be a name for `int` inside the module body, but this information is hidden from the rest of the program, because the rest of the program gets its bindings from the module interface.

So `-(x,0)` is not well-typed, because the main program does not know that values of type `from m1 take t` are actually values of type `int`.

Let's change the program to remove the arithmetic operation, getting

```
module m1
 interface
  [opaque t
   z : t
   s : (t -> t)
   is-z? : (t -> bool)]
 body
  [type t = int
   z = 33
   s = proc (x : t) -(x,-1)
   is-z? = proc (x : t) zero?(-(x,z))]

proc (x : from m1 take t)
  (from m1 take is-z? x)
```

Now we have a well-typed program that has type (from m1 take t ->
bool).

By enforcing this abstraction boundary, the type checker guarantees that
no program manipulates the values provided by the interface except through
the procedures that the interface provides. This gives us a mechanism to
enforce the distinction between the users of a data type and its implementation, as discussed in chapter 2. We next show some examples of this technique.

Example 8.8 If a program uses a module definition

```
module colors
 interface
  [opaque color
   red : color
   green : color
   is-red? : (color -> bool)]
 body
  [type color = int
   red = 0
   green = 1
   is-red? = proc (c : color) zero?(c)]
```

there is no way the program can figure out that from colors take
color is actually int, or that from colors take green is actually 1
(except, perhaps, by returning a color as the final answer and then printing
it out).

Example 8.9 The program

```
module ints1
 interface
  [opaque t
   zero : t
   succ : (t -> t)
   pred : (t -> t)
   is-zero : (t -> bool)]
 body
  [type t = int
   zero = 0
   succ = proc(x : t) -(x,-5)
   pred = proc(x : t) -(x,5)
   is-zero = proc (x : t) zero?(x)]

let z = from ints1 take zero
in let s = from ints1 take succ
   in (s (s z))
```

has type `from ints1 take t`. It has value 10, but we can manipulate this value only through the procedures that are exported from `ints1`. This module represents the integer k by the expressed value $5 * k$. In the notation of section 2.1, $\lceil k \rceil = 5 * k$.

Example 8.10 In this module, $\lceil k \rceil = -3 * k$.

```
module ints2
 interface
  [opaque t
   zero : t
   succ : (t -> t)
   pred : (t -> t)
   is-zero : (t -> bool)]
 body
  [type t = int
   zero = 0
   succ = proc(x : t) -(x,3)
   pred = proc(x : t) -(x,-3)
   is-zero = proc (x : t) zero?(x)]

let z = from ints2 take zero
in let s = from ints2 take succ
   in (s (s z))
```

has type `from ints2 take t` and has value -6.

Example 8.11 In the preceding examples, we couldn't manipulate the values directly, but we could manipulate them using the procedures exported by the module. As we did in chapter 2, we can compose these procedures to do useful work. Here we combine them to write a procedure to-int that converts a value from the module back to a value of type int.

```
module ints1 ...as before...

let z = from ints1 take zero
in let s = from ints1 take succ
in let p = from ints1 take pred
in let z? = from ints1 take is-zero
in letrec int to-int (x : from ints1 take t) =
              if (z? x)
              then 0
              else -((to-int (p x)), -1)
in (to-int (s (s z)))
```

has type int and has value 2.

Example 8.12 Here is the same technique used with the implementation of arithmetic ints2.

```
module ints2 ...as before...

let z = from ints2 take zero
in let s = from ints2 take succ
in let p = from ints2 take pred
in let z? = from ints2 take is-zero
in letrec int to-int (x : from ints2 take t)
              = if (z? x)
                then 0
                else -((to-int (p x)), -1)
in (to-int (s (s z)))
```

also has type int and value 2.

We show in section 8.3 how to abstract over these two examples.

Example 8.13 In the next program, we construct a module to encapsulate a data type of booleans. The booleans are represented as integers, but that fact is hidden from the rest of the program, as in example 8.8.

```
module mybool
  interface
    [opaque t
     true : t
     false : t
     and : (t -> (t -> t))
     not : (t -> t)
     to-bool : (t -> bool)]
  body
    [type t = int
     true = 0
     false = 13
     and = proc (x : t)
             proc (y : t)
               if zero?(x) then y else false
     not = proc (x : t)
             if zero?(x) then false else true
     to-bool = proc (x : t) zero?(x)]

let true = from mybool take true
in let false = from mybool take false
in let and = from mybool take and
in ((and true) false)
```

has type `from mybool take t`, and has value 13.

Exercise 8.12 [⋆] In example 8.13, could the definition of and and not be moved from inside the module to outside it? What about `to-bool`?

Exercise 8.13 [⋆] Write a module that implements arithmetic using a representation in which the integer k is represented as $5 * k + 3$.

Exercise 8.14 [⋆] Consider the following alternate definition of `mybool` (example 8.13):

```
module mybool
  interface
   [opaque t
    true : t
    false : t
    and : (t -> (t -> t))
    not : (t -> t)
    to-bool : (t -> bool)]
  body
   [type t = int
    true = 1
    false = 0
    and = proc (x : t)
           proc (y : t)
            if zero?(x) then false else y
    not = proc (x : t)
           if zero?(x) then true else false
    to-bool = proc (x : t)
               if zero?(x) then zero?(1) else zero?(0)]
```

Is there any program of type `int` that returns one value using the original definition of `mybool`, but a different value using the new definition?

Exercise 8.15 [⋆ ⋆] Write a module that implements a simple abstraction of tables. Your tables should be like environments, except that instead of binding symbols to Scheme values, they bind integers to integers. The interface provides a value that represents an empty table and two procedures `add-to-table` and `lookup-in-table` that are analogous to `extend-env` and `apply-env`. Since our language has only one-argument procedures, we get the equivalent of multiargument procedures by using Currying (exercise 3.20). You may model the empty table with a table that returns 0 for any query. Here is an example using this module.

```
module tables
  interface
   [opaque table
    empty : table
    add-to-table : (int -> (int -> (table -> table)))
    lookup-in-table : (int -> (table -> int))]
  body
   [type table = (int -> int)
    ...]

let empty = from tables take empty
in let add-binding = from tables take add-to-table
in let lookup = from tables take lookup-in-table
```

```
in let table1 = (((add-binding 3) 300)
                  (((add-binding 4) 400)
                   (((add-binding 3) 600)
                     empty)))
in -(((lookup 4) table1),
     ((lookup 3) table1))
```

This program should have type `int`. The table `table1` binds 4 to 400 and 3 to 300, so the value of the program should be 100.

8.2.2   Implementation

We now extend our system to model transparent and opaque type declarations and qualified type references.

Syntax and the Interpreter

We add syntax for two new kinds of types: named types (like `t`) and qualified types (like `from m1 take t`).

$$Type ::= Identifier$$
$$\boxed{\texttt{named-type (name)}}$$

$$Type ::= \texttt{from } Identifier \texttt{ take } Identifier$$
$$\boxed{\texttt{qualified-type (m-name t-name)}}$$

We add two new kinds of declarations, for opaque and transparent types.

$$Decl ::= \texttt{opaque } Identifier$$
$$\boxed{\texttt{opaque-type-decl (t-name)}}$$

$$Decl ::= \texttt{transparent } Identifier \texttt{ = } Type$$
$$\boxed{\texttt{transparent-type-decl (t-name ty)}}$$

We also add a new kind of definition: a type definition. This will be used to define both opaque and transparent types.

$$Defn ::= \texttt{type } Identifier \texttt{ = } Type$$
$$\boxed{\texttt{type-defn (name ty)}}$$

The interpreter doesn't look at types or declarations, so the only change to the interpreter is to make it ignore type definitions.

defns-to-env : *Listof(Defn)* × *Env* → *Env*

```
(define defns-to-env
  (lambda (defns env)
    (if (null? defns)
      (empty-env)
      (cases definition (car defns)
        (val-defn (var exp) ...as before...)
        (type-defn (type-name type)
          (defns-to-env (cdr defns) env))))))
```

The Checker

The changes to the checker are more substantial, since all the manipulations involving types must be extended to handle the new types.

First, we introduce a systematic way of handling opaque and transparent types. An opaque type behaves like a primitive type, such as `int` or `bool`. Transparent types, on the other hand, are transparent, as the name suggests: they behave exactly like their definitions. So every type is equivalent to one that is given by the grammar

$$Type ::= \text{int} \mid \text{bool} \mid \text{from } m \text{ take } t \mid (Type \text{ -> } Type)$$

where *t* is declared as an opaque type in *m*. We call a type of this form an *expanded type*.

We next extend type environments to handle new types. Our type environments will bind each named type or qualified type to an expanded type. Our new definition of type environments is

```
(define-datatype type-environment type-environment?
  (empty-tenv)
  (extend-tenv ...as before...)
  (extend-tenv-with-module ...as before...)
  (extend-tenv-with-type
    (name type?)
    (type type?)
    (saved-tenv type-environment?)))
```

subject to the condition that `type` is always an expanded type. This condition is an *invariant*, as discussed on page 10.

We next write a procedure, `expand-type`, which takes a type and a type environment, and which expands the type using the type bindings in the type environment. It looks up named types and qualified types in the type environment, relying on the invariant that the resulting types are expanded, and for a `proc` type it recurs on the argument and result types.

expand-type : *Type* × *Tenv* → *ExpandedType*

```
(define expand-type
  (lambda (ty tenv)
    (cases type ty
      (int-type () (int-type))
      (bool-type () (bool-type))
      (proc-type (arg-type result-type)
        (proc-type
          (expand-type arg-type tenv)
          (expand-type result-type tenv)))
      (named-type (name)
        (lookup-type-name-in-tenv tenv name))
      (qualified-type (m-name t-name)
        (lookup-qualified-type-in-tenv m-name t-name tenv)))))
```

In order to maintain this invariant, we must be sure to call `expand-type` whenever we extend the type environment. There are three such places:

- in `type-of` in the checker,

- where we process a list of definitions, with `defns-to-decls`, and

- where we add a module to the type environment, in `add-module-defns-to-tenv`.

In the checker, we replace each call of the form

```
(extend-tenv sym ty tenv)
```

by

```
(extend-tenv var (expand-type ty tenv) tenv)
```

In `defns-to-decls`, when we encounter a type definition, we expand its right-hand side and add it to the type environment. The type returned by `type-of` is guaranteed to be expanded, so we don't need to expand it again. We turn a type definition into a transparent type declaration, since in the body all type bindings are transparent. In `add-module-defns-to-tenv`, we call `extend-tenv-with-module`, adding an interface to the type environment. In this case we need to expand the interface to make sure that all the types it contains are expanded. To do this, we modify `add-module-defns-to-tenv` to call `expand-iface`. See figure 8.9.

The procedure `expand-iface` (figure 8.10) calls `expand-decls`. We separate these procedures in preparation for section 8.3.

---

defns-to-decls : *Listof(Defn)* × *Tenv* → *Listof(Decl)*
```
(define defns-to-decls
  (lambda (defns tenv)
    (if (null? defns)
      '()
      (cases definition (car defns)
        (val-defn (var-name exp)
          (let ((ty (type-of exp tenv)))
            (let ((new-env (extend-tenv var-name ty tenv)))
              (cons
                (val-decl var-name ty)
                (defns-to-decls (cdr defns) new-env)))))
        (type-defn (name ty)
          (let ((new-env
                  (extend-tenv-with-type
                    name (expand-type ty tenv) tenv)))
            (cons
              (transparent-type-decl name ty)
              (defns-to-decls (cdr defns) new-env)))))))))
```

add-module-defns-to-tenv : *Listof(ModuleDefn)* × *Tenv* → *Tenv*
```
(define add-module-defns-to-tenv
  (lambda (defns tenv)
    (if (null? defns)
      tenv
      (cases module-definition (car defns)
        (a-module-definition (m-name expected-iface m-body)
          (let ((actual-iface (interface-of m-body tenv)))
            (if (<:-iface actual-iface expected-iface tenv)
              (let ((new-env
                      (extend-tenv-with-module m-name
                        (expand-iface
                          m-name expected-iface tenv)
                        tenv)))
                (add-module-defns-to-tenv
                  (cdr defns) new-env))
              (report-module-doesnt-satisfy-iface
                m-name expected-iface actual-iface)))))))))
```

Figure 8.9 Checker for OPAQUE-TYPES, part 1

The procedure `expand-decls` loops through a set of declarations, creating a new type environment in which every type or variable name is bound to an expanded type. One complication is that declarations follow `let*` scoping: each declaration in a set of declarations is in scope in all the following declarations.

To see what this means, consider the module definition

```
module m1
  interface
    [opaque t
     transparent u = int
     transparent uu = (t -> u)
     % point A
     f : uu
     ...]
body
  [...]
```

In order to satisfy the invariant, m1 should be bound in the type environment to an interface containing the declarations

```
[transparent t = from m1 take t
 transparent u = int
 transparent uu = (from m1 take t -> int)
 f : (from m1 take t -> int)
 ...]
```

If we do this, then any time we retrieve a type from this type environment, we will get an expanded type, as desired.

At point A, immediately before the declaration of f, the type environment should bind

```
t    to   from m1 take t
u    to   int
uu   to   (from m1 take t -> int)
```

We call the type environment at points like point A above the *internal* type environment. This will be passed as an argument to `expand-decls`.

We can now write `expand-decls`. Like `defns->decls`, this procedure creates only transparent declarations, since its purpose is to create a data structure in which qualified types can be looked up.

Last, we modify `<:-decls` to handle the two new kinds of declarations. We must now deal with the scoping relations inside a set of declarations. For example, if we are comparing

```
expand-iface : Sym × Iface × Tenv → Iface
(define expand-iface
  (lambda (m-name iface tenv)
    (cases interface iface
      (simple-iface (decls)
        (simple-iface
          (expand-decls m-name decls tenv))))))

expand-decls : Sym × Listof(Decl) × Tenv → Listof(Decl)
(define expand-decls
  (lambda (m-name decls internal-tenv)
    (if (null? decls) ()
      (cases declaration (car decls)
        (opaque-type-decl (t-name)
          (let ((expanded-type
                  (qualified-type m-name t-name)))
            (let ((new-env
                    (extend-tenv-with-type
                      t-name expanded-type internal-tenv)))
              (cons
                (transparent-type-decl t-name expanded-type)
                (expand-decls
                  m-name (cdr decls) new-env)))))
        (transparent-type-decl (t-name ty)
          (let ((expanded-type
                  (expand-type ty internal-tenv)))
            (let ((new-env
                    (extend-tenv-with-type
                      t-name expanded-type internal-tenv)))
              (cons
                (transparent-type-decl t-name expanded-type)
                (expand-decls
                  m-name (cdr decls) new-env)))))
        (val-decl (var-name ty)
          (let ((expanded-type
                  (expand-type ty internal-tenv)))
            (cons
              (val-decl var-name expanded-type)
              (expand-decls
                m-name (cdr decls) internal-tenv))))))))))
```

Figure 8.10   Checker for OPAQUE-TYPES, part 2

```
[transparent t = int
 x : bool                        <:     [y : int]
 y : t]
```

when we get to the declaration of y, we need to know that t refers to the type int. So when we recur down the list of declarations, we need to extend the type environment as we go, much as we built internal-tenv in expand-decls. We do this by calling extend-tenv-with-decl, which takes a declaration and translates it to an appropriate extension of the type environment (figure 8.11).

We always use decls1 for this extension. To see why, consider the comparison

```
[transparent t = int              [opaque t
 transparent u = (t -> t)  <:      transparent u = (t -> int)
 f : (t -> u)]                     f : (t -> (int -> int))]
```

This comparison should succeed, since a module body that supplies the bindings on the left would be a correct implementation of the interface on the right.

When we compare the two definitions of the type u, we need to know that the type t is in fact int. The same technique works even when the declaration on the left is not present on the right, as illustrated by the declaration of t in the first example above. We call expand-type to maintain the invariant that all types in the type environment are expanded. The choice of module names in the last clause of extend-tenv-with-decl doesn't matter, since the only operation on qualified types is equal?. So using fresh-module-name is enough to guarantee that this qualified type is new.

Now we get to the key question: how do we compare declarations? Declarations can match only if they declare the same name (either a variable or a type). If a pair of declarations have the same name, there are exactly four ways in which they can match:

- They are both value declarations, and their types match.

- They are both opaque type declarations.

- They are both transparent type declarations, and their definitions match.

- decl1 is a transparent type declaration, and decl2 is an opaque type declaration. For example, imagine that our module has an interface that

<:-decls : *Listof(Decl)* × *Listof(Decl)* × *Tenv* → *Bool*

```
(define <:-decls
  (lambda (decls1 decls2 tenv)
    (cond
      ((null? decls2) #t)
      ((null? decls1) #f)
      (else
        (let ((name1 (decl->name (car decls1)))
              (name2 (decl->name (car decls2))))
          (if (eqv? name1 name2)
            (and
              (<:-decl
                (car decls1) (car decls2) tenv)
              (<:-decls
                (cdr decls1) (cdr decls2)
                (extend-tenv-with-decl
                  (car decls1) tenv)))
            (<:-decls
              (cdr decls1) decls2
              (extend-tenv-with-decl
                (car decls1) tenv)))))))))
```

extend-tenv-with-decl : *Decl* × *Tenv* → *Tenv*

```
(define extend-tenv-with-decl
  (lambda (decl tenv)
    (cases declaration decl
      (val-decl (name ty) tenv)
      (transparent-type-decl (name ty)
        (extend-tenv-with-type
          name
          (expand-type ty tenv)
          tenv))
      (opaque-type-decl (name)
        (extend-tenv-with-type
          name
          (qualified-type (fresh-module-name '%unknown) name)
          tenv)))))
```

Figure 8.11   Checker for OPAQUE-TYPES, part 3

declares opaque t and a body that defines type t = int. This should
be accepted. The procedure defns-to-decls turns the definition type
t = int into a transparent type declaration, so the test

```
actual-iface <: expected-iface
```

in add-module-defn-to-tenv will ask whether

$$(\texttt{transparent } t = \texttt{int}) <: (\texttt{opaque } t)$$

Since the module should be accepted, this test should return true.

This tells us that something with a known type is always usable as a thing
with an unknown type. But the reverse is false. For example,

$$(\texttt{opaque } t) <: (\texttt{transparent } t = ty)$$

should be false, because the value with an opaque type may have some
actual type other than int, and a module that satisfies opaque t may
not satisfy transparent t = int.

This gives us the code in figure 8.12. The definition of equiv-type?
expands its types, so that in examples like

```
[transparent t = int x : bool y : t] <: [y : int]
```

above, the t on the left will be expanded to int, and the match will succeed.

Exercise 8.16 [⋆] Extend the system of this section to use the language of exercise 7.24,
and then rewrite exercise 8.15 to use multiple arguments instead of procedure-
returning procedures.

Exercise 8.17 [⋆ ⋆] As you did in exercise 8.8, remove the restriction that a module
must produce the values in the same order as the interface. Remember, however, that
the definition must respect scoping rules, especially for types.

Exercise 8.18 [⋆ ⋆] Our code depends on the invariant that every type in a type environment is already expanded. We enforce this invariant by calling expand-type in
many places in the code. On the other hand, it would be easy to break the system
by forgetting to call expand-type. Refactor the code so that there are fewer calls to
expand-type, and the invariant is maintained more robustly.

```
<:-decl  :  Decl  ×  Decl  ×  Tenv  →  Bool
(define <:-decl
  (lambda (decl1 decl2 tenv)
    (or
      (and
        (val-decl? decl1)
        (val-decl? decl2)
        (equiv-type?
          (decl->type decl1)
          (decl->type decl2) tenv))
      (and
        (transparent-type-decl? decl1)
        (transparent-type-decl? decl2)
        (equiv-type?
          (decl->type decl1)
          (decl->type decl2) tenv))
      (and
        (transparent-type-decl? decl1)
        (opaque-type-decl? decl2))
      (and
        (opaque-type-decl? decl1)
        (opaque-type-decl? decl2)))))

equiv-type?  :  Type  ×  Type  ×  Tenv  →  Bool
(define equiv-type?
  (lambda (ty1 ty2 tenv)
    (equal?
      (expand-type ty1 tenv)
      (expand-type ty2 tenv))))
```

Figure 8.12   Checker for OPAQUE-TYPES, part 4

8.3   Module Procedures

The programs in OPAQUE-TYPES have a fixed set of dependencies. Perhaps module m4 depends on m3 and m2, which depends on m1. Sometimes we say the dependencies are *hard-coded*. In general, such hard-coded dependencies lead to bad program design, because they make it difficult to reuse modules. In this section, we add to our system a facility for *module procedures*, sometimes called *parameterized modules*, that allow module reuse. We call the new language PROC-MODULES.

8.3.1   Examples

Consider our three developers again. Charlie wants to use some of the facilities of Alice's module. But Alice's module uses a database that is supplied by Bob's module, and Charlie wants to use a different database, which is supplied by some other module (written by Diana).

To make this possible, Alice rewrites her code using module procedures. A module procedure is much like a procedure, except that it works with modules, rather than with expressed values. At the module level, interfaces are like types. Just as the type of a procedure in CHECKED specifies the type of its argument and the type of its result, the interface of a module procedure specifies the interface of its argument and the interface of its result.

Alice writes a new module `Alices-point-builder` that begins

```
module Alices-point-builder
  interface
   ((database : [opaque db-type
                 opaque node-type
                 insert-node : (node-type ->
                                  (db-type -> db-type))
                 ...])
    => [opaque point
        initial-point : (int -> point)
        ...])
```

This interface says that `Alices-point-builder` will be a module procedure. It will expect as an argument a module that will export two types, `db-type` and `node-type`, a procedure `insert-node`, and perhaps some other values. Given such a module, `Alices-point-builder` should produce a module that exports an opaque type `point`, a procedure `initial-point`, and perhaps some other values. The interface of `Alices-point-builder` also specifies a local name for its argument; we will see later why this is necessary.

The body of Alice's new module begins

```
body
  module-proc (m : [opaque db-type
                    opaque node-type
                    insert-node : (node-type ->
                                     (db-type -> db-type))
                    ...])
    [type point = ...
     initial-point = ... from m take insert-node ...
     ...]
```

Just as an ordinary procedure expression looks like

```
proc (var : t) e
```

a module procedure looks like

```
module-proc (m : [...]) [...]
```

In this example Alice has chosen m as the name of the bound variable in the module procedure; this need not be the same as the local name in the interface. We repeat the interface of the argument because the scope of a module interface never extends into the module body. This can be fixed (see exercise 8.27).

Now Alice rebuilds her module by writing

```
module Alices-points
  interface
   [opaque point
    initial-point : (int -> point)
    ...]
  body
   (Alices-point-builder Bobs-db-Module)
```

and Charlie builds his module by writing

```
module Charlies-points
  interface
   [opaque point
    initial-point : (int -> point)
    ...]
  body
   (Alices-point-builder Dianas-db-module)
```

Module Alices-points uses Bobs-db-module for the database. Module Charlies-points uses Dianas-db-module for the database. This organization allows the code in Alices-point-builder to be used twice. Not only does this avoid having to write the code twice, but if the code needs to be changed, the changes can be made in one place and they will be propagated automatically to both Alices-points and Charlies-points.

For another example, consider examples 8.11 and 8.12. In these two examples, we used what was essentially the same code for to-int. In example 8.11 it was

```
letrec int to-int (x : from ints1 take t)
        = if (z? x)
           then 0
           else -((to-int (p x)), -1)
```

and in example 8.12 the type of x was `from ints2 take t`. So we rewrite this as a module parameterized on the module that produces the integers in question.

Example 8.14 The declaration

```
module to-int-maker
  interface
   ((ints : [opaque t
             zero : t
             succ : (t -> t)
             pred : (t -> t)
             is-zero : (t -> bool)])
     => [to-int : (from ints take t -> int)])
  body
   module-proc (ints : [opaque t
                        zero : t
                        succ : (t -> t)
                        pred : (t -> t)
                        is-zero : (t -> bool)])
     [to-int
       = let z? = from ints take is-zero
         in let p = from ints take pred
         in letrec int to-int (x : from ints take t)
                      = if (z? x)
                        then 0
                        else -((to-int (p x)), -1)
         in to-int]
```

defines a module procedure. The interface says that this module takes as a module `ints` that implements the interface of arithmetic, and produces another module that exports a `to-int` procedure that converts `ints`'s type `t` to an integer. The resulting `to-int` procedure cannot depend on the implementation of arithmetic, since here we don't know what that implementation is! In this code `ints` is declared twice: once in the interface and once in the body. This is because, as we said earlier, the scope of the declaration in the interface is local to the interface, and does not include the body of the module.

Let's look at a few examples of to-int in action:

Example 8.15

```
module to-int-maker ...as before...

module ints1 ...as before...

module ints1-to-int
  interface [to-int : (from ints1 take t -> int)]
  body
   (to-int-maker ints1)

let two1 = (from ints1 take succ
             (from ints1 take succ
              from ints1 take zero))
in (from ints1-to-int take to-int
     two1)
```

has type int and value 2. Here we first define the modules to-int-maker, and ints1. Then we apply to-int-maker to ints1, getting the module ints1-to-int, which exports a binding for from ints1-to-int take to-int.

Here's an example of to-int-maker used twice, for two different implementations of arithmetic.

Example 8.16

```
module to-int-maker ...as before...

module ints1 ...as before...

module ints2 ...as before...

module ints1-to-int
  interface [to-int : (from ints1 take t -> int)]
  body (to-int-maker ints1)

module ints2-to-int
  interface [to-int : (from ints2 take t -> int)]
  body (to-int-maker ints2)


let s1 = from ints1 take succ
in let z1 = from ints1 take zero
in let to-ints1 = from ints1-to-int take to-int
```

```
in let s2 = from ints2 take succ
in let z2 = from ints2 take zero
in let to-ints2 = from ints2-to-int take to-int

in let two1 = (s1 (s1 z1))
in let two2 = (s2 (s2 z2))
in -((to-ints1 two1), (to-ints2 two2))
```

has type int and value 0. If we had replaced (to-ints2 two2) by (to-ints2 two1), the program would not be well-typed, because to-ints2 expects an argument from the ints2 representation of arithmetic, and two1 is a value from the ints1 representation of arithmetic.

Exercise 8.19 [⋆] The code for creating two1 and two2 in example 8.16 is repetitive and therefore ready for abstraction. Complete the definition of a module

```
module from-int-maker
  interface
   ((ints : [opaque t
             zero : t
             succ : (t -> t)
             pred : (t -> t)
             is-zero : (t -> bool)])
     => [from-int : (int -> from ints take t)])
  body
    ...
```

that converts an integer expressed value to its representation in the module ints. Use your module to reproduce the computation of example 8.16. Use an argument bigger than two.

Exercise 8.20 [⋆] Complete the definition of the module

```
module sum-prod-maker
  interface
   ((ints : [opaque t
             zero : t
             succ : (t -> t)
             pred : (t -> t)
             is-zero : (t -> bool)])
     => [plus : (from ints take t
                  -> (from ints take t
                       -> from ints take t))
         times : (from ints take t
                   -> (from ints take t
                        -> from ints take t))])
  body
    [plus = ...
     times = ...]
```

to define a module procedure that takes an implementation of arithmetic and produces sum and product procedures for that implementation. Use the definition of plus from page 33, and something similar for times.

Exercise 8.21 [⋆] Write a module procedure that takes an implementation of arithmetic ints and produces another implementation of arithmetic in which the number k is represented by the representation of $2 * k$ in ints.

Exercise 8.22 [⋆] Complete the definition of the module

```
module equality-maker
 interface
  ((ints : [opaque t
              zero : t
              succ : (t -> t)
              pred : (t -> t)
              is-zero : (t -> bool)])
   => [equal : (from ints take t
               -> (from ints take t
                   -> bool))])
   body
    ...
```

to define a module procedure that takes an implementation of arithmetic and produces an equality procedure for that implementation.

Exercise 8.23 [⋆] Write a module table-of that is similar to the tables module of exercise 8.15, except that it is parameterized over its contents, so one could write

```
module mybool-tables
 interface
  [opaque table
   empty : table
   add-to-table : (int ->
                  (from mybool take t ->
                   (table -> table)))
   lookup-in-table : (int ->
                     (table ->
                      from mybool take t))]
  body
   (table-of mybool)
```

to define a table containing values of type from mybool take t.

8.3.2   Implementation

Syntax

Adding module procedures to our language is much like adding procedures.
A module procedure has an interface that is much like a proc type.

> *Iface* ::= ((*Identifier* : *Iface*) => *Iface*)
> | proc-iface (param-name param-iface result-iface)

Although this interface looks a little like an ordinary procedure type, it
is different in two ways. First, it describes functions from module values
to module values, rather than from expressed values to expressed values.
Second, unlike a procedure type, it gives a name to the input to the function. This is necessary because the interface of the output may depend on
the value of the input, as in the type of to-int-maker:

```
((ints : [opaque t
          zero : t
          succ : (t -> t)
          pred : (t -> t)
          is-zero : (t -> bool)])
 => [to-int : (from ints take t -> int)])
```

to-int-maker takes a module ints and produces a module whose type
depends not just on the type of ints, which is fixed, but on ints itself.
When we apply to-int-maker to ints1, as we did in example 8.16, we
get a module with interface

```
[to-int : (from ints1 take t -> int)]
```

but when we apply it to ints2, we get a module with a different interface

```
[to-int : (from ints2 take t -> int)]
```

We extend expand-iface to treat these new interfaces as already
expanded. This works because the parameter and result interfaces will be
expanded when needed.

```
expand-iface : Sym × Iface × Tenv → Iface
(define expand-iface
  (lambda (m-name iface tenv)
    (cases interface iface
      (simple-iface (decls) ...as before...)
      (proc-iface (param-name param-iface result-iface)
        iface)))))
```

We will need new kinds of module bodies to create a module procedure, to refer to the bound variable of a module procedure, and to apply such a procedure.

ModuleBody ::= module-proc (*Identifier* : *Iface*) *ModuleBody*
> proc-module-body (m-name m-type m-body)

ModuleBody ::= *Identifier*
> var-module-body (m-name)

ModuleBody ::= (*Identifier* *Identifier*)
> app-module-body (rator rand)

The Interpreter

We first add a new kind of module, analogous to a procedure.

```
(define-datatype typed-module typed-module?
  (simple-module
    (bindings environment?))
  (proc-module
    (b-var symbol?)
    (body module-body?)
    (saved-env environment?)))
```

We extend value-of-module-body to handle the new possibilities for a module body. The code is much like that for variable references and procedure calls in expressions (figure 8.13).

The Checker

We can write down rules like the ones in section 7.2 for our new kinds of module bodies. These rules are shown in figure 8.14. We write ($\triangleright$ *body tenv*) = *i* instead of (interface-of *body tenv*) = *i* in order to make the rules fit on the page.

A module variable gets its type from the type environment, as one might expect. A module-proc gets its type from the type of its parameter and the type of its body, just like the procedures in CHECKED.

An application of a module procedure is treated much like a procedure call in CHECKED. But there are two important differences.

First, the type of the operand (i_2 in the rule IFACE-M-APP) need not be exactly the same as the parameter type (i_1). We require only that $i_2 <: i_1$. This is sufficient, since $i_2 <: i_1$ implies that any module that satisfies the interface i_2 also satisfies the interface i_1, and is therefore an acceptable argument to the module procedure.

value-of-module-body : *ModuleBody* × *Env* → *TypedModule*
```
(define value-of-module-body
  (lambda (m-body env)
    (cases module-body m-body
      (defns-module-body (defns) ...as before...)
      (var-module-body (m-name)
        (lookup-module-name-in-env m-name env))
      (proc-module-body (m-name m-type m-body)
        (proc-module m-name m-body env))
      (app-module-body (rator rand)
        (let ((rator-val
                (lookup-module-name-in-env rator env))
              (rand-val
                (lookup-module-name-in-env rand  env)))
          (cases typed-module rator-val
            (proc-module (m-name m-body env)
              (value-of-module-body m-body
                (extend-env-with-module
                  m-name rand-val env)))
            (else
              (report-bad-module-app rator-val)))))))))
```

Figure 8.13   value-of-module-body

IFACE-M-VAR
$$(\triangleright\ m\ tenv)\ =\ tenv\,(m)$$

IFACE-M-PROC
$$\frac{(\triangleright\ body\ [m\!=\!i_1]\,tenv)\ =\ i_1'}{(\triangleright\ (\texttt{m-proc}\ (m\!:\!i_1)\ body)\ tenv)\ =\ ((m\!:\!i_1)\ \texttt{=>}\ i_1')}$$

IFACE-M-APP
$$\frac{tenv(m_1) = ((m\!:\!i_1)\ \texttt{=>}\ i_1')\qquad tenv(m_2) = i_2 \qquad\qquad i_2 <: i_1}{(\triangleright\ (m_1\ m_2)\ tenv)\ =\ i_1'[m_2/m]}$$

Figure 8.14   Rules for typing new module bodies

Second, we substitute the operand m_2 for m in the result type i'_1. Consider the example on page 318, where we applied the module procedure `to-int-maker`, which has the interface

```
((ints : [opaque t
          zero : t
          succ : (t -> t)
          pred : (t -> t)
          is-zero : (t -> bool)])
  => [to-int : (from ints take t -> int)])
```

to `ints1` and `ints2`. When we apply `to-int-maker` to `ints1`, the substitution gives us the interface

```
[to-int : (from ints1 take t -> int)]
```

When we apply it to `ints2`, the substitution gives the interfaces

```
[to-int : (from ints2 take t -> int)]
```

as desired.

From these rules, it is easy to write down the code for `interface-of` (figure 8.15). When we check the body of a `module-proc`, we add the parameter to the type environment as if it had been a top-level module. This code uses the procedure `rename-in-iface` to perform the substitution on the result interface.

Last, we extend `<:-iface` to handle the new types. The rule for comparing `proc-iface`s is

$$\frac{i_2 <: i_1 \qquad i'_1[m'/m_1] <: i'_2[m'/m_2] \qquad m' \text{ not in } i'_1 \text{ or } i'_2}{((m_1 : i_1) \ => \ i'_1) <: ((m_2 : i_2) \ => \ i'_2)}$$

In order to have $((m_1 : i_1)\ =>\ i'_1) <: ((m_2 : i_2)\ =>\ i'_2)$, it must be the case that any module m_0 that satisfies the first interface also satisfies the second interface. This means that any module with interface i_2 can be passed as an argument to m_0, and any module that m_0 produces will satisfy i'_2.

For the first requirement, we insist that $i_2 <: i_1$. This guarantees that any module that satisfies i_2 can be passed as an argument to m_0. Note the reversal: we say that subtyping is *contravariant* in the parameter type.

What about the result types? We might require that $i'_1 <: i'_2$. Unfortunately, this doesn't quite work. i'_1 may have instances of the module variable m_1 in it, and i'_2 may have instances of m_2 in it. So to compare them, we rename both m_1 and m_2 to some new module variable m'. Once we do that, we can compare them sensibly. This leads to the requirement $i'_1[m'/m_1] <: i'_2[m'/m_2]$.

```
interface-of  : ModuleBody × Tenv → Iface
(define interface-of
  (lambda (m-body tenv)
    (cases module-body m-body
      (var-module-body (m-name)
        (lookup-module-name-in-tenv tenv m-name))
      (defns-module-body (defns)
        (simple-iface
          (defns-to-decls defns tenv)))
      (app-module-body (rator-id rand-id)
        (let ((rator-iface
                (lookup-module-name-in-tenv tenv rator-id))
              (rand-iface
                (lookup-module-name-in-tenv tenv rand-id)))
          (cases interface rator-iface
            (simple-iface (decls)
              (report-attempt-to-apply-simple-module rator-id))
            (proc-iface (param-name param-iface result-iface)
              (if (<:-iface rand-iface param-iface tenv)
                (rename-in-iface
                  result-iface param-name rand-id)
                (report-bad-module-application-error
                  param-iface rand-iface m-body))))))
      (proc-module-body (rand-name rand-iface m-body)
        (let ((body-iface
                (interface-of m-body
                  (extend-tenv-with-module rand-name
                    (expand-iface rand-name rand-iface tenv)
                    tenv))))
          (proc-iface rand-name rand-iface body-iface))))))
```

Figure 8.15   Checker for PROC-MODULES, part 1

The code to decide this relation is relatively straightforward (figure 8.16). When deciding $i_1'[m'/m_1] <: i_2'[m'/m_2]$ we extend the type environment to provide a binding for m'. We associate m' with i_1, since it has fewer components than i_2. When we call extend-tenv-with-module to compare the result types, we call expand-iface to maintain the invariant.

And now we're done. Go have a sundae, with anything that satisfies the ice cream interface, anything that satisfies the hot-topping interface, and anything that satisfies the nuts interface. Don't worry about how any of the pieces are constructed, so long as they taste good!

```
<:-iface  :  Iface  ×  Iface  ×  Tenv  →  Bool
(define <:-iface
  (lambda (iface1 iface2 tenv)
    (cases interface iface1
      (simple-iface (decls1)
        (cases interface iface2
          (simple-iface (decls2)
            (<:-decls decls1 decls2 tenv))
          (proc-iface (param-name2 param-iface2 result-iface2)
            #f)))
      (proc-iface (param-name1 param-iface1 result-iface1)
        (cases interface iface2
          (simple-iface (decls2) #f)
          (proc-iface (param-name2 param-iface2 result-iface2)
            (let ((new-name (fresh-module-name param-name1)))
              (let ((result-iface1
                      (rename-in-iface
                        result-iface1 param-name1 new-name))
                    (result-iface2
                      (rename-in-iface
                        result-iface2 param-name2 new-name)))
                (and
                  (<:-iface param-iface2 param-iface1 tenv)
                  (<:-iface result-iface1 result-iface2
                    (extend-tenv-with-module
                      new-name
                      (expand-iface new-name param-iface1 tenv)
                      tenv)))))))))))
```

Figure 8.16   Checker for PROC-MODULES, part 2

Exercise 8.24 [*] Application of modules is currently allowed only for identifiers. What goes wrong with the type rule for application if we try to check an application like `(m1 (m2 m3))`?

Exercise 8.25 [*] Extend PROC-MODULES so that a module can take multiple arguments, analogously to exercise 3.21.

Exercise 8.26 [★★] Extend the language of module bodies to replace the production for module application by

$$ModuleBody ::= (ModuleBody \; ModuleBody)$$
$$\boxed{\texttt{app-module-body (rator rand)}}$$

Exercise 8.27 [★★★] In PROC-MODULES, we wind up having to write interfaces like

```
[opaque t
 zero : t
 succ : (t -> t)
 pred : (t -> t)
 is-zero : (t -> bool)]
```

over and over again. Add to the grammar for programs a facility for named interfaces, so we could write

```
interface int-interface = [opaque t
                           zero : t
                           succ : (t -> t)
                           pred : (t -> t)
                           is-zero : (t -> bool)]
module make-to-int
 interface
  ((ints : int-interface)
   => [to-int : from ints take t -> int])
 body
  ...
```

9 *Objects and Classes*

Many programming tasks require the program to manage some piece of state through an interface. For example, a file system has internal state, but we access and modify that state only through the file system interface. Often, the piece of state spans several variables, and changes to those variables must be coordinated in order to maintain the consistency of the state. One therefore needs some technology to ensure that the various variables that constitute the state are updated in a coordinated manner. *Object-oriented programming* is a useful technology for accomplishing this task.

In object-oriented programming, each managed piece of state is called an *object*. An object consists of several stored quantities, called its *fields*, with associated procedures, called *methods*, that have access to the fields. The operation of calling a method is often viewed as sending the method name and arguments as a message to the object; this is sometimes called the *message-passing* view of object-oriented programming.

Procedures in stateful languages, like those in chapter 4 give another example of the power of programming with objects. A procedure is an object whose state is contained in its free variables. A closure has a single behavior: it may be invoked on some arguments. For example, the procedure g on page 105 controls the state of a counter, and the only thing one can do with this state is to increment it. More often, however, one wants an object to have several behaviors. Object-oriented programming languages provide support for this ability.

Often, one needs to manage several pieces of state with the same methods. For example, one might have several file systems or several queues in a program. To facilitate the sharing of methods, object-oriented programming systems typically provide *classes*, which are structures that specify the fields and methods of each such object. Each object is created as a class *instance*.

Similarly, one may often have several classes with fields and methods that are similar but not identical. To facilitate the sharing of implementation, object-oriented languages typically provide *inheritance*, which allows the programmer to define a new class as a small modification of an existing class by adding or changing the behavior of some methods, or by adding fields. In this case, we say the new class *inherits from* or *extends* the old class, since the rest of the class's behavior is inherited from the original class.

Whether program elements are modeling real-world objects or artificial aspects of a system's state, a program's structure is often clarified if it can be composed of objects that combine both behavior and state. It is also natural to associate behaviorally similar objects with the same class.

Real-world objects typically have some *state* and some *behavior* that either controls or is controlled by that state. For example, cats can eat, purr, jump, and lie down, and these activities are controlled by their current state, including how hungry and tired they are.

Objects and modules have many similarities, but they are very different. Both modules and classes provide a mechanism for defining opaque types. However, an object is a data structure with behavior; a module is just a set of bindings. One may have many objects of the same class; most module systems do not offer a similar capability. On the other hand, module systems such as PROC-MODULES allow a much more flexible way of controlling the visibility of names. Modules and classes can work fruitfully together.

9.1   Object-Oriented Programming

In this chapter, we study a simple object-oriented language that we call CLASSES. A CLASSES program consists of a sequence of class declarations followed by an expression that may make use of those classes.

Figure 9.1 shows a simple program in this language. It defines c1 as a class that inherits from object. Each object of class c1 will contain two fields named i and j. The fields are called *members* or *instance variables*. The class c1 supports three *methods*, sometimes called *member functions*, named initialize, countup, and getstate. Each method consists of its *method*

```
class c1 extends object
 field i
 field j
 method initialize (x)
  begin
   set i = x;
   set j = -(0,x)
  end
 method countup (d)
  begin
   set i = +(i,d);
   set j = -(j,d)
  end
 method getstate () list(i,j)
let t1 = 0
    t2 = 0
    o1 = new c1(3)
in begin
   set t1 = send o1 getstate();
   send o1 countup(2);
   set t2 = send o1 getstate();
   list(t1,t2)
   end
```

Figure 9.1   A simple object-oriented program

name, its *method vars* (also called *method parameters*), and its *method body*. The method names correspond to the kinds of *messages* to which instances of c1 can respond. We sometimes refer to "c1's countup method."

In this example, each of the methods of the class maintains the integrity constraint or *invariant* that $i = -j$. A real programming example would, of course, likely have far more complex integrity constraints.

The program in figure 9.1 first initializes three variables. t1 and t2 are initialized to zero. o1 is initialized to an object of the class c1. We say this object is an *instance* of class c1. An object is created using the new operation. This causes the class's initialize method to be invoked, in this case setting the object's field i to 3 and its field j to -3. The program then calls the getstate method of o1, returning the list (3 -3). Next, it calls o1's countup method, changing the value of the two fields to 5 and -5. Then the

```
class interior-node extends object
 field left
 field right
 method initialize (l, r)
  begin
   set left = l;
   set right = r
  end
 method sum () +(send left sum(),send right sum())
class leaf-node extends object
 field value
 method initialize (v) set value = v
 method sum () value
let o1 = new interior-node(
         new interior-node(
           new leaf-node(3),
           new leaf-node(4)),
         new leaf-node(5))
in send o1 sum()
```

Figure 9.2   Object-oriented program for summing the leaves of a tree

getstate method is called again, returning the list (5 -5). Last, the value of list(t1,t2), which is ((3 -3) (5 -5)), is returned as the value of the entire program.

The program in figure 9.2 illustrates a key idea in object-oriented programming: *dynamic dispatch*. In this program we have trees with two kinds of nodes, interior-node and leaf-node. To find the sum of the leaves of a node, we send it the sum message. Generally, we do not know what kind of node we are sending the message to. Instead, each node accepts the sum message and uses its sum method to do the right thing. This is called *dynamic dispatch*. Here the expression builds a tree with two interior nodes and three leaf nodes. It sends a sum message to the node o1; o1 sends sum messages to its subtrees, and so on, returning 12 at the end. This program also shows that all methods are mutually recursive.

A method body can invoke other methods of the same object by using the identifier self (sometimes called this), which is always bound to the object on which the method has been invoked. For example, in

```
class oddeven extends object
 method initialize () 1
 method even (n)
  if zero?(n) then 1 else send self odd(-(n,1))
 method odd (n)
  if zero?(n) then 0 else send self even(-(n,1))
let o1 = new oddeven()
in send o1 odd(13)
```

the methods even and odd invoke each other recursively, because when they are executed, self is bound to an object that contains them both. This is much like the dynamic-binding implementation of recursion in exercise 3.37.

9.2   Inheritance

Inheritance allows the programmer to define new classes by incremental modification of old ones. This is extremely useful in practice. For example, a colored point is like a point, except that it has additional methods to manipulate its color, as in the classic example in figure 9.3.

If class c_2 extends class c_1, we say that c_1 is the *parent* or *superclass* of c_2 or that c_2 is a *child* of c_1. Since inheritance defines c_2 as an extension of c_1, c_1 must be defined before c_2. To get things started, the language includes a predefined class called object with no methods or fields. Since object has no initialize method, it is impossible to create an object of class object. Each class other than object has a single parent, but it may have many children. Thus the relation extends imposes a tree structure on the set of classes, with object at the root. Since each class has at most one immediate superclass, this is a *single-inheritance* language. Some languages allow classes to inherit from multiple superclasses. Such *multiple inheritance* is powerful, but it is also problematic; we consider some of the difficulties in the exercises.

The genealogical analogy is the source of the term *inheritance*. The analogy is often pursued so that we speak of the *ancestors* of a class (the chain from a class's parent to the root class object) or its *descendants*. If c_2 is a descendant of c_1, we sometimes say that c_2 is a *subclass* of c_1, and write $c_2 < c_1$.

If class c_2 inherits from class c_1, all the fields and methods of c_1 will be visible from the methods of c_2, unless they are redeclared in c_2. Since a class inherits all the methods and fields of its parent, an instance of a child class can be used anywhere an instance of its parent can be used. Similarly, any instance of any descendant of a class can be used anywhere an instance of the class can be used. This is sometimes called *subclass polymorphism*. This is

```
class point extends object
 field x
 field y
 method initialize (initx, inity)
  begin
   set x = initx;
   set y = inity
  end
 method move (dx, dy)
  begin
   set x = +(x,dx);
   set y = +(y,dy)
  end
 method get-location () list(x,y)
class colorpoint extends point
 field color
 method set-color (c) set color = c
 method get-color () color
let p = new point(3,4)
    cp = new colorpoint(10,20)
in begin
    send p move(3,4);
    send cp set-color(87);
    send cp move(10,20);
    list(send p get-location(),    % returns (6 8)
         send cp get-location(),   % returns (20 40)
         send cp get-color())      % returns 87
   end
```

Figure 9.3   Classic example of inheritance: colorpoint

the design we have chosen for our language; other object-oriented languages may have different visibility rules.

We next consider what happens when the fields or methods of a class are redeclared. If a field of c_1 is redeclared in one of its subclasses c_2, the new declaration *shadows* the old one, just as in lexical scoping. For example, consider figure 9.4. An object of class c2 has two fields named y: the one declared in c1 and the one declared in c2. The methods declared in c1 see c1's fields x and y. In c2, the x in getx2 refers to c1's field x, but the y in gety2 refers to c2's field y.

```
class c1 extends object
 field x
 field y
 method initialize () 1
 method setx1 (v) set x = v
 method sety1 (v) set y = v
 method getx1 () x
 method gety1 () y
class c2 extends c1
 field y
 method sety2 (v) set y = v
 method getx2 () x
 method gety2 () y
let o2 = new c2()
in begin
    send o2 setx1(101);
    send o2 sety1(102);
    send o2 sety2(999);
    list(send o2 getx1(),      % returns 101
         send o2 gety1(),      % returns 102
         send o2 getx2(),      % returns 101
         send o2 gety2())      % returns 999
   end
```

Figure 9.4   Example of field shadowing

If a method *m* of a class c_1 is redeclared in one of its subclasses c_2, we say that the new method *overrides* the old one. We call the class in which a method is declared that method's *host class*. Similarly, we define the host class of an expression to be the host class of the method (if any) in which the expression occurs. We also define the superclass of a method or expression as the parent class of its host class.

If an object of class c_2 is sent an *m* message, then the new method should be used. This rule is simple, but it has subtle consequences. Consider the following example:

```
class c1 extends object
 method initialize () 1
 method m1 () 11
 method m2 () send self m1()
class c2 extends c1
 method m1 () 22
let o1 = new c1() o2 = new c2()
in list(send o1 m1(), send o2 m1(), send o2 m2())
```

We expect `send o1 m1()` to return 11, since o1 is an instance of c1. Similarly, we expect `send o2 m1()` to return 22, since o2 is an instance of c2. Now what about `send o2 m2()`? Method m2 immediately calls method m1, but which one?

Dynamic dispatch tells us that we should look at the class of the object bound to self. The value of self is o2, which is of class c2. Hence the call `send self m1()` should return 22.

Our language has one more important feature, *super calls*. Consider the program in figure 9.5. There we have supplied the class colorpoint with an overly specialized initialize method that sets the field color as well as the fields x and y. However, the body of the new method duplicates the code of the overridden one. This might be acceptable in our small example, but in a large example this would clearly be bad practice. (Why?) Furthermore, if colorpoint declared a field x, there would be no way to initialize the field x of point, just as there is no way to initialize the first y in the example on page 331.

The solution is to replace the duplicated code in the body of colorpoint's initialize method with a *super call* of the form `super initialize()`. Then the initialize method in colorpoint would read

```
method initialize (initx, inity, initcolor)
  begin
   super initialize(initx, inity);
   set color = initcolor
  end
```

A super call `super n(...)` in the body of a method *m* invokes a method *n* of the parent of *m*'s host class. This is not necessarily the parent of the class of self. The class of self will always be a subclass of *m*'s host class, but it may not be the same, because *m* might have been declared in an ancestor of the target object.

```
class point extends object
 field x
 field y
 method initialize (initx, inity)
  begin
   set x = initx;
   set y = inity
  end
 method move (dx, dy)
  begin
   set x = +(x,dx);
   set y = +(y,dy)
  end
 method get-location () list(x,y)
class colorpoint extends point
 field color
 method initialize (initx, inity, initcolor)
  begin
   set x = initx;
   set y = inity;
   set color = initcolor
  end
 method set-color (c) set color = c
 method get-color () color
let o1 = new colorpoint(3,4,172)
in send o1 get-color()
```

Figure 9.5   Example demonstrating a need for super

To illustrate this distinction, consider figure 9.6. Sending an m3 message to an object o3 of class c3 finds c2's method for m3, which executes super m1(). The class of o3 is c3, whose parent is c2. But the host class is c2, and c2's superclass is c1. So c1's method for m1 is executed. This is an example of *static method dispatch*. Though the object of a super method call is self, method dispatch is static, because the specific method to be invoked can be determined from the text, independent of the class of self.

In this example, c1's method for m1 calls o3's m2 method. This is an ordinary method call, so dynamic dispatch is used, so it is c3's m2 method that is found, returning 33.

```
class c1 extends object
 method initialize () 1
 method m1 () send self m2()
 method m2 () 13
class c2 extends c1
 method m1 () 22
 method m2 () 23
 method m3 () super m1()
class c3 extends c2
 method m1 () 32
 method m2 () 33
let o3 = new c3()
in send o3 m3()
```

Figure 9.6   Example illustrating interaction of `super` call with `self`

9.3   The Language

For our language CLASSES, we extend the language IMPLICIT-REFS with the additional productions shown in figure 9.7. A program is a sequence of class declarations followed by an expression to be executed. A class declaration has a name, an immediate superclass name, zero or more field declarations, and zero or more method declarations. A method declaration, like a procedure declaration in a `letrec`, has a name, a list of formal parameters, and a body. We also extend the language with multiargument procedures, multideclaration `let`, `letrec` expressions, and some additional operations like addition and `list`. The operations on lists are as in exercise 3.9. Last, we add a `begin` expression, as in exercise 4.4, that evaluates its subexpressions from left to right and returns the value of the last one.

We add objects and lists as expressed values, so we have

$$\begin{aligned} ExpVal &= Int + Bool + Proc + Listof(ExpVal) + Obj \\ DenVal &= Ref(ExpVal) \end{aligned}$$

We write *Listof(ExpVal)* to indicate that the lists may contain any expressed value.

We will consider *Obj* in section 9.4.1. Classes are neither denotable nor expressible in our language: they may appear as part of objects but never as the binding of a variable or the value of an expression, but see exercise 9.29.

$$Program \quad ::= \{ClassDecl\}^* \; Expression$$

```
a-program (class-decls body)
```

$$ClassDecl \quad ::= \texttt{class} \; Identifier \; \texttt{extends} \; Identifier$$
$$\{\texttt{field} \; Identifier\}^* \; \{MethodDecl\}^*$$

```
a-class-decl
 (class-name super-name
   field-names method-decls)
```

$$MethodDecl ::= \texttt{method} \; Identifier \; (\{Identifier\}^{*(,)}) \; Expression$$

```
a-method-decl (method-name vars body)
```

$$Expression \quad ::= \texttt{new} \; Identifier \; (\{Expression\}^{*(,)})$$

```
new-object-exp (class-name rands)
```

$$Expression \quad ::= \texttt{send} \; Expression \; Identifier \; (\{Expression\}^{*(,)})$$

```
method-call-exp (obj-exp method-name rands)
```

$$Expression \quad ::= \texttt{super} \; Identifier \; (\{Expression\}^{*(,)})$$

```
super-call-exp (method-name rands)
```

$$Expression \quad ::= \texttt{self}$$

```
self-exp ()
```

Figure 9.7   New productions for a simple object-oriented programming language

We have included four additional expressions. The `new` expression creates an object of the named class. The `initialize` method is then invoked to initialize the fields of the object. The `rands` are evaluated and passed to the `initialize` method. The value returned by this method call is thrown away and the new object is returned as the value of the `new` expression.

A `self` expression returns the object on which the current method is operating.

A `send` expression consists of an expression that should evaluate to an object, a method name, and zero or more operands. The named method is retrieved from the class of the object, and then is passed the arguments obtained by evaluating the operands. As in IMPLICIT-REFS, a new location is allocated for each of these arguments, and then the method body is evaluated within the scope of lexical bindings associating the method's parameters with the references to the corresponding locations.

A `super-call` expression consists of a method name and zero or more arguments. It looks for a method of the given name, starting in the superclass of the expression's host class. The body of the method is then evaluated, with the current object as `self`.

9.4   The Interpreter

When a program is evaluated, all the class declarations are processed using `initialize-class-env!` and then the expression is evaluated. The procedure `initialize-class-env!` creates a global *class environment* that maps each class name to the methods of the class. Because this environment is global, we model it as a Scheme variable. We discuss the class environment in more detail in section 9.4.3.

```
value-of-program : Program → ExpVal
(define value-of-program
  (lambda (pgm)
    (initialize-store!)
    (cases program pgm
      (a-program (class-decls body)
        (initialize-class-env! class-decls)
        (value-of body (init-env)))))))
```

The procedure `value-of` contains, as usual, a clause for each kind of expression in the language, including a clause for each of the four new productions.

We consider each new kind of expression in turn.

Usually, an expression is evaluated because it is part of a method that is operating on some object. In the environment, this object is bound to the pseudo-variable `%self`. We call this a *pseudo-variable* because it is bound lexically, like an ordinary variable, but it has somewhat different properties, which we explore below. Similarly, the name of the superclass of the host class of the current method is bound to the pseudo-variable `%super`.

When a `self` expression is evaluated, the value of `%self` is returned. The clause in `value-of` is

```
(self-exp ()
  (apply-env env '%self))
```

When a `send` expression is evaluated, the operands and the object expression are evaluated. We look in the object to find its class name. Then we find the method using `find-method`, which takes a class name and a method name and returns a method. That method is then applied to the current object and the method arguments.

```
(method-call-exp (obj-exp method-name rands)
  (let ((args (values-of-exps rands env))
        (obj (value-of obj-exp env)))
    (apply-method
      (find-method
        (object->class-name obj)
        method-name)
      obj
      args)))
```

Super method invocation is similar to ordinary method invocation except that the method is looked up in the superclass of the host class of the expression. The clause in `value-of` is

```
(super-call-exp (method-name rands)
  (let ((args (values-of-exps rands env))
        (obj (apply-env env '%self)))
    (apply-method
      (find-method (apply-env env '%super) method-name)
      obj
      args)))
```

Our last task is to create objects. When a `new` expression is evaluated, the operands are evaluated and a new object is created from the class name. Then its initialize method is called, but its value is ignored. Finally, the object is returned.

```
(new-object-exp (class-name rands)
  (let ((args (values-of-exps rands env))
        (obj (new-object class-name)))
    (apply-method
      (find-method class-name 'initialize)
      obj
      args)
    obj))
```

Next we determine how to represent objects, methods, and classes. To illustrate the representation, we use a running example, shown in figure 9.8.

```
class c1 extends object
 field x
 field y
 method initialize ()
  begin
   set x = 11;
   set y = 12
  end
 method m1 () ... x ... y ...
 method m2 () ... send self m3() ...
class c2 extends c1
 field y
 method initialize ()
  begin
   super initialize();
   set y = 22
  end
 method m1 (u,v) ... x ... y ...
 method m3 () ...
class c3 extends c2
 field x
 field z
 method initialize ()
  begin
   super initialize();
   set x = 31;
   set z = 32
  end
 method m3 () ... x ... y ... z ...
let o3 = new c3()
in send o3 m1(7,8)
```

Figure 9.8   Sample program for OOP implementation

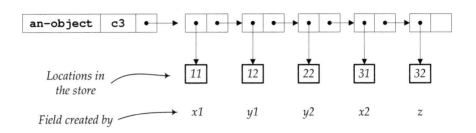

Figure 9.9 A simple object

9.4.1 Objects

We represent an object as a data type containing the object's class name and a list of references to its fields.

```
(define-datatype object object?
  (an-object
    (class-name identifier?)
    (fields (list-of reference?))))
```

We lay out the list with the fields from the "oldest" class first. Thus in figure 9.8, an object of class c1 would have its fields laid out as (x y); an object of class c2 would lay out its fields as (x y y), with the second y being the one belonging to c2, and an object of class c3 would be laid out as (x y y x z). The representation of object o3 from figure 9.8 is shown in figure 9.9. Of course, we want the methods in class c3 to refer to the field x declared in c3, not the one declared in c1. We take care of this when we set up the environment for evaluation of the method body.

This strategy has the useful property that any subclass of c3 will have these fields in the same positions in the list, because any fields added later will appear to the right of these fields. What is the position of x in a method that is defined in any subclass of c3? Assuming that x is not redefined, we know that the position of x must be 3 throughout all such methods. Thus, when a field variable is declared, the position of the corresponding value remains unchanged. This property allows field references to be determined statically, similarly to the way we handled variables in section 3.6.

Making a new object is easy. We simply create an an-object with a list of new references equal to the number of fields in the object. To determine that number, we get the list of field variables from the object's class. We initialize each location with an illegal value that will be recognizable in case the program dereferences the location without initializing it.

ClassName = *Sym*

new-object : *ClassName* → *Obj*
```
(define new-object
  (lambda (class-name)
    (an-object
      class-name
      (map
        (lambda (field-name)
          (newref (list 'uninitialized-field field-name)))
        (class->field-names (lookup-class class-name)))))))
```

9.4.2   Methods

We next turn to methods. Methods are like procedures, except that they do not have a saved environment. Instead, they keep track of the names of the fields to which they refer. When a method is applied, it runs its body in an environment in which

- The method's formal parameters are bound to new references that are initialized to the values of the arguments. This is analogous to the behavior of `apply-procedure` in IMPLICIT-REFS.

- The pseudo-variables `%self` and `%super` are bound to the current object and the method's superclass, respectively.

- The visible field names are bound to the fields of the current object. To implement this, we define

```
(define-datatype method method?
  (a-method
    (vars (list-of identifier?))
    (body expression?)
    (super-name identifier?)
    (field-names (list-of identifier?))))
```

apply-method : *Method* × *Obj* × *Listof(ExpVal)* → *ExpVal*
```
(define apply-method
  (lambda (m self args)
    (cases method m
      (a-method (vars body super-name field-names)
        (value-of body
          (extend-env* vars (map newref args)
            (extend-env-with-self-and-super
              self super-name
              (extend-env field-names (object->fields self)
                (empty-env)))))))))
```

Here we use `extend-env*` from exercise 2.10, which extends an environment by binding a list of variables to a list of denoted values. We have also added to our environment interface the procedure `extend-env-with-self-and-super`, which binds `%self` and `%super` to an object and a class name, respectively.

In order to make sure that each method sees the right fields, we need to be careful when constructing the `field-names` list. Each method should see only the last declaration of a field; all the others should be shadowed. So when we construct the `field-names` list, we will replace all but the rightmost occurrence of each name with a fresh identifier. For the program of figure 9.8, the resulting `field-names` fields look like

Class	Fields Defined	Fields	field-names
c1	x, y	(x y)	(x y)
c2	y	(x y y)	(x y%1 y)
c3	x, z	(x y y x z)	(x%1 y%1 y x z)

Since the method bodies do not know anything about x%1 or y%1, they can only see the rightmost field for each field variable, as desired.

Figure 9.10 shows the environment built for the evaluation of the method body in `send o3 m1(7,8)` in figure 9.8. This figure shows that the list of references may be longer than the list of variables: the list of variables is just `(x y%1 y)`, since those are the only field variables visible from method `m1` in `c2`, but the value of `(object->fields self)` is the list of all the fields of the object. However, since the values of the three visible field variables are in the first three elements of the list, and since we have renamed the first `y` to be `y%1` (which the method knows nothing about) the method `m1` will associate the variable `y` with the `y` declared in `c2`, as desired.

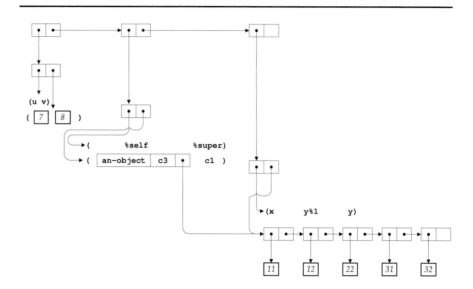

Figure 9.10   Environment for method application

When the host class and the class of `self` are the same, the list of variables is generally of the same length as the list of field locations. If the host class is higher up the class chain, then there may be more locations than field variables, but the values corresponding to the field variables will be at the beginning of the list, and the extra values will be inaccessible.

9.4.3   Classes and Class Environments

Our implementation so far has depended on the ability to get information about a class from its name. So we need a *class environment* to accomplish this task. The class environment will associate each class name with a data structure that describes the class.

The class environment is global: in our language, class declarations are grouped at the beginning of the program and are in force for the entire program. So, we represent the class environment as a global variable named `the-class-env`, which will contain a list of (class-name, class) lists, but we hide this representation behind the procedures `add-to-class-env!` and `lookup-class`.

ClassEnv = *Listof*(*List*(*ClassName*, *Class*))

the-class-env : *ClassEnv*
```
(define the-class-env '())
```

add-to-class-env! : *ClassName* × *Class* → *Unspecified*
```
(define add-to-class-env!
  (lambda (class-name class)
    (set! the-class-env
      (cons
        (list class-name class)
        the-class-env))))
```

lookup-class : *ClassName* → *Class*
```
(define lookup-class
  (lambda (name)
    (let ((maybe-pair (assq name the-class-env)))
      (if maybe-pair (cadr maybe-pair)
        (report-unknown-class name)))))
```

For each class, we need to keep track of three things: the name of its super-class, the list of its field variables, and an environment mapping its method names to its methods.

```
(define-datatype class class?
  (a-class
    (super-name (maybe identifier?))
    (field-names (list-of identifier?))
    (method-env method-environment?)))
```

Here we use the predicate (maybe identifier?) which is satisfied by any value that is either a symbol or is #f. The latter possibility is necessary for the class object, which has no superclass. The field-names will be the fields of the class, as seen by methods of that class, and methods will be an environment giving a definition to each method name that is defined for the class.

We will initialize the class environment with an entry for the class object. For each declaration, we add a new binding to the class environment, binding the name of the class to a class consisting of the name of the super-class, the field-names for the methods of that class, and the environment of methods for that class.

initialize-class-env! : *Listof(ClassDecl)* → *Unspecified*
```
(define initialize-class-env!
  (lambda (c-decls)
    (set! the-class-env
      (list
        (list 'object (a-class #f '() '()))))
    (for-each initialize-class-decl! c-decls)))
```

initialize-class-decl! : *ClassDecl* → *Unspecified*
```
(define initialize-class-decl!
  (lambda (c-decl)
    (cases class-decl c-decl
      (a-class-decl (c-name s-name f-names m-decls)
        (let ((f-names
                (append-field-names
                  (class->field-names (lookup-class s-name))
                  f-names)))
          (add-to-class-env!
            c-name
            (a-class s-name f-names
              (merge-method-envs
                (class->method-env (lookup-class s-name))
                (method-decls->method-env
                  m-decls s-name f-names)))))))))
```

The procedure append-field-names is used to create the field-names
for the current class. It appends the fields of the superclass and the fields
declared by the new class, except that any field of the superclass that is shadowed by a new field is replaced by a fresh identifier, as in the example on
page 341.

append-field-names :
    Listof(FieldName) × *Listof(FieldName)* → *Listof(FieldName)*
```
(define append-field-names
  (lambda (super-fields new-fields)
    (cond
      ((null? super-fields) new-fields)
      (else
       (cons
         (if (memq (car super-fields) new-fields)
           (fresh-identifier (car super-fields))
           (car super-fields))
         (append-field-names
           (cdr super-fields) new-fields))))))
```

9.4.4 Method Environments

All that's left to do is to write `find-method` and `merge-method-envs`.

As we did for classes, we represent a method environment by a list of (method-name, method) lists. We look up a method using `find-method`.

MethodEnv = Listof(List(MethodName, Method))

find-method : *Sym × Sym → Method*
```
(define find-method
  (lambda (c-name name)
    (let ((m-env (class->method-env (lookup-class c-name))))
      (let ((maybe-pair (assq name m-env)))
        (if (pair? maybe-pair) (cadr maybe-pair)
          (report-method-not-found name))))))
```

With this information we can write `method-decls->method-env`. It takes the method declarations of a class and creates a method environment, recording for each method its bound variables, its body, the name of the superclass of the host class, and the `field-names` of the host class.

method-decls->method-env :
   Listof(MethodDecl) × ClassName × Listof(FieldName) → MethodEnv
```
(define method-decls->method-env
  (lambda (m-decls super-name field-names)
    (map
      (lambda (m-decl)
        (cases method-decl m-decl
          (a-method-decl (method-name vars body)
            (list method-name
              (a-method vars body super-name field-names)))))
      m-decls)))
```

Last, we write `merge-method-envs`. Since methods in the new class override those of the old class, we can simply append the environments, with the new methods first.

merge-method-envs : *MethodEnv × MethodEnv → MethodEnv*
```
(define merge-method-envs
  (lambda (super-m-env new-m-env)
    (append new-m-env super-m-env)))
```

There are ways of building method environments that will be more efficient for method lookup (exercise 9.18).

```
((c3
  #(struct:a-class c2 (x%2 y%1 y x z)
    ((initialize #(struct:a-method ()
                        #(struct:begin-exp ...) c2 (x%2 y%1 y x z)))
      (m3 #(struct:a-method ()
            #(struct:diff-exp ...)) c2 (x%2 y%1 y x z))
      (initialize #(struct:a-method ...))
      (m1 #(struct:a-method (u v)
            #(struct:diff-exp ...) c1 (x y%1 y)))
      (m3 #(struct:a-method ...))
      (initialize  #(struct:a-method ...))
      (m1 #(struct:a-method ...))
      (m2 #(struct:a-method ()
            #(struct:method-call-exp #(struct:self-exp) m3 ())
            object (x y))))))
 (c2
  #(struct:a-class c1 (x y%1 y)
    ((initialize #(struct:a-method ()
                        #(struct:begin-exp ...) c1 (x y%1 y)))
      (m1 #(struct:a-method (u v)
            #(struct:diff-exp ...) c1 (x y%1 y)))
      (m3 #(struct:a-method ()
            #(struct:const-exp 23) c1 (x y%1 y)))
      (initialize #(struct:a-method ...))
      (m1 #(struct:a-method ...))
      (m2 #(struct:a-method ()
            #(struct:method-call-exp #(struct:self-exp) m3 ())
            object (x y)))))
 (c1
  #(struct:a-class object (x y)
    ((initialize #(struct:a-method ()
                        #(struct:begin-exp ...) object (x y)))
      (m1 #(struct:a-method ()
            #(struct:diff-exp ...) object (x y)))
      (m2 #(struct:a-method ()
            #(struct:method-call-exp #(struct:self-exp) m3 ())
            object (x y)))))
 (object
  #(struct:a-class #f () ()))))
```

Figure 9.11   The class environment for figure 9.8

9.4.5   Exercises

Exercise 9.1 [⋆] Implement the following using the language of this section:

1. A queue class with methods `empty?`, `enqueue`, and `dequeue`.

2. Extend the queue class with a counter that counts the number of operations that have been performed on the current queue.

3. Extend the queue class with a counter that counts the total number of operations that have been performed on all the queues in the class. As a hint, remember that you can pass a shared counter object at initialization time.

Exercise 9.2 [⋆] Inheritance can be dangerous, because a child class can arbitrarily change the behavior of a method by overriding it. Define a class `bogus-oddeven` that inherits from `oddeven` and overrides the method `even` so that `let o1 = new bogus-oddeven() in send o1 odd (13)` gives the wrong answer.

Exercise 9.3 [⋆ ⋆] In figure 9.11, where are method environments shared? Where are the `field-names` lists shared?

Exercise 9.4 [⋆] Change the representation of objects so that an *Obj* contains the class of which the object is an instance, rather than its name. What are the advantages and disadvantages of this representation compared to the one in the text?

Exercise 9.5 [⋆] The interpreter of section 9.4 stores the superclass name of a method's host class in the lexical environment. Change the implementation so that the method stores the host class name, and retrieves the superclass name from the host name.

Exercise 9.6 [⋆] Add to our language the expression `instanceof` *exp class-name*. The value of this expression should be true if and only if the object obtained by evaluating *exp* is an instance of *class-name* or of one of its subclasses.

Exercise 9.7 [⋆] In our language, the environment for a method includes bindings for the field variables declared in the host class *and* its superclasses. Limit them to just the host class.

Exercise 9.8 [⋆] Add to our language a new expression,

$$\text{fieldref } obj \; field\text{-}name$$

that retrieves the contents of the given field of the object. Add also

$$\text{fieldset } obj \; field\text{-}name = exp$$

which sets the given field to the value of *exp*.

Exercise 9.9 [⋆] Add expressions `superfieldref` *field-name* and `superfieldset` *field-name* = *exp* that manipulate the fields of `self` that would otherwise be shadowed. Remember `super` is static, and always refers to the superclass of the host class.

Exercise 9.10 [⋆ ⋆] Some object-oriented languages include facilities for named-class method invocation and field references. In a named-class method invocation, one might write `named-send c1 o m1()`. This would invoke `c1`'s `m1` method on `o`, so long as `o` was an instance of `c1` or of one of its subclasses, even if `m1` were over-ridden in `o`'s actual class. This is a form of static method dispatch. Named-class field reference provides a similar facility for field reference. Add named-class method invocation, field reference, and field setting to the language of this section.

Exercise 9.11 [⋆ ⋆] Add to CLASSES the ability to specify that each method is either *private* and only accessible from within the host class, *protected* and only accessible from the host class and its descendants, or *public* and accessible from anywhere. Many object-oriented languages include some version of this feature.

Exercise 9.12 [⋆ ⋆] Add to CLASSES the ability to specify that each field is either private, protected, or public as in exercise 9.11.

Exercise 9.13 [⋆ ⋆] To defend against malicious subclasses like `bogus-oddeven` in exercise 9.2, many object-oriented languages have a facility for *final* methods, which may not be overridden. Add such a facility to CLASSES, so that we could write

```
class oddeven extends object
  method initialize () 1
  final method even (n)
   if zero?(n) then 1 else send self odd(-(n,1))
  final method odd (n)
   if zero?(n) then 0 else send self even(-(n,1))
```

Exercise 9.14 [⋆ ⋆] Another way to defend against malicious subclasses is to use some form of *static dispatch*. Modify CLASSES so that method calls to *self* always use the method in the host class, rather than the method in the class of the target object.

Exercise 9.15 [⋆ ⋆] Many object-oriented languages include a provision for *static* or *class* variables. Static variables associate some state with a class; all the instances of the class share this state. For example, one might write:

```
class c1 extends object
  static next-serial-number = 1
  field my-serial-number
  method get-serial-number () my-serial-number
  method initialize ()
   begin
    set my-serial-number = next-serial-number;
    set next-serial-number = +(next-serial-number,1)
   end
let o1 = new c1()
    o2 = new c1()
in list(send o1 get-serial-number(),
        send o2 get-serial-number())
```

Each new object of class c1 receives a new consecutive serial number.

Add static variables to our language. Since static variables can appear in a method body, apply-method must add additional bindings in the environment it constructs. What environment should be used for the evaluation of the initializing expression for a static variable (1 in the example above)?

Exercise 9.16 [⋆ ⋆] Object-oriented languages frequently allow *overloading* of methods. This feature allows a class to have multiple methods of the same name, provided they have distinct *signatures*. A method's signature is typically the method name plus the types of its parameters. Since we do not have types in CLASSES, we might overload based simply on the method name and number of parameters. For example, a class might have two initialize methods, one with no parameters for use when initialization with a default field value is desired, and another with one parameter for use when a particular field value is desired. Extend our interpreter to allow overloading based on the number of method parameters.

Exercise 9.17 [⋆ ⋆] As it stands, the classes in our language are defined globally. Add to CLASSES a facility for local classes, so one can write something like letclass *c* = . . . in *e* . As a hint, consider adding the class environment as a parameter to the interpreter.

Exercise 9.18 [⋆ ⋆] The method environments produced by merge-method-envs can be long. Write a new version of merge-method-envs with the property that each method name occurs exactly once, and furthermore, it appears in the same place as its earliest declaration. For example, in figure 9.8, method m2 should appear in the same place in the method environments of c1, c2, c3, and any descendant of c3.

Exercise 9.19 [⋆ ⋆] Implement lexical addressing for CLASSES. First, write a lexical-address calculator like that of section 3.7.1 for the language of this section. Then modify the implementation of environments to make them nameless, and modify value-of so that apply-env takes a lexical address instead of a symbol, as in section 3.7.2.

Exercise 9.20 [⋆ ⋆ ⋆] Can anything equivalent to the optimizations of the exercise 9.19 be done for method invocations? Discuss why or why not.

Exercise 9.21 [⋆ ⋆] If there are many methods in a class, linear search down a list of methods can be slow. Replace it by some faster implementation. How much improvement does your implementation provide? Account for your results, either positive or negative.

Exercise 9.22 [⋆ ⋆] In exercise 9.16, we added overloading to the language by extending the interpreter. Another way to support overloading is not to modify the interpreter, but to use a syntactic preprocessor. Write a preprocessor that changes the name of every method *m* to one of the form *m*:@*n*, where *n* is the number of parameters in the method declaration. It must similarly change the name in every method call, based on the number of operands. We assume that :@ is not used by programmers in method names, but is accepted by the interpreter in method names. Compilers frequently use such a technique to implement method overloading. This is an instance of a general trick called *name mangling*.

Exercise 9.23 [★ ★ ★] We have treated super calls as if they were lexically bound. But we can do better: we can determine `super` calls *statically*. Since a super call refers to a method in a class's parent, and the parent, along with its methods, is known prior to the start of execution, we can determine the exact method to which any super call refers at the same time we do lexical-addressing and other analyses. Write a translator that takes each super call and replaces it with an abstract syntax tree node containing the actual method to be invoked.

Exercise 9.24 [★ ★ ★] Write a translator that replaces method names in named method calls as in exercise 9.10 with numbers indicating the offset of the named method in the run-time method table of the named class. Implement an interpreter for the translated code in which named method access is constant time.

Exercise 9.25 [★ ★ ★] Using the first example of inheritance from figure 9.5, we include a method in the class `point` that determines if two points have the same x- and y-coordinates. We add the method `similarpoints` to the point class as follows:

```
method similarpoints (pt)
  if equal?(send pt getx(), x)
  then equal?(send pt gety(), y)
  else zero?(1)
```

This works for both kinds of points. Since `getx`, `gety`, and `similarpoints` are defined in class `point`, by inheritance, they are defined in `colorpoint`. Test `similarpoints` to compare points with points, points with color points, color points with points, and color points with color points.

Next consider a small extension. We add a new `similarpoints` method to the `colorpoint` class. We expect it to return true if both points have the same x- and y-coordinates and further, in case both are color points, they have the same color. Otherwise it returns false. Here is an incorrect solution.

```
method similarpoints (pt)
  if super similarpoints(pt)
  then equal?(send pt getcolor(),color)
  else zero?(1)
```

Test this extension. Determine why it does not work on all the cases. Fix it so that all the tests return the correct values.

The difficulty of writing a procedure that relies on more than one object is known as the *binary method problem*. It demonstrates that the class-centric model of object-oriented programming, which this chapter explores, leaves something to be desired when there are multiple objects. It is called the *binary* method problem because the problem shows up with just two objects, but it gets progressively worse as the number of objects increases.

Exercise 9.26 [★ ★ ★] Multiple inheritance, in which a class can have more than one parent, can be useful, but may introduce serious complications. What if two inherited classes both have methods of the same name? This can be disallowed, or resolved by enumerating the methods in the class by some arbitrary rule, such as depth-first left-to-right, or by requiring that the ambiguity be resolved at the point such a method is called. The situation for fields is even worse. Consider the following situation, in which class c4 is to inherit from c2 and c3, both of which inherit from c1:

```
class c1 extends object
  field x
class c2 extends c1
class c3 extends c1
class c4 extends c2, c3
```

Does an instance of c4 have one instance of field x shared by c2 and c3, or does c4 have two x fields: one inherited from c2 and one inherited from c3? Some languages opt for sharing, some not, and some provide a choice, at least in some cases. The complexity of this problem has led to a design trend favoring single inheritance of classes, but multiple inheritance only for interfaces (section 9.5), which avoids most of these difficulties.

Add multiple inheritance to CLASSES. Extend the syntax as necessary. Indicate what issues arise when resolving method and field name conflicts. Characterize the sharing issue and its resolution.

Exercise 9.27 [★ ★ ★] Implement the following design for an object language without classes. An object will be a set of closures, indexed by method names, that share an environment (and hence some state). Classes will be replaced by procedures that return an object. So instead of writing send o1 m1(11,22,33), we would write an ordinary procedure call (getmethod(o1,m1) 11 22 33), and instead of writing

```
class oddeven extends object
  method initialize () 1
  method even (n)
    if zero?(n) then 1 else send self odd(-(n,1))
  method odd (n)
    if zero?(n) then 0 else send self even(-(n,1))
let o1 = new oddeven()
in send o1 odd(13)
```

we might write something like

```
let make-oddeven
  = proc ()
      newobject
        even = proc (n) if zero?(n) then 1
                          else (getmethod(self,odd) -(n,1))
        odd = proc (n) if zero?(n) then 0
                          else (getmethod(self,even) -(n,1))
      endnewobject
in let o1 = (make-oddeven) in (getmethod(o1,odd) 13)
```

Exercise 9.28 [★ ★ ★] Add inheritance to the language of exercise 9.27.

Exercise 9.29 [★ ★ ★] Design and implement an object-oriented language without explicit classes, by having each object contain its own method environment. Such an object is called a *prototype*. Replace the class `object` by a prototype object with no methods or fields. Extend a class by adding methods and fields to its prototype, yielding a new prototype. Thus we might write `let c2 = extend c1 ...` instead of `class c2 extends c1 ...`. Replace the `new` operation with an operation `clone` that takes an object and simply copies its methods and fields. Methods in this language occur inside a lexical scope, so they should have access to lexically visible variables, as usual, as well as field variables. What shadowing relation should hold when a field variable of a superprototype has the same name as a variable in a containing lexical scope?

9.5   A Typed Language

In chapter 7, we showed how a type system could inspect a program to guarantee that it would never execute an inappropriate operation. No program that passes the checker will ever attempt to apply a nonprocedure to an argument, or to apply a procedure or other operator to the wrong number of arguments or to an argument of the wrong type.

In this section, we apply this technology to an object-oriented language that we call TYPED-OO. This language has all the safety properties listed above, and in addition, no program that passes our checker will ever send a message to an object for which there is no corresponding method, or send a message to an object with the wrong number of arguments or with arguments of the wrong type.

A sample program in TYPED-OO language is shown in figure 9.12. This program defines a class `tree`, which has a `sum` method that finds the sum of the values in the leaves, as in figure 9.2, and an `equal` method, which takes another tree and recursively descends through the trees to determine if they are equal.

The major new features of the language are:

- Fields and methods are specified with their types, using a syntax similar to that used in chapter 7.

- The concept of an *interface* is introduced in an object-oriented setting.

- The concept of *subtype polymorphism* is added to the language.

- The concept of *casting* is introduced, and the `instanceof` test from exercise 9.6 is incorporated into the language.

We consider each of these items in turn.

The new productions for TYPED-OO are shown in figure 9.13. We add a
void type as the type of a set operation, and list types as in exercise 7.9; as
in exercise 7.9 we require that calls to list have at least one argument. We
add identifiers to the set of type expressions, but for this chapter, an identifier used as a type is associated with the class or interface of the same name.
We consider this correspondence in more detail below. Methods require their
result type to be specified, along with the types of their arguments, using a
syntax similar to that used for letrec in chapter 7. Last, two new expressions are added, cast and instanceof.

In order to understand the new features of this language, we must define
the types of the language, as we did in definition 7.1.1.

Definition 9.5.1 *The property of an expressed value v being of type t is defined as
follows:*

- *If c is a class, then a value is of type c if and only if it is an object, and it is an
  instance of the class c or one of its descendants.*

- *If I is an interface, then a value is of type I if and only if it is an object that is an
  instance of a class that implements I. A class implements I if and only if it has
  an* implements *I declaration or if one of its ancestors implements I.*

- *If t is some other type, then the rules of definition 7.1.1 apply.*

An object is an instance of exactly one class, but it can have many types.

- It has the type of the class that created it.

- It has the type of that class's superclass and of all classes above it in the
  inheritance hierarchy. In particular, every object has type object.

- It has the type of any interfaces that its creating class implements.

The second property is called *subclass polymorphism*. The third property
could be called *interface polymorphism*.

An interface represents the set of all objects that implement a particular set
of methods, regardless of how those objects were constructed. Our typing
system will allow a class c to declare that it implements interface I only if
c provides all the methods, with all the right types, that are required by I.
A class may implement several different interfaces, although we have only
used one in our example.

```
interface tree
 method int sum ()
 method bool equal (t : tree)

class interior-node extends object implements tree
 field tree left
 field tree right
 method void initialize(l : tree, r : tree)
  begin
   set left = l; set right = r
  end
 method tree getleft () left
 method tree getright () right
 method int sum () +(send left sum(), send right sum())
 method bool equal (t : tree)
  if instanceof t interior-node
  then if send left equal(send
                             cast t interior-node
                             getleft())
       then send right equal(send
                               cast t interior-node
                               getright())
       else zero?(1)
  else zero?(1)

class leaf-node extends object implements tree
 field int value
 method void initialize (v : int) set value = v
 method int sum () value
 method int getvalue () value
 method bool equal (t : tree)
  if instanceof t leaf-node
  then zero?(-(value, send cast t leaf-node getvalue()))
  else zero?(1)

let o1 = new interior-node (
          new interior-node (
           new leaf-node(3),
           new leaf-node(4)),
          new leaf-node(5))
in list(send o1 sum(),
         if send o1 equal(o1) then 100 else 200)
```

Figure 9.12   A sample program in TYPED-OO

ClassDecl ::= class *Identifier* extends *Identifier*
{implements *Identifier*}*
{field *Type* *Identifier*}*
{*MethodDecl*}*

```
a-class-decl (c-name s-name i-names
                     f-types f-names m-decls)
```

ClassDecl ::= interface *Identifier* {*AbstractMethodDecl*}*

```
an-interface-decl (i-name abs-m-decls)
```

MethodDecl ::= method *Type* *Identifier* ({*Identifier* : *Type*}*(,)) *Expression*

```
a-method-decl
   (res-type m-name vars var-types body)
```

AbstractMethodDecl ::= method *Type* *Identifier* ({*Identifier* :*Type*}*(,))

```
an-abstract-method-decl
   (result-type m-name m-var-types m-vars)
```

Expression ::= cast *Expression* *Identifier*

```
cast-exp (exp c-name)
```

Expression ::= instanceof *Expression* *Identifier*

```
instanceof-exp (exp name)
```

Type ::= void

```
void-type ()
```

Type ::= *Identifier*

```
class-type (class-name)
```

Type ::= listof *Type*

```
list-type (type1)
```

Figure 9.13 New productions for TYPED-OO

In figure 9.12, the classes `interior-node` and `leaf-node` both implement the interface `tree`. The typechecker allows this, because they both implement the `sum` and `equal` methods that are required for `tree`.

The expression `instanceof` e c returns a true value whenever the object obtained by evaluating e is an instance of the class c or of one of its descendants. Casting complements `instanceof`. The value of a `cast` expression `cast` e c is the same as the value of e if that value is an object that is an instance of the class c or one of its descendants. Otherwise the `cast` expression reports an error. The type of `cast` e c will always be c, since its value, if it returns, is guaranteed to be of type c.

For example, our sample program includes the method

```
method bool equal(t : tree)
  if instanceof t interior-node
  then if send left
          equal(send cast t interior-node getleft())
       then send right
              equal(send cast t interior-node getright())
       else false
  else false
```

The expression `cast t interior-node` checks to see if the value of t is an instance of `interior-node` (or one of its descendants, if `interior-node` had descendants). If it is, the value of t is returned; otherwise, an error is reported. An `instanceof` expression returns a true value if and only if the corresponding `cast` would succeed. Hence in this example the cast is guaranteed to succeed, since it is guarded by the `instanceof`. The cast, in turn, guards the use of `send ... getleft()`. The cast expression is guaranteed to return a value of class `interior-node`, and therefore it will be safe to send this value a `getleft` message.

For our implementation, we begin with the interpreter of section 9.4.1. We add two new clauses to `value-of` to evaluate `instanceof` and `cast` expressions:

```
(cast-exp (exp c-name)
  (let ((obj (value-of exp env)))
    (if (is-subclass? (object->class-name obj) c-name)
      obj
      (report-cast-error c-name obj))))

(instanceof-exp (exp c-name)
  (let ((obj (value-of exp env)))
    (if (is-subclass? (object->class-name obj) c-name)
      (bool-val #t)
      (bool-val #f))))
```

The procedure is-subclass? traces the parent link of the first class structure until it either finds the second one or stops when the parent link is #f. Since interfaces are only used as types, they are ignored in this process.

is-subclass? : *ClassName* × *ClassName* → *Bool*

```
(define is-subclass?
  (lambda (c-name1 c-name2)
    (cond
      ((eqv? c-name1 c-name2) #t)
      (else
        (let ((s-name (class->super-name
                        (lookup-class c-name1))))
          (if s-name (is-subclass? s-name c-name2) #f)))))))
```

This completes the modification of the interpreter for the language of this section.

Exercise 9.30 [⋆] Create an interface summable:

```
interface summable
  method int sum ()
```

Now define classes for summable lists, summable binary trees (as in figure 9.12) and summable general trees (in which each node contains a summable list of children).

Then do the same thing for an interface

```
interface stringable
  method string to-string ()
```

Exercise 9.31 [⋆] In figure 9.12, would it have worked to make tree a class and have the two node classes inherit from tree? In what circumstances is this a better method than using an interface like summable? In what circumstances is it inferior?

Exercise 9.32 [⋆ ⋆] Write an equality predicate for the class tree that does not use instanceof or cast. What is needed here is a *double dispatch*, in place of the single dispatch provided by the usual methods. This can be simulated as follows: Instead of using instanceof to find the class of the argument t, the current tree should send back to t a message that encodes its own class, along with parameters containing the values of the appropriate fields.

9.6   The Type Checker

We now turn to the checker for this language. The goal of the checker is to
guarantee a set of safety properties. For our language, these properties are
those of the underlying procedural language, plus the following properties
of the object-oriented portion of the language: no program that passes our
type checker will ever

- send a message to a non-object,

- send a message to an object for which there is no corresponding method,

- send a message to an object with the wrong number of arguments or with
  arguments of the wrong type.

We make no attempt to verify that the `initialize` methods actually initialize all the fields, so it will still be possible for a program to reference an
uninitialized field. Similarly, because it is in general impossible to predict
the type of an `initialize` method, our checker will not prevent the explicit
invocation of an `initialize` method with the wrong number of arguments
or arguments of the wrong type, but the implicit invocation of `initialize`
by `new` will always be correct.

The checker begins with the implementation of `type-of-program`. Since
all the methods of all the classes are mutually recursive, we proceed much as
we do for `letrec`. For a `letrec`, we first built `tenv-for-letrec-body`
by collecting the declared type of the procedure (figure 7.3). We then checked
each procedure body against its declared result type. Finally, we checked the
body of the `letrec` in `tenv-for-letrec-body`.

Here, we first call `initialize-static-class-env!`, which walks
through the class declarations, collecting all the types into a static class environment. Since this environment is global and never changes, we keep it in
a Scheme variable rather than passing it as a parameter. Then we check each
class declaration, using `check-class-decl!`. Finally, we find the type of
the body of the program.

```
type-of-program : Program → Type
(define type-of-program
  (lambda (pgm)
    (cases program pgm
      (a-program (class-decls exp1)
        (initialize-static-class-env! class-decls)
        (for-each check-class-decl! class-decls)
        (type-of exp1 (init-tenv))))))))
```

The static class environment will map each class name to a static class containing the name of its parent, the names and types of its fields, and the names and types of its methods. In our language, interfaces have no parent and no fields, so they will be represented by a data structure containing only the names and types of its required methods (but see exercise 9.36).

```
(define-datatype static-class static-class?
  (a-static-class
    (super-name (maybe identifier?))
    (interface-names (list-of identifier?))
    (field-names (list-of identifier?))
    (field-types (list-of type?))
    (method-tenv method-tenv?))
  (an-interface
    (method-tenv method-tenv?)))
```

Before considering how the static class environment is built, we consider how to extend `type-of` to check the types of the six kinds of object-oriented expressions: `self`, `instanceof`, `cast`, method calls, super calls, and `new`.

For a `self` expression, we look up the type of self using the pseudo-variable `%self`, which we will be sure to bind to the type of the current host class, just as in the interpreter we bound it to the current host object.

If an `instanceof` expression returns, it always returns a `bool`. The expression `cast` e c returns the value of e provided that the value is an object that is an instance of c or one of its descendants. Hence, if `cast` e c returns a value, then that value is of type c. So we can always assign `cast` e c the type c. For both `instanceof` and `cast` expressions, the interpreter evaluates the argument and runs `object->class-name` on it, so we we must of course check that the operand is well-typed and returns a value that is an object. The code for these three cases is shown in figure 9.14.

We next consider method calls. We now have three different kinds of calls in our language: procedure calls, method calls, and super calls. We abstract the process of checking these into a single procedure.

```
(self-exp ()
  (apply-tenv tenv '%self))

(instanceof-exp (exp class-name)
  (let ((obj-type (type-of exp tenv)))
    (if (class-type? obj-type)
      (bool-type)
      (report-bad-type-to-instanceof obj-type exp))))

(cast-exp (exp class-name)
  (let ((obj-type (type-of exp tenv)))
    (if (class-type? obj-type)
      (class-type class-name)
      (report-bad-type-to-cast obj-type exp))))
```

Figure 9.14   `type-of` clauses for object-oriented expressions, part 1

type-of-call : *Type* × *Listof(Type)* × *Listof(Exp)* → *Type*
```
(define type-of-call
  (lambda (rator-type rand-types rands exp)
    (cases type rator-type
      (proc-type (arg-types result-type)
        (if (not (= (length arg-types) (length rand-types)))
          (report-wrong-number-of-arguments
            (map type-to-external-form arg-types)
            (map type-to-external-form rand-types)
            exp))
        (for-each check-is-subtype! rand-types arg-types rands)
        result-type)
      (else
        (report-rator-not-of-proc-type
          (type-to-external-form rator-type)
          exp)))))
```

This procedure is equivalent to the line for `call-exp` in CHECKED (figure 7.2) with two notable additions. First, because our procedures now take multiple arguments, we check to see that the call has the right number of arguments, and in the `for-each` line we check the type of each operand against the type of the corresponding argument in the procedure's type. Second, and more interestingly, we have replaced `check-equal-type!` of figure 7.2 by `check-is-subtype!`.

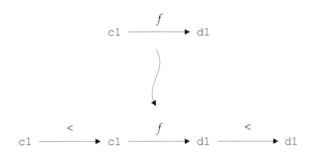

Figure 9.15   Subtyping a procedure type

Why is this necessary? The principle of subclass polymorphism says that if class c_2 extends c_1, then an object of class c_2 can be used in any context in which an object of class c_1 can appear. If we wrote a procedure proc (o : c_1) ..., that procedure should be able to take an actual parameter of type c_2.

In general, we can extend the notion of subclass polymorphism to *subtype polymorphism*, as we did with < : in chapter 8. We say that t_1 is a subtype of t_2 if and only if

- t_1 and t_2 are classes, and t_1 is a subclass of t_2, or

- t_1 is a class and t_2 is an interface, and t_1 or one of its superclasses implements t_2, or

- t_1 and t_2 are procedure types, and the argument types of t_2 are subtypes of the argument types of t_1, and the result type of t_1 is a subtype of t_2.

To understand the last rule, let t_1 be (c1 -> d1), let t_2 be (c2 -> d2), with c2 < c1 and d1 < d2. Let f be a procedure of type t_1. We claim that f also has type t_2. Why? Imagine that we give f an argument of type c2. Since c2 < c1, the argument is also a c1. Therefore it is an acceptable argument to f. f then returns a value of type d1. But since d1 < d2, this result is also of type d2. So, if f is given an argument of type c2, it returns a value of type d2. Hence f has type (c2 -> d2). We say that subtyping is *covariant* in the result type and *contravariant* in the argument type. See figure 9.15. This is similar to the definition of < : -iface in section 8.3.2.

The code for this is shown in figure 9.16. The code uses `every2?`, an extension of the procedure `every?` from exercise 1.24 that takes a two-argument predicate and two lists, and returns `#t` if the lists are of the same length and corresponding elements satisfy the predicate, or returns `#f` otherwise.

We can now consider each of the three kinds of calls (figure 9.17). For a method call, we first find the types of the target object and of the operands, as usual. We use `find-method-type`, analogous to `find-method`, to find the type of the method. If the type of the target is not a class or interface, then `type->class-name` will report an error. If there is no corresponding method, then `find-method-type` will report an error. We then call `type-of-call` to verify that the types of the operands are compatible with the types expected by the method, and to return the type of the result.

For a `new` expression, we first retrieve the class information for the class name. If there is no class associated with the name, a type error is reported. Last, we call `type-of-call` with the types of the operands to see if the call to `initialize` is safe. If these checks succeed, then the execution of the expression is safe. Since the `new` expression returns a new object of the specified class, the type of the result is the corresponding type of the class.

We have now completed our discussion of checking expressions in TYPED-OO, so we now return to constructing the static class environment.

To build the static class environment, `initialize-static-class-env!` first sets the static class environment to empty, and then adds a binding for the class `object`. It then goes through each class or instance declaration and adds an appropriate entry to the static class environment.

initialize-static-class-env! : *Listof(ClassDecl)* → *Unspecified*
```
(define initialize-static-class-env!
  (lambda (c-decls)
    (empty-the-static-class-env!)
    (add-static-class-binding!
      'object (a-static-class #f '() '() '() '()))
    (for-each add-class-decl-to-static-class-env! c-decls)))
```

The procedure `add-class-decl-to-static-class-env!` (fig. 9.18) does the bulk of the work of creating the static classes. For each class, we must collect all its interfaces, fields, and methods:

- A class implements any interfaces that its parent implements, plus the interfaces that it claims to implement.

- A class has the fields that its parent has, plus its own, except that its parent's fields are shadowed by the locally declared fields. So the `field-names` are calculated with `append-field-names`, just as in `initialize-class-env!` (page 344).

check-is-subtype! : *Type* × *Type* × *Exp* → *Unspecified*
```
(define check-is-subtype!
  (lambda (ty1 ty2 exp)
    (if (is-subtype? ty1 ty2)
      #t
      (report-subtype-failure
        (type-to-external-form ty1)
        (type-to-external-form ty2)
        exp))))
```

is-subtype? : *Type* × *Type* → *Bool*
```
(define is-subtype?
  (lambda (ty1 ty2)
    (cases type ty1
      (class-type (name1)
        (cases type ty2
          (class-type (name2)
            (statically-is-subclass? name1 name2))
          (else #f)))
      (proc-type (args1 res1)
        (cases type ty2
          (proc-type (args2 res2)
            (and
              (every2? is-subtype? args2 args1)
              (is-subtype? res1 res2)))
          (else #f)))
      (else (equal? ty1 ty2)))))
```

statically-is-subclass? : *ClassName* × *ClassName* → *Bool*
```
(define statically-is-subclass?
  (lambda (name1 name2)
    (or
      (eqv? name1 name2)
      (let ((super-name
              (static-class->super-name
                (lookup-static-class name1))))
        (if super-name
          (statically-is-subclass? super-name name2)
          #f))
      (let ((interface-names
              (static-class->interface-names
                (lookup-static-class name1))))
        (memv name2 interface-names)))))
```

Figure 9.16   Subtyping in TYPED-OO

```
(method-call-exp (obj-exp method-name rands)
  (let ((arg-types (types-of-exps rands tenv))
        (obj-type (type-of obj-exp tenv)))
    (type-of-call
      (find-method-type
        (type->class-name obj-type)
        method-name)
      arg-types
      rands
      exp)))

(super-call-exp (method-name rands)
  (let ((arg-types (types-of-exps rands tenv))
        (obj-type (apply-tenv tenv '%self)))
    (type-of-call
      (find-method-type
        (apply-tenv tenv '%super)
        method-name)
      arg-types
      rands
      exp)))

(new-object-exp (class-name rands)
  (let ((arg-types (types-of-exps rands tenv))
        (c (lookup-static-class class-name)))
    (cases static-class c
      (an-interface (method-tenv)
        (report-cant-instantiate-interface class-name))
      (a-static-class (super-name i-names
                        field-names field-types
                        method-tenv)
        (type-of-call
          (find-method-type
            class-name
            'initialize)
          arg-types
          rands
          exp)
        (class-type class-name)))))
```

Figure 9.17   type-of clauses for object-oriented expressions, part 2

- The types of the class's fields are the types of its parent's fields, plus the types of its locally declared fields.

- The methods of the class are those of its parent plus its own, with their declared types. We keep the type of a method as a `proc-type`. We put the locally declared methods first, since they override the parent's methods.

- We check that there are no duplicates among the local method names, the interface names, and the field names. We also make sure that there is an `initialize` method available in the class.

For an interface declaration, we need only process the method names and their types.

Once the static class environment has been built, we can check each class declaration. This is done by `check-class-decl!` (figure 9.19). For an interface, there is nothing to check. For a class declaration, we check each method, passing along information collected from the static class environment. Finally, we check to see that the class actually implements each of the interfaces that it claims to implement.

To check a method declaration, we first check to see whether its body matches its declared type. To do this, we build a type environment that matches the environment in which the body will be evaluated. We then check to see that the result type of the body is a subtype of the declared result type.

We are not done, however: we have to make sure that if this method is overriding some method in the superclass, then it has a type that is compatible with the superclass method's type. We have to do this because this method might be called from a method that knows only about the supertype. The only exception to this rule is `initialize`, which is only called at the current class, and which needs to change its type under inheritance (see figure 9.12). To do this, it calls `maybe-find-method-type`, which returns either the type of the method if it is found, or `#f` otherwise. See figure 9.20.

The procedure `check-if-implements?`, shown in figure 9.21, takes two symbols, which should be a class name and an interface name. It first checks to see that each symbol names what it should name. It then goes through each method in the interface and checks to see that the class provides a method with the same name and a compatible type.

The static class environment built for the sample program of figure 9.12 is shown in figure 9.22. The static classes are in reverse order, reflecting the

add-class-decl-to-static-class-env! : *ClassDecl* → *Unspecified*

```
(define add-class-decl-to-static-class-env!
  (lambda (c-decl)
    (cases class-decl c-decl
      (an-interface-decl (i-name abs-m-decls)
        (let ((m-tenv
                (abs-method-decls->method-tenv abs-m-decls)))
          (check-no-dups! (map car m-tenv) i-name)
          (add-static-class-binding!
            i-name (an-interface m-tenv))))
      (a-class-decl (c-name s-name i-names
                      f-types f-names m-decls)
        (let ((i-names
                (append
                  (static-class->interface-names
                    (lookup-static-class s-name))
                  i-names))
              (f-names
                (append-field-names
                  (static-class->field-names
                    (lookup-static-class s-name))
                  f-names))
              (f-types
                (append
                  (static-class->field-types
                    (lookup-static-class s-name))
                  f-types))
              (method-tenv
                (let ((local-method-tenv
                        (method-decls->method-tenv m-decls)))
                  (check-no-dups!
                    (map car local-method-tenv) c-name)
                  (merge-method-tenvs
                    (static-class->method-tenv
                      (lookup-static-class s-name))
                    local-method-tenv))))
          (check-no-dups! i-names c-name)
          (check-no-dups! f-names c-name)
          (check-for-initialize! method-tenv c-name)
          (add-static-class-binding! c-name
            (a-static-class
              s-name i-names f-names f-types method-tenv)))))))
```

Figure 9.18   add-class-decl-to-static-class-env!

---

check-class-decl! : *ClassDecl* → *Unspecified*

```
(define check-class-decl!
  (lambda (c-decl)
    (cases class-decl c-decl
      (an-interface-decl (i-name abs-method-decls)
        #t)
      (a-class-decl (class-name super-name i-names
                     field-types field-names method-decls)
        (let ((sc (lookup-static-class class-name)))
          (for-each
            (lambda (method-decl)
              (check-method-decl! method-decl
                class-name super-name
                (static-class->field-names sc)
                (static-class->field-types sc)))
           method-decls))
        (for-each
          (lambda (i-name)
            (check-if-implements! class-name i-name))
          i-names)))))
```

Figure 9.19   check-class-decl!

---

order in which the class environment is built. Each of the three classes has its methods in the same order, with the same type, as desired.

This completes the presentation of the checker.

Exercise 9.33 [⋆] Extend the type checker to enforce the safety property that no instanceof or cast expression is ever performed on a value that is not an object, or on a type that is not a class.

Exercise 9.34 [⋆] The expression cast *e* *c* cannot succeed unless the type of *e* is either a descendant or an ancestor of *c*. (Why?) Extend the type checker to guarantee that the program never evaluates a cast expression unless this property holds. Extend the checker for instanceof to match.

Exercise 9.35 [⋆] Extend the type checker to enforce the safety property that an initialize method is called only from within a new-object-exp.

Exercise 9.36 [⋆] Extend the language to allow interfaces to inherit from other interfaces. An interface should require all the methods required by all of its parents.

check-method-decl! :

MethodDecl × *ClassName* × *ClassName* × *Listof*(*FieldName*) × *Listof*(*Type*)
  → *Unspecified*

```
(define check-method-decl!
  (lambda (m-decl self-name s-name f-names f-types)
    (cases method-decl m-decl
      (a-method-decl (res-type m-name vars var-types body)
        (let ((tenv
                (extend-tenv
                  vars var-types
                  (extend-tenv-with-self-and-super
                    (class-type self-name)
                    s-name
                    (extend-tenv f-names f-types
                      (init-tenv))))))
          (let ((body-type (type-of body tenv)))
            (check-is-subtype! body-type res-type m-decl)
            (if (eqv? m-name 'initialize) #t
              (let ((maybe-super-type
                      (maybe-find-method-type
                        (static-class->method-tenv
                          (lookup-static-class s-name))
                        m-name)))
                (if maybe-super-type
                  (check-is-subtype!
                    (proc-type var-types res-type)
                    maybe-super-type body)
                  #t)))))))))
```

Figure 9.20 `check-method-decl!`

Exercise 9.37 [★★] Our language TYPED-OO uses dynamic dispatch. An alternative design is *static dispatch*. In static dispatch, the choice of method depends on an object's type rather than its class. Consider the example

```
class c1 extends object
 method int initialize () 1
 method int m1 () 11
 staticmethod int m2 () 21
class c2 extends c1
 method void m1 () 12
 staticmethod int m2 () 22
```

---

check-if-implements! : *ClassName* × *InterfaceName* → *Bool*

```
(define check-if-implements!
  (lambda (c-name i-name)
    (cases static-class (lookup-static-class i-name)
      (a-static-class (s-name i-names f-names f-types
                              m-tenv)
        (report-cant-implement-non-interface
          c-name i-name))
      (an-interface (method-tenv)
        (let ((class-method-tenv
                (static-class->method-tenv
                  (lookup-static-class c-name))))
          (for-each
            (lambda (method-binding)
              (let ((m-name (car method-binding))
                    (m-type (cadr method-binding)))
                (let ((c-method-type
                        (maybe-find-method-type
                          class-method-tenv
                          m-name)))
                  (if c-method-type
                    (check-is-subtype!
                      c-method-type m-type c-name)
                    (report-missing-method
                      c-name i-name m-name)))))
            method-tenv))))))
```

Figure 9.21   check-if-implements

```
let f = proc (x : c1) send x m1()
    g = proc (x : c1) send x m2()
    o = new c2()
in list((f o), (g o))
```

When f and g are called, x will have type c2, but it is bound to an object of class c2. The method m1 uses dynamic dispatch, so c2's method for m1 is invoked, returning 12. The method m2 uses static dispatch, so sending an m2 message to x invokes the method associated with the type of x, in this case c1, so 21 is returned.

Modify the interpreter of section 9.5 to handle static methods. As a hint, think about keeping type information in the environment so that the interpreter can figure out the type of the target expression in a send.

```
((leaf-node
  #(struct:a-static-class
     object
     (tree)
     (value)
     (#(struct:int-type))
     ((initialize #(struct:proc-type
                      (#(struct:int-type))
                      #(struct:void-type)))
      (sum #(struct:proc-type () #(struct:int-type)))
      (getvalue #(struct:proc-type () #(struct:int-type)))
      (equal #(struct:proc-type
                 (#(struct:class-type tree))
                 #(struct:bool-type))))))
 (interior-node
  #(struct:a-static-class
     object
     (tree)
     (left right)
     (#(struct:class-type tree) #(struct:class-type tree))
     ((initialize #(struct:proc-type
                      (#(struct:class-type tree)
                       #(struct:class-type tree))
                    #(struct:void-type)))
      (getleft #(struct:proc-type ()
                   #(struct:class-type tree)))
      (getright #(struct:proc-type ()
                    #(struct:class-type tree)))
      (sum #(struct:proc-type () #(struct:int-type)))
      (equal #(struct:proc-type
                 (#(struct:class-type tree))
                 #(struct:bool-type))))))
 (tree
  #(struct:an-interface
     ((sum #(struct:proc-type () #(struct:int-type)))
      (equal #(struct:proc-type
                 (#(struct:class-type tree))
                 #(struct:bool-type))))))
 (object
  #(struct:a-static-class #f () () () ())))
```

Figure 9.22   Static class environment built for the sample program

Exercise 9.38 [★★] Why must the class information be added to the static class environment before the methods are checked? As a hint, consider what happens if a method body invokes a method on `self`?)

Exercise 9.39 [★★] Make the typechecker prevent calls to `initialize` other than the implicit call inside `new`.

Exercise 9.40 [★] Modify the design of the language so that every field declaration contains an expression that is used to initialize the field. Such a design has the advantage that a checked program will never refer to an uninitialized value.

Exercise 9.41 [★★] Extend the typechecker to handle `fieldref` and `fieldset`, as in exercise 9.8.

Exercise 9.42 [★★] In the type checker, static methods are treated in the same way as ordinary methods, except that a static method may not be overridden by a dynamic one, or vice versa. Extend the checker to handle static methods.

A *For Further Reading*

Here are some of the readings that taught, influenced, or inspired us in the creation of this book. We hope you will enjoy at least some of them as much as we did.

Those new to recursive programming and symbolic computation might look at *The Little Schemer* (Friedman & Felleisen, 1996), or *The Little MLer* (Felleisen & Friedman, 1996), or for the more historically minded, *The Little LISPer* (Friedman, 1974). *How to Design Programs* (Felleisen *et al.*, 2001) provides an in-depth treatment of how to program recursively, intended as a first course in computing.

Using induction to define sets and relations is a long-standing technique in mathematical logic. Our bottom-up and rules-of-inference styles are largely modeled after the work of Plotkin (1975, 1981). Our "top-down" style is patterned after an alternative technique called *coinduction* (see Gordon, 1995; Jacobs & Rutten, 1997), used also by Felleisen *et al.* (2001).

Context-free grammars are a standard tool in both linguistics and computer science. Most compiler books, such as Aho *et al.* (2006), have an extensive discussion of grammars and parsing algorithms. The idea of separating concrete and abstract syntax is usually credited to McCarthy (1962), who emphasized the use of an interface to make the parse tree abstract.

Our *Follow the Grammar* slogan is based on *structural induction*, which was introduced by Burstall (1969). *Subgoal induction* (Morris & Wegbreit, 1977) is a useful way of proving the correctness of recursive procedures even if they do not Follow the Grammar. Subgoal induction also works when an invariant constrains the possible inputs to the procedures.

Generalization is a standard technique from mathematics, where one often proves a specific statement as a special case of a more general one. Our characterization of extra arguments as abstractions of the context is motivated by the use of *inherited attributes* in attribute grammars (Knuth, 1968).

Our `define-datatype` and `cases` constructs were inspired by ML's `datatype` and pattern-matching facilities described in Milner *et al.* (1989) and its revision Milner *et al.* (1997).

The lambda calculus was introduced by Church (1941) to study mathematical logic, but it has become the inspiration for much of the modern theory of programming languages. Introductory treatments of the lambda calculus may be found in Hankin (1994), Peyton Jones (1987), or Stoy (1977). Barendregt (1981, 1991) provides an encyclopedic reference.

Contour diagrams, as in figure 3.13, have been used for explaining lexical scope and were first presented by Johnston (1971). The nameless interpreter and translator are based on de Bruijn indices (de Bruijn, 1972).

Scheme was introduced by Sussman & Steele (1975). Its development is recorded in Steele & Sussman (1978); Clinger *et al.* (1985a); Rees *et al.* (1986); Clinger *et al.* (1991); Kelsey *et al.* (1998). The standard definitions of Scheme are provided by the IEEE standard (IEEE, 1991) and the *Revised[6] Report on the Algorithmic Language Scheme* (Sperber *et al.*, 2007).

Dybvig (2003) provides a short introduction to Scheme that includes many insightful examples.

The idea of an interpreter goes at least as far back as Turing, who defined a "universal" machine that could simulate any Turing machine. This universal machine was essentially an interpreter that took a coded description of a Turing machine and simulated the encoded machine (Turing, 1936). A classical von Neumann machine (von Neumann, 1945) is likewise an interpreter, implemented in hardware, that interprets machine language programs.

The modern use of interpreters dates back to McCarthy (1960), who presented a metacircular interpreter (an interpreter written in the defined language itself) as an illustration of the power of Lisp. Of course, such an interpreter brings with it an important difficulty: if a language is being defined in terms of itself, we need to understand the language in order to understand the language definition. Indeed, the same problem arises even if the interpreter is not metacircular. The reader still needs to understand the language in which the definition is written before he or she can understand the thing being defined.

Over the years, a variety of techniques have been used to resolve this difficulty. We treat our interpreters as transcriptions of equational specifications (Goguen *et al.*, 1977) or big-step operational semantics in the style of Plotkin (1975, 1981). This relies only on fairly straightforward mathematics.

Denotational semantics is another technique that defines a language in terms of mathematics. In this approach, the interpreter is replaced by a function that translates each program in the defined language into a mathematical object that defines its behavior. Plotkin (1977) provides an indispensable introduction to this technique, and Winskel (1993) gives a more leisurely exploration. Milne & Strachey (1976) is an encyclopedic study of how this technique can be used to model a wide variety of language features.

Another approach is to write the interpreter in a subset of the language being defined. For example, our interpreters in chapter 4 rely on Scheme's store to explain the concept of a store, but they use only a single global mutable object, rather than the full power of Scheme's mutable variables.

The idea of computing as manipulating a store goes back to the beginning of modern computing (see von Neumann, 1945). The design of EXPLICIT-REFS is based on the store model of ML (Milner *et al.*, 1989), which is similar to that of Bliss (Wulf, 1971). The design of IMPLICIT-REFS is close to that of most standard programming languages, such as Pascal, Scheme, or Java, that have mutable local variables.

The terms "L-value" and "R-value," and the environment-store model of memory, are due to Strachey (1967).

Fortran (Backus *et al.*, 1957) was the first language to use call-by-reference, and Algol 60 (Naur *et al.*, 1963) was the first language to use call-by-name. Friedman & Wise (1976) gave an early demonstration of the power of pervasive lazy evaluation. Haskell (Hudak *et al.*, 1990) was the first practical language to use call-by-need. Plotkin (1975) showed how to model call-by-value and call-by-name in the lambda calculus. To model call-by-name, Ingerman (1961) invented *thunks*. We used them with an effect to model call-by-need. This is similar to memoization (Michie, 1968).

Monads, introduced by Moggi (1991) and popularized by Wadler (1992), provide a systematic model of effects in programming languages. Monads provide an organizing principle for nonfunctional behavior in the functional language Haskell (Peyton Jones, 2001).

Reynolds (1993) gives a fascinating history of the several independent discoveries of continuations. Strachey & Wadsworth (1974) is probably the most influential of these. Reynolds (1972) transforms a metacircular interpreter into CPS and shows how doing this avoids some of the problems of metacircularity. The translation of programs in tail form to imperative form dates back to McCarthy (1962) and its importance as a programming technique was emphasized in Abelson & Sussman (1985, 1996).

Plotkin (1975) gave a very clean version of the CPS transformation and worked out its theoretical properties. Fischer (1972) presented a very similar version of the transformation. The connection between continuations and accumulators, as in the `fact` example at the end of section 6.1, was first explored by Wand (1980b).

The idea of making the continuation available to the program goes back to the J-operator of Landin (1965a) (see also Landin 1965b), and was used extensively in Lisp and early versions of Scheme (Steele & Sussman, 1978). Our `letcc` is based on Scheme's `call-with-current-continuation`, which first appeared in Clinger *et al.* (1985b).

Wand (1980a) showed how continuations could be used as a model for lightweight processes or threads. Continuations may also be used for a variety of purposes beyond those discussed in the text, such as coroutines (Haynes *et al.*, 1986).

Our treatment of threads approximates POSIX threads (see, for example, Lewis & Berg, 1998). Exercise 5.56 is based on the Erlang message-passing concurrency model (Armstrong, 2007).

Steele's RABBIT compiler (Steele, 1978) used CPS conversion as the basis for a compiler. In this compiler, the source program was converted into CPS and then transformed to use data-structure representations of the continuations. The resulting program, like our registerized programs, could be compiled easily. This line of development led to the ORBIT compiler (Kranz *et al.*, 1986) and to the Standard ML of New Jersey compiler (Appel & Jim, 1989).

The CPS algorithm in chapter 6 is based on the first-order compositional algorithm of Danvy & Nielsen (2003). There is a long history of CPS translations, including Sabry & Wadler (1997), which improved on Sabry & Felleisen (1993), which in turn was motivated by the CPS algorithm of chapter 8 of the first edition of this book. Exercise 6.30 is based on the higher-order compositional CPS algorithm of Danvy & Filinski (1992). A-normal form (Exercise 6.34) as an alternative to CPS was introduced by Sabry & Felleisen (1992); Flanagan *et al.* (1993).

Most current work in typed programming languages can be traced back to Milner (1978), who introduced types in ML as a way of guaranteeing the reliability of computer-generated proofs. Ullman (1998) gives a good short introduction. A complementary treatment is Felleisen & Friedman (1996); see also Paulson (1996); Smith (2006).

Type inference has been discovered several times. The standard reference is Hindley (1969), though Hindley remarks that the results were known to Curry in the 1950s. Morris (1968) also proposed type inference, but the widespread use of type inference did not happen until Milner's 1978 paper.

The separation of type inference into equation generation and solving was first articulated by Wand (1987). The system in Milner (1978), known as Hindley-Milner polymorphism, is essentially the same as the system of exercise 7.28. The two volumes of Pierce (2002, 2004) give an encyclopedic treatment of types.

The idea of data abstraction was a prime innovation of the 1970s and has a large literature, from which we mention only Parnas (1972) on the importance of interfaces as boundaries for information-hiding. An implementation of a data type was any set of values and operations that satisfied the specification of that data type. Goguen *et al.* (1977) showed that any data type could be implemented as a set of trees that recorded how a value was constructed, and that there was a unique mapping from such a set of trees to any other implementation of the data type. Conversely, any data type can be implemented using a procedural representation, in which the data is represented by its action under the observers, and in which there is a unique mapping from any other implementation of the data type to the procedural representation (Giarratana *et al.*, 1976; Wand, 1979; Kamin, 1980).

The use of types to enforce data abstraction appeared in Reynolds (1975) and types were used in CLU (Liskov *et al.*, 1977). This grew into the module system of Standard ML (Milner *et al.*, 1989) (see also Paulson, 1996; Ullman, 1998). Our module system is based on that of Leroy (1994), which is used in CAML (see Smith, 2006), another variation of ML.

Simula 67 (Birtwistle *et al.*, 1973) is generally regarded as the first object-oriented language. The object-oriented metaphor was extended by Smalltalk (Goldberg & Robson, 1983) and by Actors (Hewitt, 1977). Both use human interaction and sending and receiving messages as the metaphor for explaining their ideas. Scheme grew out of Sussman and Steele's attempts to understand Hewitt's actor model. Abelson & Sussman (1985, 1996) and Springer & Friedman (1989) provide further examples of object-oriented programming in Scheme and discuss when functional and imperative programming styles are most appropriate. Steele (1990) and Kiczales *et al.* (1991) describe CLOS, the powerful object-oriented programming facility of Common Lisp.

The language in chapter 9 is based on the object model of Java. The standard reference is Arnold & Gosling (1998), but Gosling *et al.* (1996) is the specification for the serious reader.

Ruby (see Thomas *et al.*, 2005) Python (van Rossum & Drake, 2006), and Perl (Wall *et al.*, 2000; Dominus, 2005), and are untyped languages with both objects and procedures, roughly comparable to our CLASSES. C# is a typed language that adds many features to Java, most notably *delegates*, which are similar to procedures, and the ability for a programmer to specify that certain calls should be tail calls.

Abadi & Cardelli (1996) define a very simple object calculus that is a useful foundation for the study of types in object-oriented systems. Flatt *et al.* (1998) formalize a subset of Java. Another useful subset is *Featherweight Java* (Igarashi *et al.*, 1999).

Gamma *et al.* (1995) give a fascinating handbook of useful organizational principles for writing object-oriented programs.

The ACM has run three conferences on the history of programming languages, in 1978 (Wexelblatt, 1978), 1996 (Bergin & Gibson, 1996), and 2007 (Hailpern, 2007). These conferences contain papers describing the history of a wide variety of programming languages. The *IEEE Annals of the History of Computing* contains scholarly articles on various aspects of computing history, including programming languages. Knuth & Pardo (1977) give a fascinating history of very early programming languages.

There are numerous conferences in which new developments in programming languages are reported. The three leading conferences, at least for the topics discussed in this book, are the *ACM Symposium on Principles of Programming Languages* (POPL), the *ACM SIGPLAN International Conference on Functional Programming* (ICFP), and the *ACM SIGPLAN Conference on Programming Language Design and Implementation* (PLDI). Major academic journals for programming languages include *ACM Transactions on Programming Languages and Systems*, the *Journal of Functional Programming*, and *Higher-Order and Symbolic Computation*. In addition to these, there are web sites devoted to almost every aspect of programming languages.

B The SLLGEN Parsing System

Programs are just strings of characters. In order to process a program, we need to group these characters into meaningful units. This grouping is usually divided into two stages: *scanning* and *parsing*.

Scanning is the process of dividing the sequence of characters into words, punctuation, etc. These units are called *lexical items*, *lexemes*, or most often *tokens*. Parsing is the process of organizing the sequence of tokens into hierarchical syntactic structures such as expressions, statements, and blocks. This is much like organizing a sentence into clauses.

SLLGEN is a package for generating scanners and parsers in Scheme. In this appendix, we first review the basics of scanning and parsing, and then consider how these capabilities are expressed in SLLGEN.

B.1 Scanning

The problem of scanning is illustrated in figure B.1. There we show a small portion of a program, and the way in which it is intended to be divided into atomic units.

The way in which a given stream of characters is to be separated into lexical items is part of the language specification. This part of the language specification is sometimes called the *lexical specification*. Typical pieces of lexical specification might be:

- Any sequence of spaces and newlines is equivalent to a single space.

- A comment begins with % and continues until the end of the line.

- An identifier is a sequence of letters and digits starting with a letter.

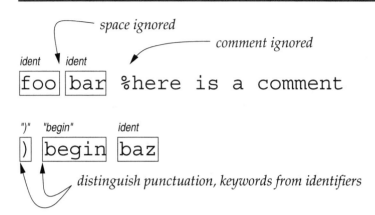

Figure B.1   The task of the scanner

The job of the scanner is to go through the input and analyze it to produce data structures with these items. In a conventional language, the scanner might be a procedure that, when called, produces the "next" token of the input.

One could write a scanner from scratch, but that would be tedious and error-prone. A better approach is to write down the lexical specification in a specialized language. The most common language for this task is the language of *regular expressions*. We define the language of regular expressions as follows:

$$R ::= Character \mid R\,R \mid R \cup R \mid R^* \mid \neg\,Character$$

Each regular expression matches some strings. We can use induction to define the set of strings matched by each regular expression:

- A character c matches the string consisting of the character c.

- $\neg c$ matches any 1-character string other than c.

- RS matches any string that consists of a string matching R followed by a string matching S. This is called *concatenation*.

- $R \cup S$ matches any string that either matches R or matches S. This is sometimes written $R\vert S$, and is sometimes called *alternation*.

- R^* matches any string that is formed by concatenating some number n ($n \geq 0$) of strings that match R. This is called the *Kleene closure* of R.

Some examples may be helpful:

- *ab* matches only the string ab.

- *ab* ∪ *cd* matches the strings ab and cd.

- (*ab* ∪ *cd*)(*ab* ∪ *cd* ∪ *ef*) matches the strings abab, abcd, abef, cdab, cdcd, and cdef.

- (*ab*)* matches the empty string, ab, abab, ababab, abababab, ...

- (*ab* ∪ *cd*)* matches the empty string, ab, cd, abab, abcd, cdab, cdcd, ababab, . . . cdcdcd, ...

The examples above illustrate the precedence of the different operations. Thus, *ab** ∪ *cd* means (*a*(*b**)) ∪ (*cd*).

The specifications for our example may be written using regular expressions as

whitespace = (*space* ∪ *newline*) (*space* ∪ *newline*)*
comment = % (¬*newline*)*
identifier = *letter* (*letter* ∪ *digit*)*

When scanners use regular expressions to specify a token, the rule is always to take the *longest* match. This way xyz will be scanned as one identifier, not three.

When the scanner finds a token, it returns a data structure consisting of at least the following pieces of data:

- A *class*, which describes what kind of token it has found. The set of such classes is part of the lexical specification. SLLGEN uses Scheme symbols to distinguish these classes; other syntactic analyzers might use other data structures.

- A piece of data describing the particular token. The nature of this data is also part of the lexical specification. For our system, the data is as follows: for identifiers, the data is a Scheme symbol built from the string in the token; for a number, the datum is the number described by the number literal; and for a literal string, the datum is the string. String data are used for keywords and punctuation. In an implementation language that did not have symbols, one might use a string (the name of the identifier), or an entry into a hash table indexed by identifiers (a *symbol table*) instead.

- Some data describing the location of this token in the input. This information may be used by the parser to help the programmer identify the location of syntactic errors.

In general, the internal structure of tokens is relevant only to the scanner and the parser, so we will not describe it in any further detail.

B.2   Parsing

Parsing is the process of organizing the sequence of tokens into hierarchical syntactic structures such as expressions, statements, and blocks. This is like organizing or diagramming a sentence into clauses. The syntactic structure of a language is typically specified using a BNF definition, also called a *context-free grammar* (section 1.1.2).

The parser takes as input a sequence of tokens, and its output is an abstract syntax tree (section 2.5). The abstract syntax trees produced by an SLLGEN parser can be described by `define-datatype`. For a given grammar, there will be one data type for each nonterminal. For each nonterminal, there will be one variant for each production that has the nonterminal as its left-hand side. Each variant will have one field for each nonterminal, identifier, or number that appears in its right-hand side. A simple example appears in section 2.5. To see what happens when there is more than one nonterminal in the grammar, consider a grammar like the one in exercise 4.22.

$$
\begin{aligned}
\textit{Statement} \;::=&\; \{\ \textit{Statement} \;;\; \textit{Statement}\ \} \\
::=&\; \texttt{while}\ \textit{Expression}\ \texttt{do}\ \textit{Statement} \\
::=&\; \textit{Identifier}\ :\!=\ \textit{Expression} \\
\textit{Expression} \;::=&\; \textit{Identifier} \\
::=&\; (\textit{Expression}\ \textrm{-}\ \textit{Expression})
\end{aligned}
$$

The trees produced by this grammar could be described by this data type:

```
(define-datatype statement statement?
  (compound-statement
    (stmt1 statement?)
    (stmt2 statement?))
  (while-statement
    (test expression?)
    (body statement?))
  (assign-statement
    (lhs symbol?)
    (rhs expression?)))
```

```
(define-datatype expression expression?
  (var-exp
    (var symbol?))
  (diff-exp
    (exp1 expression?)
    (exp2 expression?)))
```

For each nonterminal in a right-hand side, the corresponding tree appears as a field; for each identifier, the corresponding symbol appears as a field. The names of the variants will be specified in the grammar when it is written in SLLGEN. The names of the fields will be automatically generated; here we have introduced some mnemonic names for the fields. For example, the input

```
{x := foo; while x do x := (x - bar)}
```

produces the output

```
#(struct:compound-statement
  #(struct:assign-statement x #(struct:var-exp foo))
  #(struct:while-statement
    #(struct:var-exp x)
    #(struct:assign-statement x
      #(struct:diff-exp
        #(struct:var-exp x)
        #(struct:var-exp bar)))))
```

B.3   Scanners and Parsers in SLLGEN

Specifying Scanners

In SLLGEN, scanners are specified by regular expressions. Our example would be written in SLLGEN as follows:

```
(define scanner-spec-a
  '((white-sp (whitespace) skip)
    (comment ("%" (arbno (not #\newline))) skip)
    (identifier (letter (arbno (or letter digit))) symbol)
    (number (digit  (arbno digit)) number)))
```

If the scanner is used with a parser that has keywords or punctuation, like `while` or `=`, it is not necessary to put these in the scanner manually; the parser-generator will add those automatically.

A scanner specification in SLLGEN is a list that satisfies this grammar:

Scanner-spec   ::= ({*Regexp-and-action*}*)
Regexp-and-action ::= (*Name* ({*Regexp*}*) *Action*)
Name   ::= *Symbol*
Regexp   ::= *String* | `letter` | `digit` | `whitespace` | `any`
                       ::= (`not` *Character*) | (`or` {*Regexp*}*)
                       ::= (`arbno` *Regexp*) | (`concat` {*Regexp*}*)
Action   ::= `skip` | `symbol` | `number` | `string`

Each item in the list is a specification of a regular expression, consisting of a name, a sequence of regular expressions, and an action to be taken on success. The name is a Scheme symbol that will become the class of the token.

The second part of the specification is a sequence of regular expressions, because the top level of a *regexp* in a scanner is almost always a concatenation. A regular expression may be a string; one of four predefined testers: `letter` (matches any letter), `digit` (matches any digit), `whitespace` (matches any Scheme whitespace character), and `any` (matches any character); the negation of a character; or it may be a combination of regular expressions, using a Scheme-like syntax with `or` and `concat` for union and concatenation, and `arbno` for Kleene star.

As the scanner works, it collects characters into a buffer. When the scanner determines that it has found the longest possible match of all the regular expressions in the specification, it executes the *action* of the corresponding regular expression.

An action can be one of the following:

- The symbol `skip`. This means this is the end of a token, but no token is emitted. The scanner continues working on the string to find the next token. This action is used for whitespace and comments.

- The symbol `symbol`. The characters in the buffer are converted into a Scheme symbol and a token is emitted, with the class name as its class and with the symbol as its datum.

- The symbol `number`. The characters in the buffer are converted into a Scheme number, and a token is emitted, with the class name as its class and with the number as its datum.

- The symbol `string`. The characters in the buffer are converted into a Scheme string, and a token is emitted, with the class name as its class and with the string as its datum.

If there is a tie for longest match between two regular expressions, `string` takes precedence over `symbol`. This rule means that keywords that would otherwise be identifiers are treated as keywords.

Specifying Grammars

SLLGEN also includes a language for specifying grammars. The simple grammar above would be written in SLLGEN as

```
(define grammar-a1
  '((statement
      ("{" statement ";" statement "}")
      compound-statement)
    (statement
      ("while" expression "do" statement)
      while-statement)
    (statement
      (identifier ":=" expression)
      assign-statement)
    (expression
      (identifier)
      var-exp)
    (expression
      ("(" expression "-" expression ")")
      diff-exp)))
```

A grammar in SLLGEN is a list described by the following grammar:

Grammar ::= ({*Production*}*)
Production ::= (*Lhs* ({*Rhs-item*}*) *Prod-name*)
Lhs ::= *Symbol*
Rhs-item ::= *Symbol* | *String*
            ::= (arbno {*Rhs-item*}*)
            ::= (separated-list {*Rhs-item*}* *String*)
Prod-name ::= *Symbol*

A grammar is a list of productions. The left-hand side of the first production is the start symbol for the grammar. Each production consists of a left-hand side (a nonterminal symbol), a right-hand side (a list of *rhs-item*'s)

and a production name. The right-hand side of a production is a list of symbols or strings. The symbols are nonterminals; strings are literal strings. A right-hand side may also include `arbno`'s or `separated-list`'s; these are discussed below. The production name is a symbol, which becomes the name of the `define-datatype` variant corresponding to the production.

In SLLGEN, the grammar must allow the parser to determine which production to use knowing only (1) what nonterminal it's looking for and (2) the first symbol (token) of the string being parsed. Grammars in this form are called *LL*(1) grammars; SLLGEN stands for Scheme *LL*(1) parser GENerator. This is somewhat restrictive in practice, but it is good enough for the purposes of this book. SLLGEN produces a warning if the input grammar fails to meet this restriction.

SLLGEN Operations

SLLGEN includes several procedures for incorporating these scanners and grammars into an executable parser. Figure B.2 shows a sample of SLLGEN used to define a scanner and parser for a language.

The procedure `sllgen:make-define-datatypes` is responsible for generating a `define-datatype` expression for each production of the grammar, for use by `cases`. The procedure `sllgen:list-define-datatypes` generates the `define-data-type` expressions again, but returns them as a list rather than executing them. The field names generated by these procedures are uninformative because the information is not in the grammar; to get better field names, write out the `define-datatype`.

The procedure `sllgen:make-string-scanner` takes a scanner and a grammar and generates a scanning procedure. The resulting procedure may be applied to a string and produces a list of tokens. The grammar is used to add keywords to the resulting scanning procedure. This procedure is useful primarily for debugging.

The procedure `sllgen:make-string-parser` generates a parser. The parser is a procedure that takes a string, scans it according to the scanner, parses it according to the grammar, and returns an abstract syntax tree. As with `sllgen:make-string-scanner`, the literal strings from the grammar are included in the scanner.

SLLGEN can also be used to build a read-eval-print-loop (section 3.1). The procedure `sllgen:make-stream-parser` is like the string version, except that its input is a stream of characters and its output is a stream of tokens. The procedure `sllgen:make-rep-loop` takes a string, a procedure of one

```
(define scanner-spec-1 ...)

(define grammar-1 ...)

(sllgen:make-define-datatypes scanner-spec-1 grammar-1)

(define list-the-datatypes
  (lambda ()
    (sllgen:list-define-datatypes scanner-spec-1 grammar-1)))

(define just-scan
  (sllgen:make-string-scanner scanner-spec-1 grammar-1))

(define scan&parse
  (sllgen:make-string-parser scanner-spec-1 grammar-1))

(define read-eval-print
  (sllgen:make-rep-loop  "--> " value-of--program
    (sllgen:make-stream-parser scanner-spec-1 grammar-1)))
```

Figure B.2   Using SLLGEN

argument, and a stream parser, and produces a read-eval-print loop that produces the string as a prompt on the standard output, reads characters from the standard input, parses them, prints the result of applying the procedure to the resulting abstract syntax tree, and recurs. For example:

```
> (define read-eval-print
    (sllgen:make-rep-loop  "--> " eval-program
      (sllgen:make-stream-parser
        scanner-spec-3-1
        grammar-3-1)))
> (read-eval-print)
--> 5
5
--> add1(2)
3
--> +(add1(2),-(6,4))
5
```

The way in which control is returned from this loop to the Scheme read-eval-print loop is system-dependent.

arbno and separated-list **Pattern Keywords**

An arbno keyword is a Kleene star in the grammar: it matches an arbitrary number of repetitions of its entry. For example, the production

$$statement ::= \{\ \{statement\ ;\}^*\ \}$$

could be written in SLLGEN as

```
(define grammar-a2
  '((statement
      ("{" (arbno statement ";") "}")
      compound-statement)
    ...))
```

This makes a compound statement a sequence of an arbitrary number of semicolon-terminated statements.

This arbno generates a single field in the abstract syntax tree. This field will contain a *list* of the data for the nonterminal inside the arbno. Our example generates the following data types:

```
(define-datatype statement statement?
  (compound-statement
    (compound-statement32 (list-of statement?)))
  ...)
```

A simple interaction looks like:

```
> (define scan&parse2
    (sllgen:make-string-parser scanner-spec-a grammar-a2))

> (scan&parse2 "{x := foo; y := bar; z := uu;}")
(compound-statement
  ((assign-statement x (var-exp foo))
   (assign-statement y (var-exp bar))
   (assign-statement z (var-exp uu))))
```

We can put a sequence of nonterminals inside an arbno. In this case, we will get several fields in the node, one for each nonterminal; each field will contain a list of syntax trees. For example:

```
(define grammar-a3
  '((expression (identifier) var-exp)
    (expression
      ("let" (arbno identifier "=" expression) "in" expression)
      let-exp)))
```

```
(define scan&parse3
  (sllgen:make-string-parser scanner-spec-a grammar-a3))
```

This produces the data type

```
(define-datatype expression expression?
  (var-exp (var-exp4 symbol?))
  (let-exp
    (let-exp9 (list-of symbol?))
    (let-exp7 (list-of expression?))
    (let-exp8 expression?)))
```

Here is an example of this grammar in action:

```
> (scan&parse3 "let x = y u = v in z")
(let-exp
  (x u)
  ((var-exp y) (var-exp v))
  (var-exp z))
```

The specification (arbno identifier "=" expression) generates two lists: a list of identifiers and a list of expressions. This is convenient because it will let our interpreters get at the pieces of the expression directly.

Sometimes it is helpful for the syntax of a language to use lists with separators, not terminators. This is common enough that it is a built-in operation in SLLGEN. We can write

```
(define grammar-a4
  '((statement
      ("{" (separated-list statement ";") "}")
      compound-statement)
    ...))
```

This produces the data type

```
(define-datatype statement statement?
  (compound-statement
    (compound-statement103 (list-of statement?)))
    ...)
```

Here is a sample interaction:

```
> (define scan&parse4
    (sllgen:make-string-parser scanner-spec-a grammar-a4))
> (scan&parse4 "{}")
(compound-statement ())
```

```
> (scan&parse4 "{x:= y; u := v ; z := t}")
(compound-statement
  ((assign-statement x (var-exp y))
   (assign-statement u (var-exp v))
   (assign-statement z (var-exp t))))
> (scan&parse4 "{x:= y; u := v ; z := t ;}")
Error in parsing: at line 1
Nonterminal <seplist3> can't begin with string "}"
```

In the last example, the input string had a terminating semicolon that did not match the grammar, so an error was reported.

As with arbno, we can place an arbitrary sequence of nonterminals within a separated-list keyword. In this case, we will get several fields in the node, one for each nonterminal; each field will contain a list of syntax trees. This is exactly the same data as would be generated by arbno; only the concrete syntax differs.

We will occasionally use nested arbno's and separated-list's. A nonterminal inside an arbno generates a list, so a nonterminal inside an arbno inside an arbno generates a list of lists.

As an example, consider a compound-statement similar to the one in grammar-a4, except that we have parallel assignments:

```
(define grammar-a5
  '((statement
      ("{"
        (separated-list
          (separated-list identifier ",")
          ":="
          (separated-list expression ",")
          ";")
      "}")
    compound-statement)
    (expression (number) lit-exp)
    (expression (identifier) var-exp)))

> (define scan&parse5
    (sllgen:make-string-parser scanner-spec-a grammar-a5))
```

This generates the following data type for statement:

```
(define-datatype statement statement?
  (compound-statement
    (compound-statement4 (list-of (list-of symbol?)))
    (compound-statement3 (list-of (list-of expression?)))))
```

A typical interaction looks like:

```
> (scan&parse5 "{x,y := u,v ; z := 4; t1, t2 := 5, 6}")
(compound-statement
  ((x y) (z) (t1 t2))
  (((var-exp u) (var-exp v))
   ((lit-exp 4))
   ((lit-exp 5) (lit-exp 6))))
```

Here the `compound-statement` has two fields: a list of lists of identifiers, and the matching list of lists of expressions. In this example we have used `separated-list` instead of `arbno`, but an `arbno` would generate the same data.

Exercise B.1 [⋆] The following grammar for ordinary arithmetic expressions builds in the usual precedence rules for arithmetic operators:

Arith-expr	::= *Arith-term {Additive-op Arith-term}**
Arith-term	::= *Arith-factor {Multiplicative-op Arith-factor}**
Arith-factor	::= *Number*
	::= (*Arith-expr*)
Additive-op	::= + | -
Multiplicative-op	::= ⋆ | /

This grammar says that every arithmetic expression is the sum of a non-empty sequence of terms; every term is the product of a non-empty sequence of factors; and every factor is either a constant or a parenthesized expression.

Write a lexical specification and a grammar in SLLGEN that will scan and parse strings according to this grammar. Verify that this grammar handles precedence correctly, so that, for example `3+2⋆66-5` gets grouped correctly, as $3 + (2 \times 66) - 5$.

Exercise B.2 [⋆ ⋆] Why can't the grammar above be written with `separated-list`?

Exercise B.3 [⋆ ⋆] Define an interpreter that takes the syntax tree produced by the parser of exercise B.1 and evaluates it as an arithmetic expression. The parser takes care of the usual arithmetic precedence operations, but the interpreter will have to take care of associativity, that is, making sure that operations at the same precedence level (e.g. additions and subtractions) are performed from left to right. Since there are no variables in these expressions, this interpreter need not take an environment parameter.

Exercise B.4 [⋆ ⋆] Extend the language and interpreter of the preceding exercise to include variables. This new interpreter will require an environment parameter.

Exercise B.5 [⋆] Add unary minus to the language and interpreter, so that inputs like `3⋆-2` are handled correctly.

Bibliography

Abadi, Martín, & Cardelli, Luca. 1996. *A Theory of Objects*. Berlin, Heidelberg, and New York: Springer-Verlag.

Abelson, Harold, & Sussman, Gerald Jay. 1985. *The Structure and Interpretation of Computer Programs*. Cambridge, MA: MIT Press.

Abelson, Harold, & Sussman, Gerald Jay. 1996. *Structure and Interpretation of Computer Programs*. Second edition. Cambridge, MA: McGraw Hill.

Aho, Alfred V., Lam, Monica S., Sethi, Ravi, & Ullman, Jeffrey D. 2006. *Compilers: Principles, Techniques, and Tools*. Second edition. Boston: Addison-Wesley Longman.

Appel, Andrew W. & Jim, Trevor. 1989. Continuation-Passing, Closure-Passing Style. Pages 293–302 of: *Proceedings ACM Symposium on Principles of Programming Languages*.

Arnold, Ken, & Gosling, James. 1998. *The Java Programming Language*. Second edition. The Java Series. Reading, MA: Addison-Wesley.

Armstrong, Joe. 2007. *Programming Erlang: Software for a Concurrent World*. The Pragmatic Programmers Publishers.

Backus, John W., *et al.* 1957. The Fortran Automatic Coding System. Pages 188–198 of: *Western Joint Computer Conference*.

Barendregt, Henk P. 1981. *The Lambda Calculus: Its Syntax and Semantics*. Amsterdam: North-Holland.

Barendregt, Henk P. 1991. *The Lambda Calculus*. Revised edition. Studies in Logic and the Foundations of Mathematics, no. 103. Amsterdam: North-Holland.

Bergin, Thomas J., & Gibson, Richard G. (eds.). 1996. *History of Programming Languages*. New York: Addison-Wesley.

Birtwistle, Graham M., Dahl, Ole-Johan, & Myhrhaug, Bjorn. 1973. *Simula Begin*. Philadelphia: Auerbach.

Burstall, Rod M. 1969. Proving Properties of Programs by Structural Induction. *Computer Journal*, **12**(1), 41–48.

Church, Alonzo. 1941. *The Calculi of Lambda Conversion*. Princeton, NJ: Princeton University Press. Reprinted 1963 by University Microfilms, Ann Arbor, MI.

Clinger, William D., *et al.* 1985a. The Revised Revised Report on Scheme or The Uncommon Lisp. Technical Memo AIM-848. Massachusetts Institute of Technology, Artificial Intelligence Laboratory.

Clinger, William D., Friedman, Daniel P., & Wand, Mitchell. 1985b. A Scheme for a Higher-Level Semantic Algebra. Pages 237–250 of: Reynolds, John, & Nivat, Maurice (eds.), *Algebraic Methods in Semantics: Proceedings of the US-French Seminar on the Application of Algebra to Language Definition and Compilation (Fontainebleau, France, June, 1982)*. Cambridge: Cambridge University Press.

Clinger, William D., Rees, Jonathan, *et al.* 1991. The Revised[4] Report on the Algorithmic Language Scheme. *ACM Lisp Pointers*, **4**(3), 1–55.

Danvy, Olivier, & Filinski, Andrzej. 1992. Representing Control: A Study of the CPS Transformation. *Mathematical Structures in Computer Science*, **2**(4), 361–391.

Danvy, Olivier, & Nielsen, Lasse R. 2003. A First-order One-pass CPS Transformation. *Theoretical Computer Science*, **308**(1-3), 239–257.

de Bruijn, N. G. 1972. Lambda Calculus Notation with Nameless Dummies: A Tool for Automatic Formula Manipulation, with Application to the Church-Rosser Theorem. *Indagationes Mathematicae*, **34**, 381–392.

Dominus, Mark Jason. 2005. *Higher-Order Perl: Transforming Programs with Programs*. San Francisco: Morgan Kaufmann Publishers.

Dybvig, R. Kent. 2003. *The Scheme Programming Language*. Third edition. Cambridge, MA: MIT Press.

Felleisen, Matthias, & Friedman, Daniel P. 1996. *The Little MLer*. Cambridge, MA: MIT Press.

Felleisen, Matthias, Findler, Robert Bruce, Flatt, Matthew, & Krishnamurthi, Shriram. 2001. *How to Design Programs*. Cambridge, MA: MIT Press.

Fischer, Michael J. 1972. Lambda-Calculus Schemata. Pages 104–109 of: *Proceedings ACM Conference on Proving Assertions about Programs*. Republished in *Lisp and Symbolic Computation*, **6**(3/4), 259–288.

Flanagan, Cormac, Sabry, Amr, Duba, Bruce F., & Felleisen, Matthias. 1993. The Essence of Compiling with Continuations. Pages 237–247 of: *Proceedings ACM SIGPLAN 1993 Conf. on Programming Language Design and Implementation, PLDI'93, Albuquerque, NM, USA, 23–25 June 1993*, vol. 28(6). New York: ACM Press.

Flatt, Matthew, Krishnamurthi, Shriram, & Felleisen, Matthias. 1998. Classes and Mixins. Pages 171–183 of: *Proceedings ACM Symposium on Principles of Programming Languages*.

Friedman, Daniel P. 1974. *The Little LISPer*. Palo Alto, CA: Science Research Associates.

Friedman, Daniel P., & Felleisen, Matthias. 1996. *The Little Schemer*. Fourth edition. Cambridge, MA: MIT Press.

Friedman, Daniel P., & Wise, David S. 1976. *Cons* should not Evaluate its Arguments. Pages 257–284 of: Michaelson, S., & Milner, R. (eds.), *Automata, Languages and Programming*. Edinburgh: Edinburgh University Press.

Gamma, Erich, Helm, Richard, Johnson, Ralph, & Vlissides, John. 1995. *Design Patterns: Elements of Reusable Object-Oriented Software*. Reading, MA: Addison Wesley.

Giarratana, V., Gimona, F., & Montanari, U. 1976. Observability Concepts in Abstract Data Type Specifications. Pages 576–587 of: Mazurkiewicz, A. (ed.), *Mathematical Foundations of Computer Science 1976*. Lecture Notes in Computer Science, vol. 45. Berlin, Heidelberg, New York: Springer-Verlag.

Goguen, Joseph A., Thatcher, James W., Wagner, Eric G., & Wright, Jesse B. 1977. Initial Algebra Semantics and Continuous Algebras. *Journal of the ACM*, **24**, 68–95.

Goldberg, Adele, & Robson, David. 1983. *Smalltalk-80: The Language and Its Implementation*. Reading, MA: Addison-Wesley.

Gordon, Andrew D. 1995. A Tutorial on Co-induction and Functional Programming. Pages 78–95 of: *Functional Programming, Glasgow 1994*. Berlin, Heidelberg, and New York: Springer Workshops in Computing.

Gosling, James, Joy, Bill, & Steele, Guy L. 1996. *The Java Language Specification*. The Java Series. Reading, MA: Addison-Wesley.

Hailpern, Brent (ed.). 2007. *HOPL III: Proceedings of the Third ACM SIGPLAN Conference on History of Programming Languages*. New York: ACM Press.

Hankin, Chris. 1994. *Lambda Calculi: A Guide for Computer Scientists*. Graduate Texts in Computer Science, vol. 3. Oxford: Clarendon Press.

Haynes, Christopher T., Friedman, Daniel P., & Wand, Mitchell. 1986. Obtaining Coroutines with Continuations. *J. of Computer Languages*, **11**(3/4), 143–153.

Hewitt, Carl. 1977. Viewing Control Structures as Patterns of Passing Messages. *Artificial Intelligence*, **8**, 323–364.

Hindley, Roger. 1969. The Principal Type-Scheme of an Object in Combinatory Logic. *Transactions of the American Mathematical Society*, **146**, 29–60.

Hudak, Paul, *et al*. 1990. Report on the Programming Language HASKELL. Technical Report YALEU/DCS/RR-777. Yale University, CS Dept.

IEEE. 1991. *IEEE Standard for the Scheme Programming Language, IEEE Standard 1178-1990*. IEEE Computer Society, New York.

Igarashi, Atshushi, Pierce, Benjamin C., & Wadler, Philip. 1999. Featherweight Java: A Minimal Core Calculus for Java and GJ. Pages 132–146 of: Meissner, Loren (ed.), *Proceedings of the 1999 ACM SIGPLAN Conference on Object-Oriented Programming, Systems, Languages & Applications (OOPSLA '99)*.

Ingerman, Peter Z. 1961. Thunks, A Way of Compiling Procedure Statements with Some Comments on Procedure Declarations. *Communications of the ACM*, **4**(1), 55–58.

Jacobs, Bart, & Rutten, Jan. 1997. A Tutorial on (Co)Algebras and (Co)Induction. *Bulletin of the European Association for Theoretical Computer Science*, **62**, 222–259.

Johnston, John B. 1971. The Contour Model of Block Structured Processes. *SIGPLAN Notices*, **6**(2), 55–82.

Kamin, Samuel. 1980. Final Data Type Specifications: A New Data Type Specification Method. Pages 131–138 of: *Proceedings ACM Symposium on Principles of Programming Languages*.

Kelsey, Richard, Clinger, William D., & Rees, Jonathan. 1998. Revised[5] Report on the Algorithmic Language Scheme. *Higher-Order and Symbolic Computation*, **11**(1), 7–104.

Kiczales, G., des Rivières, J., & Bobrow, D. G. 1991. *The Art of the Meta-Object Protocol*. Cambridge, MA: MIT Press.

Knuth, Donald E. 1968. Semantics of Context-Free Languages. *Mathematical Systems Theory*, **2**, 127–145. Correction, 5:95–96, 1971.

Knuth, Donald E., & Pardo, L. T. 1977. The Early Development of Programming Languages. Pages 419–493 of: Belzer, J., Holzman, A. G., & Kent, D. (eds.), *Encyclopedia of Computer Science and Technology*, vol. 6. New York: Marcel Dekker.

Kranz, David A., Kelsey, Richard, Rees, Jonathan A., Hudak, Paul, Philbin, James, & Adams, Norman I. 1986. Orbit: An Optimizing Compiler for Scheme. Pages 219–223 of: *Proceedings SIGPLAN '86 Symposium on Compiler Construction*.

Landin, Peter J. 1965a. Correspondence between ALGOL 60 and Church's Lambda-notation: Part I. *Commun. ACM*, **8**(2), 89–101.

Landin, Peter J. 1965b. A Generalization of Jumps and Labels. Technical Report. UNIVAC Systems Programming Research. Reprinted with a foreword in *Higher-Order and Symbolic Computation*, **11**(2):125–143, 1998.

Leroy, Xavier. 1994. Manifest Types, Modules, and Separate Compilation. Pages 190–122 of: *Proceedings ACM Symposium on Principles of Programming Languages*.

Lewis, Bil, & Berg, Daniel J. 1998. *Multithreaded Programming with PThreads*. Englewood Cliffs, NJ: Prentice-Hall.

Liskov, Barbara, Snyder, Alan, Atkinson, R., & Schaffert, Craig. 1977. Abstraction Mechanisms in CLU. *Communications of the ACM*, **20**, 564–576.

McCarthy, John. 1960. Recursive Functions of Symbolic Expressions and their Computation by Machine, Part I. *Communications of the ACM*, **3**, 184–195.

McCarthy, John. 1962. Towards a Mathematical Science of Computation. Pages 21–28 of: Popplewell (ed.), *Information Processing 62*. Amsterdam: North-Holland.

Michie, Donald. 1968. "Memo" Functions and Machine Learning. *Nature*, **218**(1–3), 218–219.

Milne, Robert, & Strachey, Christopher. 1976. *A Theory of Programming Language Semantics*. London: Chapman and Hall.

Milner, Robin. 1978. A Theory of Type Polymorphism in Programming. *Journal of Computer and Systems Science*, **17**, 348–375.

Milner, Robin, Tofte, Mads, & Harper, Robert. 1989. *The Definition of Standard ML*. Cambridge, MA: MIT Press.

Milner, Robin, Tofte, Mads, Harper, Robert, & MacQueen, David B. 1997. *The Standard ML Programming Language (Revised)*. Cambridge, MA: MIT Press.

Moggi, Eugenio. 1991. Notions of Computation and Monads. *Information and Computation*, **93**(1), 55–92.

Morris, Jr., James H. 1968. Lambda Calculus Models of Programming Languages. Ph.D. thesis, MIT, Cambridge, MA.

Morris, Jr., James H., & Wegbreit, Ben. 1977. Subgoal Induction. *Communications of the ACM*, **20**, 209–222.

Naur, Peter, *et al*. 1963. Revised Report on the Algorithmic Language ALGOL 60. *Communications of the ACM*, **5**(1), 1–17.

Parnas, David L. 1972. A Technique for Module Specification with Examples. *Communications of the ACM*, **15**(5), 330–336.

Paulson, Laurence C. 1996. *ML for the Working Programmer*. Second edition. New York: Cambridge University Press.

Peyton Jones, Simon L. 1987. *The Implementation of Functional Programming Languages*. Englewood Cliffs, NJ: Prentice-Hall International.

Peyton Jones, Simon L. 2001. Tackling the Awkward Squad: Monadic Input/Output, Concurrency, Exceptions, and Foreign-Language Calls in Haskell. In: Hoare, C.A.R., Broy, Manfred, & Steinbruggen, Ralf (eds.), *Engineering Theories of Software Construction, Marktoberdorf Summer School*. Amsterdam, The Netherlands: IOS Press.

Pierce, Benjamin C. 2002. *Types and Programming Languges*. Cambridge, MA: MIT Press.

Pierce, Benjamin C. 2004. *Advanced Topics in Types and Programming Languges*. Cambridge, MA: MIT Press.

Plotkin, Gordon D. 1975. Call-by-Name, Call-by-Value and the λ-Calculus. *Theoretical Computer Science*, **1**, 125–159.

Plotkin, Gordon D. 1977. LCF Considered as a Programming Language. *Theoretical Computer Science*, **5**, 223–255.

Plotkin, Gordon D. 1981. A Structural Approach to Operational Semantics. Technical Report FN 19, DAIMI, Department of Computer Science. University of Aarhus, Aarhus, Denmark.

Pratt, Terrence W., & Zelkowitz, Marvin V. 2001. *Programming Languages: Design and Implementation*. 4th edition. Englewood Cliffs, NJ: Prentice-Hall.

Rees, Jonathan A., Clinger, William D., *et al.* 1986. Revised[3] Report on the Algorithmic Language Scheme. *SIGPLAN Notices*, **21**(12), 37–79.

Reynolds, John C. 1972. Definitional Interpreters for Higher-Order Programming Languages. Pages 717–740 of: *Proceedings ACM National Conference*. Reprinted, with a foreword, in *Higher-Order and Symbolic Computation* **11**(4) 363-397 (1998).

Reynolds, John C. 1975. User-Defined Types and Procedural Data Structures as Complementary Approaches to Data Abstraction. In: *Conference on New Directions on Algorithmic Languages*. IFIP WP 2.1, Munich.

Reynolds, John C. 1993. The Discoveries of Continuations. *Lisp and Symbolic Computation*, **6**(3/4), 233–248.

Sabry, Amr, & Felleisen, Matthias. 1992. Reasoning about Programs in Continuation-Passing Style. Pages 288–298 of: *Proceedings 1992 ACM Conf. on Lisp and Functional Programming*. New York: ACM Press.

Sabry, Amr, & Felleisen, Matthias. 1993. Reasoning about Programs in Continuation-Passing Style. *Lisp and Symbolic Computation*, **6**(3/4), 289–360.

Sabry, Amr, & Wadler, Philip. 1997. A Reflection on Call-by-Value. *ACM Transactions on Programming Languages and Systems*, **19**(6), 916–941.

Scott, Michael L. 2005. *Programming Language Pragmatics*. Second edition. San Francisco: Morgan Kaufmann.

Sebesta, Robert W. 2007. *Concepts of Programming Languages*. 8th edition. Boston: Addison-Wesley Longman Publishing Co., Inc.

Smith, Joshua B. 2006. *Practical OCaml*. Berkeley, CA: Apress.

Sperber, Michael, Dybvig, R. Kent, Flatt, Matthew, & van Straaten, Anton. 2007. *Revised[6] Report on the Algorithmic Language Scheme*. www.r6rs.org.

Springer, George, & Friedman, Daniel P. 1989. *Scheme and the Art of Programming*. New York: McGraw-Hill.

Steele, Guy L. 1978. Rabbit: A Compiler for Scheme. Artificial Intelligence Laboratory Technical Report 474. Massachusetts Institute of Technology, Cambridge, MA.

Steele, Guy L. 1990. *Common Lisp: the Language*. Second edition. Burlington, MA: Digital Press.

Steele, Guy L., & Sussman, Gerald Jay. 1978. The Revised Report on SCHEME. Artificial Intelligence Memo 452. Massachusetts Institute of Technology, Cambridge, MA.

Stoy, Joseph E. 1977. *Denotational Semantics: The Scott-Strachey Approach to Programming Language Theory*. Cambridge, MA: MIT Press.

Strachey, Christopher. 1967. *Fundamental Concepts in Programming Languages*. Unpublished notes from International Summer School on Programming Languages, Copenhagen. Reprinted, with a foreword, in *Higher-Order and Symbolic Computation* **13**(1–2) 11–49 (2000).

Strachey, Christopher, & Wadsworth, Christopher P. 1974. Continuations: A Mathematical Semantics for Handling Full Jumps. Technical Monograph PRG-11. Oxford University Computing Laboratory. Reprinted, with a foreword, in *Higher-Order and Symbolic Computation* **13**(1–2) 135–152 (2000).

Sussman, Gerald J., & Steele, Guy L. 1975. SCHEME: An Interpreter for Extended Lambda Calculus. Artificial Intelligence Memo 349. Massachusetts Institute of Technology, Cambridge, MA. Reprinted, with a foreword, in *Higher-Order and Symbolic Computation* **11**(4) 405-439 (1998).

Thomas, Dave, Fowler, Chad, & Hunt, Andy. 2005. *Programming Ruby: The Pragmatic Programmers' Guide*. Second edition. Raleigh, NC: The Pragmatic Bookshelf.

Turing, A. M. 1936. On Computable Numbers, with an Application to the Entscheidungsproblem. *Proc. London Math. Soc.*, **42**(1), 230–265.

Ullman, Jeffrey D. 1998. *Elements of ML Programming*. ML97 edition. Englewood Cliffs, NJ: Prentice-Hall.

van Rossum, Guido, & Drake, Fred L. Jr. 2006. *The Python Language Reference Manual (Version 2.5)*. Bristol, UK: Network Theory Ltd.

von Neumann, John. 1945. First Draft of a Report on the EDVAC. Technical Report. Moore School of Electrical Engineering, University of Pennsylvania.

Wadler, Philip. 1992. The Essence of Functional Programming. Pages 1–14 of: *Proceedings ACM Symposium on Principles of Programming Languages*.

Wall, Larry, Christiansen, Tom, & Orwant, Jon. 2000. *Programming Perl*. 3rd edition. Cambridge, MA: O'Reilly.

Wand, Mitchell. 1979. Final Algebra Semantics and Data Type Extensions. *Journal of Computer and Systems Science*, **19**, 27–44.

Wand, Mitchell. 1980a. Continuation-Based Multiprocessing. Pages 19–28 of: Allen, J. (ed.), *Conference Record of the 1980 LISP Conference*. Palo Alto, CA: The Lisp Company. Republished by ACM. Reprinted, with a foreword, in *Higher-Order and Symbolic Computation* **12**(3) 285–299 (1999).

Wand, Mitchell. 1980b. Continuation-Based Program Transformation Strategies. *Journal of the ACM*, **27**, 164–180.

Wand, Mitchell. 1987. A Simple Algorithm and Proof for Type Inference. *Fundamenta Informaticae*, **10**, 115–122.

Wexelblatt, R. L. (ed.). 1978. *Special Issue: History of Programming Languages Conference*. Vol. 13. New York: ACM Press.

Winskel, Glynn. 1993. *The Formal Semantics of Programming Languages*. Cambridge, MA: MIT Press.

Wulf, William. 1971. BLISS: A Language for Systems Programming. *Communications of the ACM*, **14**(12), 780–790.

Index